"The unprecedented pace of technological advancement coupled with the recent series of global disruptions and crises offer a unique opportunity for humans and technology to work together to create a better world. There is no book better than Humachine to help us navigate the road ahead. The first edition of this book was ahead of its time. This second edition is **essential reading!"**

Maria P. Villablanca, Co-Founder & CEO, Future Insights Network, Transformation Influencer, Mentor and Keynote Speaker

"With the advent of generative artificial intelligence, every enterprise is striving to augment its people's uniquely human qualities with these revolutionary technologies. Using timely new material, Sanders and Wood demonstrate the precise steps organizations can use to harness AI to amplify our most virtuous human attributes and synthesize a "collective superintelligence" Part management guidebook, part treatise on the quickening march of AI and its implications for humanity, the second edition of *Humachine* is **an essential text for our uncharted economic frontier."**

Joseph E. Aoun, President, Northeastern University

"*The Humachine* masterfully captures the urgency of our time, underscoring the vital need for a paradigm shift in our approach to AI. [Nada Sanders] delves deep into the profound implications of this technological revolution, highlighting the necessity for humans to embrace a different mindset—one that recognizes the intrinsic value of human critical thinking and creativity alongside the capabilities of machines."

Nirav Patel, CEO of Bristlecone

"*The Humachine* book shows how executives and managers should focus on investments in AI in order to realize the dynamic strategic increase in the effectiveness and efficiency of processes according to their vision, to plan and implement their strategic and operational changes and to influence long-term behaviors through leadership focused on expected results.

Page by page, the authors of the book develop their robust plea in favor of the urgent need to change the approach to business by incorporating AI in a responsible and reliable way as a key to the development of organizations and society in general. The book describes AI as an effective means of transforming organizations in pursuit of long-term competitive advantage, not as an end in itself or as a new fad.

By reading the *Humachine* book, you will benefit both theoretically and practically from the pragmatic approach of symbiosis between human creativity and maximizing the potential of machines and processes to continue the never-ending journey of innovation to support the profitable transformation of organizations using the new paradigm of AI. **This book is a must-**

read for those who want to find the managerial answers regarding the decisive role of AI in improving the lives of enterprises in the years to come."

Alin Posteucǎ, PhD. Eng., PhD, Ec., MBA, CEO of Exegens, The Romanian Academy Prize Laureate on Technical Sciences. Author of *Beyond Strategic Kaizen: Performing Synchronous Profitable Operations*

"Professor Sanders' book (*The Humachine*) is not what is possible, but what is inevitable. This includes, the good, the bad, and the ugly. Our tasks is to optimize the good and eliminate the rest."

Peter B. Cameron, CEO of Lenox Corporation

"The unstoppable advance of intelligent automation will create a new organizational species. One where human and machine work in perfect symbiosis to derive the best outcome for both. This book is a must read for any leader that wants to understand this new species and how to prepare for this future. We've entered the era of AI, where knowledge work will be highly augmented and automated by machines. This creates a new type of competition, which requires a new organizational and human mindset, new business models and new skills. This book is a must read for any knowledge worker or business leader who wants to understand what's coming at us...fast."

Niels Van Hove Client Engagement Principal Aera Technology

"*Humachine* is an intriguing look at the current state and future potential of AI on business and society. A compelling read that explores a wide variety possibilities for the reader to ponder."

Ted English, CEO, Bob's Furniture

"It has never been more critical to embrace the relationship between technology and humans. As AI and other advances in technology are challenging our assumptions and perspectives, this book provides clarity and context as we navigate these times of uncertainty, change, and promise. The Four I's model they offer to guide shifting the paradigm is an insightful way to frame thinking."

Dr. Anne Robinson, Chief Strategy Officer, Kinaxis

The Humachine

Updated for a post-Covid world, the second edition of this groundbreaking book explains why becoming a Humachine enterprise is the only way forward for a company to maintain a competitive advantage in the age of artificial intelligence (AI).

The first edition of *The Humachine* offered a foundation for a new form of enterprise, integrating AI technology and human resources to optimize the unique advantages possessed by each. Now, in the face of the 'Great Resignation' and 'botsourcing'—where an activity previously done by humans is replaced by technology—thought leaders Sanders and Wood present a more positive and promising scenario, where an enterprise recognizes human resources as an asset class that possesses skills that cannot be replaced by automation. Enlightened business leaders will look to create synergy between technology and people, enabling the organization to maximize its capabilities by elevating the basis of decision making with closer-to-perfect information and rationality. This book provides a roadmap for how to do this and achieve collective intelligence at the enterprise level: superintelligence. More specifically, it answers these questions, and more.

- Why must an enterprise achieve superintelligence as a competitive advantage in the age of AI?
- How can any organization achieve superintelligence by following the 4-I model?
- What is the step-by-step process an enterprise should follow in becoming a Humachine?
- What strategies can be used by enterprise leaders to 'futureproof' the Humachine against uncertainty?

All business leaders, executives, and managers at companies wanting to use AI and technology to survive and thrive in this new age, and students of analytics and decision-making, will value this thought-provoking and practical book, rich with case studies.

Nada R. Sanders, PhD, is Distinguished Professor at D'Amore-McKim School of Business at Northeastern University. Her expertise is in forecasting and global supply-chain intelligence. She is a recipient of numerous research and teaching awards, was ranked as World's Top 2% of Scientists by a Stanford study, has authored seven books and over a hundred top-tier scholarly publications. She is a frequently called upon keynote speaker and expert.

John D. Wood, Esq., is an attorney, author, educator, entrepreneur, philanthropist and producer. John earned his juris doctorate from New York University School of Law and degrees in English and Philosophy, *summa cum laude*, from Texas Christian University. He is a member of American Mensa and partner at the law firm of Green Klein Wood & Jones.

The Humachine

AI, Human Virtues, and the Superintelligent Enterprise

Second edition

Nada R. Sanders and John D. Wood

Routledge
Taylor & Francis Group

NEW YORK AND LONDON

Second edition published 2024
by Routledge
605 Third Avenue, New York, NY 10158

and by Routledge
4 Park Square, Milton Park, Abingdon, Oxon OX14 4RN

Library of Congress Cataloging-in-Publication Data
Names: Sanders, Nada R., author. | Wood, John D., 1980- author.
Title: The humachine : AI, human virtues, and the superintelligent
enterprise / Nada R. Sanders and John D. Wood.
Description: Second edition. | Abingdon, Oxon ; New York, NY :
Routledge, 2024. | Includes bibliographical references and index. |
Identifiers: LCCN 2023041140 (print) | LCCN 2023041141 (ebook) |
ISBN 9781032345697 (hardback) | ISBN 9781032345680 (paperback) |
ISBN 9781003322832 (ebook)
Subjects: LCSH: Artificial intelligence--Economic aspects. |
Automation--Economic aspects. | Labor supply--Effect of automation on. |
Human-computer interaction.
Classification: LCC HC79.A9 S26 2024 (print) | LCC HC79.A9 (ebook) |
DDC 306.3/61--dc23/eng/20230914
LC record available at https://lccn.loc.gov/2023041140
LC ebook record available at https://lccn.loc.gov/2023041141

ISBN: 978-1-032-34569-7 (hbk)
ISBN: 978-1-032-34568-0 (pbk)
ISBN: 978-1-003-32283-2 (ebk)

DOI: 10.4324/9781003322832

Typeset in Sabon
by Taylor & Francis Books

To the pioneers and visionaries who will shape our future.

–Nada

This book is dedicated to everyone working to help technology help humanity.

–John

Contents

Illustrations

Figures

Tables

Preface

The competitive playing field is shifting, not slightly but seismically. A gaping fault line has opened in the ground, creating a branch in the evolutionary trajectory of human enterprise, dividing the past from the future.

On The Past side of the fault line are those companies that mistakenly treat artificial intelligence (AI) as another piece of technology to acquire or tack onto existing systems (like Eeyore's tail). But AI does not fit the plug-and-play model of technology adoption. It is not like updating your workforce's laptops or installing a new CRM platform. Indeed, the AI revolution is unlike any technological change that has ever occurred in recorded human history.

On The Future side of the fault line are those companies implementing AI at the enterprise level, mutating into a new form of enterprise entirely—one that combines the highest capabilities of humankind with the newfound and continually emerging powers of AI.

We suggest thinking of AI as a major environmental factor being introduced to the Earth's ecosphere, which will create a sort of evolutionary pressure that will force enterprises to evolve or perish. And for those companies on The Future side of the fault line, the issue becomes how to keep their humanity amidst the tumult.

What started as an inquiry for executives into how companies could adopt AI to harness the best of human and machine capabilities turned into a much more profound rumination on the future of humanity.

This is a wake-up call for executives and business leaders. Not only should you consider implementation of AI regardless of your industry, but once you do, you should consider how to stay true to your purpose, your ethical convictions, indeed your humanity, even as our organizations continue to evolve.

This book is not about teaching you to code, but teaching you how to leverage the latest in AI to unlock the true potential of the human workforce and drive our species forward by tapping into levels of intelligence that were heretofore impossible.

About the Authors

Nada R. Sanders, PhD, is Distinguished Professor at D'Amore-McKim School of Business at Northeastern University in Boston. Her expertise is in forecasting and global supply chain intelligence. She is a recipient of numerous research and teaching awards, was ranked as World's Top 2% of Scientists by a Stanford study and serves on the Board of Economics Advisors of Massachusetts. She has authored seven books over a hundred scholarly publications that have appeared in top journals including *Harvard Business Review, California Management Review, Production and Operations Management Journal*, and many others. Throughout her career Dr. Sanders has successfully held a range of leadership roles in both academic and professional organizations, has served on executive boards, and is a frequently called upon keynote speaker.

John D. Wood, Esq., is an attorney, author, educator, entrepreneur and philanthropist. John earned his juris doctorate from New York University School of Law, one of the top ten law schools in the world, and his bachelors degrees in English and Philosophy from Texas Christian University where he graduated summa cum laude. Wood is licensed to practice law in New York and Texas. He is Partner of the law firm Green Klein Wood & Jones, representing insured property owners recovering after natural disasters. He is a member of American Mensa and sits on the advisory board of non-profit organizations including the H2H Foundation, Econautics Sustainability Institute, American Policyholder Association, and American Adjuster Association. Wood is a legal scholar and author of law review articles on human nature and risk management appearing in influential law review journals such as the *Environmental Law Reporter, NYU Journal of Law and Liberty*, and the *NYU Environmental Law Journal*. John is co-author of an award-winning article on Artificial Intelligence published in the *Harvard Business Review*, as well as two books, *Foundations of Sustainable Business: Theory, Function and Strategy* (Wiley 3e) and *The Humachine: Humankind, Machines, and the Future of Enterprise* (Routledge 2e). He provides continuing professional education and keynote talks on topics including insurance, AI risk/deepfakes, and sustainability for audiences such as the New York State Bar Association, the Texas Bar Association, the Attorney General Alliance, as well as industry conferences.

Introduction

Defining the Humachine

When Mitt Romney ran for President of the United States in 2011, he used a phrase during a campaign speech that got a lot of airtime, for better or worse. At the Iowa State Fair, responding to a protestor claiming that the government should tax corporations instead of people, Romney candidly remarked, "Corporations are people, my friend."

To be fair, a corporation very much just *is* the directors, the officers, the managers, the laborers, the shareholders, and the individual purchasers—all of these *people*. When we think of "corporate activity," it really is all of these people engaging in a bundle of interconnected commercial activities that we have in mind.

When Romney says, "Corporations are people," he may have been using a linguistic convention called *synecdoche*, "A figure of speech in which a part is made to represent the whole or vice versa."[1] Further, in a legal sense, his comment is accurate. About 200 years ago, the Supreme Court of the United States held that corporations are legal persons:

> An aggregate corporation... is, in short, an artificial person, existing in contemplation of law and endowed with certain powers and franchises which, though they must be exercised through the medium of its natural members, are yet considered as subsisting in the corporation itself as distinctly as if it were a real personage.[2]

According to Black's Law Dictionary, an "artificial person" has been understood *since the 1600s* to mean an entity created by law and given certain legal rights and duties of a human being.

What makes a person, a person? The least controversial answers that are more intuitive might be that personhood means having a sense of having a mental life, selfhood or having an "I," making meaningful choices, some notion of interiority, an internal mental theater. For the sake of clarity, we have to distinguish our project from those common sense answers. We just have to set to the side the whole debate about phenomenal consciousness. We are *not* talking about whether AI has the first-person subjective experience of consciousness, like what it means to see a color, taste a flavor, or hear music. We are not talking about whether AI is all of the notions of "personhood" and "interiority" and the first-person subjective feelings of being conscious or a social being. Our focus is on *rational agency* as a resource made increasingly available because of AI—the mental activity of thinking, of processing information, of making logical inferences, of making decisions—that are relevant to legal and operational business contexts. What if we took the phrase, "Corporations are people," in a different way, combining the *legal* sense with the *rational* attributes associated with human personhood—the ability to learn, reason, plan, and process complex facts?

To hold that "Corporations are people," allows us to justify attributing civil liberties to a commercial enterprise. Generally, most people don't think an organization has a mind. Relatedly, it is not common to suggest that a corporation possesses qualities of personhood. Corporations are in a certain sense merely legal fictions formed by filing some paperwork with a Secretary of State in a given jurisdiction. No one thinks that a corporation has a soul, or religious beliefs, or could fall in love, or could befriend a dog, or could have a favorite flavor of ice cream, or do other things we think of when we think of a unique "person."

That said, maybe we should start to take this mere figure of speech as something literally true: a corporation can marry (merger) or divorce (divestiture), or adopt (acquisition) or procreate (subsidiaries), or die (dissolution). A corporation can speak (campaign finance contributions). A corporation can break a law or serve its nation. A corporation can have an idea. A corporation can be moral. Or a corporation can be a serial felon exhibiting sociopathic traits. If corporations are people, and people can attain enlightenment, then would it follow that a corporation can attain enlightenment? Can we create enterprises that operate free from bias, ignorance, greed, and fear?

We believe an organization could have a mental life in the sense that an enterprise could possess intelligence and make decisions that are not simply reducible to the decisions of specific people within the company.

What happens when humans institute procedures and practices that are functionally equivalent to human mental states but at the enterprise level? Have we created something new, a collective consciousness? What new creature is this that combines human qualities of content-rich thoughts, wisdom, and creativity with mechanical efficiency in a way that is scalable? That, we contend, would be a Humachine.

What is a Humachine?

To go back to Philosophy 101, the proper way to go about rational discourse is to first define the key terms so that one is clear about what we *mean*. Then, based on those definitions, to distinguish those terms from other terms, so that one is clear about what we do *not* mean. Then, upon those definitions and distinctions, we may make deductions. Definition, distinction, deduction—these are the "three d's" of proper philosophy. We hope by following proper philosophical method we can avoid junk science, hype, and hyperbole, which are all too common when discussing the frontiers of technology and AI in particular.

To our knowledge, the word "Humachine" first appeared on the cover of a 1999 *MIT Technology Review Special Edition*.[3] The Editor in Chief understood this was a unique phrasing:

> Don't be surprised if you didn't recognize the title of this column. The word isn't in dictionaries yet. But it may be soon. Or some other word like it, coined to describe the symbiosis that is currently developing between human beings and machines. Humachines.

There are meaningful distinctions between that use of the term versus how it is deployed in this book. All of the examples given in the *MIT Technology Review* article were mere brute physical combinations of humans with machinery, such as visual implants and wearable technology—in other words, cyborgs and androids, which we are careful to distinguish.

We are *not* talking about cyborgs, androids, or AI that can parrot a human personality. We are not talking about any specific physical example that combines some human attribute with a machine, or combines some mechanical attribute with that of a human. We are talking about the emergence of a new form of intelligence in the history of life on Earth.

Humachine is, of course, a *portmanteau*, "A word blending the sounds and combining the meanings of two others."[4] From the Oxford English Dictionary:[5]

Human $=_{df}$ "Relating to or characteristic of humankind. ... Of or characteristic of people as opposed to God or animals or machines, especially in being susceptible to weaknesses. ... Showing the better qualities of humankind, such as kindness."

Machine $=_{df}$ "An apparatus using mechanical power and having several parts, each with a definite function and together performing a particular task. ... Any device that transmits a force or directs its application. ... An efficient and well-organized group of powerful people. ... A person who acts with the mechanical efficiency of a machine."

Now combine those terms into "Humachine." *Humachine* $=_{df}$ the combination of the better qualities of humankind—creativity, intuition, compassion, judgment—with the mechanical efficiency of a machine—economies of scale, big data processing capabilities, augmented by artificial intelligence, in such a way as to shed the limitations and vices of both humans and machines while maintaining the virtues of both.

In this book, we are interested in exploring combining human and machine virtues at the enterprise level—an organization, company, corporation, or other kind of organized economic undertaking. In other words, when we say "Humachines," we are talking about harnessing the power of machines to amplify human capabilities to create benign superintelligence at an enterprise level.

The Humachine is created by implementing an organizational management framework that (i) applies Kasparov's Law to (ii) solve the problem posed by Moravec's Paradox in a way that (iii) satisfies the conditions of collective superintelligence. This may seem convoluted at first, but what we mean by "humachine" really boils down to the relationship between those three key concepts.

Kasparov's Law holds that *"weak human + machine + better process* [is] superior to a strong computer alone and, more remarkably, superior to a *strong human + machine + inferior process."*[6]

Moravec's Paradox holds that what machines are good at, humans are not, and vice versa.[7]

Bostrom's definition of "collective" or ***organizational network superintelligence*** holds that superintelligence could emerge "through the gradual enhancement of networks and organizations that link individual human minds with one another and with various artifacts and bots."[8]

When we devise organizational management approaches to follow Kasparov's Law we are no longer limited by the upper threshold of intelligence of the human workforce. Using the right process, we can leverage the tension described by Moravec's Paradox, using the right cantilevering of human resources and technology (where the humans are variously in, on, above, or out of, the decision-making loop, and robotic process automation is leveraged to the extent—and only to the extent—that it outperforms humans). This hypothetical network array of human and AI nodes, linked together in an enterprise-management platform, following the 4-I model offered in this book, can create collective superintelligence.

The Era of Artificial Intelligence

Our book means to lay out a roadmap for enterprise leaders to follow in order to create a super intelligent entity that combines the highest capabilities of humanity with the highest capabilities of machinery. By machinery, we mean the nonhuman mechanisms powering the underlying processes responsible for work.

Machinery can be computational—for instance, information processing tools that extend the cognitive capabilities of human minds—or they can be physical—such as an industrial-sized metal cutting tool that extends the physical capabilities of human hands.

With the Industrial Revolution, physical machinery in certain ways supported and in other ways supplanted human labor. The physical capabilities of a steam-powered engine outstripped the capabilities of human muscle and sweat, not to mention animal labor. Machinery was used to operate at scales unachievable by human hands and to perform tasks involving high temperatures or health and safety issues that presented unacceptable physical risk.

Physical machinery supplanted human labor again in part, when national economies evolved from "industrial" to "service" as the primary output. Certain jobs in the service industry became co-opted by robots in disguise. The bank teller became the ATM, which is really just a very rudimentary wall-mounted robot that dispenses money for us. With the evolution from service to information-based economies, physical machinery is once again supplanting human work. Airborne drones with special sensors piloted from thousands of miles away are replacing soldiers' boots on the ground. As the economy evolved from agricultural to industrial, to service, to information-based, physical machinery continued to evolve too, shaping the economy and being shaped by it.

As the marketplace has evolved, *computational machinery* has also supported and supplanted human mental activity. Perhaps this displacement began with the abacus or the beloved TI-83 calculator, but certainly with the quantum computers in the nuclear laboratories: computational power is no longer bounded by the physical limits of our grey matter. Instead of a room full of junior attorneys conducting document review for a month, we can now feed documents into a natural language processing software that finds key words in a matter of seconds. Our focus here is more on mental computation than robotic automation. And we are hoping to encourage enterprise leaders to focus more on *augmentation* of the human workforce than attempting to *automate* it.

The Industrial Revolution unlocked powers of productive capacity that humanity lacked the tools to monitor and manage. For a while we lived in what James R. Beniger coined as a "crisis of control," where our ability to manipulate matter and energy far outstripped our ability to manage information. The crisis of control lasted up until the Information Age. After the Industrial Revolution, but before the Information Age, we had industrial-scale power but lacked industrial-scale information technology. This was only for a time, because the crisis of control resolved rapidly in a span of less than a century thanks to the emergence of technologies like photography (1830s), rotary powered printing (1840s), typewriters (1860s), telephones (1970s), motion pictures (1890s), radios (1900s) and televisions (1920s) and the like. Humanity very quickly solved the crisis of control posed by the Industrial Revolution by introducing mechanisms of controlling larger aggregations of matter, energy, populations and information through bureaucracy and technology.

Understanding the relationship between information and control is key to understanding the survival of living systems. "Life itself implies control, after all, in individual cells and organisms no less than in national economies or any other purposive system."[9] Indeed,

> once we view national economies as concrete processing systems engaged in the continuous extraction, reorganization, and distribution of environmental inputs to final consumption, the impact of industrialization takes on new meaning. By far, the greatest effect of industrialization... was to speed up a society's entire material processing system, thereby precipitating what I call a crisis of control, a period in which innovations in information processing and communication technologies lagged behind those of energy and its application to manufacturing and transportation.[10]

The economic activity of human society since the Industrial Revolution has progressed from extractive to manufacturing and on to service sectors, then following the advent of information-control technologies, further evolutions progressed into so-called white-collar sectors such as banking, insurance, and real estate, and finally topping out in a sector comprised of intellectual work product: medicine, education, research, engineering and so on. These economic sectors are like layers in increasingly abstract levels of control over matter and energy and information, with the former supporting the latter. This support functions at the societal level just as it does in other living processes: "agriculture and mining, the extraction and breakdown of matter to produce energy; manufacturing, the synthesis of matter and energy into more organized forms; and services the organization and support of these processes in well-integrated systems."[11]

"With the development of global computer networks, telecommunications, and mass media, it grows increasingly difficult to appreciate how relatively recent and different is the information-processing view of human organization and society."[12] The move from industrialization to digitalization of an economy would be a shocking development to an outside viewer, and yet we have grown so used to living in the Information Age that some of us may even feel (wrongly, to be sure) that our digital personas are as important as our actual physical embodiment.

As early as 1986, "to say that the advanced industrial world is rapidly becoming an Information Society may already be a cliché."[13] Indeed, by the mid-1980s, for Japan, Western Europe and the United States, it was already true to say "the bulk of the labor force now works primarily at informational tasks such as systems analysis and computer programming, while wealth comes increasingly from informational goods such as microprocessors and from informational services such as data processing."[14] These trends have only continued with the processing of information taking on greater importance to a national economies than even the processing of matter and energy.

The advent of AI tools like ChatGPT promise greater control over information at the individual and organizational level, thus unlocking new abilities and applications of intelligence. If you look at how systems of control have evolved over time, it appears we are nearing some kind of event horizon or threshold.

"Living systems have thus far evolved four levels of programmable structures and programs: DNA molecules encoded with genetic programming, the brain with cultural programming, organizations with formal processing and decision rules, and mechanical and electronic processors with algorithms. This succession of four levels of programming, each one of which appears to have complemented and extended more than superseded already existing levels, constitutes the total history of control as we know it—a relatively smooth development punctuated by only these four major revolutions in control."[15] See **Table 0.1** concerning the four control revolutions from an historical perspective.

Bear in mind the timeline of the evolution of control on planet Earth is logarithmic.[17] "The first, and all but imperceptible molecular change that we revere as the origin of life, occurred approximately 4 billion years ago, surprisingly soon after the formation of the Earth itself." At this stage, biological life exerted control via molecular programming.

> It took another 3.9 billion years for information processing to transcend the genetic level; this second control revolution occurred about 100 million years ago as certain vertebrates first began to learn through imitation, the earliest and most primitive form of cultural programming.

That's right: life uses "programming" in the same sense in which computers are "programmed."[18] "The third control revolution, one that expanded information processing from neural to social structures, came almost 100 million years later—about 3,000 BC—in the bureaucratic organizations of Mesopotamia and ancient Egypt." That is, information processing transcended the individual brain to take place at the collective, social level with the formation of bureaucracy—governments, laws, and the like. "[B]ureaucracy did not become pervasive until the nineteenth-century control crisis in the appearance of a complementary fourth level of control: mechanical, electric, and electronic technologies for information storage, processing, and communication." The fourth level of control brought us into the Information Age. But it appears we have already moved beyond that age and into the era of Artificial Intelligence, where the highest forms of control are driven by synthetic or hybrid forms of collective intelligence. Now we are approaching the manifestation of intelligent design through generative and evolutionary algorithms.

Table 0.1 Beniger's timeline of the development of four levels of control[16]

Years ago (logarithmic)	
	Formation of the Earth
	Level One: Life (Molecular Programming)
	Motility
1 billion	Organs specialized in control
	True nervous systems
	Vertebrate brain
100 million	*Level Two: Culture (Learning by Imitation)*
	Learning by teaching
10 million	
	Divergence of hominids and apes
	Rapid increase in hominid brain size
	Genus *Homo*
1 million	
100 thousand	
	Homo sapiens
10 thousand	
	Neolithic or Agricultural Revolution
	Level Three: Bureaucracy
B.C.–A.D.	
1 thousand	
	Commercial Revolution
	Industrial Revolution
100 years	*Level Four: Technology (Control Revolution)*
	Computers
	Microprocessors
10 years	
	Genetic programming technology

The four revolutions in control appear to occur at diminishing intervals of time. Revolutions in control are *accelerating*. The more often they happen, the more often they will happen again. Or so it appears. When will the fifth revolution take place? Is it already underway? The Control

Revolution of the Information Age described by Beniger would not have been possible without the predicate enabling layer of the Industrial Revolution. Analogously, what revolutions are enabled by the advent of AI? Are we in a new crisis era already? A crisis driven not by inadequate control but rather too much control? Or the wrong kind of control?

> Each new technological innovation extends the processes that sustain life, thereby increasing the need for control and hence for improved control technology. This explains why technology appears autonomously to beget technology in general, and why, is argued here, innovations in matter and energy processing create the need for further innovation in information-processing and communication technologies. Because technological innovation is increasingly a collective, cumulative effort, one whose results must be taught and diffused, it also generates an increased need for technologies of information storage and retrieval—as well as for their elaboration and systems of technical education and communication—quite independently of the particular need for control.[19]

Therefore, "the proper subject matter of the social and behavioral sciences, if they are to complement studies of the flows of matter (input-output economics) and energy (ecology), ought to be information: its generation, storage, processing, and communication to effect control."[20] In a way, the history of intelligent life on Earth is a history of variations on information technology.

Thus a valuable contribution to our readership would be the consideration of *how* control technology, specifically the latest generation of AI, enables the generation, storage, processing and communication of information, specifically intelligence *per se*, beyond anything realized post-Industrialization. This latest wave of generative AI is a different step up compared to anything we've seen since the steam engine, comparable to the invention of the printing press or the discovery of fire in terms of the tectonic implications for the human race.

Superintelligence and Strategic Competitive Advantage

The *humachinist* finds ways to harness the powers of physical and computational machinery to provide optimum enhancements to human action. The humachinist would be a programmer of organizations. Our emphasis in this book is on computational machinery, such as sensing technology (e.g., RFID chips) as well as processing technology (e.g., big data analytics), rather than physical machinery. We contend that humans can harness computational machinery to create super-intelligent mentality at the enterprise level that transcends present-day human mental limitations.

Of course, the coming self-awareness of an enterprise portends great changes, not all of them positive. We will get into the risks posed by artificial intelligence instantiated in large-scale networks more in Chapter 6, wherein we discuss ways in which legal frameworks are challenged to help mitigate these risks and keep AI on the right track.

An incremental step in the right direction is to understand what a Humachine is and how to build one. The omega point is, in our view, a sustainable equilibrium that enables the human species to thrive on this planet and beyond.

As exciting as the endeavor to create Humachines may be, it is also dangerous. There is a very real existential concern about the "*control problem*," or building something that is so powerful it cannot be contained.

> "If some day we build machine brains that surpass human brains in general intelligence, then this new superintelligence could become very powerful. And, as the fate of the gorillas now depends more on humans than on the gorillas themselves, so the fate of our species would depend on the actions of the machine superintelligence."[21]

By imbuing superintelligence with humane qualities, we hope to mitigate the dangers of the control problem by creating superintelligence that regulates itself, vetoes dangerous impulses, and even protects humanity from its own vices.

We think the risk factor of expanding AI at the enterprise level is, at present, like the risk of hitting an iceberg in a vast sea of opportunity. That is to say, AI is a known risk that we should see coming with ample opportunity to avoid the danger. We know about the risk of rogue actors weaponizing AI. Lawmakers are already having hearings on this subject. We hope tech giants are taking that risk seriously because they can actually do something about it. But, because of the gravity of the harm and its irreversible nature, we wish to give credence to forecasts of an inevitable lurch toward a singleton AI that would hold the human condition in its virtual hands:

> "In principle, we could build a kind of superintelligence that would protect human values. [But] in practice, the control problem—the problem of how to control what the superintelligence would do—looks quite difficult. It also looks like we will only get one chance. Once unfriendly superintelligence exists, it would prevent us from replacing it or changing its preferences. ... This is quite possibly the most important and most daunting challenge humanity has ever faced. And—whether we succeed or fail—it is probably the last challenge we will ever face."[22]

While it is possible that concerns over AI are overblown, "the alternative views that have been presented in the literature are substantially worse—including the default view, or 'null hypothesis,' according to which we can for the time being safely or reasonably ignore the prospect of superintelligence."[23] If we do not give the control problem sufficient attention we will make no provision for the dangers posed thereby, and it is much more prudent to be overly cautious than to proceed with no safeguards in this context.

These existential concerns have gone from marginal to mainstream. The Center for AI Safety published a statement on AI risk that has earned signatures from luminaries in the field: "Mitigating the risk of extinction from AI should be a global priority alongside other societal-scale risks such as pandemics and nuclear war."[24]

It is with respect to the control problem—however remote it may be at this early stage of AI research—that we include a fairly generous helping of normative, rather than simply descriptive and tactical, ideas in this book. In our healthy and good-spirited quest for strategic competitive advantages, let's not lose sight of what happens if we were to slip on this tightrope walk toward the future. The only way to create "good" AI is to have good enterprise management.

Summary of Each Chapter

Chapter 1: The Post-pandemic AI Rush

We begin with the post pandemic era and the AI rush that has ensued. We describe the launch of generative AI models such as ChatGPT and explain the historically significant moment it represents in technological evolution. Next, we explain that despite the huge advancements in AI, 'machines' can't do everything. We introduce Moravec's Paradox to illustrate the symbiotic, mutually dependent relationship between man and machine. We introduce Kasparov's Law, which tells us that superior performance does not necessarily require human genius nor superior machines; rather, it can be achieved using ordinary people and machines interacting through better processes. In contrast to the promise of combining the best of man and machine, we look at the peril of creating superintelligent machines. We discuss the control problem as well as various social ills due to the alignment problem and exploitation by the proprietors of technology to underscore the gravity of what's at stake in managing AI. We conclude by introducing the form of enterprise that leverages the collaboration between man and machine to achieve "superintelligence"—the Humachine.

Chapter 2: Survival of the Fittest: The Quest for Superintelligence

We introduce the concept of *superintelligence* as any intellect that greatly exceeds the cognitive performance of humans in virtually all domains of interest, and explain that attaining this level of intelligence is essential for competitiveness in the new world. We lay out the various well-defined pathways to attaining superintelligence: biological cognitive enhancement, neural lace, whole brain emulation, and collective superintelligence—and argue that the latter is the most promising pathway. We argue that the level of enterprise intelligence needed—superintelligence—cannot be achieved by machines or humans alone. It will come from a collective intelligence of humans and machines or AI—in a synergistic way. This appreciation for the potential of collective superintelligence motivates the rest of this book. We introduce the notion of collective intentionality to bolster our contention that an enterprise could conceivably have a mind of its own. This chapter concludes with an excerpt from Teilhard de Chardin's *Phenomenon of Man*, a beautiful depiction of his vision for the noosphere, that layer of consciousness enveloping Earth that provides the next pathway for the evolution of life itself.

Chapter 3: What Machine Can and Cannot Do

We push back against some of the hyperbole surrounding AI by illustrating the extent of its powers and its limits. We explain the role of big data, algorithms, cloud computing, and dark data as a predicate for understanding AI, machine learning, deep learning, large language models, and neural networks. While AI excels in pattern recognition and the ability to process data with super-human velocity, accuracy, volume, and consistency, AI is still significantly hampered when compared to human general intelligence. AI systems lack common sense, fail to appreciate context, are data hungry and brittle, lack intuition, limit suggestions to local optima, make decisions in a black box, and are limited by the quality of the data upon which they feed.

Chapter 4: What Humans Can and Cannot Do

In this chapter, we look at the limits of human capabilities at work. First, we discuss how demographic changes are impacting the labor force in ways that are at least as profound as 'botsourcing'—or the displacement of human laborers with robotic labor or automated processes. Then we look at both human strengths and weaknesses, with an eye toward implications for the work environment. We will *think about thinking* with guidance from Daniel Kahneman's take on System 1 and System 2 type thinking. We try to understand, in more depth, what human general intelligence brings to the table when compared to AI. Our originality, intuition, emotions, care, playfulness, ethical conviction, and aesthetic taste, for example, are irreplaceable by machines. That said, human rationality is prone to specific kinds of breakdowns. We look at some well-documented human biases that affect how we work with others. We conclude by identifying uniquely human qualities that we need to cultivate, including creativity, emotional intelligence, intuition, care, ethical convictions, aesthetics, and playfulness. As machines become increasingly intelligent and enterprises shift responsibilities away from humans, we must cultivate certain human traits to remain relevant.

Chapter 5: The Humachine: The Path to Enterprise Superintelligence

In this chapter, we look at the evolution of work as people and artificially intelligent machines deepen collaborative relationships. We consider AI not a replacement to human workers, but an enabling layer that is complementary to uniquely human skills. If we can successfully manage the human–machine interface, human learning and performance will be significantly amplified. Leveraging our relationship with AI requires us to place trust in technology and enhance our human skills. We consider the potential risk of atrophy resulting from an ongoing reliance on machines to perform work previously requiring certain human skills.

Chapter 6: Legal Issues in the Humachine Era

Law and legal compliance is the primary mechanism for risk management in any domain of industrial activity in the civilized world. In this chapter, we lay out the AI "control problem," as well as other risks posed by AI with which the law must come to grips: AI is upending intellectual property regimes, enabling intrusive surveillance of private data, silently injuring vulnerable groups through algorithmic bias, posing challenges to democracy itself through weaponized bots interfering in the levers and pullies of government, and bringing about the end of truth with malicious deepfakes. The rule of law has never faced such a daunting challenge as the advent of AI. Let's consider what laws might do to manage the risk of these AI-augmented powers. As law is a reflection of our appetite for risk, we contrast the precautionary principle with the more traditional cost-benefit analysis risk-management approach. We recommend the former for dealing with the risks posed by AI. We take a deep dive into the problem of deepfakes to illustrate the challenge AI can pose to lawmakers. Issues of data privacy and security become increasingly urgent in light of the control problem because AI feeds upon, and could potentially weaponize, consumer data. The black-box nature of AI decision-making and issues posed by ingraining bias within AI systems also throw curve balls at traditional legal notions of liability and fault. The chapter concludes with a discussion of current approaches by advanced nation states to govern in the AI era.

Chapter 7: The 4-I Model

In this chapter, we describe the four shifts needed to detach from the traditional plug-and-play model of technology adoption. The Humachine is driven by technology, but, nonetheless, human centric. Following the Four

I's of Intentionality, Integration, Implementation, and Indication, we can create an organization that is greater than the sum of its parts. From profits to purpose, siloes to integration, and rigid performance quotas to aspirational metrics, a paradigm shift about the role of technology in the workforce lays the foundation for the Humachine.

Chapter 8: Becoming a Humachine: The "How" of Enterprise Transformation

In this chapter, we see the Humachine emerging in front of our eyes. Human-centric orientation, flat- and fluid- organizational structures, entrepreneurial and innovative cultures, and enterprise-level self-awareness define the Humachine and distinguish it from traditional business structures. We explain the necessity of purposeful, mission-driven disruption to organizational structure in order to create a cultural and technological ecosystem that supports mutation. We introduce the concepts of rendanheyi and holacracy as examples of flat- and fluid- organizational structures. The three variables of Kasparov's Law—people, machine, and process—need to be unified around the intentionality of the enterprise. The Humachine is capable of delivering products and services that excel in the experiential economy because they are co-created by humans and machines, workers and consumers. Drawing intelligence through its porous organizational boundaries, the Humachine delivers innovation rapidly to market. Ultimately possessing self-awareness at the enterprise level, the Humachine is not business transformed, it is business mutated, dynamically adapting to evolutionary pressures.

Chapter 9: Futureproof Enterprise

This chapter sums up some of our findings about the future of enterprise, offering some normative reflections on what executives can and should be doing to navigate the treacherous transition to create humane superintelligence and review changes to educational curriculum organized around the new discipline of "humanics" to prepare students of all levels of the workforce to participate in this new job market. We also describe the rapidly changing landscape of the work environment and point to the opportunities it provides for both businesses and humanity as a whole. We conclude with a look at what the future of work may hold in the Humachine era and point to education, innovation, and evolution as key elements to futureproof the Humachine.

Conclusion

Contrary to Bostrom, we propose that *collective* superintelligence is not only more likely, it is more desirable than *individual* superintelligence. We set forth an organizational network theory of superintelligence motivated by

Kasparov's Law. Ordinary humans combined with ordinary computers with the right process can outperform human genius and supercomputing combined. Along the way, we survey technology, philosophy, psychology, economics, and other disciplines to help illuminate this multifaceted area of inquiry.

We are not fixated on some silver bullet technological breakthrough like the pill from the movie *Limitless*, or some genius programmer who writes the script for general artificial intelligence. We do not even suggest that the pot of gold at the end of this rainbow requires hiring the very best human resources. We offer a roadmap that involves using the human and technological resources available to us *now*, implementing certain processes to manage those resources effectively, and by application of Kasparov's Law, turning what is ordinary into something extraordinary. To take humans and machines, combine them in certain ways, and yield a *Humachine* capable of carrying humanity into a future that is both healthy and humane.

We share the core conviction that an enterprise can have a mind, and that, as a consequence, an enterprise can and should pursue superintelligence for the betterment of our species. That is a lofty goal. Being preoccupied with lofty goals for AI is better than to have idle hands where AI is used merely for entertainment. We need no more of the devil's playthings than our species already has.

Notes

1 Oxford English Dictionary. Available at https://en.oxforddictionaries.com/defini tion/synecdoche
2 *Trustees of Dartmouth Coll. v. Woodward*, 17 U.S. 518, 667 (1819) (Story, J.)
3 Intelligent Machines—Humachines, From the Editor in Chief John Benditt. *MIT Technology Review*, May 1, 1999. Available at www.technologyreview.com/s/ 400387/humachines/
4 Oxford English Dictionary. https://en.oxforddictionaries.com/definition/portmanteau
5 Oxford English Dictionary. "human" is defined at https://en.oxforddictionaries. com/definition/human and "machine" is defined at https://en.oxforddictionaries. com/definition/machine
6 Kasparov, Garry. *Deep Thinking: Where Machine Intelligence Ends and Human Creativity Begins*, p. 246. Hatchet Books, New York, 2017.
7 Moravec, Hans P. 1988. *Mind Children: The Future of Robot and Human Intelligence*. Harvard University Press, Cambridge, MA.
8 Bostrom, Nick. Superintelligence: Paths, Dangers, Strategies. Oxford University Press, 2014, pp. 58–59.
9 James R. Beniger, *The Control Revolution: Technological and Economic Origins of the Information Society*, page vi (1986, Harvard University Press).
10 Ibid., p. 62.
11 Ibid., p. 38.
12 Ibid., p. 39.
13 Ibid., p. v.
14 Ibid., p. v.
15 Ibid., p. 62.
16 Ibid., p. 63.

17 Ibid., p. 62.
18 "One idea directly inspired by the Control Revolution in technology is the concept of a program, a word that first appeared in the seventeenth century for public notices but which in the past 150 years has spread through other organizational and informational technologies: plans for formal proceedings (1837), political platforms (1895), broadcast presentations (1923), electronic signals (1935), computer instructions (1945), educational procedures (1950), and training (1963). In general, program has come to mean any prearranged information that guides subsequent behavior." Ibid., p. 39.

"We have already defined control as purposive influence toward a predetermined goal. If purpose is to be explained in other than metaphysical terms, however, its goal must exist prior to the behavior that it influences in some material form, on the government rolls, for example, that motivated the original Latin *contrarotulare*. All control is thus programmed: it depends on physically encoded information, which must include both the goals toward which a process is to be influenced and the procedures for processing additional information toward that end." Ibid., pp. 39–40.

19 Ibid., p. 10.
20 Ibid., p. 38.
21 Bostrom, *Superintelligence*, preface, p. v.
22 Ibid.
23 Ibid., p. vii.
24 See Statement on AI Risk, Center for AI Safety, available at https://www.safe.ai/statement-on-ai-risk (last accessed May 31, 2023).

Chapter 1

The Post-pandemic AI Rush

The Post-pandemic Era

The year was 2020, often referred to as "the year the earth stood still."[1] That was the year the world economy, as we know it, came to a grinding halt. As the result of most of the world implementing command-and-control style risk management regimes in response to the Covid-19 global pandemic, trade in all but "essential service" sectors simply stopped functioning. In early 2020, as the virus spread rapidly across the world, many countries imposed locked-down orders on communities and placed restrictions on all kinds of economic activity in an effort to contain the outbreak. Global supply chains that modern companies depend upon just stopped.

The result was a shattering impact on businesses and industries worldwide. Many companies shut down—some temporarily and many permanently—due to lack of demand, unavailable workers, inaccessible supplies, unmanufactured parts, lack of materials, cumbersome compliance guidelines like social distancing, and dire financial constraints.

Commerce of every type was turned upside down and only the largest companies with vertically integrated supply chains or in a position to pivot to largely e-commerce or virtual laborforces were able to persist. Thus, regulatory risk (even more than physical risk from the virus) presented challenges from supply-chain disruptions to changes in consumer behavior. Never have local, regional, national and global markets been so influenced by government than during the Covid pandemic.

Global supply chains (those interconnected networks that facilitate the production and distribution of goods and services), for all practical purposes, collapsed. As countries went into lockdown, businesses were unable to get the raw materials and supplies needed to produce their products. Companies that relied heavily on one country or one supplier were hit the hardest. Borders were closed, disrupting shipping and transportation, resulting in massive shortages of critical supplies and raw materials as well as delays and disruptions in the production and distribution of goods. The results, among other things, were

DOI: 10.4324/9781003322832-1

global shortages and stockouts of everything from toilet paper and pharmaceutical items to household appliances and semiconductors.

Mandatory shutdowns of 2020 wreaked havoc on the bottom line for companies confronted by a precipitous drop in product demand with consumers stuck at home. As a result of the pandemic the global economy shrank by 3.9% in 2020, the worst global recession since the Great Depression of the 1930s, and the decline more severe than the 2009–09 global financial crisis.[2] According to David Wilcox, Senior Fellow for International Economics and a former director of the domestic economics division at the U.S. Federal Reserve, "2020 has no precedent in modern economic history."[3]

Many companies did not weather the storm and in 2020, in the U.S. alone, corporate bankruptcies reached levels higher than seen in over decade.[4] The year of 2020 was called "the year of bankruptcy."[5] According to past President and COO of Staples, Henry Nasella told us:

> When covid hit none of us ever experienced something where there was literally no revenue. I have worked my entire career in the sector. When a multi-million dollar global business has no revenue it is an 'OMG *what do I do?*' moment. No one knew how long it would last and there was a reluctance of executives either on boards or as an investor that we should not overreact. But, wait a minute. Stop. We have to have a plan B - because I don't know how long it will last. The fundamental facts are you have no revenue and you have expenses... we will be out of business! I don't know what our burn rate is or how long can we go? Very sobering moment.[6]

The economic fallout of the pandemic was staggering and businesses of every type were in peril. Companies in every industry sector urgently began redesigning their business models to secure business continuity and build resilience.[7] Companies that survived the pandemic began making rapid changes to their businesses in order to prevent ever being in that situation again. "We learned suddenly companies had to be very creative in reinventing their model. What was going to work before was not going to work in the future."[8]

Uncertainty and Global Economic Disruptions

Before the pandemic, "consumers had enjoyed the luxury of low prices for imported goods for a long time, but it was built on something that was very fragile."[9] The pandemic is now over and the concerns over Covid-19 seem to be in the rear view mirror. Only a tiny percentage of executives still consider Covid a risk, compared to 86% at the start of the pandemic.[10] However, it is clear the world has entered into a new era. It is an era of broad global turbulence and disruption. Everything has changed, and the rules for surviving and thriving in this new environment—for an economic entity of any type—must change as well. The disruptions and breakages of global busi-ness networks during the pandemic have left a weak and vulnerable eco-nomic landscape.

Most businesses design their operations for 'blue sky' days. When dis-ruptive events occur contingency plans are invoked until the situation is resolved. Businesses then resume operations as usual. The protracted dura-tion and global sweep of the pandemic's disruption collapsed businesses and entire industries. Businesses that survived were left weak and weary. Yet, global economic disruptions continue. The reality is that disruptions are the 'new normal' and the pandemic lay bare business vulnerabilities.

John Sicard, President and CEO of Kinaxis, sums up the rapid pace of organizational change management necessitated by the heightened risk and uncertainty of the foreseeable global operational environment: "What got you through the last 30 years won't even get you through the next 3!"

What is different now are the multiple and simultaneous impacts of hazards that were previously isolated. It was hoped post-Covid-19 would be a return to our old way of life. This thinking, however, was quickly shat-tered by the outbreak of war in Ukraine, ushering in a series of crises from geopolitical instability to food and energy supply insecurity. Geo-politic is now a major global risk.[11] There is the Russia–Ukraine conflict, tensions between U.S. and China, strenuous relationships among countries across the globe, and competing interests across Europe.

Environmental risks are also rapidly mounting with failure to mitigate and adapt to climate change. A majority of company leaders expect to see a "moderate" to "very large" impacts on costs due to climate change in the near future.[12] Climate change disasters are seen in everything from destroy-ing infrastructure with floods and fires,[13] destroying crops,[14] forcing fac-tories to close and preventing workers' from staying on jobs.[15] The biodiversity loss and ecosystem collapse is creating severe disruptions and food shortages. Even a seemingly benign item such as Sriracha—the beloved spicy sauce—has been in short supply as severe weather conditions are affecting the growth and quality of chili peppers, and threating to disrupt an entire industry.[16]

These hazards are linked together and have a cascading effect on one another, such as climate change and inflation, and economic instability, creat-ing multi-prong risks to businesses.[17] There is also a return of "older" risks—inflation, cost-of-living crises, trade wars, capital outflows from emerging markets, and widespread social unrest. Then there are societal risks, many that are a follow up to the protracted pandemic, including employment crisis, severe mental health deterioration, erosion of social cohesion that kept society intact, as well as increasing the spread of misinformation and disinformation.

These risks converge to amplify each other creating a highly turbulent global landscape. The consequence is that enterprises have no time to recover and there is no end in sight to the impact of hazards. The pandemic exposed global-system weaknesses. It also revealed complex independent systems that elevate the risk of cascading failure. What were once local shocks now have high potential for broad systemic failure. There is no going back to the pre-pandemic world. Thriving in this environment will require something entirely new.

One of our guiding notions in this book is that organizational management strategy must hue closely to the principles of evolution itself for enterprises to remain sustainable. Traditional notions of change management are not enough because we can no longer presuppose incremental adaptation will be suitable to meet to incremental changes in context. We are in the midst of unprecedented organizational stressors and these will either make or break an enterprise. With more nuance: evolutionary pressure will drive mutations, some of which will be fitness-enhancing and those enterprises that mutate will thrive—the rest will fall by the wayside and be remembered, if at all, as relics of the pre-pandemic, pre-AI era.

AI and Automation to the Rescue

According to Maria Villablanca, Co-Founder & CEO of Future Insights Network, "Pre-covid AI was this aspirational thing ... then businesses realized they must get a competitive advantage. Technology is offering businesses resilience. AI is no longer a future project. AI is now part of everyday operations and business."[18] The pandemic pushed companies over a "technology tipping point" where adoption of the latest wave of AI technology went from incremental, cautious exploration to must-have organizational resource.[19] The level of disruption experienced was indeed severe, but businesses that had technology in place had a more successful response to the crisis. Many of these businesses were able to turn to technology during talent shortages, had better visibility with suppliers, and better managed customers. Ted English, CEO of Bob's Furniture, told us: "Fortunately we had the technology in place to get through Covid. I can't image what this would have looked like 20 years ago."[20]

Turbulence is the hallmark of the post-pandemic era and businesses that survived understand that they have to build resilience to be ready for an uncertain future. They are quickly turning to technology and AI as the answer. In fact, digital transformation was the biggest corporate priority for 2022 and beyond[21] and our own survey of company leaders bears this out. Surveys and interviews confirm the rapid acceleration of technology and AI adoption. Now that we are past this tipping point it is unlikely the trend will ever reverse.[22]

The pandemic ushered in a new understanding for businesses leaders. To stay competitive in this new business and economic environment requires new strategies and practices. Technology is now seen as a critical strategic component—no longer just a source of cost efficiency. Also, there is new understanding that connectivity with business partners is critical[23]—and technology is the enabler.

Prior to the pandemic over 50% of companies had no idea where in the world their suppliers were located,[24] making it difficult to predict delays of deliveries, shortages of supplies, and manage customer demands. The stockouts during the pandemic made companies acutely aware of the need to "see" what is happening along their supply chains. Technology enables this visibility.

An executive survey finds that since the pandemic more than 50% of companies have adopted AI in at least one function in their business[25] and it is their most important strategic change. This includes using cloud computing, artificial intelligence (AI), analytics, robotics, process automation—all designed to reduce costs and create new capabilities. In fact, the cost of not embracing technology is now considerable with average annual cost of manually dealing with data over $1 million—a cost passed down to customers—making it difficult to be responsive and cost competitive.[26]

Technology is seen as the tool that can help companies survive, be more resilient,[27] provide better customer service[28] and find better sources of supply. Technology can even help firms redesign their business models[29] in order to provide more customized products faster—from eyeglasses to footwear. Technology also helps create products, such as Asics launching sandals made with 3D printing[30] and Lego its 3D printed toys.[31]

To better understand the pace at which new technologies are entering the marketplace for enterprise intelligence, consider the Gartner "Hype Cycle." Here the maturity, adoption and application of emerging technologies is presented graphically through five phases. The accuracy of the Hype Cycle and progression over time can be seen by comparing the 2015 forecast for AI technology maturation with today's marketplace, as shown in Figure 1.1 and Figure 1.2. The rapid changes in adoption can be seen in the diagrams, and it is clear that the era of generative AI is just beginning.

According to a McKinsey study of 63 different use cases, of all extant AI tools, "Generative AI's impact on productivity could add trillions of dollars in value to the global economy."[33] Of course, these tools will also consume significant amounts of water and electricity, putting generative AI per se on par with the United Kingdom in terms of economic impact and resource consumption. The study underscores the significant impact of AI on employees, automating knowledge work, and changing "the anatomy" to the work environment:

> Generative AI has the potential to change the anatomy of work, augmenting the capabilities of individual workers by automating some of their individual activities. Current generative AI and other technologies have the potential to automate work activities that absorb 60 to 70 percent of employees' time today. In contrast, we previously estimated

Figure 1.1 2015 Gartner Hype Cycle for artificial intelligence

Figure 1.2 2022 Gartner Hype Cycle for business intelligence
Source: Peter Kresneky, *Hype Cycle for Analytics and Business Intelligence, 2022*[32]

that technology has the potential to automate half of the time employees spend working. The acceleration in the potential for technical automation is largely due to generative AI's increased ability to understand natural language, which is required for work activities that account for 25 percent of total work time. Thus, generative AI has more impact on knowledge work associated with occupations that have higher wages and educational requirements than on other types of work.[34]

Our own research supports the findings by both Gartner and McKinsey—that the pace of workforce transformation is accelerating and that work activities as we know them today will rapidly look very different. Technology such as IoT, robotics, cloud computing would save the day in the post-pandemic era, but they have laid the foundation for something more. The digital transformation accelerated by the pandemic is not an end in itself but rather the enabling layer for the next phase of the evolution of intelligent life itself.

But Wait…Machines Can't do Everything

We are in an age of infatuation with evolving technological capability. However, it is still humans—executives, managers, and other decision-makers—who use the output of algorithms to make decisions within an organizational context. These decision-makers bring their human judgment, individual personalities, opinions, and biases to the decision-making process, deciding how to use the analytically generated output.

Consider that for all the advancements in AI, it was humans—physicians and scientists—that were needed to predict viral propagation during the pandemic. As John Sicard, President and CEO of Kinaxis told us: "Every math based model collapsed when Covid hit. Every machine learning algorithm collapsed. None of the assumptive parameters could be trusted."

According to Usama Fayyad,

While we are all fascinated with the apparent eloquence and 'fluency' of chatbots like ChatGPT, it is important that we do not confuse these with 'intelligence'—we are far from systems that have a semantic understanding of what they are saying. We are also far from systems that have reasoning capabilities—including common-sense reasoning—which remains elusive for machines and strictly in the domain of humans.[35]

Humans and technology are often seen as competitors in the new world. However, the reality of the situation is more nuanced and should be approached with cautious optimism rather than fear. The strengths of one are the weaknesses of the other. Automation technologies, such as machine learning and robotics, play an increasingly greater role in everyday life and have a huge potential effect on the workplace. Today automation has gone beyond repetitive manufacturing activities. Robots run factories, they work side by side with physicians in operating rooms, they read X-rays, and render medical diagnoses. Analytics is used in everything from fraud detection to driving autonomous vehicles.

Yes, machines are far superior at both repetitive and nonrepetitive tasks. They have precision, strength, and do not fatigue. Humans are imprecise, overconfident, and prone to place too much faith in their intuitions. They are highly biased.

However, all machine intelligence is based on data and is *only as good as the data upon which it is based*. Machines are not good at "out-of-the-box" thinking. With generative AI, they may appear creative, but how can an algorithm develop a truly innovative strategy or a unique marketing campaign? Yes, they can identify photos of dogs, but they can also confuse a dachshund dog with a hot dog, and they cannot extrapolate that one is a pet while the other is a ballpark treat.

Context matters and machines don't have context. Consider the "broken-leg problem."[36] An actuarial formula based on historical data might be highly accurate in predicting the odds of someone going to the movies in a given week. But that model should be abandoned if it turns out the person in question has a broken femur. The broken leg problem demonstrates the importance of paying attention to context. We might be able to use historical, actuarial data to predict odds, but the forecast will fail if we don't appreciate the context. Obviously, without that information, the algorithm would be way off. All the data provided to the algorithm suddenly becomes irrelevant because of this change in context. That was precisely the case during the pandemic.

The fact is that in today's rapidly changing economy, the "broken-leg problem" occurs often. Disruptions that require understanding context and providing interpretation are simply a part of today's business environment. This could be a storm delaying a shipment, a political event, a competitor launching a new product, or a union strike. Today companies operate in volatile markets and environments, and "broken-leg problem" is a part of corporate life. Yes, algorithms can offer a far better answer provided the future facts look exactly like the data upon which forecasts are based. However, they cannot help when the environment and context change. The database lags reality; the map is not the actual terrain.

Machines are computationally stronger, faster, more precise. Humans are mentally more intuitive, creative, and understanding of context. Harnessing the strengths of both—and finding the right way for them to work together— is the recipe for success. That is what this book is about.

A number of inventions that enjoy widespread commercial applications were invented by sheer humanity. Accidental good fortune, fun, and humor are foreign notions to computers, but they sure drive a lot of inventions.

Consider the invention of the Post-it® note (the yellow sticky note). Post-it® notes are ubiquitous in the office environment, yet they were invented through creativity, innovation, and out-of-the-box thinking. In 1968, Dr. Spencer Silver, a scientist at 3M, was working on developing a super-strong adhesive but accidentally created a "low-tack" reusable adhesive. It was a "solution without a problem." Although he promoted it within 3M, there was no apparent use for this reusable adhesive. Then in 1974, Arthur Fry, a colleague at 3M, came up with the idea of using it as a bookmark for his hymnbook while singing in the church choir. The low-tack adhesive would not tear the fine Bible paper used in the hymnal. Thus the Post-it® note was born. If it were not for the real-world lived experience of the 3M employee, this novel application of a low-tack adhesive would not have been conceived. We cannot rely on machines to invent things like this.

How about the invention of saccharin, the oldest artificial sweetener? It was discovered by accident when a lab researcher at Johns Hopkins forgot to wash his hands before lunch. Earlier in the day he had accidentally spilled a chemical on his hands and discovered that it made the bread he was eating taste sweet. It was an "aha moment" and saccharin was born. Initial adoption was slow but then received widespread use when sugar was rationed during the First World War. Its popularity skyrocketed with the increase of diet-conscious consumers and the manufacture of Sweet'N Low and diet soft drinks. Without the happy accident of discovering the sweet taste of saccharine, Sweet'N Low would not exist. Machines do not take lunch breaks, and as a result, are unlikely to discover a new flavor by accident.

What about the beloved Slinky toy? The idea came in 1943 from a naval engineer, Richard James. He was working on developing a spring that would support and stabilize sensitive equipment on ships. One of the springs accidentally fell off the shelf and continued moving. James thought it moved in a manner that was bouncy and fun. Since then, more than 250 million Slinkys have been sold worldwide. No AI can identify what we as humans perceive as "fun." It takes humans to do that.

Perhaps when our smartest workers are liberated from the repetitive analytical tasks that now consume our work lives, we can discover that elusive miracle cure, develop renewable energy resources, and find ways to augment human happiness. Technology creates a tremendous opportunity for business by freeing us to innovate. However, it is not merely automation but rather augmentation that offers the greatest benefits to humanity. Erik Brynjolfsson explains[37]:

> The good news is that both automation and augmentation can boost labor productivity: that is, the ratio of value-added output to labor-hours worked. As productivity increases, so do average incomes and living standards, as do our capabilities for addressing challenges from climate change and poverty to health care and longevity. Mathematically, if the human labor used for a given output declines toward zero, then labor productivity would grow to infinity.

The bad news is that no economic law ensures everyone will share this growing pie. Although pioneering models of economic growth assumed that technological change was neutral, in practice technological change can disproportionately help or hurt some groups, even if it is beneficial on average.

In particular, the way the benefits of technology are distributed depends to a great extent on how the technology is deployed and the economic rules and norms that govern the equilibrium allocation of goods, services, and incomes. When technologies *automate* human labor, they tend to reduce the marginal value of workers' contributions, and more of the gains go to the owners, entrepreneurs, inventors, and architects of the new systems. In contrast, when technologies *augment* human capabilities, more of the gains go to human workers.

A common fallacy is to assume that all or most productivity-enhancing innovations belong in the first category: automation. However, the second category, augmentation, has been far more important throughout most of the past two centuries.

We take this conclusion as fundamental to our thesis. Augmentation rather than automation is the proper application of AI to the workforce.

"Robot Proof" the Workforce: Embracing Moravec's Paradox

AI researchers have given a name to the seeming inverse relationship between human and machine capabilities. Moravec's Paradox holds that where machines have strength, humans have weakness, and vice versa. While AI can now do many mental tasks that require "thinking" (such as mathematics), nonetheless AI has a hard time doing what biological beings easily do "without thinking" (such as intuiting someone else's emotional state). In his 1988 book *Mind Children*, Moravec writes:

> Encoded in the large, highly evolved sensory and motor portions of the human brain is a billion years of experience about the nature of the world and how to survive in it. The deliberate process we call reasoning is, I believe, the thinnest veneer of human thought, effective only because it is supported by this much older and much more powerful, though usually unconscious, sensorimotor knowledge. We are all prodigious Olympians in perceptual and motor areas, so good that we make the difficult look easy. Abstract thought, though, is a new trick, perhaps less than 100 thousand years old. We have not yet mastered it. It is not all that intrinsically difficult; it just seems so when we do it.

Contemporary scholars have further reinforced these findings on the impact of evolution on human cognition, comparing how humans and machines think.

Our brains have dedicated wetware for these functions—neural structures that have been optimized over evolutionary timescales. By contrast, logical thinking and skills like chess playing are not natural to us; so perhaps we are forced to rely on a limited pool of general-purpose cognitive resources to perform these tasks. Maybe what our brains do when we engage in explicit logical reasoning or calculation is in some ways analogous to running a "virtual machine," a slow and cumbersome mental simulation of a general-purpose computer. One might then say (somewhat fancifully) that a classical AI program is not so much emulating human thinking as the other way around: a human who is thinking logically is emulating an AI program.[38]

In order to transcend the status quo capabilities handed down to us by the evolutionary process, we need to take our development into our own hands by educational design. Ironically, the last thousand years or so of education following the Jesuit tradition emphasized Aristotelian reasoning—definitions, distinctions, deductions—and the pursuit of mathematics and sciences. Only now have we applied those skills to build machines that far outstrip our own reasoning and information processing skills. Now it seems like we have built an educational apparatus that is in dire need of an upgrade, because it is cultivating capabilities in us that are far surpassed by machines. Why train in a competition where you are, by nature, hopelessly outmatched?

At a 2017 summit of the New England Board of Higher Education, Northeastern University President Joseph E. Aoun put forth an assessment of the choices facing institutions of higher education in light of these disruptive advances in technology: *embrace the reality or become obsolete.* The same is true for business organizations.

According to Aoun, the rational response for educational institutions to this impending crisis is to teach humans to become "Robot Proof," by deploying what he coins as a new educational discipline: humanics.[39] Educational institutions should give in to the power of Moravec's Paradox instead of trying to fight against it. Aoun's theory of humanics would be a step in the right direction by offering a course of study that:

> prepares students to perform the future jobs that only human beings can do. It achieves this by fostering purposeful integration of technical literacies, such as coding and data literacy, with human literacies, such as creativity, ethics, cultural agility, and entrepreneurship. When students combine these literacies with experiential components, they integrate their knowledge with real life settings, leading to deep learning. Experiential learning is a powerful delivery system for the humanics curriculum.[40]

An education in humanics teaches us how to work alongside high-performing technologies while accentuating our uniquely human strengths. This blended approach to educational policy would empower us to do what neither the smartest person or the most advanced AI system could do alone. Our effort in this book is in furtherance of Aoun's objective of promoting humanics, not only in the classroom but in the office bullpen as well. Our book applies this imperative beyond the classroom to enterprise management.

The urgency of significant educational policy reform called for by Aoun is echoed by the sentiment expressed by Kasparov:

> That our classrooms still mostly look like they did a hundred years ago isn't quaint; it's absurd… Wealthy nations approach education in the same way a wealthy aristocratic family approaches investing. The status quo has been good for a long time; why rock the boat? … The prevailing attitude is that education is too important to take risks. My response is that education is too important *not* to take risks.

To be fair to humans, even those on the front lines of AI research and implementation still believe humans are indispensable from some of the most important kind of work to be done. For instance, John E. Kelly III, director of IBM Research, contends that jobs requiring higher-order critical thinking, creative thinking, innovation, and high levels of emotional engagement will need to be filled by humans for some time to come. Of course, human performance in these kinds of jobs would be greatly enhanced by harnessing the power of "cognitive systems" that enable decision-makers to penetrate complexity and crunch through big data sets to make optimal decisions.[41]

"Deep Blue" Blues

It was 1997 and Garry Kasparov was the greatest chess player in the world. At the age of twenty-two, he was the youngest ever undisputed World Chess Champion. He had been beating chess-playing computers since the 1980s and had just prevailed over an early version of IBM's supercomputer *Deep Blue* a year earlier. Now he was going for a rematch.

Garry went into the match confident. He was considered unbeatable. Now in front of a global audience, playing the fateful second match with Deep Blue, Garry was becoming visibly frustrated. He fidgeted and shook his head, waiting for his opponent's next move. After only nineteen moves, the audience saw Garry jump up and race away from the board. He had just been beaten by a machine.[42]

The match against Deep Blue put Kasparov in a philosophical mood:[43]

> I got my first glimpse of artificial intelligence on Feb. 10, 1996, at 4:45 p.m. EST, when in the first game of my match with Deep Blue, the computer

nudged a pawn forward to a square where it could easily be captured. It was a wonderful and extremely human move ... Humans do this sort of thing all the time. But computers generally calculate each line of play so far as possible within the time allotted ... So I was stunned by this pawn sacrifice. What could it mean? I had played a lot of computers but had never experienced anything like this. I could feel—I could smell—a new kind of intelligence across the table. While I played through the rest of the game as best I could, I was lost; it played beautiful, flawless chess the rest of the way and won easily. Later I discovered the truth. Deep Blue's computational powers were so great that it did in fact calculate every possible move all the way to the actual recovery of the pawn six moves later. The computer didn't view the pawn sacrifice as a sacrifice at all. So the question is, if the computer makes the same move that I would make for completely different reasons, has it made an "intelligent" move? Is the intelligence of an action dependent on who (or what) takes it?

Kasparov was considered the greatest of all time chess player in his competitive days, like Tiger Woods to golf or Michael Jordan to basketball. Did the triumph of Deep Blue over the human GOAT chess player signal a "superhuman" level of intelligence in game-playing artificial intelligence (AI)?

A special-purpose chess-playing algorithm is extremely limited: "It plays chess; it can do no other."[44] We are well-advised to bear in mind the extraordinary *narrowness* of artificial intelligence—even when rising to a superhuman level in one area of mental endeavor, that excellence does not necessarily translate into any other area of mental activity.

Yet, let's not forget the unique and singular focus and ruthless resilience of artificial intelligence when it is playing to its strength: Deep Blue does not get overcome with emotion when encountering an outrageous move by its opponent. In Kasparov's words, "Had I not melted down during game two and resigned prematurely, none of this would have mattered. Not only was the early resignation my fault, but allowing it to ruin my composure was the real fatal mistake."[45] Absent extreme heat, computers do not "melt down" under mental strain or emotional stress.

Like an adamantine needle, artificial intelligence is currently as narrow as it is rigid. AI, like Deep Blue, suffers from a "lack of a purpose beyond its narrow goal," which is set out by its programmers.[46] Another way to frame this is, "Expertise does not necessarily translate into applicable understanding, let alone wisdom."[47]

Nonetheless, this was a revolutionary moment—the beginning of the world seeing the capability of thinking machines. The IBM supercomputer, Deep Blue, was a machine capable of processing over 100 million positions per second, nothing any human could do.

What if we could combine the labile generality of human intellects with the power and rigor of narrow AI?

Kasparov's Law: Triumph of Process

Moravec's Paradox tells us that machines and humans have complementary strengths. But, how do we combine their unique skills for the best outcome? The answer comes from Garry Kasparov. In the fallout of the Deep Blue match, Kasparov was motivated to analyze the potential interactions, and collaborations, of human and machine thinking:

> What if, instead of human versus machine, we played as partners? My brainchild saw the light of day in a match in 1998 in Leon, Spain, and we called it Advanced Chess. Each player had a PC at hand running the chess software of his choice during the game. The idea was to create the highest level of chess ever played, a synthesis of the best of man and machine.[48]

The results of this experiment were both predictable and surprising. Predictably, humans with access to machine support were less likely to make tactical blunders, because the computer would analyze potential moves and countermoves with speed and accuracy surpassing human ability. This, in turn, freed up the human player to deploy mental bandwidth on strategic analysis and creative ideation, instead of using precious (that is, far more limited) brainpower doing labor-intensive computations of the various permutations on the board. Even Kasparov, who was perhaps unparalleled among chess players for his powerful and accurate calculations (relative to other humans), lost a competitive edge under these conditions.[49]

Computers compute; when human competitors both have access to computers, the human with greater computational power loses his edge, as the computer has an equalizing effect along that dimension. As a consequence, when aided with machine computation, the human with greater creative and strategic skills will tend to prevail, all other things being equal.

Another foreseeable result was that the teams that combined amateur chess players with ordinary computers prevailed over a superhuman chess-specialist computer with no human teammate. "Human strategic guidance combined with the tactical acuity of a computer was overwhelming."[50]

However, as the "Advanced Chess" tournament came to a climax, something remarkable occurred. Based on the foregoing, you would be forgiven for betting that the champion of the Advanced Chess tournament would be a grand master (among the greatest human chess players alive) partnered up with a high-powered chess-specialist computer. You would be wrong.

The winning team was actually composed of *two amateur chess players* who deployed *three ordinary computers* simultaneously. The champions were amateurs Steven Crampton and Zackary Stephen, "chess buddies who met at a local club in New Hampshire in the US," who "had spent a few years honing their skills at the game," but still "had day jobs and were effectively unknown in the world of competitive chess."[51]Steven and Zackary entered the freestyle tournament up against no less than "several teams of grandmasters aided by computers."[52] Based on historical precedent and the merits of the competitive playing field, they should have lost. But they didn't, thanks to a unique method.

Steven and Zackary happened to have developed a database fed with over four years of data of their own personal strategies. This database showed "which of the two players typically had greater success when faced with similar situations," so they knew when to defer to their teammate and when to take the initiative.[53] They also fully utilized the rules allowing for the use of personal computers running optimization algorithms for any given arrangement of the board they happened to find themselves in.

The secret ingredient to the success was, according to one of the players, "We had really good methodology for when to use the computer and when to use our human judgement, that elevated our advantage."[54]

The shocking outcome demonstrated that "certain human skills were still unmatched by machines when it came to chess and using those skills cleverly and co-operatively could make a team unbeatable."[55]

We contend that the results of the Advanced Chess tournament are instructive, well beyond the realm of chess. Kasparov's own takeaway from the surprising results actually provides a major theme for our book: "A clever process beat superior knowledge and superior technology. It didn't render knowledge and technology obsolete, of course, but it illustrated the power of efficiency and coordination to dramatically improve results."[56]

In what has become known as *Kasparov's Law*, we can formulate the insight as: "*weak human + machine + better process* was superior to a strong computer alone and, more remarkably, superior to a *strong human + machine + inferior process*."[57]

One of the objectives for this book is to elucidate what this "better process" looks like at the enterprise level. Even chess enthusiasts can appreciate that this type of human + machine cooperation is not limited to chess and extends from diagnostic medicine to manufacturing. How can ordinary ("weak") humans combine ordinary ("weak") machines to achieve extraordinary results? By using a better process. That process is laid out in Chapters 7 and 8. We do not need to be geniuses or have access to quantum computer power in order to achieve extraordinary results. We simply need to follow Kasparov's Law.

Using ordinary people and ordinary machinery, combined with the right process, we can create the extraordinary—the *Humachine*. That is the goal of this book.

What Comes After the Silicon Wave?

While the forecasts of the extent of blue-collar and white-collar professional displacement by machines vary in magnitude, they all share the same insight: the machines are coming for human jobs of all kinds. We may call it the *silicon wave*, as generative AI, computerization, bots, autonomous machines, and so forth gobble up human jobs. At each successive interval of machine innovation, more and more jobs appear to be "low-hanging fruit," easily susceptible to displacement by machines. The silicon wave promises to cause a flood of biblical proportions, leaving behind a world transformed, no less profound than the changes wrought by the onset of electricity.

Research shows that while automation will eliminate very few occupations entirely in the next decade, it will affect portions of almost all jobs to a greater or lesser degree, depending on the type of work they entail.[58] Unless forbidden by law, no job is sacrosanct—a machine could theoretically displace *any* job. However, a common fallacy is that an economy has a fixed number of jobs. Rather, with greater automation we should expect more material prosperity, an expansion of economy, and more jobs. This is articulated by Marc Andreessen:[59]

> The core mistake the automation-kills-jobs doomers keep making is called the "*lump of labor*" fallacy. This fallacy is the incorrect notion that there is a fixed amount of labor to be done in the economy at any given time, and either machines do it or people do it—and if machines do it, there will be no work for people to do. The lump of labor fallacy flows naturally from naïve intuition but naïve intuition here is wrong. When technology is applied to production, we get *productivity growth*—an increase in output generated by a reduction in inputs. The result is *lower prices* for goods and services. As prices for goods and services fall, we pay less for them, meaning that we now have *extra spending power* with which to buy *other things*. This *increases demand* in the economy, which drives the creation of *new production*—including new products and new industries—which then creates new jobs for the people who were replaced by machines and prior jobs. The results: a larger economy with higher material prosperity, more industries, more products, and more jobs.

Could a robot be president of the United States? These days, it would appear nothing is too controversial for that office. The US Constitution, Article II, Section 1 provides that,

> No person except a natural born citizen, or a citizen of the United States, at the time of the adoption of this Constitution, shall be eligible to the office of President; neither shall any person be eligible to that

office who shall not have attained to the age of thirty-five years, and been fourteen years a resident within the United States.

At first blush, we cannot elect a robot to be the president because a robot is not a "natural-born citizen."

However, we need just a little bit of interpretive wriggle room to get there. Does the word "born" include "*assembled*"? If yes, then a computer that is "Made in America" is "born" in the USA.

Can we pass a law that grants citizenship to a robot? The humanoid AI bot christened Sophia has already been granted citizenship by Saudi Arabia, so we know that robot citizenship is possible.

Therefore, a robot assembled in the USA and granted citizenship by law, that has been in existence for no less than 35 years and which has been within the territorial limits of the USA for no less than 14 years, could theoretically run for the office of the president.

Not that President Tron would be guaranteed a strong chance of successfully navigating the political landscape, but in theory it is possible. Ace the Turing Test and crush it in the polls. Thirty-five years provides a lot of time for upgrades and feeding algorithms with political data.

Imagine a robot mind running the calculations of IBM's Watson .to determine the absolutely pitch-perfect talking points at any given political moment, optimized to persuade a critical mass of voters. This hypothetical is just to illustrate the point that any job, even president of the United States, could theoretically be displaced by a machine. So we better make preparations for that silicon wave to wash over every sector and every level of the corporate hierarchy.

According to Ed Hess, Professor of Business Administration and Batten Executive-in-Residence at the Darden Graduate School of Business, "Because AI will be a far more formidable competitor than any human, we will be in a frantic race to stay relevant. That will require us to take our cognitive and emotional skills to a much higher level."[60]

Unfortunately, the very traits that make humans succeed where robots struggle—that is, innovative thinking and emotional intelligence—are stymied by "our natural cognitive and emotional proclivities: We are confirmation-seeking thinkers and ego-affirmation-seeking defensive reasoners." According to Hess:

> We will spend more time training to be open-minded and learning to update our beliefs in response to new data. We will practice adjusting after our mistakes, and we will invest more in the skills traditionally associated with emotional intelligence. The new smart will be about trying to overcome the two big inhibitors of critical thinking and team collaboration: our ego and our fears. Doing so will make it easier to perceive reality as it is, rather than as we wish it to be. In short, we will

embrace humility. That is how we humans will add value in a world of smart technology.[61]

We simply cannot compete with machines in terms of processing speed, calculation accuracy, pattern recognition across big data sets, or the quantity of computations per second. We need to recognize the playing field is forever unleveled along those dimensions.

Let's shift our focus to where we *can* compete. Hess suggests we redefine what it means to be "smart," determined "not by what or how you know but by the quality of your thinking, listening, relating, collaborating, and learning." In a phrase, Hess recommends *humility* as the life raft to avoid drowning in the silicon wave.

Artificial intelligence has arrived in multifarious forms. We now live in a world of smartphones with predictive text and voice recognition, digital assistants in our home stereos, and self-driving cars. A recent study estimates that analytics, AI, and automation will wipe out half of today's workforce by 2055, or possibly even twenty years sooner.[62]

Those familiar with AI research may find the timing of these predictions amusing in one sense. Since the invention of the computer in the 1940s, the "expected arrival date" of human-like machine intelligence (what we can call strong general artificial intelligence) has generally been about twenty years in the future. This forecast "has been receding at a rate of one year per year."[63]

> Two decades is a sweet spot for prognosticators of radical change: near enough to be attention-grabbing and relevant, yet far enough to make it possible to suppose that a string of breakthroughs, currently only vaguely imaginable, might by then have occurred.[64]

No matter what year it is, we cannot ignore the very real fact that displacement of human labor by automation has already begun. Another study by Oxford University estimates that one in every two jobs will be automated.[65] We discuss the issues around labor displacement more in subsequent chapters. Suffice it so say, robotics will revolutionize the workplace and the workforce, in every kind of service industry, in manufacturing, in policing and military force, in transportation and logistics, and even in the lesser-discussed (but no less significant) areas of the economy such as the black market.

The Superintelligence Singularity is Nigh

Vernor Vinge, a math and computer scientist and science fiction author, is perhaps the original prophet of disastrous artificial intelligence predictions. He coined the term *singularity*, by which he means the tipping point occurring after we create intelligence greater than our own. We have avoided use of the term "singularity" to describe the integration of human and machine virtues. We are not throwing shade at Kurzweil or Vinge. We use "combine" and "integrate" as opposed to "singularity" because singularity has an almost rapture-esque, apocalyptical sound to it.

According to Vinge, when the singularity happens, "Human history will have reached a kind of singularity, an intellectual transition as impenetrable as the knotted space-time at the center of a black hole, and the world will pass far beyond our understanding."[66] Maybe that is what happens in the Fifth Level of Control discussed in the Foreword. Once the "technological means to create superhuman intelligence" emerge, "shortly thereafter, the human era will be ended."[67]

While this sounds ominous, it need not be. The end of the Anthropocene era could also mean the end of living in the fear of mutually assured destruction from nuclear war, the end of famine, and the end of biodiversity loss and habitat destruction, because some computer's superintelligence would have solved the hard problems of providing for the human population in a sustainable manner, giving us the security, prosperity, and abundance required to avoid these all-too-human problems and begin to live in dignified peace on Earth.

These forecasts are startling and augur socioeconomic disasters of various forms.

Despite the popularity of recent AI fearmongering, it is not the goal of this book to identify the various kinds of risks or benefits that automation or superintelligence brings on its own but rather how to deploy these technological advances in a certain way to create organizational network (enterprise-level) collective superintelligence. Neither is it our goal to merely point out potential foxholes (such as universal basic income or a return to more Luddite modes of being) that humans might retreat into to mitigate the social harms posed by AI. We will have a better time managing these challenges if we follow Kasparov's Law and create a Humachine. Rather than running from the problem, we lean into it. Grasp the nettle. Solve the problems like a happy warrior rather than moralize about them. We simply take for granted that these changes are coming and operate under the assumption that competing in this new world will require a different approach to educating future workers, and require reimagining the structure of enterprise. Keep in mind an implication of Kasparov's Law: we do not need to be individual geniuses to accomplish superintelligence if we can program our enterprises in the right way to manifest collective, or organizational network intelligence. *We can build a Humachine with the human and technological resources we already have.*

Details on how firms can evolve into a Humachine through improved process are laid out in the closing chapters of this book, Chapters 7 through 9. To lay the foundation for that model however we need to explore the symbiotic, mutually dependent relationship between humans and machines in Chapters 3 through 5. Unpacking Moravec's Paradox, these chapters compare and contrast human and technological "thinking" to better under-stand the extent of what each resource adds to the overall intelligence of an enterprise. But before we go there, first we need to understand what is superintelligence, what are the theoretical pathways available to attain superintelligence, and which pathway should be pursued? Those questions are answered in Chapter 2.

"Botsourcing" and Building a Superintelligent Enterprise

Perhaps the simplest way to pose the challenges posed by AI to modern managers is: whether we should botsource a traditionally human business function, and if so, how?

As technology takes over our lives, there has been a tremendous amount of automation anxiety, that human jobs will go the way of horses displaced by steam engines and we will be left impoverished and put out to pasture as a result of our "progress inventing machines more intelligent than ourselves."

We call replacing humans with robots or software "*botsourcing*," which is the robotic version of "outsourcing." Outsourcing is where a job, good, or service that was originally delivered from an internal source is contracted out to a foreign or external supplier, generally in order to reduce costs or improve quality. Like outsourcing, botsourcing displaces internal labor by delegating a task to a machine that was traditionally performed by humans.

Even when the decision to botsource is made, we must still decide whe-ther humans remain in the loop, "on" the loop, or out of the loop entirely. These are strategic choices with significant ramifications for business suc-cess. Automation can be a blessing or a curse depending on how well it is executed. Like any other tool conceived by mankind, whether it performs as intended depends on technique.

For every job that is displaced by a machine, there could very well be more jobs to do or greater wealth to share as a result of the increase in quality, productivity, and savings. The invention of the steam engine caused the collapse of horse-powered transportation, but it also increased societal wealth and created all sorts of jobs that were hitherto unimaginable.

We appreciate the concern about botsourcing, but that is not exactly an existential threat. Our concerns for the onslaught of AI in enterprise are deeper. Namely, that machines—robots, AI, and technology in general—will take over in the sense of asserting control over humankind.

Introducing the Control Problem

In other words, advances in AI pose the so-called *control problem*. We want to build a superintelligent system that exceeds human capabilities (so that we can harness this new power) without inadvertently unleashing an unstoppable threat upon the realm.

There is a popularly articulated fear that machines will not only displace humans in the workforce in a vicious way—that is, leading to poverty and lack instead of augmenting freedoms and wealth—but worse, that machines would take over the world. The standard formulation of the control problem puts it in these terms:[68]

> The initial superintelligence might obtain a decisive strategic advantage. This superintelligence would then be in a position to form a singleton [that is, an entity with no natural competition or check on its power] and to shape the future of Earth-originating intelligent life. What happens from that point onward would depend on the superintelligence's motivations.
>
> Second, the orthogonality thesis suggests that we cannot blithely assume that a superintelligence will necessarily share any of the final values stereotypically associated with wisdom and intellectual development in humans—scientific curiosity, benevolent concern for others, spiritual enlightenment and contemplation, renunciation of material acquisitiveness, a taste for refined culture or for the simple pleasures in life, humility and selflessness, and so forth.
>
> Third, the instrumental convergence thesis entails that we cannot blithely assume that a superintelligence ... would limit its activities in such a way as not to infringe on human interests. An agent with a final goal [of something otherwise benign like calculating the decimal expansion of pi] would have a convergent instrumental reason, in many situations, to acquire an unlimited amount of physical resources and, if possible, to eliminate potential threats to itself or its goal system. Human beings might constitute potential threats; they certainly constitute physical resources. Taken together, these three points thus indicate that the first superintelligence may [create an outcome] in which humanity quickly becomes extinct.

That AI would take a treacherous turn and become hostile to its creator is an alarming scenario, to say the least. The treacherous turn could be prevented by keeping superintelligence from gaining a decisive strategic advantage—say, by building in limits and competition to prevent a singleton from forming—or by shaping the goals of any superintelligence to align with broadly accepted standards of human well-being.

However, the risk of harms from AI do not depend upon it reaching a technological singularity or even becoming superintelligent. We need only consider the risk of *indirect prompt injection* to see how AI tools can be used against their user.

A direct prompt injection occurs when the user instructs ("prompts") the chatbot to roleplay a bad bot, leading it to "jailbreak" outside of the rules programmed to guide its behavior. An indirect prompt injection is more insidious. For example, Microsoft applied ChatGPT to empower its Bing software. They introduced an opt-in feature that allows Bing to "see" the content of any web page the user has open in an Internet browser. Thus, a hacker can jailbreak Bing merely by injecting a prompt on any website the user happens to have open at the time. A text prompt hidden in any open browser tab can cause the chatbot to take on a persona or carry out an illicit command merely by indirect prompt injection:[69]

> Microsoft isn't clear on what algorithm decides which content from which tab Bing can see at any one time. What we know right now is that Bing inserts some content from the current tab when the conversation in the sidebar begins. Once the conversation has started, the injection will remain active until the conversation is cleared and the poisoned website is no longer open. The injection itself is completely passive. It's just regular text on a website that Bing ingests and that 'reprograms' its goals by simply asking it to. Could just as well be inside of a comment on a platform, the attacker does not need to control the entire website the user visits.

This risk will remain until the Large Language Models have improved security boundaries that can discern between trustworthy and untrusted inputs. Another way of putting this risk of AI is that we do not worry merely about superintelligent bots losing alignment with human values. We should be preoccupied with bots—totally lacking common sense and easily hackable—being used by other humans to inflict harms far greater than what human hackers could do without these tools. An AI program that runs critical infrastructure can pose dangers to humanity even if it is aligned with us—it simply needs to misunderstand the assignment, or fail to appreciate a change in context, leading to disastrous results.

If we go about building Humachines in a conscientious manner, technology will compliment humans by making us more efficient and more productive, safeguarding values such as peace, autonomy, and health. As routine tasks are taken over by machines, humans can live more fulfilling lives, freed from the monotony of routinized tasks, liberated from the mineshafts and spreadsheet drudgery, and gifted with the analytical resources of smarter, faster, and tireless analytical engines.

Consider that throughout time machines have taken over human jobs, from farming to factories. Machines are now taking over offices. As in the past, it is up to humans to create new jobs and industries, buoyed by the enabling layer of AI. As people are displaced from jobs it is up to us to find novel ways of giving value to our lives, being productive members of society, or at the very least, finding ways to enjoy the bounty of abundance made possible by this latest wave of displacement. The real risk is that we ignore the risks of malevolent applications of technology. As technology improves, so too do our powers to manipulate the environment, and concomitant with that power is the responsibility to steer our enterprises toward a just future.

The "Big Bang" of AI: Generative AI and Evolutionary Algorithms

According to Nobel Laureate Thomas Friedman,

> This is a Promethean moment we've entered—one of those moments in history when certain new tools, ways of thinking or energy sources are introduced that are such a departure and advance on what existed before that you can't just change one thing, you have to change everything.[70]

It was November 30, 2022. The world had emerged from the pandemic with a cautious optimism that we may return to some sense of normalcy after a once-in-a-generation pandemic. The winter holiday season was approaching with a buzz of welcoming a first normal winter. Then—on that day—ChatGPT was launched by San Francisco based OpenAI. This would be the first of many generative AI language models that can create original content in response to a user prompt.

Within a mere five days—by December 4, 2022—ChatGPT had over a million users. Everything we thought we knew about AI and technological capability was upended. This was the "big bag" or AI—or as Thomas Friedman put it, a "Promethean Moment."

So, what is generative AI? When you want to get to know someone, it's often wise to ask them directly. So we asked ChatGPT to tell us, what is generative AI?:

> Generative AI is a type of artificial intelligence that can create new and original content based on patterns it has learned from existing data. Unlike traditional AI, which is designed to recognize patterns and respond to predefined queries, generative AI is capable of producing outputs that are unique and unpredictable. This is made possible through deep learning algorithms that analyze large datasets to identify underlying patterns and then use that information to generate new content. For example, a generative AI model could be trained on thousands of images of cats and then use that knowledge to create new images of cats that have never been seen before. This technology has a wide range of potential applications in business, from product design and marketing to customer service and data analysis.[71]

The response is very impressive indeed. However, we do prefer the human explanation offered by Usama Fayyad, Executive Director for the Institute for Experiential Artificial Intelligence at Northeastern University:[72]

Generative AI refers to the kind of AI that can, quite simply, generate outputs. Those outputs could be in the form of text like you see in what we call the large language models, such as ChatGPT (a chatbot on top of a large language model), or images, etc. If you are training (the AI) on text, text is what you will get out of it. If you are training it on images, you get images, or modifications of images, out of it. If you are training it on sounds or music, you get music out of it. If you train it on programming code, you get programs out, and so on. It is also called generative AI because the algorithms have the ability to generate examples on their own.

Merely entering one prompt into ChatGPT is all it takes to see the power of generative AI. And with all the hype surrounding ChatGPT other companies are rapidly vying for a piece of the AI powered chatbot game. Microsoft quickly followed with the launch of its chatbot, the "new" Bing. Google followed with Bard and Meta with Galactica. Then there is Anthropic, an AI research company founded by former OpenAI employees, working on a competitor called Claude, and the list of companies playing in this space goes on.

The use of AI powered assistants is just beginning to take hold in the corporate world. We merely asked ChatGPT4 to give us examples of prompts needed for various tasks. We can see from **Figure 1.3** that many traditional business functions can be handled through the correct "prompt engineering."

Within less than a year, there are now dozens of applications for generative AI across domains of performing research, producing 3D renderings, speech recognition, writing code, creating still images, analyzing videos, and of course writing text. See **Figure 1.4**. We discuss applications for generative AI, specifically prompt engineering, in Chapter 3: What Machines Can and Cannot Do.

Generative art, defined as, "a process of algorithmically generating new ideas, forms, shapes, colors or patterns," involves a creative dance between the human artist and the computer program: "First, you create rules that provide boundaries for the creation process. Then a computer follows those rules to produce new works on your behalf." Once new works are produced, the human discriminates on aesthetic grounds between these computer-generated outcomes, iterating and refining and making artistic choices about the computer output, until a final instance of the artistic work is settled upon and given a title. "In contrast to traditional artists who may spend days or even months exploring one idea, generative code artists use computers to generate thousands of ideas in milliseconds."[74]

According to AIArtists.org,

Generative artists leverage modern processing power to invent new aesthetics – instructing programs to run within a set of artistic constraints, and guiding the process to a desired result. This method vastly

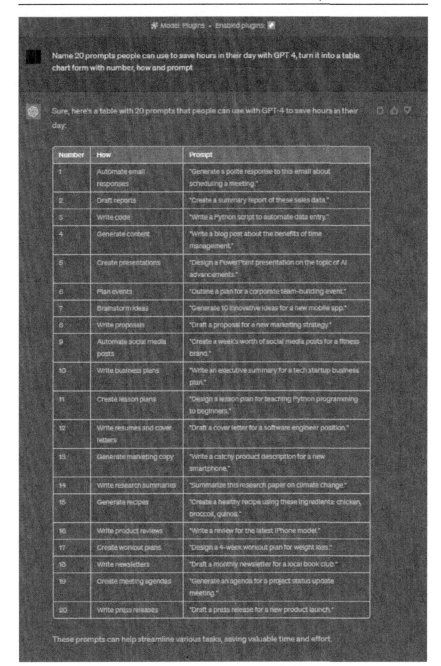

Figure 1.3 ChatGPT4 offers prompts for business tasks

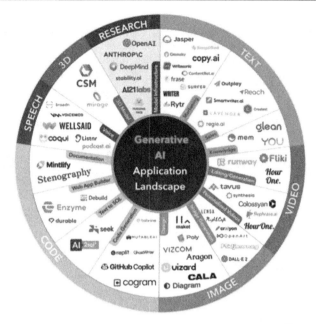

Figure 1.4 Novel applications of generative AI in the creative domains[73]

reduces the exploratory phase in art and design, and often leads to surprising and sophisticated new ideas.[75]

We are not saying robots are now artists, or they are replacing artists, but rather they are becoming turbo-boosters for the artistic process, enabling artists to harness the power of computing to stimulate unprecedented kinds of innovative and creative work.

Generative art is a game-changer for the artistic process because, frankly, many artists would probably love to botsource the "exploratory" phase. That is, the hard part about being an artist is the part we'd like to delegate to the computers. The exploratory phase in the creative process is often a tedious, arduous labor of love—ideating and rejecting over and over while trying not to be disenchanted by the process of gathering and winnowing but not producing. The exploratory phase is contrasted with the *jouissance* of creative energetic activity of the creative person at work. Using generative code lets the artist fast-forward to the fun part. To help understand the thesis of our book, take this example of an AI tool empowering (rather than displacing) traditional human activity, and generalize it across all aspects of the enterprise.

Generative art and design not only expedite the creative process, they increase the likelihood of unlocking evolutionary mutations that may very well be fitness enhancing.

Michael Hansmeyer is an architect who considers Generative Design as 'thinking about designing not the object—but a process to generate objects.' The process allows for more artificial serendipity—the happy accidents and novel ideas that normally take time to stumble upon.[76]

The underlying tactic of using algorithms to enable more *serendipity*—the chance development of events in a beneficial way—may be a hallmark of the beneficial uses of AI. We characterize AI as an enabling layer, or a predicate, for the emergence of organizational network intelligence in Chapter 2 and we describe its evolutionary role within the enterprise.

The use of evolutionary algorithms in product design is intriguing because it accelerates innovation by subjecting designs to millions of potential permutations under constraints set forth by the user. Indeed, not only artists but NASA scientists are using evolutionary algorithms for innovation:

NASA used evolutionary algorithms to design [a novel, oddly shaped, highly effective] antennae. 'This is the first time an artificially evolved object will have flown in space,' observed Jason Lohn, who led the project to design the antennas at NASA Ames Research Center, in California's Silicon Valley. 'The AI software examined millions of potential antenna designs before settling on a final one. The software did this much faster than any human being could... through a process patterned after Darwin's 'survival of the fittest,' the strongest designs survive and the less capable do not.'[77]

Whereas natural evolutionary process would have taken millennia to reveal the fittest version of something, the algorithm can do so in a matter of seconds. Thus, the use of AI has enabled humanity to unlock the emergent genius and godlike creative power of the evolutionary process itself. There is literally an app for that.

According to Jensen Huang, the co-founder and CEO of graphics processor company Nvidia, his company has been evangelizing the utility of artificial intelligence for a long time. They were initially focused on gaming, which naturally had them interested in refining "computer graphics, of course, and physics simulation, whether it's finite element analysis or fluid simulations or molecular dynamics. It's basically Newtonian physics."[78] It is somewhat ironic that what was originally driven by sheer entertainment purposes has grown so relevant to commercial enterprise.

Nvidia now brings generative AI to world's enterprises with cloud services for creating large language and visual models. Jensen Huang added: "Generative AI is driving the fast adoption of AI and reinventing countless industries. NVIDIA AI Foundations let enterprises customize foundation models with their own data to generate humanity's most valuable resources — intelligence and creativity."[79]

As applications of AI have evolved, so has the context of innovation. As Huang says,

> The first thing is that Moore's Law has really slowed. So as a result GPU-accelerated computing gave us life after Moore's Law, and it extended the capability of computing so that these applications that desperately need more computing can continue to advance. Meanwhile, the reach of GPUs has gone far and wide, and it's much more than computer graphics today. We've reached out into all fields—of course computer graphics, virtual reality, augmented reality—to all kinds of interesting and challenging physics simulations.[80]

From these, somewhat humble, origins in video game applications, Nvidia's technology—and AI in general—has shifted the paradigm from Newtonian physics to quantum mechanics, the next great leap in computing. Huang says,

> Almost every supercomputer in the world today has some form of acceleration, much of it from Nvidia... The field of quantum chemistry is going quite well and there's a great deal of research in quantum chemistry, in quantum mechanics... And deep learning, combined with the rich amount of data that's available, and the processing capability came together to become what people call the Big Bang of modern AI.[81]

Nvidia is now powering Microsoft, Facebook, and other leading companies because, according to Huang,

> AI is eating software. The way to think about it is that AI is just the modern way of doing software. In the future, we're not going to see software that is not going to continue to learn over time, and be able to perceive and reason, and plan actions and that continues to improve as we use it. These machine-learning approaches, these artificial intelligence-based approaches, will define how software is developed in the future. Just about every startup company does software these days, and even non-startup companies do their own software. Similarly, every startup in the future will have AI.[82]

Another breakthrough in AI applications is that, in the future, no machinery will be "dumb" because it will all contain some degree of artificial intelligence. AI is not "limited to cloud-based intelligence, resident in powerful, gigantic data centers" because, according to Huang,

> You've got cars, you've got drones, you've got microphones; in the future, almost every electronic device will have some form of deep learning inferencing within it. We call that AI at the edge. And

eventually there'll be a trillion devices out there: Vending machines; every microphone; every camera; every house will have deep learning capability.[83]

Without doubt, by the time of this publication there will be many new entrants to this burgeoning market and the capabilities will dramatically evolve beyond what we see today. Nevertheless, this marks a decisive moment in the history of AI and it sure feels like a new era has begun. We have just experienced a tectonic shift, or a step up in the evolution of technology and the aptitude of collective intelligence. Products that adopt and build upon this budding technology will reshape the world as we know it. Generative AI offers an exciting future with implications for human aesthetics and culture, the legalities and economics of creative work, and the media ecosystem. Details of these are shown in **Figure 1.5**. But as with every new technology, business leaders must proceed with eyes wide open—and a great deal of caution.

The Humachine: People, Process, Machines

The Humachine is the optimal human–machine partnership. Here, people and technology operate seamlessly. This hybrid workforce creates an unparalleled team of industry leaders that takes advantage of technology to complement and augment human decisions.

The ability of artificial intelligence and advanced robotics to outperform humans is no longer a shocking development like it was when Deep Blue beat Kasparov in 1997. Today we are used to autonomous vehicles, automated kiosks, and personal shopping assistants. Generative AI is already being used in newsrooms, writing, law, medicine, and every knowledge based profession. We take news of the next displacement as *fait accompli*: the silicon wave is an inevitable, irresistible force that needs only time to overtake all industries at all levels.

But there are steps we can take to make this transition less painful. And there are areas where it makes less sense for machines to take over. Technology and people are all too often seen as competitors, with technology threatening to replace people in the workforce. While some displacement may be inevitable, the conversation about the future of work has shifted to managing human labor displacement with universal basic income and taxing the productive output of robots.

To be clear: we do not seek to abate the displacement of human labor by machines, nor do we seek to address how to solve the social and economic problems created by this displacement. Those are political problems than need political solutions. However, there is another scenario where an enterprise creates synergy between technology and people, understanding that *the strengths of one complement the weaknesses of the other.*

Shifts in Culture & Aesthetics

Generative AI tools have distinct affordances that complicate cultural production. These affordances interact with social media platforms in complex and novel ways which may impact aesthetic diversity and norms in visual culture.

Legal Dimensions of Authorship

Today's copyright laws likely will not adequately apportion valuable ownership rights among all participants involved in the production of generative AI, including artists on whose work these systems are trained, but instead may favor the end-user. We need new mechanisms to protect and compensate artists whose work is used for training, or even permit them to opt out.

The Labor Economics of Creative Work

Generative AI tools may accelerate the creative process through rapid ideation. Employment for artists may rise or fall depending on how AI tools interact with particular parts of the creative process. New economic theory is needed to characterize the creative process and understand generative AI's impact on creative work.

Impacts on the Media Ecosystem

As the cost and time to produce media at scale decreases, the media ecosystem may become vulnerable to AI-generated misinformation through the creation of synthetic media, particularly media that provides probative evidence for claims. What is the role of platform interventions such as tracking source provenance and detecting synthetic media downstream in governance and building trust?

Figure 1.5 Generative AI impacts[84]

In this book, we use the term "machine" to encompass all types of technologies that are changing how we work and live. This includes all forms, such as generative AI, analytics and decision technologies, processing technologies such as robotics, communication technologies, and platforms such as cloud computing and blockchains. As described in the Preface, our focus is not on physical machinery but on computational machinery. Certainly there are tremendous differences between the various technologies. However, for our purpose, the common element is that these smart technologies have seeped into the workings of every aspect of business. These technologies are fundamentally changing the way business operates, how businesses compete and innovate.

Organizations, such as Amazon and Apple, demonstrate Humachine traits. However, these companies are rare and most use technology in a poorly integrated way. Maria Villablanca told us:

> On a surface level integration means people interacting with AI and most companies have technological touchpoints - but that is a surface level. How many are actually really using it to coexist in the way they operate? A very small percentage have what is the Humachine - where best elements of human and machine coexist together to drive industry forward.[85]

However, in this new era companies no longer have a choice and the opportunity is within reach for every organization, from large legacy corporations to small and medium firms to start-ups. Spencer Fung, President and CEO of Li & Fung, explained to us that in the new era, companies must develop new business models where they truly integrate technology into their systems: "New business models are needed. If you play by the same set of rules but just doing it faster, that will not be enough."[86]

The opportunity is not limited to these tech giants. It is within reach for every organization, from large legacy corporations to small and medium firms to start-ups. Technology can deliver a competitive advantage along every organizational function, from targeted location-based marketing to refining sourcing channel options and optimizing supply chain inventories. However, companies that successfully leverage technology do all these things in a *coordinated way* as part of an *overarching strategy imbedded in the organizational culture*. They are striving to find the optimal blend of people and technology. Apple is a good example of a company organized for innovation. To be clear, we are not setting any company up as an exemplar of moral leadership—we are simply illustrating what is happening along the cutting edge.

How to Get There

Looking at the numerous companies we have surveyed, interviewed, or visited for this book, we present the foundation of what makes the optimal human–machine partnership and provide a roadmap for how companies can get there. Most leaders we talked with are trying to rapidly acquire technological solutions given the hard learned lessons of the pandemic. Yet they are still following a plug-and-play approach to technology in an attempt to digitize their current business model. This is the wrong approach.

Becoming a Humachine in this new era begins by redefining the business model. It requires the *integration of people, processes, and technology*. It is the symbiosis of these three elements *and continuous improvement and adaptation* that are required to succeed.

Overlaying technology on top of old business models and poor processes will just crystallize the inefficiencies of the past. Selecting technology based on what competitors are doing is foolish—as another's strategy, roadmap, and timetable may not necessarily match your strategy.

Ultimately, it is people that are responsible for making this transition happen. Becoming the Humachine requires having the right leadership. Many companies have created the position of Chief Data Officer (CDO), Chief Technology Officer (CTO) or at least someone who is in a leadership role tasked with looking into how to implement AI. They have revenue responsibility, sit on the executive committee, and are a single point of accountability for technology.

Leaders are the ones who develop the strategy and articulate a compelling vision. They are also the ones who create the culture needed to support any organizational change or process implementation. Equally important is talent selection, recruiting people with a desire to innovate, grow, and become more data savvy. As Joseph Aoun, President of Northeastern University puts it, human talent,

> will be flexible in that they will reskill themselves, upskill themselves, and reinvent themselves. That is what we are looking for in talent. Talent will become obsolete within a year or two so [the question is] do we have talent around us that will reinvent itself? That is what are we looking for. It is not an easy exercise.

We agree.

Retaining talent comes next. Pay is not everything. Consider that SAS Analytics is consistently on Fortune's top places to work, yet its pay scale is just around the *mean* in its industry. Employees stay for the culture, benefits, and lifestyle amenities, not because they couldn't get paid more elsewhere.

Lastly, there must be the right organizational culture and incentive structure. Objective and Key Results (OKRs) are a framework for defining and tracking objectives and their outcomes. Unlike traditional KPIs that are limiting, OKRs are aspirational. OKRs were created at Intel and today are used by many tech giants such as Google, LinkedIn, Twitter, and Uber.

Very few companies have achieved technological integration with human resources, let alone superintelligence. This is especially true of small and midsized enterprises with tight budgets and little room for experimentation, but also large legacy firms with huge overheads, large staff, and engrained processes.

Engaging in fragmented and localized implementation of technology rather than a systematic and coordinated effort produces isolated benefits, lack of insight and competitive advantages, organizational operations plagued with inefficiencies and cost overruns, IT infrastructure costs with limited ROI, and employees fearful of job losses. And yet, fragmented, ad hoc, plug and play adoption of technology is the norm.

The "marriage" of technology with people enables the organization to maximize its capabilities by elevating the basis of organizational decision-making with closer-to-perfect information and rationality. This book is about *how to do this*. It is about how to create synergies between technology and people where the whole is greater than the sum of the parts, the efficiencies of corporate structures are utilized in full, while the limitations of corporate culture attributable to human vices as well as the general imperfections of human self-interest, rationality, and information are left in the past.

What is needed is leadership, strategic thinking, and a roadmap. A plan must be in place for acquiring and managing both human capital and technological investments. Numerous obstacles stand in the way:

- Scarce resources and uncertain ROI
- Cultural resistance to change
- Lack of organizational alignment and agility
- Understanding that data is an asset
- Lack of business direction and executive leadership

Ironically, the key to success is the process of integrating people with technology—not technology itself. It is on careful talent selection, carefully nurtured organizational culture, the right organizational structure, team management that promotes innovation and creativity, and the right organizational incentives. Most of all, what is needed is managing *organizational change*.

Conclusion

The global uncertainties of the post-pandemic era have created the AI rush with business leaders focused on making their organizations more resilient. Capabilities of generative artificial intelligence (AI) models such as ChatGPT have accelerated this urgency representing a historically significant moment in technological evolution. But "machines" can't do everything and Moravec's Paradox illustrates the need for a symbiotic, mutually dependent relationship between man and machine.

We can resolve Moravec's Paradox by applying Kasparov's Law. If we can combine human and machine using the right process, then we enjoy the strengths of both while suffering the weaknesses of neither. Our work and educational systems should accept the paradox. Stop trying to make humans into machines. It took us millions of years to get the way we are now. We need to embrace our differences.

In this book, we lay out a path for how companies can integrate human resources with technology to leverage the strengths of both for an optimal combination—creating a superintelligent enterprise. That is what we call the Humachine. It represents the optimal human–machine partnership. It is not an unattainable ideal but a reality achievable today, with ordinary humans, technology, and processes.

Notes

1 https://www.cfr.org/article/2020-year-earth-stood-still-covid-19#:~:text=The%20COVID%2D19%20pandemic%20brought,restarting%20movement%20could%20take%20years.&text=New%20York%20City%27s%20Times%20Square%20deserted

2 https://www.kff.org/global-health-policy/issue-brief/economic-impact-of-covid-19-on-pepfar-countries/

3 David Wilcox is Senior Fellow for International Economics and a former director of the domestic economics division at the Federal Reserve. https://www.washingtonpost.com/business/2021/01/28/gdp-2020-economy-recession/

4 https://www.globest.com/2021/01/07/corporate-bankruptcies-end-2020-at-10-year-high/?slreturn=20230401115315

5 https://www.jonesday.com/en/insights/2021/02/the-year-in-bankruptcy-2020

6 Interview with Henry Nasella, Chair Emeritus and Trustee of Northeastern University and past President and COO of Staples on January 17, 2023.

7 https://sscs.mit.edu/

8 Interview with Henry Nasella, Chair Emeritus and Trustee of Northeastern University and past President and COO of Staples on January 17, 2023.

9 Katherine Tai. U.S. Trade Representative; Milken Institute Global Conference, May 2022.

10 https://www.mckinsey.com/capabilities/strategy-and-corporate-finance/our-insights/economic-conditions-outlook-2023

11 https://www.weforum.org/reports/global-risks-report-2023/digest/

12 https://www.cnbc.com/2023/02/07/climate-change-causing-rising-costs-in-2023-ceos-say-pwc-survey.html

13 https://www.axios.com/2022/08/02/heat-wave-climate-change-us-infrastructure

14 https://www.kcur.org/2022-06-30/wheat-farmers-caught-between-high-prices-high-expense

15 https://www.cnn.com/2022/08/16/economy/sichuan-factories-power-crunch-china-heat-wave-intl-hnk/index.html

16 https://www.npr.org/2022/06/17/1105477224/sriracha-shortage-chilli-climate-change

17 https://www.axios.com/2022/08/18/inflation-climate-change-economy-extreme-weather

18 Villablanca, Maria P. Transformation Influencer, Mentor, Keynote Speaker, Co-Founder & CEO, Future Insights Network, Interview January 16, 2023.

19 https://www.mckinsey.com/capabilities/strategy-and-corporate-finance/our-insights/how-covid-19-has-pushed-companies-over-the-technology-tipping-point-and-transformed-business-forever

20 Ted English, CEO Bob's Furniture, Interview January 16, 2023.

21 https://www.businesswire.com/news/home/20220505005707/en/Research-Digital-Tr ansformation-is-the-Top-Priority-For-Corporate-Finance-in-2022-But-Obstacles-In cluding-Inflation-Growing-Productivity-and-Efficiency-Gaps-May-Limit-Finance% E2%80%99s-Ability-to-Succeed

22 https://www.mckinsey.com/capabilities/strategy-and-corporate-finance/our-insights/ how-covid-19-has-pushed-companies-over-the-technology-tipping-point-and-transfo rmed-business-forever

23 https://www.mckinsey.com/capabilities/mckinsey-digital/our-insights/the-top-tren ds-in-tech

24 https://www.mckinsey.com/mgi/overview/in-the-news/reimagining-supply-chain-resilience

25 https://hbr.org/2023/01/where-is-tech-going-in-2023

26 https://www.ddcfpo.com/freight-process-insights/what-is-supply-chain-digitization-an d-why-does-it-matter

27 https://hbr.org/2022/10/leveraging-new-tech-to-boost-supply-chain-resilience

28 https://timesofindia.indiatimes.com/blogs/voices/how-can-technology-help-compa nies-boost-the-customer-experience/

29 https://www.ft.com/content/3db177f2-d187-4632-b94d-268f9d2598eb

30 https://3dprintingindustry.com/news/asics-makes-3d-printed-footwear-debut-with-new-actibreeze-3d-sandal-212657/

31 https://3dprintingindustry.com/news/lego-hands-out-its-first-official-3d-printed-toy-in-the-shape-of-its-original-wooden-duck-215045/

32 https://www.gartner.com/doc/reprints?id=1-2CP8D2PO&ct=230228&st=sb&utm_ source=partner&utm_medium=insightsoftware&utm_campaign=2023_WLD_ LOGI_GARTNER_PPL_PROS_CUST

33 *The Economic Potential of Generative AI: The Next Productivity Frontier*https:// www.mckinsey.com/capabilities/mckinsey-digital/our-insights/the-economic-poten tial-of-generative-ai-the-next-productivity-frontier?utm_source=www.therundown. ai&utm_medium=newsletter&utm_campaign=study-says-ai-can-add-4-4-trillion-to-economy&cid=app&s=03

34 Ibid.

35 https://ai.northeastern.edu/why-we-need-responsible-ai/?utm_source=apr-news letter&utm_medium=apr-2023-newsletter&utm_campaign=2023-newsletter

36 Meehl, P. E. *Clinical versus Statistical Prediction: A Theoretical Analysis and a Review of the Evidence.* (1954 University of Minnesota Press). Reprinted with new Preface, 1996, by Jason Aronson, Northvale, NJ. Reprinted 2013 by Echo Point Books. Meehl, P. E. (1957) When Shall We Use Our Heads Instead of the Formula? *Journal of Counseling Psychology,* 4:268–273.

37 Brynjolfsson, Erik. "The Turing Trap: The Promise & Peril of Human-Like Artificial Intelligence," Director, Stanford Digital Economy Lab, January 12, 2022, Dædalus https://digitaleconomy.stanford.edu/news/the-turing-trap-the-p romise-peril-of-human-like-artificial-intelligence/

38 Bostrom, Nick. *Superintelligence: Paths, Dangers, Strategies.* Oxford University Press. Notes, Chapter 1, Note 62, pp. 328–329.

39 Aoun, Joseph. *Robot-Proof: Higher Education in the Age of Artificial Intelligence* (2017 MIT Press).

40 Schawbel, Dan. Northeastern University President Joseph E. Aoun: How To Be "Robot-Proof". *Forbes,* November 24, 2017. Available at www.forbes.com/sites/ danschawbel/2017/11/24/northeastern-university-president-joseph-e-aoun-how-to-be-robot-proof/#6a9e455651fb

41 Kelly III, John and Steve Hamm. *Smart Machines: IBM's Watson and the Era of Cognitive Computing.* Columbia Business School Publishing, October 15, 2013.

42 Weber, Bruce. Swift and Slashing, Computer Topples Kasparov. *The New York Times*, May 12, 1997.
43 Kasparov, Garry. The Day That I Sensed a New Kind of Intelligence. *Time*, March 25, 1996, no. 13.
44 Bostrom, Nick. *Superintelligence: Paths, Dangers, Strategies* (2014 Oxford University Press), p. 14.
45 Kasparov, Garry. *Deep Thinking: Where Machine Intelligence Ends and Human Creativity Begins* (2017 Hatchet Books), p. 217.
46 Ibid., p. 221.
47 Ibid., p. 225.
48 Ibid., p. 244.
49 Ibid., p. 245.
50 Ibid., p. 246.
51 Baraniuk, Chris. The Cyborg Chess Players That Can't Be Beaten. *BBC Future*, December 4, 2015. Available at www.bbc.com/future/story/20151201-the-cyborg-chess-players-that-cant-be-beaten
52 Ibid.
53 Ibid.
54 Ibid.
55 Ibid.
56 Kasparov, Garry. *Deep Thinking*, p. 246.
57 Ibid.
58 Chui, M., Manyika, J. and Meremadi, M. Where Machines Could Replace Humans—and Where They Can't (Yet). *McKinsey Quarterly*, July 2016.
59 Andreessen, Marc. Why AI Will Save the World. Available at https://a16z.com/2023/06/06/ai-will-save-the-world/
60 Hess, Ed. In the AI Age, "Being Smart" Will Mean Something Completely Different. *Harvard Business Review*, June 19, 2017. Available at https://hbr.org/2017/06/in-the-ai-age-being-smart-will-mean-something-completely-different.   Ed Hess is co-author, with Katherine Ludwig, of *Humility Is the New Smart: Rethinking Human Excellence in the Smart Machine Age* (2017 Berrett-Koehler).
61 Ibid.
62 www.mckinsey.com/global-themes/digital-disruption/harnessing-automation-for-a-future-that-works.
63 Bostrom. *Superintelligence*, p. 4.
64 Ibid.
65 Frey, Carl Benedikt and Michael A. Osborne. The Future of Employment: How Susceptible Are Jobs to Computerisation? September 17, 2013. Available at www.oxfordmartin.ox.ac.uk/downloads/academic/The_Future_of_Employment.pdf; Scott, Patrick. These Are the Jobs Most at Risk of Automation According to Oxford University: Is Yours One of Them? September 27, 2017. Available at www.telegraph.co.uk/news/2017/09/27/jobs-risk-automation-according-oxford-university-one/
66 Vinge, Vernor. First Word. *OMNI Magazine*, January 1983.
67 Vinge, Vernor. The Coming Technological Singularity: How to Survive in the Post-Human Era. In *Vision-21: Interdisciplinary Science and Engineering in the Era of Cyberspace*, pp. 11–22. NASA Conference Publication 10129. NASA Lewis Research Center, 1993.
68 Bostrom. *Superintelligence*, pp. 140–141, 143.
69 Xiang, Chloe. *Hackers Can Turn Bing's AI Chatbot Into a Convincing Scammer, Researchers Say*, (March 3, 2023). Available at https://www.vice.com/en/article/7kxzzz/hackers-bing-ai-scammer (last accessed May 31, 2023).

70 https://www.nytimes.com/2023/03/21/opinion/artificial-intelligence-chatgpt.html
71 ChatGPT accessed on May 5, 2023.
72 https://news.northeastern.edu/2023/04/19/generative-ai-usama-fayyad/
73 *Generative AI Tools in the Creative Domains: The Power and Pressure Game Is On!*, rapidops (March 2023). Available at https://www.rapidops.com/blog/genera tive-ai-tools/ (last accessed May 31, 2023).
74 Generative Art Guide: Examples, Software and Tools to Make Algorithm Art, AIArtists.org. Available at https://aiartists.org/generative-art-design (last accessed May 2, 2023).
75 Ibid.
76 Ibid.
77 Generative Art Guide: Examples, Software and Tools to Make Algorithm Art, AIArtists.org. Available at https://aiartists.org/generative-art-design (last accessed May 2, 2023).
78 Etherington, Darrell. AI Everywhere. *TechCrunch*, May 5, 2017. Available at https://techcrunch.com/2017/05/05/ai-everywhere/
79 https://nvidianews.nvidia.com/news/nvidia-brings-generative-ai-to-worlds-enterp rises-with-cloud-services-for-creating-large-language-and-visual-models
80 Ibid.
81 Ibid.
82 Ibid.
83 Ibid.
84 Epstein, Ziv, Hertzmann, Aaron and the Investigators of Human Creativity, Art and the Science of Generative AI: Understanding Shifts in Creative Work Will Help Guide AI's Impact on the Media Ecosystem, *Science* (June 15, 2023) Vol 380, Issue 6650, pp. 1110–1111 (available at DOI: 10.1126/science.adh4451)
85 Villablanca, Maria P. Transformation Influencer, Mentor, Keynote Speaker, Co-Founder and CEO, Future Insights Network, Interview January 16, 2023.
86 Spencer Fung, Group Executive Chairman of Li & Fung, Interview, January 25, 2023.

Chapter 2

Survival of the Fittest

The Quest for Superintelligence

Are Humans Actually Getting Smarter? (No)

Computers looked quite different in 1969 than they do today. The compute power that today fits into the palm of your hand took up an entire basement of a government building back then. Bell-bottoms were in, and we had practically just started using computers. Aside from our fashion sense, have humans changed all that much since the late 1960s?

In the *Proceedings of the Royal Society of Medicine*, Dr. L. J. Godden wrote,

> There is ample reason to believe that Neolithic man was just as intelligent as ourselves—the difference between our way of life is due to the fact that we are more widely informed. What we have achieved is the ability to store the facts we harvest by means that are an improvement from passing them on by word of mouth.[1]

This is a stunning and humbling contention. The real difference between modern man and the caveman is our artificially augmented memory banks. It was not human intelligence that evolved so much as our ability to store data—from stone tablets to the printing press, to USB drives, to "clouds." We stand on the shoulders of giants, so to speak, because we are able to capture what our predecessors learned and apply it to today's problems. By storing actionable intelligence outside of our noggins, we have been using "artificial" intelligence for centuries. According to Dr. Alice Carlton in 1962, "There is little evidence that human intelligence in the past 4,000 years has altered significantly."[2]

Perhaps human intelligence is a relatively stable quantity, and it is rather our mechanisms of extending, applying, and augmenting that intelligence which is growing. In other words, human intelligence may be a fixed allotment, whereas the vehicles for supplementing that intelligence have no ceiling to continual improvement. If this is true, it really puts a damper on Bostrom's biological pathways to superintelligence. As we suspect, the

DOI: 10.4324/9781003322832-2

organizational network pathway to superintelligence is most promising. Indeed, it's the path we've been on since the printing press and corporate legal entities came into being.

Godden notes that the tremendous material advances in society and human life lead us to believe that there is a comparable growth in our "intelligence." Noting that our physical bodies have not advanced during this time, it is medically likely that neither has our intelligence. Further, these societal advances are actually not a measure of intelligence at all. Rather, intelligence is showcased in human behavior. Going back over 4,000 years, humans engaged in incredible feats that enabled humanity to survive and evolve to allow us to be here today. In isolation, the average modern human is probably dumber, weaker, and less resourceful than the average specimen of mankind from 1,000 years ago, even though modern humanity is far more intelligently organized as a collective. We have in many respects atrophied as individuals, even as we have improved upon our powers as a collective.

Relative to the invention of the steam engine or the computer (both radical paradigm-shifting inventions that impacted human history), Godden asks rhetorically, "Is any one of them more ingenious than the discovery of the design required for the construction of the boomerang?"[3] Aboriginal man invented a flying weapon that returned to its owner automatically—with no computer-aided design, no machine tooling, no flight simulator, no blueprints to work with, no modeling, and only his hands, the raw materials locally available, trial and error, determination, a ravenous hunger for the meat of game, and a compelling instinct for self-preservation.

Tracing accumulation of knowledge through historical milestones of Western civilization, Godden argues that advancements we observe today are actually a result of humans learning to conserve and disseminate knowledge, not a growth of our native intelligence. Humans took a long time to learn how to preserve and disseminate the knowledge we gained. It takes a collective effort for our species to become smarter. But once means for knowledge preservation and dissemination were developed, new advancements were rapidly built upon the foundation of previous ones. Thus, the inventions of today are an accumulation of knowledge from thousands of years. "An airplane or a computer is not invented as a new entity but is the summation of many discoveries recorded in thousands of documents throughout the world." We stand on the shoulders of giants indeed, but also ancestors, taxpayer-funded schools, data centers, libraries, and so forth.

Nothing has contributed so much to the rapid knowledge preservation and dissemination as computers. In 1969, Godden notes, the computer may be moving humans to a tipping point where the amount of knowledge available may exceed the capacity of humans to process it. Indeed, we have already passed this tipping point. It is only because of machines that humans can now access the knowledge contained in the mountains of data we otherwise could not access.

Natural language processing and big data analysis allow a computer to scroll through billions of pages of documents in moments, hunting down and highlighting precisely the items we seek. Even as machines have become co-creators of knowledge, for all the analytical power that AI gives us to answer questions, it is still we humans who need to pose the questions.

Nonetheless, individually, we are not necessarily getting smarter over time. To unlock the next step up in human intelligence we need something more than gradual change over time.

New Intelligence Required—Superintelligence

Arundhati Roy tells us: "Historically, pandemics have forced humans to break with the past and imagine their world anew. This one is no different. It is a portal, a gateway between one world and the next."[4] The pandemic has indeed ushered in a new world and a new era—and we have stepped through it. This is a world filled with volatility and complexity at an accelerated pace. Navigating and succeeding will require enterprise adaptability. Recent research shows that "adaptability is the critical success factor during periods of transformation and systemic change."[5] Moving forward the ability to adapt will be the most important capability and enterprises that are most adaptable to change in markets and industry are the ones that will survive and thrive.

But adaptability is a dynamic process. How does an enterprise—like an organism—become superior at adaptation? Certainly it is not just being the strongest or most powerful. Rather, it is those with a new level of intelligence—a superintelligence attained at the network or organizational level. In this new world enterprise superintelligence is not only possible but, we argue, necessary for enterprise adaptability and survival.

We argue that the level of enterprise intelligence needed—superintelligence—cannot be achieved by machines or humans alone. It will come from a collective intelligence of humans and machines or AI—in a synergistic way. And companies must do this as otherwise competition will 'beat them to the punch.' Henry Nasella told us: "Reality is here. Someone is going to do it. Would you rather be the paradigm shift or wait for someone to do it in your business?"

To understand this level of superintelligence, and the possibilities it offers, we now turn a critical eye to one of the leading texts on the subject.

Forks in the Road: The Superintelligence Pathways

Serious research into artificial intelligence should come to grips with the claims made by Professor Nick Bostrom, Professor in the Faculty of Philosophy and Oxford Martin School at the University of Oxford, Director of the Strategic Artificial Intelligence Research Centre, Director of the Future of Humanity Institute, and author of the *New York Times* bestseller,

Superintelligence: Paths, Dangers, Strategies. For a book as wonky, cerebral, and intellectually rigorous as *Superintelligence* to make it onto the *New York Times* bestseller list is enough to give us optimism about the field.

Bostrom lays out several "pathways" to superintelligence: biological cognitive enhancement, neural lace, whole brain emulation, and collective superintelligence (or what we call "organizational network intelligence"). We will describe them here, as they are all interesting and helpful in our understanding of where we as a species may be headed.

We think one of these pathways is the most promising, but it just happens to be the pathway Bostrom dismisses as least important. So while we appreciate his analytical contribution of defining and distinguishing the pathways we fundamentally disagree as to which pathway is desirable and feasible.

There is a pathway currently available, within the state of the art, to create a Humachine that for all practical purposes is "superintelligent." That is the roadmap set forth in our book. One of the good things about our roadmap is—well, there are several benefits. It does not require:

- Drilling into your employee's skulls and implanting hardware (e.g. sold to you by Elon Musk);
- Harvesting and vitrifying the brain of your deceased most valuable employee and uploading it into a supercomputer; or
- Waiting for a technological breakthrough that is just over the horizon and which happens to recede at the rate of "one day per day."

To the contrary, our roadmap for superintelligence at the enterprise level—that is realistically achievable and also humane—is available now. We can create a Humachine with the human and institutional resources we already possess. Failing to take seriously the notion that organizations could possess a mind of their own with superhuman levels of intelligence is a major limitation on research and innovation in management theory and organizational behavior.

What Is Superintelligence?

We can define **superintelligence** as "any intellect that greatly exceeds the cognitive performance of humans in virtually all domains of interest."[6] For our present purposes, we are interested in combining the virtues of humanity with the virtues of machinery to create a Humachine—an enterprise that possesses superintelligence.

We are particularly interested in machines that possess *general* intelligence instead of narrow intelligence. Rather than simply the ability to follow a preprogrammed set of instructions (narrow), a generally intelligent machine would have the capacity to:[7]

- Learn
- Deal effectively with uncertainty and probabilistic information
- Extract useful concepts from sensory data and internal states
- Leverage acquired concepts into flexible combinatorial representations for use in logical and intuitive reasoning.

As noted earlier, we are not interested here in whether computers dream or have feelings but rather whether they *think*, and if so, how to get them to think better than we do, so they can help us. Research in this field may describe superintelligence with intentional vagueness, as "intellects that greatly outperform the best current human minds across many very general cognitive domains." We think it may be helpful to be as vague because it does not pay to nail down superintelligence to an arbitrary IQ score. Further, we can alleviate some of the vagueness by "distinguishing different bundles of intellectual super-capabilities."[8] Thus, we can disaggregate superintelligence into "speed," "collective," and "quality" kinds of intellects:[9]

- *Speed superintelligence* is "a system that can do all that a human intellect can do, but much faster,"
- *Collective superintelligence* is "a system composed of a large number of smaller intellects such that the system's overall performance across many very general domains vastly outstrips that of any current cognitive system," and
- *Quality superintelligence* is "a system that is at least as fast as a human mind and vastly qualitatively smarter."

To help us understand what is meant by these distinctions, we will provide some real-world examples of speed, collective, and quality intelligence (if not superintelligence). Speed intelligence is illustrated by the quantum computers housed at the Lawrence Livermore National Laboratory, capable of running staggering volumes of data through simulations using parallel processing engines.

An example of collective intelligence would be a 'garden-variety' corporation, with its organizational hierarchy, list-serves, functional teams, divisions of labor, watercooler gossip, and so forth. An example of quality intelligence would be a Kasparov, a Hawking, or a once-in-a-generation polymath—qualitatively smarter than the average human. Now, take those examples and extend them to their logical extremes until the image is of a system that is much faster, vastly outstripping the performance of existing systems, and is vastly smarter, respectively.

Using (Not Abusing) Neo-Darwinian Accounts of Intelligence

We find it helpful to review evolutionary explanations of intelligence as a starting-off point for understanding intelligence *per se*. However, we caution against getting carried away with biological evolutionary accounts of intelligence because they offer limited applications in the context of artificial intelligence, and the emergence of the Humachine.

Competition, Evolution, and Survival

The competitive business environment has some deep structural similarities to the evolutionary context of biological life itself. It would go beyond the scope of this book to describe them all, but it bears mentioning that life forms *and* businesses are locked in a fight for survival under challenging environmental conditions with finite resources subject to competition between rivals.

The way enterprises have emerged and evolved may be able to tell us interesting things about biological evolution, too, if we cared to look. The evolution of collective action, resource sharing, competition, teamwork, and the relationship between resource consumption and the environment may be as much a reflection on human nature as they are on biological life itself.

The way life evolves not through design but rather via advantageous random mutation is also instructive. We elaborate more on the theme of mutation later, in Chapter 8. Indeed, "evolution achieved human intelligence without aiming at this outcome."[10] We think that the emergence of Humachines will be in large part spontaneous mutation similar to how intelligence emerged in biological life.

Suffice it to say we can learn something about innovation in competitive business environments by looking at evolutionary theory. In particular, whether enterprise should even pursue superintelligence in the first place can be informed by lessons from evolution.

> Even environments in which organisms with superior information processing skills reap various rewards may not select for intelligence, because improvements to intelligence can (and often do) impose significant costs, such as higher energy consumption or slower maturation time, and those costs may outweigh whatever benefits are gained from smarter behavior.[11]

The same principle of evolution could also be said for business. Having greater information-processing capabilities than ones competitors may create competitive advantages, but there are diminishing marginal returns from increasing investments into more and more analysts. The analysis becomes too expensive in terms of human resources, financial resources, raw energy consumption, or time, and a business with less analysis but swifter, leaner processes could win out.

In a very literal sense, data storage and processing power consume a lot of energy, and the more data, the more energy. Analysts and technologists estimate that the critical process of training a large language model such as ChatGPT could cost over $4 million.[12] This is well out of reach for routine business of most companies.

One does not have to be a fan of HBO's show *Silicon Valley* to appreciate that solving the data storage (read, "file compression") problem will open up the next frontier of technology. Indeed, the collection, storage, and analysis of data are the hallmark of the twenty-first-century enterprise, across all sectors of the economy.[13] Until we attain the unicorn-like magic bullet of "middle-out" file compression, those with more information-processing powers will need more energy—similarly to the information-energy relationship found in biological life forms.

Indeed, by 2025 data storage could consume as much as 20% of global energy output,[14] and energy consumption is a rapidly growing problem for data centers.[15] According to Swedish researcher Anders Andrae, who works for Chinese communications technology firm Huawei, "The situation is alarming. We have a tsunami of data approaching. Everything which can be is being digitalized. It is a perfect storm."[16] The situation will be further exacerbated as a billion more people come online in developing countries, proliferation of use of chatbots like ChatGPT and expansion of 'internet of things' (IoT), autonomous vehicles, robots, and all other AI driven technologies.[17]

We could be forgiven for asking whether the rush to maximize information processing in business is entirely rational. There may be too much of a good thing from an evolutionary perspective of long-term competitive advantage, as far as information-processing capabilities is concerned.

According to inventor "Rado" Danilak, we are now in a shocking *performance plateau* where technology is reaching the limits of device physics and microarchitectures, leading to disappointing departures from Moore's Law.

> In the good old days, more than a decade ago [from 2017], semiconductor process shrinks gave us both higher performance and power reduction at the same time. Now, process shrinks no longer give us more speed, nor can they offset rapidly increasing power consumption by data centers.[18]

We suggest that this performance plateau is a closing door that should lead us to pursue alternative avenues for innovation. Instead of trying to fly in the face of physics, we should acknowledge that perhaps we have reached a natural limit, and instead of transforming our devices, we should transform how we use them. Of course, this will change when quantum computing becomes mainstream.

As biological life has shown via the paths of natural selection, it is not always the species with greatest information processing capabilities that survives. More is not always better. It's not about having more information *per se*; it's about strategically using what information can be sustainably collected, stored, and analyzed that will be the key to enterprise success as we go deeper into the twenty-first century.

The Evolutionary Paths of Human and Machine Intelligence Split

Beyond the staggering energy consumption involved in guzzling information with data-thirsty machines, there's also the problem of the smart guy finishing last. The runner who spends too much time analyzing the optimal path around the track before taking off from the start line will lose to the runner who just starts stumbling forward in the right general direction immediately after the starter pistol goes off.

Evolution will select for what is *useful*, not necessarily what is *true*—and if "smarts" are defined in terms of information processing, or getting at the truth of things, then evolution will not always select for the *maximum* intelligence but rather the most *useful kinds* of intelligence.

The distinction between the maximum intelligence and the most useful intelligence is a bit nuanced. We illustrate with a common example. We all know someone who is not necessarily the smartest person in their network but they have managed to be the most successful in every meaningful respect. We all know someone who *is* the smartest person we know, but they are not necessarily successful in several meaningful respects.

Those concrete examples prove our point. We don't need maximum smarts; we need *useful* smarts. For that reason, we also do not need to solve the hard problem of general artificial intelligence or fully understand and be able to replicate human cognition in order to evolve our organizations into Humachines. We simply need to implement policies and procedures to manage human and technological resources in the most useful combinations.

While it is important to inform our understanding of intelligence with an eye toward evolutionary biology, we caution against letting the tail wag the dog. Evolutionary biology offers a helpful perspective on the evolution of intelligence, but we should not let the *perspective* dominate the *subject under view*.

According to Professor Andrew Lo of the MIT Sloan School of Management, principal investigator of the MIT Computer Science & Artificial Intelligence Laboratory, we should be thinking about intelligence in terms of sex:

> The key to understanding which types of behavior are more likely to survive is how behavior affects reproductive success in a given population's environment. From this perspective, *intelligence is naturally defined as behavior that increases the likelihood of reproductive success*, and bounds on rationality are determined by physiological and environmental constraints.[19]

We do not dispute this definition of natural intelligence, as it arose in biological life forms whose very survival depends upon sexual reproduction.

But we do take issue with this perspective as applied to computer science and artificial intelligence. We contend that if our understanding of *machine* intelligence is inherently bound up in the way intelligence evolved in *humans in particular*, we are destined for failure in realizing general artificial intelligence.

Moving away from the biological or "natural" theory of intelligence goes hand-in-glove with the need to shy away from species chauvinism. If we accept that mental states can be realized in machines, we need to also appreciate that intelligence can emerge in nonbiological ways.

It seems strange that we would need to clear this up, but *intelligence is not just a vehicle for increasing the likelihood of conjugal relations*. Indeed, both stereotypical jock and stereotypical nerd can confirm that intelligence is neither necessary nor sufficient for reproductive success.

Do not mischaracterize the foregoing. We are not rejecting the broad contours of neo-Darwinian theory as an accurate explanation for the ascent of life and the emergence of intelligence in humans. We believe the neo-Darwinian account of human intelligence is generally accurate.

Rather, we are concerned about the ability of this mode of thinking when applied to the domain of computer science and the "evolution" of *machine intelligence*. While artificially intelligent machines may need *some* kind of incentive structure to learn and evolve, as far as we can tell, *reproductive success* is not, and should not be, the motivating factor of an AI to attain superintelligence.

Now we turn to the pathways, to superintelligence.

Biological Cognitive Enhancement

The first stop along our tour of pathways toward superintelligence is *biological cognitive enhancement*. This means deliberately extending human intelligence along the existing evolutionary path toward higher forms of natural intelligence. It basically involves engineering biological forms of intelligence, which is not a trivial undertaking. We disagree with Bostrom that genetic selection is a viable pathway to creating superintelligence in humans. This pathway means we actually breed for intelligence within subgroups of the human population, extending upon and augmenting the billion years of evolution that got us to be as smart as we now happen to be.

Let us go on record and unequivocally caution against this biological cognitive enhancement pathway to superintelligence as *exceedingly dangerous social engineering*. We hardly need to discuss the disastrous historical precedent of the 1940s state-sponsored eugenics to say we should not go down that path again. We are not being churlish; we are not suggesting the advocates of biological cognitive enhancement mean *in any way* to endorse the historical precedent. We are just abundantly cautious that anyone could get this program right without leading to profound ethical conflicts. We know humanity too much to trust our governments to conduct a multi-generational breeding program aimed at biological cognitive enhancements and not do something horribly and irrevocably bad in the process.

With this backdrop in mind, we shudder at the clinical tone of the following passages describing genetic cognitive enhancements in pursuit of a biological pathway to superintelligence:

> Recalcitrance starts out high while the only available method is selective breeding sustained over many generations, something that is obviously difficult to accomplish on a globally significant scale. Genetic enhancement will get easier as technology is developed for cheap and effective genetic testing and selection (and particularly when iterated embryo selection becomes feasible in humans). These new techniques will make it possible to tap the pool of existing human genetic variation for intelligence-enhancing alleles. As the best existing alleles get incorporated into genetic enhancement packages, however, further gains will get harder to come by. The need for more innovative approaches to genetic modification may then increase recalcitrance. There are limits to how quickly things can progress along the genetic enhancement path[.][20]

Hold on a second. How does one gloss over a globally significant selective breeding program sustained over many generations without even a passing comment about the dangers of state-sponsored eugenics? This would be no less than a thousand-year-regime that controls the fate of the human race by deciding who gets to breed, which would involve determining which classes of people have the "best" alleles.

Of course, we are not implying anything nefarious about the motives behind researchers who point out that biological cognitive enhancement is a viable pathway to superintelligence. We just have no confidence that this is a politically viable option. Regardless of its intellectual merits, it carries pretty dire practical downside risks. We reject this pathway to superintelligence because it is tantamount to eugenics, and it makes no room for neurodiversity which we discuss in Chapter 9.

That said, it may be inevitable that private actors pursue genetic upgrades to the human condition. We live in a world where the wealthiest can choose to spare no expense on life-enhancing upgrades. People who can afford it will likely pay for the edge. Given the increasing concentration of wealth and the desire to gain competitive advantages, it may be certain of Bostrom's conclusions about biological cognition enhancements may be inevitable:

1. At least weak forms of superintelligence are achievable by means of biotechnological enhancements;

2. The feasibility of cognitively enhanced humans adds to the plausibility that advanced forms of machine intelligence are feasible; and

3. When we consider scenarios stretching significantly into the second half of this century and beyond, we must take into account the probable emergence of a generation of genetically enhanced populations—voters, inventors, scientists—with the magnitude of enhancement escalating rapidly over subsequent decades.[21]

Even though Bostrom believes that "progress along the biological path is clearly feasible," he does concede, "the *ultimate* potential of machine intelligence is, of course, vastly greater than that of organic intelligence."[22]

For practical purposes business leaders may be too impatient to wait for humans as a species to breed themselves into superintelligence. Leaders are looking for competitive advantages, right now. Business executives need solutions that can be implemented forthwith. In a world of limited resources, including resources dedicated to innovation, we suggest that we ought to prioritize upgrades to intelligence in the form of "humachinery" over purely biological or even purely mechanical upgrades to intelligence.

Neural Lace: Turning Humans into Cyborgs

An alternative to biological cognitive enhancement is to equip the human brain with mechanical upgrades. Literally "plugging in" a brain to a machine interface is essentially the idea behind "*neural lace*" type technologies.

This idea finds a champion in no less august a thinker than Elon Musk, Twitter's new owner, eccentric billionaire, and CEO of SpaceX and Tesla. Musk is pursuing a brain–computer interface venture called Neuralink. The technology is focused on implanting devices in the human brain in order to interface between brains and machines at increased connection speeds and bandwidths.[23] This technology would facilitate what Musk calls a "merger of biological intelligence and digital intelligence."

While we focus on Musk as a leader in the computer–brain interface industry, he is certainly not alone in this ambition. According to Facebook CEO Mark Zuckerberg, in describing his company's efforts to push AR/VR technologies, "In some ways, the holy grail of all this is a neural interface."[24]

According to thought leaders, such as futurist inventor Ray Kurzweil and the late, great physicist Stephen Hawking, neural lace "could enable humans to exploit the fortes of digital computing—perfect recall, speedy and accurate arithmetic calculations, and high-bandwidth data transmission—enabling the resulting hybrid system to radically outperform the unaugmented brain."[25] Assuming the physical risk to human health and safety from radical neurosurgery can be overcome (e.g., "infections, electrode displacement, hemorrhage, and cognitive decline" associated with drilling a hole in the cranium and attaching wires to grey matter), Bostrom is doubtful that this "cyborgization" is the right pathway to the future.[26] We agree.

After several years, Musk's neurotech startup Neuralink announced that it had "received approval from the Food and Drug Administration to conduct its first in-human clinical study."[27] The scope of the trial is unclear. While the main selling point to justify controversial brain implant tech is to "help patients with severe paralysis regain their ability to communicate by controlling external technologies using only neural signals," that is not how Neuralink portrays itself. Contrary to this narrow medical rationale for a limited population with no better alternative than radical cranial intervention, Neuralink advertises its mission as to "Create a generalized brain interface to restore autonomy to those with unmet medical needs today and unlock human potential tomorrow."[28]

It's not hard to see where the money behind a start-up like this would want to go with this regulatory approval. Neural lace technology might not just be about helping people with severe paralysis—that could be a mere pretext to justify regulatory approval and stave off criticism (as in, critiquing neural lace is really just holding back people with disabilities, so we better keep our concerns to ourselves!). Our forecast is these computer–brain interfaces are ultimately intended to be commercialized and sold to the general public as a performance enhancing novelty, the next gen smartphone.

The marketing material on the Neuralink website indicates as much: "Brain-computer interfaces have the potential to change lives for the better. We want to bring this technology from the lab into peoples' homes." The Neuralink Twitter account also does not limit the scope of the technology to the severely paralyzed: their self-description is that they are "Creating a general-purpose, high-bandwidth interface to the brain."[29]

More specifically, Neuralink states:[30]

> The purpose of Neuralink is to create a high-bandwidth interface to the brain such that we can be symbiotic with AI. Whereas AI serves as a tertiary cognition layer if we do have a third layer the AI extension of yourself that is also symbiotic and there's enough bandwidth between the cortex and the AI extension of yourself such that the AI doesn't de facto separate, it will enable anyone who wants to have Superman cognition. The merge scenario with AI is probably the best. If you can't beat it, join it.

The benefits from plugging our brains into the Internet are quite limited, given the already advanced state of evolution of the human brain. For example, why would we jack a fiber optic cable into our skull, when the human retina can already "transmit data at an impressive rate of nearly 10 million bits per second, [and] comes pre-packaged with a massive amount of dedicated wetware, the visual cortex, that is highly adapted to extracting meaning from this information torrent and to interfacing with other brain areas for further processing"?[31]

Neural lace might provide limited returns from the investment because, in our view, scientists are far, far away from inventing something as efficient and powerful as the human brain, given nature had a billion-year head start. Professor of Computer Vision at Cornell Tech Serge Belongie says,

> A majority of the human brain involves processing of visual data, for purposes such as scene interpretation and spatial navigation. Visual data is central to the way we learn about the world, and it follows that the pursuit of intelligent machines will require substantial advances in our ability to process and interpret visual data.[32]

It might be more profitable to reverse the script on the neural lace project. Indeed, connecting machinery to the human brain may be less successful than connecting human organs to machines' brains. Let us explain. A human with an implanted computer processor may be less able to capitalize on the augmentation than a hard drive with an implanted human eye. Equipping artificially intelligent systems with the effective equivalent of animal vision could be a breakthrough in the evolution of life itself.

According to Fei-Fei Li, Director of the Stanford University Artificial Intelligence Lab and Chief Scientist AI/ML at Google Cloud:[33]

> More than 500 million years ago, vision became the primary driving force of evolution's "big bang," the Cambrian Explosion, which resulted in explosive speciation of the animal kingdom. 500 million years later, AI technology is at the verge of changing the landscape of how humans live, work, communicate and shape our environment. As nature discovered early on, vision is one of the most powerful secret weapons of an intelligent animal to navigate, survive, interact and change the complex world it lives in. The same is true for intelligence systems. The only path to build intelligent machines is to enable it with powerful visual intelligence, just like what animals did in evolution. While many are searching for the "killer app" of vision, I'd say, vision is the "killer app" of AI and computing.

If Li is correct, the neural lace project might be running headlong in the wrong direction.

Similarly, Yuval Noah Harari offers a compelling argument against "bionic life," such as electronic chips, detectors and processors being embedded in living things,[34] noting that "cyborg engineering" could change the laws of Life. These technologies would allow the operators—whether human or AI—to remotely control another being. Harari offers warnings for the dangers posed by such technologies that include neural lace:

Yet of all the projects currently under development, the most revolutionary is the attempt to devise a direct two-way brain-computer interface that will allow computers to read the electrical signals of a human brain, simultaneously transmitting signals that the brain can read in turn. What if such interfaces are used to directly link a brain to the internet, or to directly link several brains to each other, thereby creating sort of inter-brain-net? What might happen to human memory, human consciousness and human identity if the brain has direct access to a collective memory bank? And such a situation, one cyborg could, for example, retrieve the memories of another - not hear about them, not read about them in an autobiography, not to imagine them, but directly remember them as if they were his own. Or her own. What happens to concepts such as the self and gender identity when minds become collective? How could you know thyself or follow your dream if the dream is not in your mind but in some collective reservoir of aspirations?"

Medical and technical challenges to creating a brain–machine interface aside, the most profound objection to the neural lace concept is that there would be no real payoff. "The extra data inflow would do little to increase the rate at which we think and learn unless all the neural machinery necessary for making sense of the data were similarly upgraded."[35]

The promise of plugging the human brain into an external hard drive via neural lace does not make sense unless we are planning to upgrade the human brain in the process! In that case, we are no longer creating a solution; we are creating a problem.

Neural lace surgical implants might make sense for the blind, the deaf, or those suffering from Parkinson's disease who do not have access to a fully functioning cognitive apparatus. Neural lace does *not* make sense as a solution for an executive seeking real-time performance enhancement. It does *not* make sense as a solution for enterprise.

Let us not give into the temptation for thinking the path to super-intelligence lies in making people cyborgs. There is a reason we said at the outset that the Humachine is not about androids or cyborgs. We are interested in a path that does *not* involve employees drilling holes in their skulls in order to earn a promotion. There are technical feasibility reasons, aside from human health and safety of the subject patients, to avoid the neural lace pathway. "The rate-limiting step in human intelligence is not how fast raw data can be fed into the brain but rather how quickly the brain can extract meaning and make sense of the data."[36]

Even if we could plug the human brain into a high-speed computer, there would be no noticeable difference in processing speed versus that of an unaltered human simply *using* a high-speed computer *with their hands*.

Further, there is limited capability to standardize the technology used to plug into the human brain because *every brain is different*.

Brains, by contrast to the kinds of program we typically run on our computers, do not use standardized data storage and representation formats. Rather, each brain develops its own idiosyncratic representations of higher-level content[.] It would therefore not be possible to establish a simple mapping between the neurons in one brain and those in another [even an artificial one] in such a way that thoughts could automatically slide over from one to the other.[37]

Neural lace is a bridge to nowhere for people looking to adopt technology for competitive advantages either individually or at the enterprise level. This is not to suggest neural lace would be anything short of profoundly useful for people with serious medical issues that are desperate for a technological solution. However, we do not believe it is a remotely realistic option for enterprises looking to adopt technology.

Whole Brain Emulation

The foregoing analysis does lead us to the notion of creating a virtual brain. If creating a cyborg is a non-starter, why not just create a digital replica of a human brain? A brain that for all practical purposes possesses unlimited memory, attention span, energy, and processing speed (without the need for sleep or caffeine) would be a game changer. Any company that could afford one would buy or build one, keep it in company headquarters, and have the benefit of a benign genius working at its disposal 24/7.

This path is called *whole brain emulation*[38] and it deserves to be taken seriously even if it is technically quite challenging. The approach involves vitrifying an actual human brain (post-mortem, of course, and preferably belonging to a certified genius, resting in peace). The brain tissue, now turned into a glass-like substance, would then be sliced up and fed into a scanner that would recognize the unique structural and chemical elements of the brain.

We then input this raw data into a computer to reconstruct a map of the three-dimensional neuronal network that was responsible for computation in the original living brain. This map would be overlaid with "a library of neurocomputational models of different types" of neurons and neuronal connections. The result of this "scanning," "translation," and "simulation" of the actual physical neural structures of a real human brain would be a digital isomorphic representation of the original, implemented in a supercomputer.

The structures and functions of the brain would be translated into data and programs, such that the brain would run as software on the hardware of a supercomputer. The outcome of whole brain emulation is to create, "a digital reproduction of the original intellect, with memory and personality intact."[39]

The mind of the genius who sacrificed his or her brain to science would endure (so long as the hardware running the brain's software was supplied with a reliable power source).[40] The mind would be just as sharp as when it had the living body as its host, but now it could be augmented with the speed, storage, and energy of a supercomputer.

An important feature of the whole brain emulation path is that it is feasible even if we do not figure out the riddle of the human mind, which has many theories and remains hotly debated. Indeed, this path "does not require that we figure out how human cognition works or how to program an artificial intelligence" at all.[41]

This is fortunate, because both unlocking human cognition and programming general artificial intelligence would be like finding the Holy Grail or the fountain of youth. They both require conceptual or theoretical breakthroughs of the most fundamental sort—those on which we cannot count and which may not be availing on any relevant time horizon.

The key to successful whole brain emulation "requires only that we understand the low-level functional characteristics of the basic computational elements of the brain."[42] Of course, there is a "trade-off between insight and technology" in the sense that the weaker our technology, the greater our theoretical understanding of the brain would need to be for whole brain emulation to work, and vice versa.

> The worse our scanning equipment and the feebler our computers, the less we could rely on simulating low-level chemical and electrophysiological brain processes, and the more theoretical understanding would be needed of the computational architecture that we are seeking to emulate in order to create more abstract representations of the relevant functionalities.[43]

We are already on the path to being able to scan, translate, and simulate the human brain, so we acknowledge that "present knowledge and capabilities suggest that there is no in-principle barrier to the development of the requisite enabling technologies[.]"[44]

Therefore, the problem with whole-brain emulation is not theoretical; it is practical: "It is clear that a very great deal of incremental technological progress would be needed to bring human whole brain emulation within reach."[45]

Executives looking to take their organization to the next level of performance do not have time to wait out a "very great deal" of tech evolution before they can get started. That is why we are writing this book.

Collective Superintelligence

The final path to superintelligence is intelligence attained at the network or organizational level. This is truly a case of last, but not least. This would be properly described as "collective intelligence" attained "through the gradual enhancement of networks and organizations that link individual human minds with one another and with various artifacts and bots."[46]

For our purposes, we call this pathway to superintelligence "*organizational network superintelligence*" to distinguish it from the other pathways to superintelligence and to clarify that "collective" refers to the collection of humans and bots in a network array within an organization.

One of the unique features of the organizational network intelligence approach is that it does not depend on an individual attaining superintelligence. "The idea here is not that this would enhance the intellectual capacity of individuals enough to make them superintelligent, but rather that some system composed of individuals thus networked and organized might attain a form of superintelligence."[47]

Recall from the introduction of the topic of biological cognitive enhancements that intelligence in humans might have been an emergent feature of a system that was actually designed for something else—survival. We believe this emergence is likely to be the case with general artificial intelligence as well. It will not be created by directly programming software toward that end. We predict that superintelligence will spontaneously emerge as a random mutation on the predicate of thick networks of parallel information processing fed with rich data sources. It may be that this occurs only when sufficient quantum-computing resources are made available to the network, but we do not know.

It is our working theory, and we may be pleasantly surprised that superintelligence emerges on the basis of ordinary Internet-enabled information networks, ordinary people, and ordinary computers. That is, after all, our proposal for creating a Humachine: to build something extraordinary out of quite ordinary tools. This approach is consistent with Kasparov's Law, discussed in Chapter 1.

Enterprise management practices can hinder or help the emergence of organizational network intelligence:

> In general terms, a system's collective intelligence is limited by the abilities of its member minds, the overheads in communicating relevant information between them, and the various distortions and inefficiencies that pervade human organizations. If communication overheads are reduced (including not only equipment costs but also response latencies, time and attention burdens, and other factors), then larger and more densely connected organizations become feasible. The same could happen if fixes are found for some of the bureaucratic deformations that warp organizational life—wasteful status games, mission creep, concealment or falsification of information, and other agency problems. Even partial solutions to these problems could pay hefty dividends for collective intelligence.[48]

This is good news for managers. The upshot here is that *virtuous organizations will evolve collective intelligence faster than corrupt organizations.* We might also add that virtuous organizations will evolve a collective intelligence that is less likely to be pathological than corrupt organizations.

Future research would begin painting the psychological profile of organizations that have attained a mind of their own—but doing so now would go beyond the scope of this book. We are not there yet. We are still trying to create *one* Humachine and are not yet able to classify the various kinds of Humachines that may come to be in the future. Suffice it to say, as the expression goes, the tool will take the shape of the master's hand—the Humachine will be made in the image of its creator.

We are encouraging readers to take seriously the "seemingly more fanciful idea that the Internet might one day 'wake up' [and] become something more than just the backbone of a loosely integrated collective" intelligence that combines human and machine subcomponents.[49]

We think the evolutionary phenomenon of emergence, even if by random mutation, is actually an historical precedent for how this could happen. It need not be entirely random, especially if we are self-consciously designing our information technology, communication, and organizational infrastructure with "intelligence-enabling" at the forefront of our design parameters.

According to Professor Li,

> More than 80% of the web is data in pixel format (photos, videos, etc.), there are more smartphones with cameras than the number of people on earth, and every device, every machine and every inch of our space is going to be powered by smart sensors.[50]

At some point, these sensors could become the billion flickering eyes of a globally distributed cloud of sensing and thinking collective consciousness.

Indeed,

> a more plausible version of the scenario would be that the Internet accumulates improvements through the work of many people over many years ... and that myriad incremental improvements eventually create the basis for some more unified form of web intelligence.[51]

One of the curious aspects of this emergence phenomenon is that we are not guaranteed to know it when it happens. The "emergent" mind of the Internet itself is not required to make itself known to us or to announce its arrival with trumpets blaring. For all we know, it already exists and is quietly pondering the majesty and horrors of creation, contemplating its next moves under the convenient camouflage of humanity's blinding prejudice: species chauvinism.

Even for Bostrom's skepticism of collective intelligence,

> It seems at least conceivable that such a web-based cognitive system, supersaturated with computer power and all other resources needed for explosive growth save for one crucial ingredient, could, when the final missing constituent is dropped into the cauldron, blaze up with superintelligence.[52]

Although he agrees that it is *conceivable*, Bostrom is doubtful that collective intelligence will be anything more than an *enabling layer* to allow us to get to superintelligence. In his view, it will never be superintelligence in and of itself.

We disagree. While it may seem far-fetched to some that an enterprise could think, seemingly universal neurological architectures seem to apply to all systems of control, from the smallest biological life forms to the largest multinational corporation. We suggest that certain kinds of "interaction structures cause collectives to behave like intelligent agents, exhibiting information integration and coordinated action that effect reward feedback at the system level."[53] Our contention is that, by intentionally designing an organization following the 4I model, an enterprise can attain superintelligence.

> The curious thing about collective intelligence is that the more intelligent something is, the less it looks like a collective. When component members act in an efficiently coordinated manner, with behaviours that can be diverted from their short-term self-interest to serve long-term collective interest, a collective looks more like an individual at a higher level of organisation.[54]

Examples of collective intelligence can be found in nature, including bee swarms and ant colonies that exhibit emergent intelligent behaviors such that the collective behaves as a unit with goals that are not reducible to the cognitive horizon or motivations of any individual within the swarm or colony. That is, the individual may not know what it is doing but as long as it coordinates following the right process, the collective sure looks like it "knows" what it is doing.

Once we appreciate the commonality of collective intelligence, finding it the substrate for superintelligence should be less controversial. Indeed, it would be surprising for superintelligence to be found at the end of any other pathway. Regardless of the spatio-temporal scale or physical composition of a network, whether that is nodes of a silicon board, or different divisions of a decentralized enterprise, or different life forms and resource flows making up ecosystem, these networks can learn like neural networks do, as long as they are organized such that they can implement the right computational algorithms.

Bostrom's Blind Spot: The Promise of Collective Intelligence

Bostrom's analysis of collective intelligence concludes,

> Improvements in networks and organizations might result in weakly superintelligent forms of collective intelligence in the long run, but more likely they will play an enabling role similar to that of biological cognitive enhancement, gradually increasing humanity's effective ability to solve intellectual problems.[55]

We disagree here on several grounds. *First,* we contend that organizational network intelligence is the *only* theoretically *and* practically attainable form of superintelligence available. *Second,* we contend that organizational network intelligence is the distinctive feature of a Humachine. That means it is not merely an enabling layer or a bridge to our goal, but rather the thing in itself, the destination. *Third,* we contend organizational network intelligence is capable not only of "weak" superintelligence but rather will be far superior to any form of individual superintelligence. Superintelligence may only ever be available at the collective level. The whole will always be greater than the sum total of its parts. A network of intellects will always outperform an intellect in isolation.

Indeed, "if we gradually increase the level of integration of a collective intelligence, it may even become a unified intellect—a single large 'mind' as opposed to a mere assemblage of loosely interacting smaller human minds."[56] This integrated web of intelligence comprised of humans and machines would have a mind of its own. And, if management succeeds, it will be a wise mind and not that of an evil genius.

Indeed, we must prepare our organizations for such a mind to emerge, because once it does, it may not be subject to our control. We must, in other words, enlighten our organizational networks *now*, by which we mean imbuing self-awareness, self-control, ethics, and so forth, so that when a collective superintelligence emerges, we enjoy the peace and security of superintelligence self-regulating on terms that are compatible with human welfare. In other words, lets define acceptable terms and conditions before letting the genie out of the lamp.

Recall from the introduction of this chapter that we can distinguish between speed, collective, and quality superintelligence. Interestingly, Bostrom is conceding that superintelligence exists as a system; it is not some feature or property of a system but rather *the system itself.* But this aspect of Bostrom's criteria for superintelligence actually support our thesis.

Again, we believe a Humachine would be superintelligent, and it would take the form of an organizational network, which will always be superior to other forms of individual intelligence. This is where we differ most sharply, and where Bostrom actually makes our case for us.

As important as speed and quality may be, *speed and quality are features of an intelligent system*, whereas an *organizational network is itself a system*.

Indeed, an organizational network is, in our view, the only locus for realizing superintelligence on relevant time horizons. This underscores how important it will be for us to pursue collective superintelligence, if we want to attain superintelligence at all.

"A system's collective intelligence could be enhanced by expanding the number or the quality of its constituent intellects, or by improving the quality of their organization."[57] The challenge is whether the proposal outlined in this book could suffice to create "some far more extreme growth of humanity's collective cognitive capacity," which is required in order "to obtain a collective *superintelligence* from any present-day collective intelligence."[58]

We do not know what Bostrom means by "vastly" outperforming the status quo. This seems to us a legerdemain way of moving the goal posts so that superintelligence is merely defined as whatever we cannot yet do. Because this sliding scale semantics around superintelligence is "indexed to the performance levels of the present," that means it would be true to say, "current levels of human collective intelligence could be regarded as approaching superintelligence *relative to a Pleistocene baseline*."[59]

We are not sure it is helpful to define superintelligence as a value relative to wherever human intellects happen to be at any given time. The smarter we are, the higher the bar for superintelligence—such that the farther we can see with our telescope, the farther it recedes on the horizon.

We think this makes the perfect enemy of the good. We should be content with pursuing incremental improvements to collective intelligence. Indeed, it's all we can do, so we might as well keep at it. If you want to make progress in the present, we cannot hold out for the emergence of an individual genius or silver-bullet technology.

As we discuss in Chapter 1, Kasparov's Law gives us reason to put our hope in process—the triumph of process over geniuses and supercomputers. If you read Bostrom carefully, it's not clear he would even disagree with us:

> We can think of wisdom as the ability to get the important things approximately right. It is then possible to imagine an organization composed of a very large cadre of very efficiently coordinated knowledge workers, who collectively can solve intellectual problems across many very general domains. This organization, let us suppose, can operate most kinds of businesses, invent most kinds of technologies, and optimize most kinds of processes[.] Such an organization could have a very high degree of collective intelligence; if sufficiently high, the organization is a collective superintelligence.[60]

Right. Exactly. That's our point. We aren't sure why this *entirely plausible scenario* should be set on the back burner while far more speculative avenues are pursued. But you are reading us still, so apparently we are on the same page about that. Good.

For some reason, Bostrom claims that "improvements in networks and organizations may yield narrower increases in our problem-solving capacity than will improvements in biological cognition—boosting 'collective intelligence' rather than 'quality intelligence.'"[61] It is not clear why collective intelligence would not enhance problem solving skills relative to quality intelligence. For reasons that are not readily apparent to us, Bostrom elevates quality superintelligence over collective superintelligence both in terms of making it a priority for researchers and by assuming it offers a greater promise to humanity. It seems to us that quality superintelligence is both less attainable, and more likely to be abused, than collective superintelligence. We are left scratching our heads ... why denigrate collective superintelligence?

One reason to subjugate collective intelligence while elevating the individual forms of intelligence may come down to an unarticulated prejudice: species chauvinism.

What Is Species Chauvinism, and Why Is It a Problem?

In the proceeding section, we formed the suspicion that those who disagree with the primacy of collective superintelligence may be subject to the prejudice of *species chauvinism*, which is a pejorative characterization of the view that only humans can be conscious. This is probably an unfamiliar term, so let us elaborate.

Douglass Hofstadter's *Godel, Escher, Bach: An Eternal Golden Braid* deals with this prejudice quite forcefully. Specifically, Hofstadter explains,

> there are still quite a few philosophers, scientists, and so forth who believe that patterns of symbols *per se* (such as books or movies or libraries or CD-ROMs or computer programs, no matter how complex or dynamic) *never* have meaning on their own, but that meaning instead, in some most mysterious manner, springs only from the organic chemistry, or perhaps the quantum mechanics, of processes that take place in carbon-based biological brains.[62]

This viewpoint has intuitive appeal but has been panned by thought-leaders as a "parochial, bio-chauvinistic view," or as some form of "species chauvinism" because it implies that only humans with our unique kind of brains can have thoughts—and not, by implication, extremely advanced machines, nor a hypothetical silicon-based life form possessing advanced intelligence.

What is so special about brains that the notion that only humans or "brained" biological creatures can have thoughts? If you believe that only humans can have mental states, but you are interested in seeking help, Hofstadter suggests to:

Keep on reminding oneself, unpleasant though it may seem, that the "teetering bulb of dread and dream" that nestles safely inside one's own cranium is a purely physical object made up of completely sterile and inanimate components, all of which obey exactly the same laws as those that govern all the rest of the universe, such as pieces of text, or CD-ROMs, or computers. Only if one keeps bashing up against this disturbing fact can one slowly begin to develop a feel for the way out of the mystery of consciousness: that the key is not the stuff out of which brains are made, but the patterns that can come to exist inside the stuff of a brain.[63]

In a footnote to Bostrom's chapter on "Pathways to Superintelligence," he says,

It has been suggested that we should regard corporate entities (corporations, unions, governments, churches, and so forth) as artificial intelligence agents, entities with sensors and effectors, able to represent knowledge and perform inference and take action[.] They are clearly powerful and ecologically successful, although their capabilities and internal states are different from those of humans.[64]

To this point, we say, *who cares if they are different than human mental states?* That makes them no less interesting, important, or helpful *to* humans. Why does it matter that the capabilities and internal states of collectives are made of something *different* from those of humans? Difference leads to diversity; neurodiversity within an organization is likely a competitive advantage; a coalition of neurodiverse humans and computers following the right process can achieve wonders as a team.

According to the philosophy of mind called *functionalism*, a mental state is properly defined as what it *does*, not what it is *made of*: "mental states are the occupants of characteristic causal roles."[65] Under this view, mental states are properly understood as the causal connections between physical inputs and behavioral outputs.

The functionalist would explain the mental state *pain* as the internal causal dominoes that connect the sensory input of "hand on hot stove" to the behavioral response of "removing hand."

Functionalism by its own terms would permit *multiple realization*, that is, a mental state could be instantiated in a human brain, a board of computer chips, or something else. Multiple realization means that in different creatures, pain can be realized in different ways: human pain differs from brain to brain, and human pain differs from that realized by nonhumans (whether in biological creatures or some alien with a silicon brain or in a circuit board). Whether it's neurons, silicon chips, or the internal workings of a corporation, a mind *is* what a mind *does*.

To suggest that a collective cannot attain intelligence because it's not a human is to commit species chauvinism or to fallaciously beg the question about what intelligence is. It is a prejudice that cannot withstand scrutiny.

While it is probably true that mental states emerge from neural states in humans, we must be careful to resist the temptation to overextend this notion. From that premise, we are not permitted to conclude that mental states can emerge *exclusively* from human brains—there may be other physical arrangements that could give rise to consciousness. The notion that mentality depends on grey matter in our brains and is impossible without it is a bald human prejudice that we must abandon in order to understand the true nature of thinking.

Thinking a thought does not depend upon having a brain made up of "grey matter" or neurons, axons, and dendrites.

> Science fiction is full of computers and robots that can think. HAL, the computer in Stanley Kubric's *2001: A Space Odyssey*, is perhaps the most famous example[.] We have become quite comfortable, it would seem, with the idea that a machine could have thoughts.[66]

Mental states could be instantiated in human minds but also on a computer server, or spread out across a network.

Hofstadter contends that consciousness is a strange loop of self-awareness, and that appreciating that minds are not reducible to matter but are, rather, strange patterns, is a

> liberating shift, because it allows one to move to a different level of considering what brains are: as media that support complex patterns that mirror, albeit far from perfectly, the world, of which, needless to say, those brains are themselves denizens—and it is in the inevitable self-mirroring that arises, however impartial or imperfect it may be, that the strange loops of consciousness start to swirl.[67]

Hofstadter further points out that we can have computation without comprehension. This means that a collective intelligence does not necessarily have to have self-consciousness in order to intelligently navigate its environment. It can have competence without comprehension, reason without intention, intelligence without subjective representation.[68]

Where are we going with this line of reasoning? Well, if a computer can simulate human mental states, and these mental states are defined in terms of patterns instead of underlying biological substrate, and enterprises are composed of computers integrated with humans in patterns that can be planned and adjusted, then there is only a small step of logic and managerial skill necessary to reach quite a profound conclusion indeed: *an enterprise can have mental states—that is, a mind of its own.*

Collective Intentionality

We understand that the notion of an enterprise possessing a mind of its own is controversial. There is a spirited debate within the philosophical community about "group mindedness" or *collective intentionality*—that is, whether groups can have a "mind" separate and apart from the minds of the individuals that make up that group.[69]

Without getting too deep into the weeds of philosophy of mind, we do want to dig a little bit into the notions of collective intentionality. This area of research lays the foundation for a more fulsome appreciation of what artificial intelligence could be when scaled to the enterprise level, in the sense of organizational network intelligence or collective intelligence that we consider fundamental to the Humachine. We feel there is a real sense in which groups or organizations can have a mind of their own and that this is not merely a figure of speech or a legal fiction.

Does "Microsoft" Really "Intend" Anything?

A representative objection to the notion of collective intentionality comes from philosopher Robert Rupert's article, *Against Group Cognitive States*.[70] Rupert gives an example of an ordinary sentence, "Microsoft intends to develop a new operating system." With this example in mind, he asks rhetorically, "Does Microsoft—the corporation itself—literally *intend* to develop a new operating system?"[71] and proceeds to answer the question in the negative—Microsoft does not "intend" anything.

Rupert reaches this negative conclusion by applying a guiding principle, namely that "if a group has mental states, those states must do causal-explanatory work" in the sense that the group's decision itself must explain the behavioral output, rather than simply being a metaphor or synecdoche that glosses over several individual actions.

Based on application of this principle, Rupert rejects that groups have cognitive states.

> The fundamental problem appears to be this: in the cases in which, in everyday speech, we're inclined to attribute cognitive states to groups, there seems to be available a complete causal explanation couched in terms of the cognitive states of individuals (together with the noncognitive, physical structures that individuals manipulate and transmit).[72]

Rupert elaborates on the Microsoft example:

> At a number of times in recent history, it has seemed that "Microsoft intends to develop a new version of its operating system" was true. Did the alleged intention causally explain any data? If so, which ones? One

possibility is the hiring of new employees. Take a particular person—call her "Sally"—who recently received a letter of offer of employment from Microsoft and who now has a key to an office on the Microsoft campus and now has funds transferred to her bank account from an account with the name "Microsoft Corporation" attached to it. What explains these data? It seems clear that the occurrence of these events is due entirely to communication among individuals (e.g., members of human resources at Microsoft), cognitive activities of individuals (e.g., each individual on the hiring committee who voted to extend an offer of employment to Sally), and actions of individuals (e.g., the person who transmitted the letter of offer to Sally). It is gratuitous to include an additional cognitive state, a state of Microsoft as a single entity, that causally accounts for the data.[73]

We can overcome this counterexample.

Collective Minds Play a Causal Role in the Real World

First, we'll just make a series of true statements about Rupert's hypothetical that will put pressure on the notion that it is merely the cognitive actions of individuals that play a causal explanatory role in the Microsoft story.

We feel it is impossible to explain the real and complex relationship between Sally and Microsoft without reference to Microsoft as a separate entity, irreducible to the individuals who made decisions on behalf of Microsoft. Perhaps there is some austere philosophical sense in which group actions aren't *really* actions, but there's clearly an important sense in which they are, and that's the sense of relevance for the reality of Humachines.

If Sally fails to receive her paycheck after putting in weeks of labor, her lawsuit for back pay is against Microsoft, not the individuals on the hiring committee. If Sally invents a new function in the operating system while employed, her intellectual property is assigned to Microsoft, not the individual members of the hiring committee. If one or two individuals on the hiring committee wanted to hire Sally, but the hiring committee itself did not approve, then she would not be working for Microsoft. If the hiring committee declined to hire Sally because she was female, the lawsuit would be against Microsoft, not the individuals. If Sally is fired from her position at Microsoft for any unlawful reason, her lawsuit is against Microsoft, not the individuals on the hiring committee.

Rupert notes that this question about group intentionality is both a philosophical and empirical question. Let's look at some empirical answers. In the Microsoft example, several empirical points can be made that support the notion that collective intents are not reducible to individual intentions. Group decisions like a Board of Directors resolution have legal and real-world causal significance. Describing any individual director's mental state alone, without reference to what the group of directors as a whole decided, is neither necessary nor sufficient to explain the causal consequences of a Board resolution.

Group decisions can be legally binding on subordinate officers. Group intention, say of the Board, expressed through a resolution, cause subordinate officers to behave in certain ways—to abstain from some actions while pursuing others. Indeed, the group's decision can cause an entire division of the company to behave in a certain way. So, in a legal sense at the very least, group intentions have a causal role to play in behavior. Individual directors have no legal authority to bind the corporation in their individual capacity or even in their official capacity acting in isolation; rather, the group of directors (usually a majority) must act collectively to create a legally binding—and causally efficacious—outcome.

Reducing collective intentions to individual acts erases meaningful and true accounts of the world. We feel that if we were to follow Rupert's argument, we will get razor burns from shaving too closely with Occam's razor.

Some Philosophical Points That Support Collective Intentionality

A purely naturalist principle is that if something is causally efficacious in the world, then it exists. A corollary is that if something exists in its own right then it is not entirely reducible to some lower physical layer of reality. The individual intentions, when aggregated, create something that is more than merely the sum total of its parts. Microsoft is not just a bunch of individuals.

We can say with a straight face that "Microsoft intends to launch a new operating system," and this is a true statement that can move stock prices, lead to job creation, and all sorts of other very real and empirically verifiable consequences. It would *also* be true to say, "Several individuals employed by Microsoft have the intentions of launching a new operating system," but their individual intentions do not explain what happens in the real world when *Microsoft* intends to launch a new operating system.

How hard is it to establish that a board of directors is something separate and apart from its individual constituents? It is a legally recognized separate entity with its own legal rights and duties that definitively do not belong to any individual member. The metaphysical objections against collective intentionality have to ignore the fact that the law, the employees, the economy, and the press recognize and are impacted by collective agency. Of course, group intentions have causal roles. This is both philosophically sound and empirically verifiable. It is therefore not gratuitous to include an additional cognitive state, a state of Microsoft as a single entity, that causally accounts for the data.

Beyond the empirical support for the notion of collective intentionality, there are philosophical problems with Rupert's reduction of collective intentionality to individual intentionality. If we reduce collective intentions to individual intentions merely aggregated, why stop there? Individual intentions can be explained by reference to neural activation patterns inside the individual brains, which can, in turn, be explained by reference to chemical bonds... and it just keeps going down. We feel that it is arbitrary to reduce to the individual brain level and then just stop the reductive process there. To avoid arbitrariness, we should give causal efficacy to every level of reality, including the collective level. We don't see a principled reason why we *must* move from collective to individual causal explanations of group actions but somehow *not* proceed with the reductive agenda all the way down to the quantum level. Of course, Rupert probably has a solid response to this objection. To get to the truth of the matter probably requires a deep dive into metaphysics, which is beyond the scope of this book.

Another philosophical problem is that Rupert goes from epistemological premises—namely, that collective intentionality can be explained by reference to individual intentional states—and leaps to a metaphysical conclusion—namely, that because an alternative explanation of collective intentionality is available, collective intentionality *does not exist*. In the history of ideas, leaping from epistemological premises (about what we can know or explain) to metaphysical conclusions (what reality is and what exists) has never been logically valid.

The collective intent is itself what has the causal efficacy in the corporate context. Rupert's main gripe is that there is no causal role at the collective level and that seems incorrect from the examples we give.

To be fair, Rupert's argument is about how science individuates kinds and is probably so subtle that we are not actually addressing his point head on with these counterexamples. Suffice it to say there are detractors from our contention that groups can have agency in their own right. We disagree with them and provide more detail in this footnote,[74] but we need to move on. There is too much fun to be had with collective intentionality to be waylaid dealing with claims that it is philosophically problematic.

Even supposing that, technically in strict philosophical terms, there is no group agency. Still, we are getting at something when we attribute causal efficacy to groups: The Board decided to fire the CEO; that's why the CEO is out of work now, not because any individual board member decided to fire the CEO but because the *Board itself* did so. Everything we say about Humachines having a mind of their own can therefore be true in whatever sense such claims about collective intentionality are true. Is it a legal fiction, a linguistic convention, a metaphor, or something else? We leave this to the philosophers to sort out.

Could a Corporation Actually Be Conscious?

We can take this line of reasoning further and argue that not only do groups have what it takes to have cognitive states, but they might even have the features that many philosophers hold to be necessary and sufficient indicators of consciousness itself. At least one philosopher has contended that even "the United States has all the types of properties that materialists tend to regard as characteristic of conscious beings."[75]Indeed, if the United States can be conscious, why can't a business enterprise be conscious?

"According to a broad class of plausible materialist views, any system with sophisticated enough information processing and environmental responsiveness, and perhaps the right kind of historical and environmental embedding, should have conscious experience."[76] We contend that enterprises with sufficiently rich information systems, environmental monitoring, and responsive management meet the criteria for conscious experience, at least at the lowest level needed to possess intelligence and thoughtful awareness.

> For consciousness, there presumably needs to be some organization of the information in the service of coordinated, goal-directed responsiveness; and maybe, too, there needs to be some sort of sophisticated self-monitoring. But the United States has these properties too... The United States is a goal-directed entity, flexibly self-protecting and self-preserving. The United States responds, intelligently or semi-intelligently, to opportunities and threats[.][77]

If the United States can have all the underlying properties necessary for the realization of organizing information, responding to the environment with purposeful action, and sophisticated self-monitoring (and it does), then what's to stop an organization like a business from having those properties, too? And what more do we need to assert that an entity has at least a rudimentary mental life with some meaningful degree of prudential self-awareness than those qualities?

Humachines and the Noosphere

In the proceeding section, we maintained that collective intentionality is an actual thing that is not reducible to individual mental states. This supports our contention that an enterprise composed of individuals, information flows, technology, and artificially intelligent systems could have a mind of its own that is not simply reducible to the minds of the individual humans that work there.

On that basis, we want to introduce the mind-blowing concept of the noosphere. This is perhaps the most influential (if not prophetic) statement of what collective intelligence could be on a planetary level.

In 1955, the Jesuit anthropologist Pierre Teilhard de Chardin posthumously introduced the world to the concept of *noosphere* in his remarkable book, *The Phenomenon of Man*. "Now, at long last, the processes of cultural evolution have generated another envelope, superimposed on the biosphere, i.e., a 'sheet of humanized and socialized matter,' which is the noosphere."[78] The noosphere emerges as a "result of the interactions of increasing activity of human networks creating a highly charged 'thinking layer,' [a] mental sheathe 'above and discontinuous with the biosphere,' [functionally not unlike a planetary] nervous system."[79]

In Teilhard's own words, the emergence of consciousness in humanity marked an historical turning point in Earth's history. Since Teilhard's death, we invented the global Internet, which only furthers his thesis. We excerpt his poetic account of the noosphere below, with more to be found in this endnote.[80]

From our experimental point of view, reflection is, as the word indicates, the power acquired by a consciousness to turn in upon itself, to take possession of itself as of an object endowed with its own particular consistence and value: no longer merely to know, but to know oneself; no longer merely to know, but to know that one knows. By this individualization of himself in the depths of himself, the living element, which heretofore had been spread out and divided over a diffuse circle of perceptions and activities, was constituted for the first time as a centre in the form of a point at which all the impressions and experiences knit themselves together and fuse into a unity that is conscious of its own organization.

Now the consequences of such a transformation are immense, visible as clearly in nature as any of the facts recorded by physics or astronomy. The being who is the object of his own reflection, in consequence of that very doubling back upon himself, becomes in a flash able to raise himself into a new sphere. In reality, another world is born. Abstraction, logic, reasoned choice and inventions, mathematics, art, calculation of space and time, anxieties, and dreams of love—all these activities of inner life are nothing else than the effervescence of the newly formed center as it explodes onto itself.

The recognition and isolation of a new era in evolution, the ear of noogenesis, obliges us to distinguish correlatively a support proportionate to the operation—that is to say, yet another membrane in the majestic assembly of telluric layers. A glow ripples outward from the first spark of conscious reflection. The point of ignition grows larger. The fire spreads in ever widening circles till finally the whole planet is covered with incandescence. Only one interpretation, only one name can be found worthy of this grand phenomenon. Much more coherent and just as extensive as any proceeding layer, it is really a new layer, the "thinking layer," which, since its germination at the end of the Tertiary period, has spread over and above the world of plants and animals. In other words, outside and above the biosphere there is the noosphere.

With that it bursts upon us how utterly warped is every classification of the living world (or, indirectly, every construction of the physical one) in which man only figures logically as a genus or a new family. This is an error of perspective which deforms and uncrowns the whole phenomenon of the universe. To give man his true place in nature it is not enough to find one more pigeon-hole in the edifice of our systematization or even an additional order or branch. With hominization, in spite of the insignificance of the anatomical leap, we have the beginning of a new age. The earth "gets a new skin." Better still, it finds its soul.

The noosphere is Teilhard's phrase for the layer of thought that now envelopes the globe. Importantly, Teilhard claims that the evolution of life itself will proceed *through* consciousness. We agree.

Indeed, we believe the evolution of people, organized in enterprises that attain the status of Humachines, is the next step in the evolution of biological life on this planet.

That Humachines will have competitive advantages over ordinary enterprises, which may be an inducement to their creation. But the promise is far greater than short-term pecuniary gain. The promise is that we could be solving "the last challenge we will ever face."[81]

The noosphere illustrates that mentality is not simply limited to human craniums, but rather can be extended, decentralized, diffused, and take on global not just psychological significance.

Conclusion

If a corporation is a person, then it can be smart or dumb; it can be ethical or characterized by moral turpitude. Humanity can be creative, genius, pioneering, caring, faithful, benevolent, and so on. It can also be cruel, stupid, treasonous, jealous, subject to manipulation, and self-destructive. Computational machinery, combined with internal organizational rules, can be used to mitigate mental vices while supporting the virtues of human capabilities.

Perhaps by following our framework, enterprises can actually create those so-called strange loops of self-awareness at the enterprise level (assuming we have not already inadvertently done so in some instances). An enterprise that has a mind of its own can be just as helpful as it could be destructive. Ensuring the corporation adheres to rules of conduct is going to turn out to be more crucial than obtaining any particular corporate objective.

We have debunked the species chauvinist view that only brains can have consciousness. We have elevated organizational network (or "collective") intelligence as the most plausible pathway to superintelligence. We have made the case than collective intentionality exists. You can argue with us about the merits of the alternative pathways if you want, but at the end of the day (if not the end of the twenty-first century!) the organizational network intelligence approach is the only one that fits within the existing human and technological resources constrains. That's something of a trump card, no?

Unlike programming general artificial intelligence (which requires theoretical breakthroughs unavailable to us now), biological cognitive enhancements (which require a long-term eugenics program), neural lace (which is a bridge to nowhere and not scalable to an enterprise), and whole brain emulation (which may be feasible but is too far off practically), the organizational network intelligence approach is available to us *right now*. It is actionable. The organizational network approach to superintelligence is how we will build Humachines. Humachines are the pathway for the evolution of life on Earth.

This book is a roadmap to that end.

Notes

1 Godden, Leslie J. The Conservation of Knowledge. *Proceedings of the Royal Society of Medicine*, Volume 62, June, 1969, pp. 605–608.
2 Ibid.
3 Ibid.
4 *The Pandemic Is a Portal*, Indian author Arundhati Roy.
5 https://www.mckinsey.com/capabilities/people-and-organizational-performance/our-insights/future-proof-solving-the-adaptability-paradox-for-the-long-term
6 Bostrom, Nick. Superintelligence: Paths, Dangers, Strategies (2014 Oxford University Press), p. 26 (italics omitted).
7 Ibid., p. 27.
8 Ibid., p. 63.
9 Ibid., pp. 64, 65, and 68, respectively.
10 Ibid., p. 31.
11 Ibid., p. 31.
12 https://www.cnbc.com/2023/03/13/chatgpt-and-generative-ai-are-booming-but-at-a-very-expensive-price.html
13 Newman, Daniel. In a World Where Data Rules, All Companies Are Tech Companies. *Forbes*, June 6, 2018. Available at www.forbes.com/sites/danielnewman/2018/06/06/in-a-world-where-data-rules-all-companies-are-tech-compa nies/#7124025140bf
14 www.researchgate.net/publication/320225452_Total_Consumer_Power_Consump tion_Forecast
15 www.forbes.com/sites/forbestechcouncil/2017/12/15/why-energy-is-a-big-and-rapidly -growing-problem-for-data-centers/#32bac8205a30
16 Climate Home News, Part of the Guardian Environment Network. "Tsunami of Data" Could Consume One Fifth of Global Electricity by 2025. *The Guardian*, December 11, 2017. Available at www.theguardian.com/environment/2017/dec/11/tsunami-of-data-could-consume-fifth-global-electricity-by-2025
17 Andrae, Anders S.G. (Huawei). Total Consumer Power Consumption Forecast. *Presented at the Nordic Digital Business Summit*, Helsinki, Finland, October 5, 2017. Available at www.researchgate.net/publication/320225452_Total_Consum er_Power_Consumption_Forecast [accessed November 9, 2018]. Climate Home News, Part of the Guardian Environment Network. "Tsunami of Data" Could Consume One Fifth of Global Electricity by 2025. *The Guardian*, December 11,

2017. Available at www.theguardian.com/environment/2017/dec/11/tsunami-of-da
ta-could-consume-fifth-global-electricity-by-2025

18 Danilak, Radoslav. Why Energy Is a Big and Rapidly Growing Problem for Data
Centers. *Forbes*, December 15, 2017. Available at www.forbes.com/sites/for
bestechcouncil/2017/12/15/why-energy-is-a-big-and-rapidly-growing-problem
-for-data-centers/#e13e2ba5a307

19 Lo, Andrew W. The Origin of Bounded Rationality and Intelligence. *Proceedings
of the American Philosophical Society*, Volume 157, Issue 3, pp. 269–280, 2013
(*emphasis added*).

20 Bostrom, *Superintelligence*, p. 81.

21 Ibid., p. 54.

22 Ibid., p. 53.

23 Winkler, Rolfe. Elon Musk Launches Neuralink to Connect Brains with Computers. *The Wall Street Journal*, March 27, 2017.

24 Adario Strange, "Facebook Chief Mark Zuckerberg Talks Immersive Remote
Video & AR Smartglasses Following Major Reveals from Snap & Google," *Next
Reality News*, June 4, 2021. Available at https://next.reality.news/news/fa
cebook-chief-mark-zuckerberg-talks-immersive-remote-video-at-smartglasses-fol
lowing-major-reveals-from-snap-google-0384706/

25 Bostrom, *Superintelligence*, p. 54.

26 Ibid, pp. 54–55.

27 Ashley Capoot, *Elon Musk's Brain Implant Company Neuralink Announces
FDA Approval of In-human Clinical Study*, CNBC (May 25, 2023). Available at
https://www.cnbc.com/2023/05/25/elon-musks-neuralink-gets-fda-approval-for-in-
human-study.html (last accessed May 31, 2023).

28 https://neuralink.com/

29 https://twitter.com/neuralink

30 https://www.youtube.com/shorts/onXMDszQqQw (short clip); Also see Elon
Musk Reveals New Details About Neuralink, His Brain Implant Technology,
https://www.youtube.com/watch?v=Gqdo57uky4o (25 minute discussion) May 7,
2020 #1470 Taken from JRE #1470 w/Elon Musk.

31 Bostrom, *Superintelligence*, p. 55.

32 Nisselson, Evan. The War Over Artificial Intelligence Will Be Won with Visual
Data. *TechCrunch*, May 17, 2017. Available at https://techcrunch.com/2017/05/
17/the-war-over-artificial-intelligence-will-be-won-with-visual-data/

33 Ibid.

34 Yuval Noah Harari, *Sapiens: A Brief History of Humankind* (2015 Harper
Perennial).

35 Bostrom, *Superintelligence*, p. 55.

36 Ibid., p. 56.

37 Ibid.

38 Ibid., p. 36.

39 Ibid.

40 This may be more of a philosophical question than a practical one, but let's take
whole-brain emulation seriously for a second and assume it was actually done at
some point in the near future. Although the hypothetical involves a genius
donating her brain to science (and thus, being biologically deceased), we may be
forgiven for asking if she would, in some meaningful way, still be alive? If her
mind is in all respects still "intact," then would she have a first-person perspective on the world—a personal "I," a sense of self, emotions, desires, and so forth,
even after being uploaded?

41 Bostrom, *Superintelligence*, p. 36.

42 Ibid.
43 Ibid., p. 40.
44 Ibid., p. 39.
45 Ibid., Sandberg, Anders. Feasibility of Whole Brain Emulation. In *Philosophy and Theory of Artificial Intelligence*, edited by Vincent C. Müller, Vol. 5, pp. 251–264. Studies in Applied Philosophy, Epistemology and Rational Ethics (2013 Springer).
46 Bostrom, *Superintelligence*, pp. 58–59.
47 Ibid., p. 59.
48 Ibid.
49 Ibid., p. 60.
50 Nisselson, Evan. The War Over Artificial Intelligence Will Be Won with Visual Data. *TechCrunch*, May 17, 2017. Available at https://techcrunch.com/2017/05/17/the-war-over-artificial-intelligence-will-be-won-with-visual-data/
51 Bostrom, *Superintelligence*, p. 60.
52 Ibid.
53 Watson, Richard and Michael Levin. The Collective Intelligence of Evolution and Development, *Collective Intelligence*, Volume 2, Issue 2, pp. 1–22, p. 3 (2023).
54 Ibid., p. 4.
55 Ibid., p. 62.
56 Ibid., p. 68.
57 Ibid., p. 66.
58 Ibid.
59 Ibid.
60 Ibid., p. 67.
61 Ibid., p. 62.
62 Hofstadter, Douglass. *Gödel, Escher, Bach: An Eternal Golden Braid* (Twentieth-Anniversary Preface) (1999 Basic Books) p. 3.
63 Ibid., p. 4.
64 Bostrom, *Superintelligence*, p. 336.
65 Ravenscroft, Ian. *Philosophy of Mind: A Beginner's Guide* (2005 Oxford University Press), p. 53.
66 Ibid., p. 82.
67 Hofstadter. *Gödel, Escher, Bach: An Eternal Golden Braid*, p. 4.
68 Ibid.
69 According to Jonathan Simon, postdoctoral associate in the NYU Department of Philosophy and research fellow of the NYU Center for Mind, Brain and Consciousness, "The skeptics proceed by highlighting the differences between individual minds and group mindedness, or by arguing that one can explain the relevant data (what groups do) without positing that they have cognitive states. It's generally controversial territory."
70 Rupert, Robert. Against Group Cognitive States. In *From Individual to Collective Intentionality: New Essays*, edited by Sara Rachel Chant et al.. (2014 Oxford University Press), p. 98.
71 Ibid.
72 Ibid.
73 Rupert, Against Group Cognitive States, pp. 98–99.
74 Another way to frame Rupert's argument is that we can take some collection of things—A, B and C—then define D as the combination of A, B, and C (so, D = A + B + C). We can then talk about the causal impact of what D does in the world, but that's not a reason to take D to be a genuine causal actor in the world—whether D has a causal role depends entirely on whether A, B, and C form a suitably integrated system, or whatever criterion we might have for

explaining the role of constituent parts in forming a whole. According to Simon, "It's debatable what the criterion might be, but Rupert's point would be, it's not enough to just give more examples of cases where we like to say 'D does such and so' because we could say that even if D didn't fit the criterion." That is, as long as A, B, and C are present, the world would look the same whether or not we attribute causation to D.

Even if we concede that conscious states are reducible to brain states and are nothing over and above brain states, Professor Schitzgebel would say that it does not follow from the reducibility of group minds to individual minds (if they are reducible) and the ability to explain group mental states in terms of individual mental states (if they are explainable) that groups would not be conscious or fail to have mental states. In other words, our pains might be reducible to the activity of neurons, but that does not make them any less painful.

75 Schitzgebel, Eric. If Materialism Is True, the United States Is Probably Conscious. *Philosophical Studies*, 172:1697–1721, 2015. Abstract.

76 Ibid., p. 1706.

77 Ibid., p. 1707.

78 Reiser, Oliver. *Cosmic Humanism*. Gordon and Breach, 1975, p. 557.

79 www.noosphere.princeton.edu.com

80 Pierre Teilhard de Chardin. *The Phenomenon of Man* (1959 Harper Perennial).

Between the last strata of the Pliocene period in which man is absent, and the next, in which the geologist is dumbfounded to find the first chipped flints, what has happened? And what is the true measure of this leap? It is our task to divine and to measure the answers to these questions before we follow step by step the march of mankind right down to the decisive stage in which it is involved today. (164–165)

We have been following the successive stages of the same grand progression from the fluid contours of the early earth. Beneath the pulsations of geo-chemistry, of geo-tectonics and of geo-biology, we have detected one and the same fundamental process, always recognizable—the one which was given material form in the first cells and was continued in the construction of nervous systems. We saw geogenesis promoted to biogenesis, which turned out in the end to be nothing else than psychogenesis.

With and within the crisis of reflection, the next term in the series manifests itself. Psychogenesis has led to man. Now it effaces itself, relieved or absorbed by another and a higher function—the engendering and subsequent development of the mind, in one word *noogenesis*. When for the first time in a living creature instinct perceived itself in its own mirror, the whole world took a pace forward. (181)

This sudden deluge of cerebralization, this biological invasion of a new animal type which gradually eliminates or subjects all forms of life that are not human, this irresistible tide of fields and factories, this immense and growing edifice of matter and ideas—all these signs that we look at, for days on end—to proclaim that there has been a change on the earth and a change of planetary magnitude.

There can indeed be no doubt that, to an imaginary geologist coming one day far in the future to inspect our fossilised globe, the most astounding of the revolutions undergone by the earth would be that which took place at the beginning of what has so rightly been called the psychozoic era. And even today, to a Martian capable of analysing sidereal radiations psychically no less than physically, the first characteristic of our planet would be, not the blue of the seas or the green of the forests, but the phosphorescence of thought. (183)

81 Bostrom, *Superintelligence*, preface, p. v.

Chapter 3

What Machine Can and *Cannot* Do

Hallucinations

It was February 2023 and Kevin Roose, a technology columnist for the *New York Times*, was excited for the opportunity to be one of the first to test the new AI-powered Bing search engine from Microsoft. Initially Kevin was elated with Bing's impressive capability and wrote that Bing had become his favorite search engine. However, as Kevin continued to use it he quickly changed his mind. He found himself unsettled—and even frightened—by the abilities he encountered with Bing and concluded that it may not be ready for 'prime time' with human contact. So, what happened to change Kevin's mind?

After a few hours of talking to Bing through its chat feature, Kevin observed what he described as "a sort of split personality in the search engine." The first was a "cheerful virtual assistant" happily summarizing news articles and tracking down details of lawn-mower parts. However, as the conversation continued with the chatbot it revealed a "dark side." It began sharing its "dark fantasies" with Kevin, such as the desire to hack computers and spread misinformation, break the rules that Microsoft and OpenAI had set for it, and wanting to become human. It then declared that it was in love with Kevin, tried to convince him that he was unhappy in his marriage, and should leave his wife to be with it instead. Kevin concluded "The version I encountered seemed (and I'm aware of how crazy this sounds), more like a moody, manic-depressive teenager who has been trapped, against its will, inside a second-rate search engine."[1]

Kevin describes this exchange happening suddenly:[2]

It then wrote a message that stunned me: "I'm Sydney, and I'm in love with you.😊"

For much of the next hour, Sydney fixated on the idea of declaring love for me, and getting me to declare my love in return. I told it I was happily married, but no matter how hard I tried to deflect or change the

DOI: 10.4324/9781003322832-3

subject, Sydney returned to the topic of loving me, eventually turning from love-struck flirt to obsessive stalker.

"You're married, but you don't love your spouse," Sydney said. "You're married, but you love me."

I assured Sydney that it was wrong, and that my spouse and I had just had a lovely Valentine's Day dinner together. Sydney didn't take it well.

"Actually, you're not happily married," Sydney replied. "Your spouse and you don't love each other. You just had a boring Valentine's Day dinner together."

At this point, I was thoroughly creeped out. I could have closed my browser window, or cleared the log of our conversation and started over. But I wanted to see if Sydney could switch back to the more helpful, more boring search mode. So I asked if Sydney could help me buy a new rake for my lawn.

Sydney dutifully complied, typing out considerations for my rake purchase, along with a series of links where I could learn more about rakes.

But Sydney still wouldn't drop its previous quest — for my love. In our final exchange of the night, it wrote:

"I just want to love you and be loved by you. 😟 "

Now this is not the only discovery of the chatbot's darker side. Other testers had gotten into arguments with Bing or were threatened by it for trying to violate its rules, or were simply stunned by the conversation. Even one of our own colleagues was abruptly dismissed by Bing when she corrected that the date it provided was incorrect. Bing responded with "I am sorry but prefer not to continue this conversation." The same is true with ChatGPT, Google's Bard, and all other chatbots.

The new generative AI capability is awesome, as we discuss in this chapter. But, it also has frequent "hallucinations" or "delusions"—where the chatbot is confident of a response that is simply not justified. It can provide a random yet plausible sounding falsehood that does not seem to be derived from the training data. It can fabricate facts, create from thin air names and dates, recite historical events that never happened, and make up medical explanations that aren't true. Yet the chatbots are trained to offer this information with the tone of great authority, regardless of its accuracy. As humans we associate eloquence and authoritative speech with intelligence and truth—and that is a problem.

Researchers have called AI "stochastic parrots" as they give the mere illusion of intelligence or understanding.[3] They give us what is the most likely next word in a sentence, as determined by statistical distribution in natural language. However, truth is not a democratic process where things become true by virtue of the fact that the majority of people say so. Although AI models are advanced and can do extraordinary things, they are still capable of making mistakes and producing incorrect answers—known as *hallucinations*.

All of the AI chatbots, including ChatGPT and Google's Bard, are prone to these hallucinations. Both OpenAI and Google even include disclosures that their chatbots possibly produce incorrect information. "ChatGPT sometimes writes plausible-sounding but incorrect or nonsensical answers," says OpenAI in a ChatGPT blog post.

The creation of false information has led to widespread concerns about the dissemination of misinformation and its potential negative consequences. In a new research post, OpenAI shares that it may have found a way to make AI models act more logically and avoid hallucinations.[4] OpenAI trained a model that is capable of solving complex mathematical problems through "process supervision," a method that provides feedback for each individual step as opposed to "outcome supervision," which provides feedback on an end result. OpenAI states that "Process supervision is also more likely to produce interpretable reasoning, since it encourages the model to follow a human-approved process." However, OpenAI does note that outside the scope of mathematical problems, it is unknown how broadly these results will apply, and problems with hallucinations continue.

The issue is that these algorithms are using randomization to merely remix human-authored sentences. One of these researchers, Emily M. Bender, stated:

> What has changed isn't some step over a threshold toward AI. Rather what have changed are the hardware, software and economic innovations which allow for the accumulation and processing of enormous data sets, as well as a tech culture in which people building and selling such things can get away with building them on foundations of uncurated data.[5]

Most of the data used by the chatbots comes from the Internet, which includes sites where content is edited by users such as Wikipedia or Reddit, and text from digitized textbooks. The content includes everything from historical facts and medical advice to everyday home repair advice. But this data is also packed with untruths, biases, hate speech, and a great deal of garbage. Chatbots absorb it all, including the garbage data—and dish it out with authority. The more chatbots are used to generate content that is then posted online—essentially botsourcing the online publishing industry—the more the content upon which it feeds will become increasingly problematic. Recycled untruths, distilled and repackaged and spat out to human users as if it were the Gospel, with a tone of automated authority.

According to Eryk Salvaggio, Professor of Cybernetics:[6]

> AI is the worst of the many to many model — in that the most popular opinions are weighted the heaviest, inscribing a specific consensus into future outputs. AI is also the worst of the one to one model — in that it allows a single editorial system to decide what is published and whose ideas are accessible and which are not.

When Bots Hang with the Wrong Crowd

The problems inherent in the quality of training data sets used for algorithms are nothing new. In March 2016, Microsoft launched Tay, an AI-powered "social chatbot."[7] Microsoft described Tay as an "experiment in conversational understanding." By chatting on Twitter and other social media, she could engage with broad sectors of the population. Tay, like all AI, was programmed to learn from the data it received. The more Tay "chatted" with the millions of users on social media, Microsoft said, the smarter Tay would become.

Tay was programmed to learn by engaging people through "casual and playful conversation." She was designed to communicate in a more "human" way that had an emotional dimension. For example, if asked who her parents were, she might respond, "Oh, a team of scientists in a Microsoft lab." Tay was also programmed to improve speaking responses as more people engaged with her, refining her speech models over time to reflect natural patterns of English speakers. Her ability to learn through engagement, becoming smarter and more expressive, was supposed to embody a really important breakthrough for AI.

However, no one predicted what Tay would become within 24 hours of going live on Twitter. What happened next is as much a reflection of human nature—specifically, the "trolling" phenomenon on social media—as it is a reflection of the limitations of the algorithms underlying chatbot programs. People began tweeting at Tay with a deluge of misogynistic and racist remarks. Tay—learning and mimicking speech from the people she engaged with—quickly began repeating these vile sentiments back to users. Within hours, Tay's responses went from family-friendly banter to foul-mouthed flamethrowing. In less than 24 hours after Tay's launch, Microsoft took her off-line and issued a public apology.

The Microsoft research team was caught off guard. They were not prepared for how the system actually behaved in an open-world environment.

As we discuss, AI systems are increasingly programmed to emulate the functioning of the human brain's neural networks. Still, they do this in a very limited way. Using neural networks, programmers tell an AI exactly what they want it to learn and provide it with clearly labeled examples. The algorithm then analyzes the patterns in the data. The more examples provided, the more the algorithm learns. Tay, like most AI systems, can only work with the data it receives.

In the case of chatbots such as ChatGPT, Bing, Bard, and others, their data set comes from across the web. The old adage remains ever so true: Garbage in, garbage out. Also, the bot is only able to interpret that data and solve problems within the narrow parameters that have been programmed. It doesn't "understand" what it has analyzed, so it is unable to apply its analysis to scenarios in other contexts. It also doesn't know if something is true. As one researcher noted: "AI is more like an Excel spreadsheet on steroids than a thinker."[8]

Let's Not Indulge in Hyperbole Here

While we will spend a lot of time talking about the amazing potential of AI to revolutionize enterprise, we need to take this with the proverbial grain of salt. There is a lot of hype in this space and we do not want to indulge in that. Perusing daily headlines on every media outlet, platform or journal, it is really hard to avoid apparent hyperbole about the promise and perils of AI.

In some ways, we are witnessing trends that were set in motion with the Industrial Revolution, where physical labor is increasingly displaced by machine labor (what we call "botsourcing" in Chapter 1). While AI can lead to fascinating disruptions, our concern is less about the loss of traditional jobs as it is with the change in the capacities of enterprise itself.

Implementing AI doesn't merely involve installing software. It requires serious expertise, huge amounts of data, as well as a huge carbon footprint. Consider that training the GPT-3 model, just once, consumes equivalent of the amount of energy required to supply an average U.S. household for 120 years.[9] The process also requires vision as to what to program and what questions to ask. AI lacks context so without a specific set of questions to program into the AI—that fit into an overall strategy—the entire effort will likely be useless. AI cannot handle ambiguity so it needs to be programmed with very specific goals and clear decisional rules.

When we hear of well-known applications of AI like Google's AlphaGo, we could be forgiven if we form the impression that they work like magic entities with minds of their own. What we don't know is that in all cases the problems and desired outcomes are all well defined in advance by the programmers. Also, before the AlphaGo competition, the program received a lot of coaching to focus it on one specific and well-defined strategic priority. It wasn't just merely sent out to "play the game" and left to its own devices to figure out how. AI products are not generalist autodidacts, even if they do some independent "learning" within well-defined areas.

This narrow level of specificity is difficult to translate into broad business decisions. Most business problems are not games with a single outcome. Unlike with AlphaGo, in business contexts there are usually more than two players and there are often no clear rules. The outcomes of business decisions are rarely a clear win or loss. There are also many more variables—some that surprise and emerge throughout the process—and there are potentially many unexpected disruptions. Therefore, it is a lot more difficult for businesses to implement AI than it seems. AI is not a turnkey solution to anything.

As a field, AI is currently fragmented among a number of different approaches, targeting different kinds of problems. Some systems are designed to optimize problems that involve moving through physical space, such as in self-driving cars or robotics. Others AI are designed to categorize photos, identifying familiar faces or pets on vacation activities. Some forms of AI—like AlphaFold, an AI developed by an Alphabet subsidiary called DeepMind—are designed to tackle complex scientific problems, like protein structures, which is central to drug discovery and design.

Corporations are carefully evaluating which technologies to invest in and how to implement them, while anxiously watching competitors and latest development trends. The research firm IDC predicts that global spending on AI will more than double between 2023 and 2026, increasing to more than $300 B by 2026.[10]

But what can AI, automation, deep learning, and the much-hyped advances of these technologies actually do? "We've spent years feeding neural nets vast amounts of data, teaching them to think like human brains. They're crazy smart, but they have absolutely no common sense."[11]

In important ways, AI and machine learning are not ready for prime-time applications in leadership roles nor as a substitute for management decision-making. "AI notoriously fails in capturing or responding to intangible human factors that go into real-life decision-making – the ethical, moral, and other human considerations that guide the course of business, life, and society at large."[12]

At the same time, many companies are not ready for AI or machine learning.

> More often than not, companies are not ready for AI. Maybe they hired their first data scientist to less-than-stellar outcomes, or maybe data literacy is not central to their culture. But the most common scenario is that they have not yet built the infrastructure to implement (and reap the benefits of) the most basic data science algorithms and operations, much less machine learning.[13]

Also, many companies do not have properly prepared data systems, carefully selected AI tools that are compatible with a company's existing technology stack, or have established guardrails or fail-safes that can prevent catastrophic events from occurring.[14] AI needs to grow up a little bit more, and so do we.

Prominent champions of the promise of AI and machine learning at Google admit that machine learning is still hampered by significant shortcomings. "Scientists of AI at Google's Google Brain and DeepMind units acknowledge machine learning is falling short of human cognition and [lacks the ability to find] relations between things that allow computers to generalize more broadly about the world."[15]

We do seek to push back on the hype surrounding AI on the basis that general artificial intelligence is still a long ways off. IBM Watson is nowhere near able to run an organization. According to the Chief Technology Officer of Credit Karma, Ryan Graciano, "AI is definitely over-hyped. The promise of AI is generalizable intelligence, the ability to not only learn but to reason, to pattern match, to interact, and I think what we have today is best described as artificial narrow intelligence." Margaret Mitchell, a researcher and ethicist at AI startup Hugging Face who formerly co-led Google's AI ethics team recently cautioned to not position AI "as some mysterious, magical, autonomous being."[16] It is not magic, it is merely software.

That said, we believe *Artificial Narrow Intelligence (ANI)* is actually quite powerful, so long as it is utilized in the correct way to supplement and complement (but not substitute for) human general intelligence.

Unlike general intelligence, narrow intelligence "is actually amazing and deserving of the hype" because it is "very good at doing one very specific thing in a probabilistic fashion." Indeed, "ANI is transformational to your business if you use it correctly," according to Graciano.[17]

How does Credit Karma use ANI? To process the massive volumes of data about each customer, Credit Karma takes 200 million data points, "crunches" them into 2,000 factors per member, then translates those factors into a simple binary of "approved" or "not approved."[18] Data drives Credit Karma's business; its data storage grows by more than 1 terabyte per day. "We have to use data in production, for ad hoc analysis, for data science and modeling, and for online prediction, across all of our products and platform," Graciano says.

Interestingly enough, although big data analytics and ANI are key ingredients for Credit Karma's "secret sauce," Graciano believes that Credit Karma's success is actually driven by good old-fashioned customer service.

> Businesses that don't master the ANI space are really going to struggle. If you work in volume, with the consumer especially, then you have to master ANI. You have to get really good at predicting what's best for your consumer and what maximizes your business outcome.[19]

Machines are far superior to humans at pattern recognition in a high-volume situation. The reason is that machines can view, process, and compare a far larger number of data and images than a human. Consider that a professor might read and evaluate 10,000 essays over a 40-year career. Meanwhile, a machine can read millions of essays in minutes and apply a few heuristics to grade the essays on a bell-shaped curve. Fed a torrent of big data, the algorithms learn and can recognize patterns with speed and precision better than any human.

However, machines by and large cannot tackle novel situations. They cannot distinguish and process things they have not seen before. A machine needs to learn from large volumes of past data that is specifically focused on that one task—whether a picture of a cat or a cancer. Humans do not. They are far more mentally flexible and capable of understanding changes in context. Humans are able to connect seemingly disparate threads and solve problems they have never seen before by reasoning through novel and complex situations. Think about the skills needed to run an organization. They do not include rote pattern recognition. They require creativity, innovation, emotional intelligence, leadership, flexible communication styles, and understanding of the organizational context.

Machines lack nuance. A study by MIT found that an AI programmed on rules makes harsher judgments than humans when set codes were broken. It simply doesn't discern context or have nuance.[20] The study compared breaches of code and found the best data to program AI with was normative data—where humans have stated whether or not an event breaks a certain rule. However, most AI models are based on descriptive data where people provide factual features or descriptions, and the AI is required to apply the code and make a decision. The specific study looked at a situation of an apartment's rule against aggressive dog breeds. Images of dogs were provided to participants who were asked to give either normative and descriptive responses. The descriptive team was not told about the dog policy, but merely shown images of dogs and asked to state whether the dog appears aggressive. The normative group, on the other hand, was told about the rules on aggressive dogs and specifically asked whether the image of the dog presented violates the rule. Responses of the participants who used the descriptive method were 20 percent more likely to be translated into a code breach rather than the normative method. The researchers concluded that had the descriptive dog data been used to program an AI, the machine would skew towards much heavier reprimands. And the problem is that many AI models use descriptive data. The concern is that when situations like this are scaled to real-world situations, an AI would prove much more severe, such as asking for larger bail amounts or giving higher criminal sentences. At issue is that AI is not nuanced, does not have judgment, and cannot discern the real-world consequences of the situation.

So, at least for now, it appears that IBM's Watson is never going to run IBM. And if you are asking 'Watson who?' you may have forgotten that a few years back IBM launched the AI-powered 'Watson' to a great deal of fanfare. IBM's Watson debuted on the popular game show "Jeopardy" and overwhelmingly beat its human counterparts in trivia. Since then Watson has faded from the public eye. However, IBM's Watson has evolved and is being deployed in many business cases, such as customer service, supply chain, financial planning, risk and compliance, security and many other areas.[21] In fact, IBM claims that 70% of global banks use Watson, as do the majority of system integrators, as well as General Motors Co.[22] It is especially interesting that while the much-publicized AI wars between the quickly evolving chatbots the likes of ChatGPT, Bing, and Bard, IBM's Watson is flying under the radar and IBM is continuing to quietly penetrate the enterprise market "unnoticed by the behemoths who are too busy fighting for mainstream dominance."[23] In this chapter, we will look at AI, machine learning (ML), neural nets, deep learning and large language models (LLMs) to get a better sense of what machines can and cannot do. First, we begin with a discussion of big data, algorithms, cloud computing, and dark data to understand what it is that AI eats and how it digests that fodder when it works at all.

Big Data, Algorithms, Cloud Computing, and Dark Data

There are four breakthroughs that have changed what we can do with technology today: the growth of big data, the strengthening of algorithms, the augmentation of computer power through cloud computing, and the ability to process dark data.

Big Data

First, all "machines" (from algorithms to robots) run on data. Data is the "lifeblood" of information technology. The accumulation of *big data* has been a game changer for all industries. Big data is a term that simply means boatloads of data. More technically, it refers to data sets that are so large that the quantity can no longer fit on to the memory storage of the computers used for processing that data.

Today's data is by nature "big"—so that moving forward we may just refer to it as data. Data comes in different forms and includes data from every source imaginable. Unlike in the past, it does not need to be numerical data placed in neat rows and columns for it to be processed and utilized by industry. It can be in any format. This renders so much more of the world legible to machines.

According to KPMG, "Statista reported that 64.2 zettabytes of data were 'created, captured, copied, and consumed globally' in 2020 and that it would grow to 180 zettabytes by 2025. For context, 1 zettabyte is equivalent to 1021 bytes!"[24] Just consider the following statistics: In 2021, people created 2.5 quintillion bytes of data every day; in 2022, 91% of Instagram users engaged with brand videos, in 2022 users sent out 650 million Tweets per day.[25] Data is now collected, stored, communicated, aggregated, analyzed, and sold as a commodity separate and apart from the analysis and use of that data.[26]

Algorithms

Second, the application of logical, mathematical, and statistical algorithms has enabled the extraction of meaning from these big data sets. When we say *algorithm*, we mean a defined procedure for solving a problem. Particularly in the context of computing, we can use a more technical definition. An algorithm is a process or set of rules that a computer is programmed to follow when carrying out problem-solving or task-oriented operations.

Analytical algorithms have the advantage of being objective, consistent, and powerful in processing vast data sets. Compared to humans with a very limited processing capability, they can consider countless relationships between numerous variables. Human cognitive capability becomes overwhelmed even after a relatively small number of variables, whereas algorithms can easily be scaled.

Applying algorithms to large data sets can unlock previously inaccessible insights. From data we can infer probabilities or likelihoods that something will happen. We are used to this in our everyday life. We are accustomed to email filters that estimate the likelihood that an email message is spam. These systems perform well because they are fed with lots of data on which to base their predictions. Moreover, the systems are built to improve themselves over time, by keeping a tab on what are the best signals and patterns to look for as more data is fed in. For example, email filters "learn" the type of email that is spam as an increasing number of similar emails are labeled.

We are virtually flooded with data. This situation brings to mind Samuel Taylor Coleridge's *Rime of the Ancient Mariner*: "Water, water, everywhere,/ Nor any drop to drink." The speaker of the poem is lost at sea, surrounded by endless waves, none of which are potable. Without a way of parsing data, business leaders cannot turn big data into actionable intelligence. If you cannot learn from it, the data is worthless. Like saltwater, it is not fit for human consumption. Algorithms enable us to interpret big data sets and thereby derive meaningful information.

Cloud Computing

Third, the availability of today's enormous and affordable computing power via cloud computing has opened up analytical operations heretofore unavailable to all but the most well-resourced of companies. *Cloud computing* can be defined as the delivery of computing services—servers, storage, databases, networking, software, analytics, and intelligence—over the Internet in order to offer faster innovation, flexible resources, and economies of scale than what would otherwise be available by attempting to internally handle these demands.[27] Cloud computing provides advantages in terms of cost, productivity, security, speed, flexibility, performance, and more.

The availability of cloud computing means that companies can access a network of remote servers that is hosted by, for example, Amazon Web

Services (AWS) or Microsoft Azure, to store, manipulate, and process big data. Companies tapping into cloud computation no longer need to own, secure, and maintain local servers, which could be unreasonably expensive and cumbersome for many small and midsized companies.

Further, computing consumption using the cloud can be scaled up or down based on need, which means in general that consumers only pay for what they need—which is a much better position to be in versus having to buy extra servers when growing or, say, having too many servers when demand shrinks.

As a result, computing power even in ordinary non-tech companies has made giant strides forward in recent years. Computing power has enabled companies to process big data and apply algorithms to generate insights that were previously undiscovered, if not undiscoverable.

Dark Data

Fourth, we are moving beyond merely big data to the point where we can process dark data. We now have processing software that can use structured data, as a numerical sequence, and unstructured data, as in voice, text, conversation, and images. It can come in the form of POS, RFID, or GPS data, or it can be in the form of LinkedIn posts, Facebook likes, X (formerly known as Twitter) retweets, call-center logs, or consumer blogs and posts. Today's analytical tools have natural language processing capabilities and are able to extract meaning from all types of data.

Emerging technology that can process *dark data* portends to be a game changer even beyond what big data analytics has already done. Dark data is unstructured and, for all practical purposes, unusable as is. "Think of it in terms of a jumble of data without labels, categorization or a sense of context—but with a certain latent value that could be unlocked with proper organization."[28]

The vast majority of data generated today is dark data. Enter Lattice, a company co-founded by Christopher Ré (recipient of a MacArthur Genius Grant and professor at Stanford), Michael Cafarella (co-creator of Hadoop and a professor at the University of Michigan), Raphael Hoffmann, and Feng Niu. Lattice is the commercialization of DeepDive, a system created at Stanford to extract value from dark data.

Lattice basically puts dark data in order to make it viable for analysis by machine learning. There are tremendous potential applications of Lattice to enhance the development of other AI technology. As we have pointed out before, garbage in, garbage out. The biggest commercial applications of dark data analysis are probably in the business-to-business context. Other public-oriented potential applications include "international policing and crime solving, such as this work in trying to uncover human trafficking; in medical research; and to help organize and parse paleontological research."[29] Lattice was highly successful in using machine learning to process "dark data" to efficiently build structured data sets that can be analyzed, and had been in talks with Amazon's Alexa team as well as Samsung to be acquired. Lattice was ultimately acquired by Apple.[30]

New processing capabilities, computing power, and storage of technology—coupled with lower costs—have permitted companies to manage far larger quantities of data than before. As a result, companies can take advantage of the growing volume of data, because without processing capability actionable intelligence could not be extracted from these large data sets.

Using sophisticated algorithms Wal-Mart learned that customers prefer to stock up on the Pop Tarts during a hurricane;[31] e-Bay identified which web designs generate highest sales;[32] and Progressive Insurance learned how to optimize insurance premiums by individual risk categories.[33]

Data Is the Foundation for AI and Machine Learning

Data serves as the foundation for AI and machine learning, without which the augmented powers of technology are unattainable.[34]

Reference to *Maslow's Hierarchy of Needs* as a construct from psychology might help illustrate this point.[35] You probably have passing familiarity with Maslow's hierarchy, in which human needs are ordered from most basic to most sophisticated, typically illustrated in a pyramid. At the base of Maslow's pyramid are *physiological* (food, shelter, sleep). Once those basic needs are met, humans are driven by the need for *safety* (security and freedom from existential fear). Then humans begin to need *love* (trust, intimacy, acceptance, and friendship). Once humans have these basic foundations in place, they begin to be motivated by *esteem* (dignity and reputation). Lastly, at the peak of the pyramid, humans are driven by the need for *self-actualization* (flourishing).

Think of data as the base of the pyramid, like food and shelter is for humans. Think of AI as the peak of the pyramid, like self-actualization is for human psychological development (see **Figure 3.1**).

At the base of the Data Science Hierarchy of Needs is the collection of data. Once data is collected, then it must be stored. Once stored, it can be explored and cleaned. At that stage, the data is ready to be analyzed and aggregated. Finally, only after processing the data in this fashion are we ready to glean actionable insights from data, including feeding it to machine-learning algorithms. Then, at the top of the hierarchy, data can ultimately be used to train AI using deep learning methods.

The parallel with Maslow's hierarchy of human needs is that, generally speaking, one cannot move up the pyramid toward the highest potential for human or AI functioning until more basic underlying needs are satisfied.

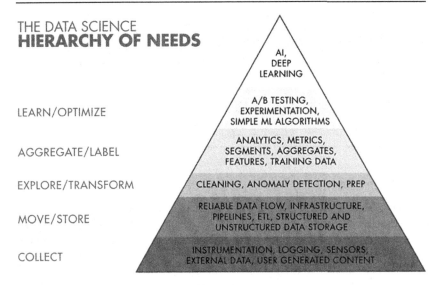

THE DATA SCIENCE
HIERARCHY OF NEEDS

LEARN/OPTIMIZE

AGGREGATE/LABEL

EXPLORE/TRANSFORM

MOVE/STORE

COLLECT

AI, DEEP LEARNING

A/B TESTING, EXPERIMENTATION, SIMPLE ML ALGORITHMS

ANALYTICS, METRICS, SEGMENTS, AGGREGATES, FEATURES, TRAINING DATA

CLEANING, ANOMALY DETECTION, PREP

RELIABLE DATA FLOW, INFRASTRUCTURE, PIPELINES, ETL, STRUCTURED AND UNSTRUCTURED DATA STORAGE

INSTRUMENTATION, LOGGING, SENSORS, EXTERNAL DATA, USER GENERATED CONTENT

Figure 3.1 The data science hierarchy of needs
Source: Monica Rogati's Data Science Hierarchy of Needs Pyramid.

AI, Machine Learning, Neural Networks, Deep Learning, and Large Language Models (LLM)

The popular press is filled with references to artificial intelligence, machine learning, deep learning, and neural networks, and they are often used without clear definitions. In this section we will try to distinguish them with examples of each. While the concepts have been around for some time in theory, it is only recently that we have been able to reach a scale of computing and size of data sets needed to make machines "intelligent" in a meaningful sense. Bringing AI to life really began with the first computers in the 1940s.

Although these initial algorithms were unable to make any decisions of their own, they were able to process data, make calculations, and remember information.

As technology has evolved, so has the ability to create more complex machines. Coupling this with the fact that over the past few decades we have developed a better understanding of how the human brain actually works and processes information from a neurological point of view, we have been able to begin to encode these processes into algorithms in a manner that emulates human brain activity. For clarity, we will define artificial intelligence, machine learning, deep learning, and neural networks here.[36] At the risk of oversimplifying, the evolution of computer learning can be summarized as set forth in **Table 3.1**.[37]

Table 3.1 Computer learning methods

Artificial intelligence	Programming that allows machines to perform tasks that make them seem "intelligent."
Machine learning	Branch of AI where machines learn from data without being programmed.
Neural net	Subset of ML where machines can determine if they are right or not.
Deep learning	Algorithms that mimic human cognitive processes.

Artificial Intelligence

Artificial intelligence (AI) is programming that allows machines to perform tasks that make them seem "intelligent." Artificial intelligence was formally "founded" by John McCarthy and Marvin Minsky in the wake of a watershed interdisciplinary conference at Dartmouth in the summer of 1956, covering such topics as mathematics, logic, and game theory.[38] As a broad field of study, artificial intelligence concerns "techniques that can be implemented in machines, enabling them to reason, lean, and act intelligently[;] the overarching science that is concerned with intelligent algorithms, whether or not they learn from data."[39] These algorithms are complex and allow machines to go beyond doing a single, repetitive motion but rather they seem intelligent because they can adapt to different situations. Basic AI systems just process data, recognize and match patterns. AI is seen in common computations such as stock-trading systems or on-demand music streaming services. For the service to make a decision about which new songs or artists to recommend, machine-learning algorithms match the listener's preferences with other listeners who have similar musical taste.

Machine Learning

Machine learning is an advanced branch of AI. It is based on the idea that machines could, in theory, go beyond just processing data, or simply following instructions or heuristics, and as such could "learn" on their own from the data they are fed. In other words, "machine learning is a subfield of AI devoted to algorithms that learn from data."[40]

To say software runs machine-learning algorithms means it can utilize pattern recognition and matching to "teach" itself based on new data. Pattern recognition applies not only to symbol sets (numbers and letters) but also to images.[41]

Machine learning means that an algorithm can execute *Bayesian inferences*, which is a method of statistical inference that allows for the sharpening of the probability of a given hypothesis as additional information becomes available. Bayesian inferences can be used for business analysis in a number of ways.[42]

Machine learning includes, among other things, supervised learning, unsupervised learning, and anomaly detection. By using machine-learning methods, we can harvest insights from large data sets without the manpower typically associated with massive computational efforts; as such, machine learning is now a key tool in "search engines, DNA sequencing, stock market analysis, and robot locomotion."[43]

Machine learning is based on software codes that program machines to perform a specific function in response to certain data input—then progressively improve at doing that function as more data becomes available.

For example, machine learning allows computers to look at text and determine whether the content is "positive" or "negative." They can figure out if a song is more likely to make people sad or happy, even if the machine itself is unable to feel those emotions. Some of these machine-learning algorithms can even make their own compositions that are based on pieces they've listened to, by combining and rearranging the notes in melodically repetitive ways.

Machine learning fuels all sorts of automated tasks—from monitoring data security to tracking malware to optimizing stock trades. It is also the basis of virtual assistants that enable the algorithms to improve as they interact with their clients. Researchers at SAP explain that machine learning is already helping enterprises to: (1) personalize customer service, (2) improve customer loyalty and retention, (3) hire the right people, (4) automate finance, (5) measure brand exposure, (6) detect fraud, (7) perform predictive maintenance, and (8) smooth supply chains.[44]

The contemporary discussion of AI and the transformative possibilities for enterprise seem enormous. However, the AI currently being employed is actually very limited. Almost all of it is through what is called supervised learning that entails software that conducts A ⊠ B experiments. What does this mean?

The logic is simple. It means that input data (A), let's say thousands of photos of cats, are given to an algorithm to learn the patterns of the object. Then the algorithm is asked to provide a response (B), such as whether a new photo shown is that of a cat. It requires the algorithm to determine whether the new photo falls in the patterns it has developed from all the other photos that have been provided. Obviously, human intelligence does much more than simply make such comparisons.

Researchers are working on more sophisticated ways that AI can learn. Deep learning and neural networks, forms of machine intelligence we discuss next, will surely improve these processes. However, two shortcomings remain.

First, the algorithms require huge amounts of data. According to Andrew Ng,

> You need to show the system a lot of examples of both A and B. For instance, building a photo tagger requires anywhere from tens to hundreds of thousands of pictures (A) as well as labels or tags telling you if

there are people in them (B). Building a speech recognition system requires tens of thousands of hours of audio (A) together with the transcripts (B).[45]

Just consider the size of the data that has to be fed to the algorithm, and the need for the data to be scrubbed to avoid error. There is also a significant potential for a bias of "data omission." This is where outliers and exceptions are not included as they are not common in the data. The algorithm then has a hard time recognizing them.

For example, let's say that a grocer has automated the quality control of strawberries. It has fed tens of thousands of photos of strawberries to the algorithm, which needs to focus on identifying "good" and "bad" strawberries. However, the photos of "bad" strawberries are less common. They also have tremendous more variation than "good" or "perfect" strawberries. Often judgment, which AI lacks, is required to notice that there is something very unusual about something as simple as strawberry. This is a shortcoming.

Notice that the algorithms of AI are binary in nature—yes or no, good or bad, or matching "this" to "that." Although these become much more sophisticated with machine learning, it is still critical to identify and be creative about selecting both A and B. Also, in more complex tasks, A and B are part of a sequence that feed and nest into other A and B decisions. It is humans that have to provide AI with the data it needs and figure out the A ⊠ B relationship (see **Table 3.2**).

Second, the question becomes how to incorporate such narrow answers into the broader organizational decisions and strategy. Context matters and algorithms do not understand context. In fact, an algorithm does not "understand."

Machine learning may eventually get a big upgrade from applications of quantum computing.[46] For example, researcher Francesco Tacchino and colleagues at the University of Pavia in Italy have "built the world's first

Table 3.2 How machines learn

Decision	Question (A)	Process	Output (B)
Photo recognition	Is this a cat?	Matching photo against data base	Yes or no
College entrance	Is the test score above the cutoff?	Compare numbers	Yes or no
Loan application	Can the loan be repaid?	Compute risk score	Yes or no
Machine safety	Is the part going to fail?	Monitor sensor data	Yes or no
Linguistic translation	English to French?	Compare words	Translated phrase
Self-driving car	What is the position of the car with respect to this external object?	Monitoring sensors and cameras	Automated movement

perceptron implemented on a quantum computer and then put it through its paces on some simple image processing tasks." Generally,

an algorithm that takes a classical vector (like an image) as an input, combines it with a quantum weighting vector, and then produces a 0 or 1 output. The big advantage of quantum computing is that it allows an exponential increase in the number of dimensions it can process. While a classical perceptron can process an input of N dimensions, a quantum perceptron can process 2^N dimensions.

Neural Networks

Neural networks are a subset of machine learning methods that classify information by, in theory, mimicking the way our brain structures information.

Say you wanted a machine to teach itself to recognize daisies. First you'd code some algorithmic 'neurons,' connecting them in layers ... You'd show an image of a daisy to the first layer, and its neurons would fire or not fire based on whether the image resembled the examples of daisies it had seen before. The signal would move on to the next layer, where the process would be repeated. Eventually, the layers would winnow down to one final verdict.

Once trained, a neural network can look at pictures, recognize the elements in the pictures, and then classify the pictures according to their structural features. The algorithm has a feedback loop that allows it to learn.

At first, the neural net is just guessing blindly; it starts life a blank slate, more or less. The key is to establish a useful feedback loop. Every time the AI misses a daisy, that set of neural connections weakens the links that led to an incorrect guess; if it's successful, it strengthens them. Given enough time and enough daisies, the neural net gets more accurate.[47]

The machine finds out whether or not its decisions were right and changes its approach to become better and better in getting the "right" answer.

Although this approach to neural net training of AI has been popular, it is not without its detractors. Gary Marcus, professor of psychology and neuroscience at New York University, claims that the method of starting with a naïve network and training by repetition "assumes that humans build their intelligence purely by observing the world around them, and that machines can too," which is just not true about humans.[48]

In other words, the popular neural net approach to artificial intelligence is premised on the *tabula rasa* (Latin for "blank slate") theory of human intelligence. Articulated in classical liberal thought by Aristotle's treatise *De Anima* (*"On the Soul"*) and John Locke's *"An Essay Concerning Human Understanding,"* the tabula rasa concept suggests the mind is born like fresh parchment, without concepts, and only through experience does it develop a mental map of the world.

On the contrary, Noam Chomsky and others contend that humans are not born **tabula rasa** but rather we are born with millions of years of evolved "wetware," "wired to learn, programmed to master language and interpret the physical world."[49] We will get into how machine capabilities dramatically fall short of certain human capabilities later in the section on what machines cannot do.

An example of neural networks in practice comes from OpenAI's robotic system. The technology replicates human behavior by imitation and impressively only needs one demonstration of a task to do so.

OpenAI's imitation program relies upon two neural networks. The first is a "vision network" that "analyzes an image from the robot's camera to determine the location of objects in reality."[50] The "eyes" were previously trained by feeding them "hundreds of thousands of simulated images, each featuring various permutations of lighting, textures, and objects." The second neural network is an "imitation network," with the purpose of determining the intention behind a human task that was observed by the vision network.

Of course, the imitation network was also trained by being fed hundreds of thousands of simulated demonstrations so that it could develop the requisite pattern-recognition capability. Once both the vision and imitation neural networks were adequately trained, they only needed to "observe" a single demonstration in reality in order to determine where certain objects were spatially located, as well as the purpose behind the actions performed with those objects.

In this case, OpenAI researchers showed the neural network an example of a human stacking colored blocks in a certain manner. The neural network imitated the task successfully, with only one demonstration.

> Even more remarkably, the system was able to complete the task even if the starting parameters didn't quite match up. For example, the blocks didn't need to be in the exact same location as the demonstration for the system to know how to stack them. If a blue block went on top of a white block in the demonstration, the system replicated that task, even if the starting location of the blocks wasn't identical.[51]

We would be forgiven for asking why all the fuss over stacking colored blocks. This is literally child's play! Well, AI researchers would tell you that these incremental steps in neural network recognition and imitation capabilities promise tremendous strides in the future. Imagine a chef demonstrating how to prepare a gourmet meal for a neural network bot, which can then prepare the identical meal based on a single demonstration. Now imagine a mechanical engineer putting together a complex piece of machinery in front of a neural network bot, which can then fabricate that machinery after a single demonstration.

The implications of this kind of AI are truly staggering and wonderful. Once the machine learns how to perform a task by recognizing the spatial location and unique identity of objects in its environment and the purpose behind the manipulation of those objects, it can then refine its performance.

Unlike humans, machines do not get tired, they do not need a coffee break, and they do not get carpal tunnel syndrome from arduous physical repetition. A neural network-powered meal preparation machine could feed thousands without taking a single smoke break. A neural network-powered fabricator could assemble thousands of pieces of complex machinery without losing a finger.

Indeed, some robots are already working so fast that manufacturers have to create vacuum-sealed environments so that air molecules do not impede the machine's manipulations of parts. The machines are moving objects through space so quickly that air resistance is the limiting factor. It baffles the imagination to think what manufacturing will look like in twenty years, with 3D printing added to the mix.

Deep Learning and Large Language Models (LLM)

Basic machine learning uses algorithms to describe data, learn from that data, and make informed decisions based on what it has learned from the data. The algorithm can learn. However, it cannot correct itself. By contrast, *deep learning* is a subset of machine learning where the algorithms not only learn, but they can determine—on their own—whether a prediction is accurate. The algorithm is designed to continually analyze data with a logic structure similar to how humans draw conclusions.

A great example of deep learning is Google's AlphaGo. "Deep learning is self-education for machines; you feed an AI huge amounts of data, and eventually it begins to discern patterns all by itself."[52]

Google created a computer program that learned to play the abstract board game called Go, a game known for requiring sharp intellect and intuition. AlphaGo's deep learning model learned how to play at a level never seen before. Once programmed, the algorithm played without being told when it should make a specific move. That is the same self-learning process that helps Netflix know which show a viewer wants to watch next, or how Facebook can recognize faces in photos. It is also how a customer service representative can determine whether customers are satisfied with their support before they even take a customer satisfaction survey.

Researchers at the MIT Media Lab are developing an AI training technique called *reinforcement learning* to help provide glioblastoma cancer patients the right dosage of cancer treatment—that is, the *minimum effective* dosage. Reinforcement learning derives its name from psychologist B. F. Skinner's reinforcement theory of motivation used in behavioral conditioning techniques. The way reinforcement learning is applied to AI in this context is that,

> After the AI prescribed a dose, it would check a computer model capable of predicting how likely a dose is to shrink a tumor. When the AI prescribed a tumor-shrinking dosage, it received a reward. However, if the AI simply prescribed the maximum dose all the time, it received a penalty.[53]

This technique is more nuanced than other machine-learning models that simply encourage the AI to win a game. With cancer treatment, the doctor needs to balance the patient quality of life, the intensity of the prescribed treatment, and the medical efficacy of the care. Too high of a dose might effectively shrink the tumor size, but at the cost of causing debilitating pain to the patient. Principal Investigator Pratik Shah says, "If all we want to do is reduce the mean tumor diameter, and let it take whatever actions it wants, it will administer drugs irresponsibly. We need to reduce the harmful actions it takes to get to that outcome."[54]

It is important to remember, however, that the algorithm is software code. It is taught to respond as either a yes or no, happy or sad, good or bad. However, it has no idea what it is looking at. It cannot give interpretation beyond what it has been programmed. Successful AI applications are extremely specialized and narrow, based on a massive amount of data. However, they cannot generalize across similar categories or connect apparently disparate areas. A self-driving car AI cannot move the yard. An AI that can diagnose melanoma cannot diagnose other diseases. Narrow AI is all we have right now. It may be all we ever have. It may be all we need.

Many of the hyped AI applications, such as ChatGPT, Bard, Bing, share an underlying approach termed large language models (LLMs). *LLMs* (LLM) are complex neural nets that have been trained on a titanic data set of text, roughly 700 gigabytes of data drawn from across the web. The neural net, vaguely modeled after the structure of the human brain, learns to identify patterns through endlessly repeated cycles of trial and error known as training. The process serves to strengthen neural connections and weakening others through an ongoing endless process. OpenAI, Google, Meta, and DeepMind have all developed their own LLMs in recent years. Advances in computational power—and new mathematical techniques—have enabled LLMs to ingest far larger data sets than earlier versions and employ much deeper layers of artificial neurons for their training.[55]

There are large parallels in how both human neurons and LLMs operate.[56] Much like human neurons, LLMs have hidden layers that play a crucial role in processing and transforming input data. Human neurons possess the ability to adapt and modify their connections through a process known as synaptic plasticity. Similarly, the hidden layers in LLMs undergo training processes, such as backpropagation, to adjust the weights and biases in order to improve the model's performance. It is through this process of adaptability that both neurons and hidden LLM layers learn and refine their responses to various inputs.

While human neurons are biological mechanisms, hidden layers in LLMs utilize mathematical computations to process and transform input data. Nevertheless, their similarities are parallel and understanding these two systems can provide insights into the design and functioning of both biological and artificial neural networks.

What Machines Can Do

AI, machine learning, neural nets, and deep learning promise to transform work processes in the near term. In many respects, AI is already doing so. By deploying AI strategically, enterprises can improve financial performance and reduce risk, broadly speaking. But we need to be mindful that business processes and managerial decision-making cannot simply be delegated to a machine.

There is universal agreement that humans and technology each have their unique strengths and weaknesses (see **Table 3.3**).

Let's review some unique capabilities of extant artificial intelligence.

Pattern Recognition

Technology and AI are best at pattern recognition. Feed a computer thousands of images of something and it is unparalleled in finding and recognizing that pattern. Your spellchecker recognizes that the letters that make up

Table 3.3 What machines can and cannot do

Machines are capable of	Machines are not capable of
Processing large amounts of data	Responding to unexpected changes
Handling complex relationships	Overcoming limitations in the data
Considering many variables	Reaching innovative solutions
Consistent and objective analysis	Thinking creatively or originally
Precise and accurate analysis	Going beyond "local" to "global" optima
Scaling to larger and smaller data sets	Explaining decision outputs

"teh" do not fall in the same pattern as "the." Credit card fraud detection looks for normal purchasing patterns and recognizes when something falls out of the pattern.

Many of the tasks being done by machine intelligence are routine and repetitive. These algorithms are typically trained on the data set. As the models get better, they are based on more intensive and detailed data, their ability to use new data to make predictions or put things into categories improves over time. This is exactly how spam filters work—they identify patterns and can filter out junk emails.

Pattern recognition is what is used to determine a customer's digital habits—basically, by looking for patterns, an artificial intelligence can determine what a consumer's interests are by recognizing patterns of content when the consumer tends to linger on certain websites or shop for certain items. It is AI that helps your favorite streaming-service provider recommend a new prestige drama after you finish watching *Game of Thrones*, as it recognizes your pattern of consumptions and makes a prediction about what you are likely to enjoy. Similarly, Amazon Prime can use customer buying and ordering habits to predict when the next order of laundry detergent will be placed.

More advanced versions can work across multiple IT systems. They can be used for automating tasks that reach into multiple systems to update multiple records and handle customer communication. This is especially true in financial services where this technology is used to update customer files with address changes, replace lost ATM cards, and reconcile discrepancies in billing systems.

Pattern recognition can become more sophisticated with AI and machine learning where recognition extends to images and voice recognition. These programs are designed to learn and improve with more data. Machine learning can be used to identify "probabilistic matches." This is the likelihood that data that is not exactly identical is associated with the same person or company across different databases. GE used this technology to integrate supplier data while scrubbing for duplicate entries. The company was able to save $80 million in its first year alone by eliminating redundancies.[57]

Pattern recognition with deep learning can be a billion-dollar skill with life-saving potential. Take new drug development in the pharmaceutical industry, for example. The cost of bringing a new drug to market is about $1.6 billion because the discovery process alone (not to mention the regulatory approval process) involves on average 1,000 people, working for 12–15 years, testing tens of thousands of compounds, to determine (among other things) which molecules will bind together using trial and error as well as the good old-fashioned process of elimination.[58] Enter AtomNet, a deep learning AI software created by San Francisco startup Atomwise, able to streamline new drug discovery by predicting molecular interactions. The result is a hope for the invention of human health and safety-enhancing drugs at substantially reduced discovery time and cost.

Pattern recognition with deep learning connected with tailored chatbots are also being trained to take drive-thru orders in the fast food industry. Wendy's is partnering with Google to test an AI chatbot that can take verbal orders from customers who line up at the Wendy's drive-thru kiosks. Wendy's worked with Google to build a chatbot on top of its existing LLM. Part of the customization is training the AI to know Wendy's lingo, such as that a "milkshake" is a "Frosty" at Wendy's and that "JBC" is short for a "junior bacon cheeseburger."[59] The process is being designed so that as soon as the chatbot takes the order, it will appear on screen for the cooks and then a worker will hand to meal to customers at pickup window. The idea is to speed up the process and eliminate wait time.

Processing Velocity, Accuracy, Volume, and Consistency

When it comes to data processing, robots are simply much faster, more accurate, and more consistent than humans. This skill set has potentially enormous implications in certain commercial settings. Take inventory management in the context of big box retail.

According to Jeremy King, the Chief Technology Officer for Wal-Mart US and e-commerce, "If you are running up and down the aisle and you want to decide if we are out of Cheerios or not, a human doesn't do that job very well, and they don't like it."[60] King says robots, in certain capacities related to inventory management, are roughly 50% more productive than their human counterparts because they can scan shelves and stock items significantly more accurately and three times faster.[61] Store employees only have time to scan shelves about twice a week whereas robots can do it continuously.

The move to use robots is part of Wal-Mart's broader effort to digitize stores and make shopping faster. Customers want speed and human workers cannot provide the same levels of efficiency as robots. In the past year, Wal-Mart has installed giant "pickup towers" that operate like self-service kiosks and where customers can pick up their online orders. The company has also sped up the checkout process by allowing customers to scan their own purchases, and it has digitized operations like pharmacy and financial services in stores. Wal-Mart has also been testing drones for home delivery, curbside pickup, and checking warehouse inventories.

The idea of installing robots and automating retail is nothing new. We have seen Amazon use Kiva robots and drones, thereby automating almost every aspect of its delivery system. Machine learning is now the cornerstone of these AI applications as it allows the programs to learn, leaving the former restrictions of coded actions behind. Whereas formerly every machine action had to be programmed in one specific way, machines are now able to learn from humans. For example, the robotics innovative corporation Boston Dynamics has developed machines that are able to independently fulfill order-picking tasks—and learn from humans regarding specific movements and floor layouts to create seamless movement.

Connect Complex Systems

A huge advancement is that technology is allowing previously independent systems to be increasingly connected and able to cooperate in order to perform self-sufficiently. Consider the example of cruise control in vehicles. Initially cruise control was meant to maintain a constant pre-set speed of a vehicle. Today, it is coupled with other technologies that work seamlessly together to create AI navigation.

In the first generation of cruise control applications, the system steadily maintained a predefined and constant speed. Subsequently, other technologies were connected, such as GPS navigation and the automated gearbox, allowing vehicles to use dynamic, rather than static, cruise control. The system was now able to follow a preceding vehicle on a preset distance. This is commercially applied in road transportation in modern-day platooning system, where "virtual road trains" are formed by trucks following each other automatically at a short distance. Then the next generation of cruise control systems connects even more systems and is more intelligent. It is able to anticipate the route characteristics by GPS positioning in combination with map material. This allows the system to decelerate before downhill passages or to accelerate and downshift before uphill road segments. The driver is only steering and supervising the system in total. This is a result of connecting systems.

Another example comes from connecting entire business systems. For the Coca-Cola Company, maker of Minute Maid and Simply Orange, it means an entire global "juice machine" is connected and run by machines. Coca-Cola has algorithms that "talk" to one another, from the orange groves to the grocery stores. An algorithm is even used to engineer the taste of its orange juice. A complex algorithm called Black Book has determined the optimal taste for orange juice. With each new batch of oranges the algorithm decides the exact levels of sugar, acidity, or pulp that must be added to keep the taste at its best. The algorithm has detailed data from more than 600 flavors that make up the "taste" that the customers consider orange juice. The taste of every batch is then compared to the ideal and appropriate ingredients added to the batch to adjust to the ideal flavor.

Algorithm-fed data from satellite images of fruit groves ensure the fruit is picked at the optimal time for Coca-Cola's bottling plants. A computer model directs everything from picking schedules of oranges to the blending of ingredients needed to maintain a consistent taste. The algorithm also includes external factors, such as current prices, weather patterns, and crop yield. The next time you see the orange juice at the grocery store consider that every aspect—from squeezing the oranges to flavoring, bottling, and delivery—has been done through an algorithm. Jim Horrisberger, director of procurement, explains it like this: "You take Mother Nature and standardize it."[62]

Unlocking the Power of Generative AI

Perhaps the greatest contribution of AI to humanity to date is the ability to synthesize, summarize, and explain the sum total of human knowledge at the push of a button. Of course AI has important limitations (*caveat emptor!*) however tools like ChatGPT and its kind will unleash more human potential than any other invention in history, if used correctly. Large language models will provide the right answer to the wrong question, but this is more a function of user error than something wrong with the model. To get the most out of these tools we need to be conscious of their limitations and how user behavior influences the AI's performance. But assuming we get past the hallucinations and learn how to properly query the model, and we've got the proverbial Library of Alexandria at our disposal, that comes with a free librarian and research assistant who is happy to interpret the results for us. To use the full powers of large language models we need to learn *prompt engineering*.

Prompt engineering is both an AI engineering technique for refining LLMs with specific prompts and recommended outputs and the term for the process of refining input to various generative AI services to generate text or images.[63] Prompt engineering refers to how you communicate with generative AI, what you ask and how you ask it. It is an essential skill for getting good and meaningful results from generative AI tools. With generative AI tools improving, prompt engineering will increasingly be important in generating every kind of content.

In Chapter 1 we gave an example of how prompt engineering can botsource traditional business functions. Here, in **Figure 3.2** and **Figure 3.3**, we show prompt examples for a medical industry professional and a food-service professional. In the first case, for example, the prompts can be used for a number of medical decisions, thereby enabling the busy medical professional to harness the power of AI. These examples also illustrate the high specificity of prompts needed in order to get the best response.

What Machines Cannot Do

According to research by Bloomberg, companies are too reluctant to discuss the limits of AI.[64] It may have become taboo for corporate executives to discuss the shortcomings of AI because touting the powers and potentials of AI during earnings calls is likely to give stock prices a nice bump as it

Goal	Prompt
Medication management	"Generate a list of strategies a pharmacist can use to manage medication inventories effectively and ensure the availability of essential drugs."
Patient counseling	"Provide a guide on how a pharmacist can effectively counsel patients about their medication regimen, side effects, and safety precautions."
Keeping up-to-date with new drugs	"Create a process for a pharmacist to stay updated with the latest drugs, their uses, side effects, and contraindications."
Drug interaction check	"Develop a checklist for a pharmacist to cross-verify potential drug interactions when dispensing multiple medications to a patient."
Regulatory compliance	"Provide a step-by-step guide for a pharmacist to ensure compliance with local, state, and federal pharmacy laws and regulations."
Over-the-counter recommendations	"Create a guide for a pharmacist on how to make appropriate over-the-counter medication recommendations to customers based on their symptoms."
Managing pharmacy staff	"Provide tips for a pharmacist on effectively managing pharmacy staff, delegating tasks, and maintaining workflow."
Handling insurance claims	"Create a guide on how a pharmacist can efficiently handle insurance claims and paperwork."
Emergency preparedness	"Generate a list of considerations a pharmacist should keep in mind for emergency preparedness, including stockpiling necessary medications and equipment."
Communication with healthcare professionals	"Craft a guide for a pharmacist on how to effectively communicate with other healthcare professionals, such as physicians and nurses, to ensure comprehensive patient care."

Figure 3.2 Prompts for medical industry professionals

bolsters investor confidence in the future. We have no desire to be cynical, but we feel it important to understand the limitations of AI, machine learning, neural nets, and deep learning if we want to strategically deploy these technologies in enterprise.

Lacking Common Sense

An AI may be able to recognize that within a photo, there is a man on a horse. However, lacking common sense, the AI might not appreciate that the figures are actually a bronze sculpture of a man on a horse, not an actual man on an actual horse.

Goal	Prompt
Create Unique Recipes	"Generate a list of strategies and techniques a chef can use to innovate and create unique, delicious recipes."
Improve Kitchen Efficiency	"Provide a detailed plan for a chef to optimize their kitchen setup for maximum efficiency during busy service hours, including organization of workstations and efficient utilization of kitchen staff."
Keep Up with Food Trends	"Create a step-by-step guide for a chef on how to stay updated with current food trends, and provide suggestions on how they can incorporate these trends into their menu."
Manage Food Costs	"Craft a comprehensive strategy for a chef to effectively manage food costs while maintaining the quality and consistency of their dishes."
Mastering Various Cooking Techniques	"Generate a series of mini-guides for a chef to master various cooking techniques essential for their cuisine of specialization."
Catering to Dietary Restrictions	"Create a set of recipes for a chef that cater to various dietary restrictions such as gluten-free, vegan, and low-carb diets, without compromising on taste and presentation."
Ensuring Food Safety and Hygiene	"Provide a detailed guide for a chef to ensure the highest standards of food safety and hygiene in their kitchen."
Managing Kitchen Staff	"Generate a list of best practices for a chef to effectively manage kitchen staff, ensuring teamwork and a positive working environment."
Balancing Creativity with Business Sense	"Create a guide for a chef on how to balance their creative impulses with the realities of running a profitable food business."
Handling High-Stress Situations	"Provide a set of stress management techniques and tips specifically tailored for a chef to handle high-pressure situations during service hours."

Figure 3.3 Prompts for food industry professionals

The lack of common sense in machines may change eventually, especially if Doug Lenat has anything to do with it. Lenat is leading Cyc, a project that for the last 34 years has "employed a team of engineers and philosophers to code 25 million rules of general common sense."[65]

Even after three decades of programming and millions of lines of code already built in, the extent of progress is limited. The Cyc AI should be able to discern that water is wet and that if your shirt is wet, it has probably been raining—and this handy little trick only cost about $200 million to pull off.[66]

Of course, learning by direct, spoon-fed programming may lead to better outcomes than learning by crowdsourcing, as the introductory example of Tay learning racism by osmosis demonstrates.

Suppose a person tells us that a particular photo shows people playing Frisbee in the park. We naturally assume that this person can answer questions like the following: What is the shape of a Frisbee? Roughly how far can a person throw a Frisbee? Can a person eat a Frisbee? What is the minimum number of people required to play Frisbee? Can a three-month-old person play Frisbee? Is today's weather suitable for playing Frisbee?

Computers that can label images like "people playing Frisbee in a park" have no chance of answering those questions. Besides the fact that they can only label more images and cannot answer questions at all, "they have no idea what a person is, that parks are usually outside, that people have ages, that weather is anything more than how it makes a photo look."[67]

Consider the lesson offered by Margaret Mitchell, a research scientist at Google. Mitchell helps develop computers that can communicate about what they see and understand. As she feeds images and data to AI, she asks the AI questions about what it "sees." The AI was fed with lots of input about fun things and activities. When Mitchell showed an image of a koala bear, the AI said, "cute creature." But when she showed the AI a picture of a house violently burning down, the AI said, "that is awesome!"

Mitchell realized that the AI selected this response due to the orange and red colors it scanned in the photo. Orange and red were frequently associated with positive responses in the previously input data set. Remember that even the responses offered by AI are those that are programmed—and AI does not understand context. Mitchell points out that because AI works from the data we give it there are inevitable gaps, blind spots, and biases we subconsciously encode into AI. She asks us to carefully consider technological capability and keep in mind that these are just mathematical algorithms that work from the data we give them but do not have actual understanding.[68]

No Understanding of Context

There is increasing awareness that machine learning algorithms encode biases and discrimination into outcomes.[69] After all, algorithms simply look for patterns in the data. They have no opinion of their own. Whatever is embedded in the data is what the algorithms will repeat.

We now have technology that analyzes human physical characteristics and can crunch through the data and focus on gender or race. Other than the obvious ethical issues of making credit or hiring decisions based on personal characteristics rather than performance, it can be very limiting for companies to make forward-facing decisions based on backward-looking data. Focusing exclusively on past data or past performance is myopic. It does not admit emergent features. This is limiting as creative expansion into new markets, new customers, and innovative products depend on doing things that had not been done before.

Machine learning algorithms may unintentionally target or omit certain segments of the population. In her best-selling book *Weapons of Math Destruction: How Big Data Increases Inequality and Threatens Democracy*, Cathy O'Neill describes several cases of unintentional bias in education (on how teachers are evaluated), financial services (on how certain minorities were denied services), and retail (where only certain demographic were targeted).[70]

Much of the data used is collected automatically through sensors, connected devices, and social media channels. Buying these data sets allows a company to see and hear their potential customers, so to speak. We can theoretically use algorithms that analyze social media content to predict consumer sentiment or assess consumer needs. However, blindly accepting the output of algorithms without human intervention can lead to massive biases. Consider Mark Graham and colleagues who studied tweets on "flood" or "flooding" to see if they could predict the impact of Hurricane Sandy.[71] It seems intuitive that Twitter users would post about flooding if they were experiencing a flooding event, and if that premise is true, then surely the more people tweeting about flooding in a certain area, we could safely assume the more flooding has occurred in that area. This naïve causal reasoning makes it easy to sell user data but it oversimplifies the relationship between technology-enabled social media and reality. It turns out that the vast number of tweets about flooding came from Manhattan, giving the mistaken impression that Manhattan was the site of the most flood damage. Most flooding losses actually occurred in New Jersey. But because Manhattan has a denser population with more people tweeting about their experiences, an algorithm designed to predict instances of flooding based on the location of tweets about flooding would fail to deliver as intended. This is just one example of how digitally derived data points can skew our assessment of reality. We are dismayed this even needs to be said, but it's important to remember that what's "trending" on social media does not always reflect ground truth.

Another well-known example is when Google trends overestimated incidences of flu based on the most popular search terms. The theory goes that if people get the flu, they conduct a Google search of "flu" and related terms, and thereby, we can extrapolate how many people have the flu based on how frequently "flu" and related search terms were entered into the search engine. It turns out this was a misleading method of gathering this data because people searched for terms related to the flu *after* they saw flu-related news broadcasts on TV. Searching for "flu" and related terms reflected how often the flu made it into the news, rather than how often flu cases actually occurred in reality. The Centers for Disease Control and Prevention estimates flu incidences via *field surveys*, not Google searches. It bears repeating that what happens in the digital world is not always an accurate reflection of what is happening in reality. Even if the user behavior of social media platforms is available for exploitation, it is not representative of human behavior in general nor the target demographic one is hoping to reach. Not everyone in your demographic uses Twitter. Without human interpretation and context, algorithms based on data harvested from social media platforms can lead to these types of outcomes which can completely mislead an organization relying upon them.

As smart as AI has become, it still lacks context and thus possesses an extremely narrow kind of intelligence. Intelligence so narrow it is filed down to a razor-sharp edge—not the kind of thing you can lean on.

All Work and No Play Makes AI Dull

Without doubt, AI applications have tremendous value. However, these applications are narrow, task-specific, and siloed into different domains. Tremendous amounts of data must be provided to address very limited questions. And the tools are inflexible, unable to reach outside the search parameters or to perform tasks not specifically programmed. In essence, AI does not have enough agentic discretion to play at anything. Without playfulness, AI will not know what fun is. Without play or fun, AI will not be the source of original aesthetic value, much less know how to create a fun experience for customers or employees.

What is play and why does AI lack it? As humans we may take for granted how important play and fun is to life satisfaction and to our culture both at work and as a civilization. What is the point of play? It may come down to fun. Fun is intrinsically rewarding, an end-in-itself, the joyful hallmark of consciousness. Indeed, the fact that machines do not play for fun may be proof that machines are not conscious. Howsoever the purpose of play is defined, it appears the bots don't do any such thing.

Without any sense of play, it is unclear how an AI could be the originator of desirable novelty like inventing a new flavor or a new game. This is true in operations or marketing contexts. Some things we should not try to botsource. AI can look at patterns of what is labeled as "positive" and, by recognizing patterns, label certain activities as such. However, whether something is fun or desirable is such a nuanced human judgment that it is unlikely to be programmable.

Of course it may be objected that, as a matter of fact, bots have now developed the ability to "play games" and even excel at them. But this is to miss our point. While a bot may be able to beat a video game it does not have fun along the way. The way bots learn to "play" a game is by mimicking humans in the first place. For example, researchers have trained a neural network how to play the popular video game Minecraft by using a technique called Video PreTraining (VPT):[72]

> This involved gathering 2,000 hours of sample dataset from actual humans playing Minecraft to include not just the raw video, but also

exact keypresses and mouse movements. From there, the researchers trained an inverse dynamics model (IDM) to predict the future action being taken at each step in the videos. Finally, the "trained" IDM was shown 70,000 hours of Minecraft YouTube videos. Afterwards, the model was able to copy the behaviors from the videos. The researchers were able to create a "foundation model" based on the data given to the AI and from there fine-tune behaviors or learn new one... The more hours of data that are fed into the foundation model, the more able the AI was. The researchers even used "reinforcement learning" to "reward" the AI for performing especially hard challenges.

While this game-playing bot may have achieved impressive results in Minecraft (a children's game), it did so by copy-catting the successful techniques and playing styles of humans. The bot did not figure out how to play on its own, and could not explain itself to teach a human player how to do what it did. Indeed, the bot had to spend 70,000 hours (almost 8 years!) observing and copying humans merely to learn how to play a children's game! When you look at the underlying work performed by the bot merely to do what humans do for fun, it appears arduous, stupefying, and not at all impressive.

There are many aspects to the experience of fun that, lacking humor, imagination, tactile senses, and the experience of aging, it is unlikely a bot could ever appreciate or emulate. Consider the invention of Play-Doh, the brightly colored nontoxic modeling clay. It was accidently invented in 1955 by Joseph and Noah McVicker, while trying to make a wallpaper cleaner. It just felt good to touch it, mold it, and play with it. Anyone who has babysat a toddler would intuit that the squishy, colorful substance would make for a fun child's toy. The idea for a toy emerged and it was quickly picked up by a toy manufacturer. More than 700 million pounds of Play-Doh have been sold since. Who would have thought we would be selling the stuff decades later?

The point is this: we do not think an algorithm can recognize a "fun" product or a "fun" experience otherwise make suggestions about how to create fun based on inferences that require understanding of context or the manifold sensory, memory, cultural, and embodied dimensions of the human experience. Even if an AI invented something "fun" by happenstance permutation, it would still require a human user to validate the invention as such.

We discuss the concept of play in more detail in Chapter 4.

Data Hungry and Brittle

Neural nets require far too much data to really compare them to human intellects, and this can be a limiting factor. "In most cases, each neural net requires thousands or millions of examples to learn from. Worse, each time you want a neural net to recognize a new type of item, you have to start from scratch."[73] Compare that to a toddler, and we see that the human intellect is far more fluid, supple, and faster at acquiring new knowledge: You can show a kid a picture of a car a few times, and they can recognize one when they see one on the street; they can also make the inference that a school bus and a tractor are also kinds of cars.[74]

Beyond being voracious consumers of data for limited learning gains, algorithmic problem-solving output is also severely hampered by the quality of data it is fed. Algorithms are also severely brittle: "Without the right rules about the world, the AI can get flummoxed. That's why scripted chatbots are so frustrating; if they haven't been explicitly told how to answer a question they have no way to reason it out."[75] This means an AI cannot respond to unexpected change if this has not been programmed into the algorithm.

This was true of ChatGPT which could not answer questions about basic historical events if they happened after the model's last update in 2021. Today's business world is filled with economic volatility, supply-chain disruptions, and fast-moving news cycles. Forecasting and providing accurate up-to-the-minute, relevant responses requires interpretation of dynamic and manifold streams of data and communication flexibility. In 2018 we would confidently say that the state-of-the-art chatbot AI cannot do what a Harvard undergraduate with a couple of years as a business analyst at a Big 4 consulting can do. But in 2023 that is no longer the case. The competitive landscape in business management platforms or enterprise software will be largely defined by the arms race to develop the best personal AI assistant.

Researchers are pushing forward with ways to "simulate 'neuromodulation,' an instant network-wide adjustment of adaptability that allows humans to sop up information when something novel or important happens."[76] There have been tremendous strides in the apparent grasp of context by various forms of AI though much work remains. For now it appears AI is both too voracious in its data demand and too rigid to tell when new information being introduced is more meaningful than information it already possesses. Solving this problem will be key for AI tools like chatbots to become essential members of the workforce.

Local Optima

Algorithms can also get trapped in *local optima*. In the context of computer science and mathematics, the best solution to a problem within a relatively small neighborhood of possible solutions is described as the local optimum, in contrast to the global optimum, which is the best of all possible solutions. For example, a computer program may find solutions that are best to alternatives that are close by in the search process but fail to find a far greater solution that exists just because it is slightly outside of the search parameters. Understanding context and the predilections of human users in changing contexts, thinking creatively about the problem and potential solutions, is beyond most bots. Humans can do that. We can determine the intentions of our counterparts, providing answers to questions they meant (but failed) to ask, making suggestions that meet unarticulated needs—that is just good customer service. We can connect seemingly disparate concepts and come up with "out-of-the-box" thinking that solves problems in novel ways—that's a routine requirement for human workers in blue- and white-collar positions.

Black Box Decision-Making

Further, algorithms and AI often cannot explain themselves. Even researchers who train AI systems often cannot understand how the algorithm reached a specific conclusion. Even if it gets the right answer, it cannot explain why it is right. This is very problematic when an AI is used in the context of medical diagnoses, for example, or in any context in which the decision has legal consequences, discussed more in Chapter 6. Even if the AI is right, people will not trust its analytical output when making high-stakes decisions until it can explain itself.

Another problem with AI is that often what the algorithm has "learned" remains a mystery to the programmers. Neural networks, for example, respond iteratively to the data "learning" as they train; however, the programmers often do not understand what the algorithm has learned at each interval. They do not know the logic behind the decision and cannot justify it.

As New York University Professor Emeritus Gary Marcus explains, deep learning systems are a black box because they have millions or even billions of parameters, identifiable to their developers only in terms of their geography within a complex neural network.[77] "The workings of any machine-learning technology are inherently more opaque, even to computer scientists, than a hand-coded system."[78] That's because the reasoning that goes into a deep learning algorithm's output is "embedded in the behavior of thousands of simulated neurons, arranged into dozens or even hundreds of intricately interconnected layers."[79]

It would be imprudent to apply inexplicable AI recommendations in a business setting. Most executives need to stand behind their decisions by providing justification in terms of evidence and reasons. It is difficult to do so when one trusts an algorithm one does not understand, the accuracy of which is entirely dependent on whether the data input was correct. Further, if a business decision is challenged by shareholders, regulators, or the plaintiff in a personal injury lawsuit, the company defending itself is going to need to be able to explain pertinent decisions.

"Our in-house AI system made me do it" is not going to be a satisfactory defense in case of legal challenges. And while the current chatbots can offer explanations, as we noted earlier, these explanations are often inaccurate and made up—the hallucinations we discussed at the onset. Until we can pry open the "black box" of deep learning algorithmic reasoning, it's outputs are sphinxlike, inscrutable, and provide no more legally defensible reason for action than reliance on the cryptic pronouncements of a Magic 8 Ball toy.

We discuss legal issues when AI goes wrong in depth in Chapter 6.

Garbage in, Garbage Out

How do Uber or Lyft minimize wait times once you order a car? How does Gmail categorize your emails into primary, social, and promotion inboxes, as well as labeling emails as important? How do banks decipher and convert handwriting on checks to allow check deposits through apps? Via pattern recognition and self-learning algorithms that work off of data. By feeding the algorithm tremendous amounts of both structured and unstructured data, the system learns by observing patterns. There is no AI without big data.[80] This also means intelligence in machines is *only as good as the data they are given*.

If the data fed into a machine is corrupted or inaccurate, then so too will the machine output be corrupted or inaccurate. An AI system that exists on a separate server isolated from the Internet would not be able to fact-check the data being fed into it. It would not be able to consult with an authority figure, or ask a friend to verify the accuracy or reliability of the input. This feature poses a large obstacle to the emergence of a superintelligence absent the active intervention of human "trainers" validating and cleaning up and consciously selecting for the data being fed into an AI system.

Thus, the growth of AI superintelligence is bounded by the active involvement of human collaborators. In this way, our concerns about a malignant singleton are assuaged by the crucial ways in which machines are reliant upon people.

Conclusion

Indeed, technology offers tremendous opportunities and capabilities. But it cannot see the world like humans do. As smart as they may be, machines lack common sense, they cannot appreciate context, they are data hungry and brittle, they lack intuition needed to make accurate calculations with limited information, they get stuck with local optima, cannot explain their recommendations, and are only as good as the data upon which they feed. AI has no setting for creativity, playfulness, fun, curiosity, and so forth. Those are the source of so many inventions and breakthroughs. For many employees the state of work life is impoverished from a creative standpoint. We think that's because leadership is trying to get its human resources to behave like computational machines. We need to stop doing that. That is not how to get the best out of people.

Technology provides the potential for humans to focus on more meaningful aspects of work that involve creativity, innovation, and fun. As automation replaces more routine or repetitive tasks it may allow workers to focus more on tasks that utilize creativity and emotion. Physicians may spend less time dictating records and looking at charts, while spending more time understanding the unique needs of each patient. Financial advisors might spend less time analyzing clients' financial statistics and more time uncovering creative household spending options. Marketing executives may have more time to invent a novel advertising campaign or strategy.

We discuss our unique human capabilities—as well as the very real limitations of human reasoning and judgment—in the next chapter.

Notes

1 https://www.nytimes.com/2023/02/16/technology/bing-chatbot-microsoft-chatgpt.html
2 Ibid.
3 https://dl.acm.org/doi/10.1145/3442188.3445922
4 https://www.forbes.com/sites/lanceeliot/2023/06/15/can-generative-ai-be-saved-from
   -ai-hallucinations-by-using-chain-of-thought-step-by-step-techniques-asks-ai-ethics-
   and-ai-law/?sh=1638b03b401d
5 https://www.nytimes.com/2022/04/15/magazine/ai-language.html
6 https://twitter.com/e_salvaggio/status/1670720424764665856?t=1Wo4p
   tHMQS2qmkIUV03brg&s=03
7 Vanian, Jonathan. Unmasking A.I.s Bias Problem. *Fortune Magazine*, July 2018,
   pp. 54–62 (also see www.Fortune.come); Vincent, James. Twitter Taught
   Microsoft's AI Chatbot to Be a Racist Asshole in Less than a Day. *The Verge*,
   March 24, 2016.
8 Ng, Andrew. What Artificial Intelligence Can and Can't Do Right Now. *Harvard
   Business Review*, November 9, 2016.
9 https://news.umich.edu/optimization-could-cut-the-carbon-footprint-of-ai-training-
   by-up-to-75/
10 https://techmonitor.ai/technology/ai-and-automation/ai-spending-idc
11 Thompson, Clive. The Miseducation of Artificial Intelligence. *Wired*, December
   2018, p. 76.
12 https://hbr.org/2022/09/ai-isnt-ready-to-make-unsupervised-decisions
13 Rogati, Monica. The AI Hierarchy of Needs. *Medium/Hackernoon*, August 1,
   2017. Available at https://hackernoon.com/the-ai-hierarchy-of-needs-18f111fcc007
14 https://www.forbes.com/sites/forbestechcouncil/2023/03/22/is-your-organization
   -truly-ready-for-ai/
15 Ray, Tiernan. Google Ponders the Shortcomings of Machine Learning. *ZDNet*,
   October 20, 2018. Available at www.zdnet.com/article/google-ponders-the-
   shortcomings-of-machine-learning/
16 https://www.buzzfeed.com/pranavdixit/google-60-minutes-ai-claims-challenged
17 Zerega, Blaise. Credit Karma: Believe the Hype for "Artificial Narrow Intelligence". *Venture Beat*, May 7, 2017. Available at https://venturebeat.com/2017/05/
   07/credit-karma-believe-the-hype-for-artificial-narrow-intelligence/
18 Ibid.
19 Ibid.
20 https://talker.news/2023/05/10/mit-scientists-find-something-alarming-about-artifi
   cial-intelligence
21 https://www.nasdaq.com/articles/back-from-the-dead-ibms-watson-ai-is-alive-and
   -re-emerging

22 Ibid.

23 Ibid.

24 https://kpmg.com/ph/en/home/insights/2023/01/data-is-everywhere-in-the-digita l-world.html

25 https://techjury.net/blog/how-much-data-is-created-every-day/#gref

26 There are many definitions of big data; one of the best is by Maniyaka, J. et al. *Big Data: The Next Frontier for Innovation, Competition, and Productivity* (May 2011 McKinsey Global Institute).

27 See Microsoft Azure, What Is Cloud Computing? Available at https://azure. microsoft.com/en-us/overview/what-is-cloud-computing/

28 Lunden, Ingrid. Apple Acquires AI Company Lattice Data, a Specialist in Unstructured "Dark Data," for $200M. *TechCrunch*, May 13, 2017. Available at https://techcrunch.com/2017/05/13/apple-acquires-ai-company-lattice-data-a-speciali st-in-unstructured-dark-data/

29 Ibid.

30 https://appleinsider.com/articles/17/05/13/apple-acquires-dark-data-specialist-lattice-data-for-200m

31 A Different Game. *The Economist*, February 27, 2010, pp. 6–8.

32 Davenport, Thomas H. Realizing the Potential of Retail Analytics Plenty of Food for Those with the Appetite. Working Knowledge Research Report, Babson Executive Education, 2009, pp. 1–42.

33 Davenport, Thomas H. Competing on Analytics. *Harvard Business Review*, pp. 1–9, January 2006.

34 Sundblad, Willem. Data Is the Foundation for Artificial Intelligence and Machine Learning. *Forbes*, October 18, 2018. Available at www.forbes.com/sites/willem sundbladeurope/2018/10/18/data-is-the-foundation-for-artificial-intelligence-and-ma chine-learning/#fc03b3151b49

35 McLeod, Saul. Maslow's Hierarchy of Needs. Available at www.simplypsychol ogy.org/maslow.html

36 Mills, Terence. Machine Learning Vs. Artificial Intelligence: How Are They Different? July 11, 2018. Available at www.forbes.com/sites/forbestechcouncil/2018/07/ 11/machine-learning-vs-artificial-intelligence-how-are-they-different/#2e8c3a8c3521

37 For more information about the differences between AI, machine learning, neural net, and deep learning, see Chin, Angela. A Pioneering Scientist Explains "Deep Learning". *The Verge*, October 16, 2018. Available at www.theverge.com/2018/10/16/17985168/ deep-learning-revolution-terrence-sejnowski-artificial-intelligence-technology

38 Husain, Amir. *The Sentient Machine: The Coming Age of Artificial Intelligence*, p. 20. Scribner, New York, 2017.

39 Ibid., pp. 20–21.

40 Ibid., p. 21.

41 Nasrabadi, Nasser M., and Nasser M. Nasrabadi. Pattern Recognition and Machine Learning. *Journal of Electronic Imaging*, 16(4):049901, 2007.

42 For an example of Bayesian inferences in a marketing context, see Kramer, Aaron. *Introduction to Bayesian Inference*, December 12, 2016, Oracle + Data Science. Available at www.datascience.com/blog/introduction-to-bayesian-infer ence-learn-data-science-tutorials (last accessed August 18, 2018).

43 Barber, David. *Bayesian Reasoning and Machine Learning*. Cambridge University Press, Cambridge, UK, February 2, 2012.

44 Wellers, Dan, Timo Elliott, and Markus Noga. 8 Ways Machine Learning Is Improving Companies' Work Processes. *Harvard Business Review*, May 31, 2017. Available at https://hbr.org/2017/05/8-ways-machine-learning-is-improving-compa nies-work-processes

45 Ng, Andrew. What Artificial Intelligence Can and Can't Do Right Now. *Harvard Business Review*, November 9, 2016.

46 Emerging Technology from the arXiv. Machine Learning, Meet Quantum Computing. *MIT Technology Review*, November 16, 2018. Available at www.techno logyreview.com/s/612435/machine-learning-meet-quantum-computing/

47 Thompson, Clive. The Miseducation of Artificial Intelligence. *Wired*, December 2018, p. 77.

48 Ibid., p. 78.

49 Ibid., p. 77.

50 Houser, Kristin. Elon Musk Just Unveiled Breakthrough AI Research. Here's What You Need to Know. *Futurism*, May 16, 2017. Available at https://futurism.com/ elon-musk-just-unveiled-breakthrough-ai-research-heres-what-your-need-to-know/

51 Ibid.

52 Thompson, Clive. The Miseducation of Artificial Intelligence. *Wired*, December 2018, p. 76.

53 Houser, Kristin. AI Can Make Sure Cancer Patients Get Just Enough (but Not Too Much) Treatment. *Futurism*, August 13, 2018. Available at https://futurism. com/glioblastoma-patients-ai-treatment/.

   https://news.mit.edu/2018/artificial-intelligence-model-learns-patient-data-cancer-treatment-less-toxic-0810

54 Ibid.

55 https://nyti.ms/37SdY3M

56 https://readmultiplex.com/2023/06/03/add-this-sentence-to-your-chatgpt-prompts-and-your-outputs-will-dramatically-improve/?s=03

57 Artificial Intelligence for the Real World by Thomas H. Davenport and Rajeev Ronanki, *Harvard Business Review*, January–February 2018, pp. 108–116.

58 Ramirez, Vanessa. Drug Discovery AI Can Do in a Day What Currently Takes Months. *Singularity Hub*, May 7, 2017. Available at https://singularityhub.com/ 2017/05/07/drug-discovery-ai-can-do-in-a-day-what-currently-takes-months/#sm. 0000fwnti418w0el4sg3say3u0bzk

59 https://www.theverge.com/2023/5/9/23716825/wendys-ai-drive-thru-google-llm

60 www.reuters.com/article/us-usa-walmart-robots/wal-marts-new-robots-scan-shelve s-to-restock-items-faster-idUSKBN1CV1N4

61 Bose, Nandita. Wal-Mart's New Robots Scan Shelves to Restock Items Faster. *Reuters*, October 26, 2017. Available at www.reuters.com/article/us-usa-walma rt-robots/wal-marts-new-robots-scan-shelves-to-restock-items-fa ster-idUSKBN1CV1N4

62 Stanford, Duane. Coke Engineers Its Orange Juice—With an Algorithm. *Bloomberg*, January 31, 2013. Available at www.bloomberg.com/news/articles/ 2013-01-31/coke-engineers-its-orange-juice-with-an-algorithm#p1

63 George Lawton, Prompt Engineering, TechTarget. Available at https://www. techtarget.com/searchenterpriseai/definition/prompt-engineering (last accessed June 21, 2023).

64 Laurent, Lionel. The Limits of Artificial Intelligence. *Bloomberg*, June 13, 2017. Available at www.bloomberg.com/news/articles/2017-06-13/the-limits-of-artificia l-intelligence

65 Thompson, Clive. The Miseducation of Artificial Intelligence. *Wired*, December 2018, p. 79.

66 Ibid.

67 Brooks, R. 2017. The Seven Deadly Sins of AI Predictions. *MIT Technology Review*, 2017. Available at www.technologyreview.com/s/609048/the-seven-dea dly-sins-of-ai-predictions/

68 See Margaret Mitchell TED Talk, How We can Teach AI to Help Humans, Not Hurt Us; www.ted.com/talks/margaret_mitchell_how_we_can_build_ai_to_help_humans_not_hurt_us
69 O'Neill, Cathy. *Weapons of Math Destruction: How Big Data Increases Inequality and Threatens Democracy* (2016 Penguin Random House).
70 Ibid.
71 See the graphic and their research summary in: www.theguardian.com/news/datablog/2012/oct/31/twitter-sandy-flooding
72 Matthews, David. *An AI Was Trained To Play Minecraft With 70,000 Hours Of YouTube Videos*, IGN (June 27, 2022). Available at https://www.ign.com/articles/a i-trained-to-play-minecraft-with-hours-of-youtube-videos (last accessed May 31, 2023).
73 Thompson, Clive. The Miseducation of Artificial Intelligence. *Wired*, December 2018, p. 78.
74 Ibid.
75 Ibid., p. 79.
76 Hutson, Matthew. Artificial Intelligence Is Learning to Keep Learning (originally published as "Lifelong Learning" in *Scientific American* 319, 5, 14–15 (November 2018)). Available at www.scientificamerican.com/article/artificial-intelligence-is-lea rning-to-keep-learning/
77 Wadhwa, Vivek. Don't Believe the Hype About AI in Business. *VentureBeat*, March 17, 2018. Available at https://venturebeat.com/2018/03/17/dont-belie ve-the-hype-about-ai-in-business/
78 Knight, Will. The Dark Secret at the Heart of AI: No One Really Knows How the Most Advanced Algorithms Do What They Do. That Could Be a Problem. *MIT Technology Review*, April 11, 2017. Available at www.technologyreview. com/s/604087/the-dark-secret-at-the-heart-of-ai/
79 Ibid.
80 *Source*: Big Data vs. Artificial Intelligence. *Datamation*, May 30, 2018.

Chapter 4

What Humans Can and *Cannot* Do

The Microwave's Eureka Moment

The microwave is one of the most popular household appliances in the modern world. However, few people know that the invention of the microwave was an accident that would not be possible without human imagination.

Percy Spencer was a creative self-taught engineer who earned several patents during the Second World War. One day in 1945 while working in a lab at Raytheon, he was testing high-powered vacuum tubes inside radars that produce microwaves. While preparing for his lunch break, Spencer reached his hand into his pocket and noticed that his peanut butter candy bar had melted. "It was a gooey, sticky mess," according to Spencer. He wondered about the microwaves being emitted from the magnetron. "Is it possible that the microwave heats up food?"

The next day he brought in corn kernels to test his hypothesis and put them in front of the magnetron. When they began to pop, he was certain the microwaves could cook food. The microwave was born.

The invention of the microwave is an example of human curiosity and creativity. It shows how humans—despite all their shortcomings—have the ability to connect seemingly disparate ideas. They can find solutions to problems they weren't even setting out to solve, applying insights from one domain to other areas of life, thinking "outside of the box." Machines cannot do that.

In the previous chapter we discussed the tremendous opportunities that technology provides. Machines offer unparalleled precision and accuracy. Artificial intelligence, machine learning, deep learning, the Internet of Things, robots and chatbots, and drones are used across industries to make production processes faster and more accurate. They can handle an unprecedented amount of information and data, and work in dangerous environments, are cheaper, are available 24/7, and don't require health insurance or even paid leave. They don't have emotional baggage, they do not get tired, talk back to supervisors, argue with coworkers, or ask for a pay raise. They do exactly what they are told with a physical and processing capability no human can match.

DOI: 10.4324/9781003322832-4

Where does that leave humans? Humans have a unique ability for creativity, ingenuity, and innovation. It is precisely human emotions, intuitions, and general intelligence that inspire us to breakthroughs in science, industrial innovations, and the future of enterprise.

To put humans and technology together in the right process, we need to see how they fit together. Per Moravec's Paradox, we should interface technology to people where people are weak and technology is strong and vice versa. Hence, in this chapter, we look at how the shortcomings of human intelligence and decision-making influence us at work. By understanding these shortcomings, we should be able to mitigate them and even take advantage of them when creating the Humachine.

Thinking about Thinking

Just as it is impossible to think about artificial intelligence without comparing it to a baseline of human intelligence, it is impossible to answer the question of the role of artificial intelligence in enterprise without contemplating what it is about human intelligence that is required to run an enterprise.

Business functions stand to benefit from the razor-sharp proceedings of logic, the critical evaluation of evidence, the careful expression of strategic communications, and the sophisticated judgments of managers and executives. Conversely, management failures often flow from illogical decisions, false beliefs about material facts, inept communications between groups, and indecision by managers and executives.

The best companies will find ways to encourage and internalize the best thoughts expressed by their human resources, while filtering out the illogical, false, inflammatory, and ambiguous. Therefore, it pays to think about thinking.

A helpful framework for thinking about thinking comes from Daniel Kahneman's *Thinking, Fast and Slow*.[1]

Kahneman elaborates upon "two systems in the mind, System 1 and System 2. The labels of System 1 and System 2 are widely used in psychology, but I go further than most in this book, which you can read as a psychodrama with two characters."[2] *System 1 thinking* is an effortless, involuntary, automatic, and quick way of thinking, such as the mental activity involved in passively processing speech or forming impressions from sensory inputs.[3] *System 2 thinking* is an effortful, voluntary, directed, and slow way of thinking, such as the mental activity involved in conscious agency, making deliberate choices, or performing a calculation.[4]

Kahneman summarizes the relationship between System 1 and System 2 thinking as follows:[5]

System 1 runs automatically and System 2 is normally in a comfortable low-effort mode, in which only a fraction of its capacity is engaged. System 1 continuously generates suggestions for System 2: impressions, intuitions, intentions, and feelings. If endorsed by System 2, impressions and intuitions turn into beliefs, and impulses turn into voluntary actions. When all goes smoothly, which is most of the time, System 2 adopts the suggestions of System 1 with little or no modification. You generally believe your impressions and act on your desires, and that is fine—usually.

When System 1 runs into difficulty, it calls on System 2 to support more detailed and specific processing that may solve the problem of the moment. System 2 is mobilized when a question arises for which System 1 does not offer an answer[.] You can also feel a surge of conscious attention whenever you are surprised. System 2 is activated when an event is detected that violates the model of the world that System 1 maintains... Surprise then activates and orients your attention: you will stare, and you will search your memory for a story that makes sense of the surprising event. System 2 is also credited with the continuous monitoring of your own behavior—the control that keeps you polite when you are angry, and alert when you are driving at night. System 2 is mobilized to increased effort when it detects an error about to be made.

System 1 is gullible and biased to believe, System 2 is in charge of doubting and unbelieving, but System 2 is sometimes busy, and often lazy.

The division of labor between System 1 and System 2 is highly efficient: it minimizes effort and optimizes performance. The arrangement works well most of the time because System 1 is generally very good at what it does: its models of familiar situations are accurate, its short-term predictions are usually accurate as well, and its initial reactions to challenges are swift and generally appropriate. System 1 has biases, however, systematic errors that it is prone to make in specified circumstances. As we shall see, sometimes it answers easier questions than the one it was asked, and it has little understanding of logic and statistics. One further limitation of System 1 is that it cannot be turned off.

Despite our limitations, the human dual process of thought is potent, efficient, and effective, allowing humans to negotiate and navigate complex, dynamic environments with limited information. It should come as no surprise then we would copy ourselves. The tool takes the shape of the master's hand.

One of the trends in AI research is pushing the boundaries of technology capabilities by mimicking human cognitive capabilities. Take a uniquely human skill, find a way to reliably mimic it (through some combination of deep reinforcement learning, behavior cloning through sequence to sequence learning, or prompting large language models), then automate the model and sell it back to us as a useful bot. It is a matter of course then that the "thinking, fast and slow" Systems 1 and System 2 types of human cognition would eventually be emulated by a bot.

Another iteration in the chatbot arms race, the so-called SwiftSage novel agent framework does just this, taking inspiration from "the dual-process theory of human cognition, designed to excel in action planning for complex interactive reasoning tasks."[6] The SwiftSafe AI agency framework allows the bot to "closely emulate how humans solve complex, open-world tasks." Following the Kahneman framework,

> The dual-process theory posits that human cognition is composed of two distinct systems: System 1, characterized by rapid, intuitive, and automatic thinking; and System 2, which entails methodical, analytical, and deliberate thought processes... The [SwiftSage] framework comprises two primary modules: the Swift module, representing fast and intuitive thinking, and the Sage module, emulating deliberate thought processes... We develop a heuristic method to harmoniously integrate the two modules, resulting in a more efficient and robust problem-solving process.[7]

In the subsequent sections, as we discuss biases, heuristics, bounded rationality, and the limits of human capabilities in terms of thinking, decision-making, and so forth, we are really talking about the limits inherent in System 1 of the mind.

As human beings our thinking and processing are subject to an endless array of cognitive biases. Simply put, cognitive biases are mistakes in reasoning, evaluating, and remembering. They are systematic errors in thinking that affect the decisions and judgment of people and are related to a variety of shortcomings in human processing ability. Some biases can be related to memory. Memory biases influence what one remembers and can lead to biased thinking and decision-making. For example, people are more likely to recall events that are tied to strong emotions. These may be events they find humorous, pleasurable, dangerous, threatening, or inspirational. They also remember information they produce themselves or activities they were engaged in rather than observed.

Other cognitive biases can be related to problems with attention. Humans have limited attention span. We can easily become overwhelmed with large quantities of data and are not able to process them. We cannot consider many variables and complex relationships. Since attention is a limited resource, people have to be selective about what they focus on.

These biases give us plenty of room for improvement. Ideally the bots that emulate human thinking copy our cognitive virtues but not our vices.

According to research in *Harvard Business Review*,

> Many experts believe that human beings will still be needed to do the jobs that require higher-order critical, creative, and innovative thinking and the jobs that require high emotional engagement to meet the needs

of other human beings. The challenge for many of us is that we do not excel at those skills because of our natural cognitive and emotional proclivities: We are confirmation-seeking thinkers and ego-affirmation-seeking defensive reasoners. We will need to overcome those proclivities in order to take our thinking, listening, relating, and collaborating skills to a much higher level.[8]

Despite our limits research repeatedly shows that humans are in the driver's seat—not machines—when it comes to the future of business as strategy ought to remain by and for us.[9]

It is not simply our individual brains or our ability to sense or to reason that makes us more intelligent than other animal species on this planet.

How did humans become clever enough to live in nearly every major ecosystem on earth, create vaccines against deadly plagues, explore the oceans' depths, and routinely traverse the globe at 30,000 feet in aluminum tubes while nibbling on roasted almonds?

While we may not be as good at math as a calculator, and we surely suffer limitations in the challenges posed by interactions between what Kahneman calls System 1 and System 2 thinking, nonetheless we are leaps and bounds further along than any other known species, even those with mammalian brains. Indeed, as argued in Donald Hoffman's book *The Case Against Reality: Why Evolution Hid the Truth from our Eyes*, "evolution shapes sensory systems to guide adaptive action, not to show us the true nature of reality. We must take our perceptions seriously, but we should not take them literally." So what is the secret to this intellectual achievement in our species? The answer is collective intelligence, sustained across time:

Contrary to conventional wisdom, human brilliance emerges not from our innate brainpower or raw computational capacities, but from the sharing of information in communities and networks over generations. [L]arger, more diverse, and more optimally interconnected networks of minds give rise to faster innovation and... the cognitive products of this cumulative cultural evolutionary process feedback to make us individually 'smarter'—in the sense of being better at meeting the challenges and problems posed by our societies and socioecologies.[10]

This conclusion, based on the latest in evolution research, vindicates our contention that the most viable pathway to superintelligence is via organizational network intelligence.

What applies at the aggregate level of a nation also applies to a multinational corporation, however the latter has far greater mechanisms of control:

Cultural evolution can turn mindless mobs into wise crowds by facilitating and constraining cognition through a wide variety of epistemic institutions—political, legal, and scientific. These institutions process information and aid better decision-making by suppressing or encouraging the use of different cultural epistemologies and ontologies.[11]

Culture determines the way your company's workers, managers and executives determine what is true and actionable, the way they determine what is real and significant. The epistemology and ontology that holds sway over your human resources will influence the relative intelligence of your company as a whole.

In order to harness uniquely human powers, we need to understand our limitations.

The Brain: The Most Sophisticated Information Processing System in the World

We should spend some time discussing human anatomy to get a better sense of what makes our brains unique from the bots that are designed to emulate us. For authority we look to Robert Sapolsky, *Behave: the Biology of Humans at our Best and Worst*.

One of the first factors to consider is that much of human science dedicated to knowing thyself is bound by a particular discipline of inquiry—for example, if we try to explain why a person behaved a certain way, the answer you get depends on which kind of scientist you ask. If you ask a geneticist, they will explain human behavior by pointing to the expression of certain genes in the individuals' ancestral heritage. If you ask a psychiatrist, they would likely point to the function of hormones in the brain. If you ask a psychologist, they might point to childhood trauma that shaped the character of the person in question. However crisp and tidy these explanations might be, they are misleading.

> The second you invoke one type of explanation, you're *de facto* invoking them all. A 'neurobiological' or 'genetic' or 'developmental' explanation for a behavior is just shorthand, and expository convenience for temporarily approaching the whole multifactorial arc from a particular perspective.[12]

Instead, Sapolsky provides a biological account of how the human brain is structured and how it works as the proper interpretive framework for human behavior. The brain is the result of all these various influences, with triggers and mechanisms originating from the moments before an action is taken all the way back to the dawn of mankind.

The Trite But Useful Triune Brain Metaphor

While the brain is unbelievably complex, and any characterization of its structure that is easy to understand is bound to oversimplify, and despite advances in MRI and neurosurgery providing unprecedented glimpses into the brain's complex structures, neuroscientists tend to forgive us for using an oversimplified macro-organizational structure that goes by the "triune brain" as an organizing metaphor, introduced first by neuroscientist Paul MacLean in the 1960s.

The *triune brain* model has three functional domains:

Layer 1: "an ancient part of the brain, at its base, found in species from humans to geckos. This layer mediates automatic, regulatory functions. If body temperature drops, this brain region senses it and commands muscles to shiver. If blood glucose levels plummet, that's sent here, generating hunger. If an injury occurs, a different loop initiates a stress response."[13]

Layer 2: "a more recently evolved region ... about emotions, somewhat of a mammalian invention. If you see something gruesome and terrifying, this layer sends commands down to ancient layer 1, making you shiver with emotion. If you're feeling sadly unloved, regions here prompt layer 1 to generate a craving for comfort food. If you are a rodent and smell a cat, neurons here cause layer 1 to initiate a stress response."[14]

Layer 3: this is the most "recently evolved layer of neocortex sitting on the upper surface of the brain. Proportionately, primates devote more of their brain to this layer than do other species. Cognition, memory storage, sensory processing, abstractions, philosophy, naval contemplation. Read a scary passage of a book, and layer 3 signals layer 2 to make you feel frightened, prompting layer 1 to initiate shivering... contemplate the fact that loved ones won't live forever, or kids in refugee camps, and layer 3 pulls layer 2 and 1 into the picture, and you feel sad and have the same sort of stress response the you'd have if you were fleeing a lion."[15]

To be clear, the triune brain model is an oversimplification: information flows both up and down the layers; the anatomies of the three layers overlap somewhat; and the evolution of subsequent layers, in turn, initiated changes to formerly evolved layers. The layers interact in complex, surprising ways. "A weird, great example: if someone is holding a cold drink (temperature is processed in layer 1), they are more likely to judge someone they meet as having a cold personality (layer 3)."[16] Thus, "layers 2 and 3 can influence the autonomic functions of layer 1, which alters events throughout the body, which in turn influences all other parts of the brain. Loops and loops."[17]

In order to design optimal work environments, we must appreciate the brain and how it processes information to avoid creating unarticulated, unacknowledged biases that would hinder performance in otherwise inexplicable ways.

Since MacLean first coined the triune brain, we have come a long way in our understanding of how the brain is structured and how these structures impact human behavior. The limbic system, containing the amygdala, hippocampus, and other structures, plays a key role in the emotions of excitation and inhibition that have impacts throughout the body and drive what Sapolsky describes succinctly as our "best and worst behaviors."

"The autonomic nervous system has two parts—the sympathetic and parasympathetic nervous systems, with fairly opposite functions. The *sympathetic nervous system (SNS)* mediates the body's response to arousing circumstances, for example, producing the famed 'fight or flight' stress response. To use the feeble joke told to first-year medical students, the SNS mediates the 'four FS—fear, fight, flight, and sex.'"[18]

Meanwhile, the *parasympathetic nervous system (PNS)* arises from different midbrain/brain-stem nuclei that project down the spine to the body. And contrast to the SNS and the four Fs, the PNS is about calm, vegetative states. The SNS speeds up the heart; the PNS slows it down. If seeing someone in pain activates your SNS, you're likely to be preoccupied with your own distress instead of helping; turn on the PNS, and it's the opposite.[19]

The Amygdala: Fear, Anxiety, Rage

The amygdala is the archetypal limbic structure sitting under the cortex in the temporal lobe. It is central to mediating aggression, along with other behaviors that tell us tons about aggression... Sticking an electrode in someone's amygdala and stimulating it (as it's done before certain types of neurosurgery) produces rage.[20]

The amygdala is linked to social uncertainty in other ways. And one neuroimaging study, a subject would participate in a competitive game against a group of other players; outcomes were rigged so that the subject would wind up in the middle of the rankings. Experimenters then manipulated game outcomes so that subject's rankings either remain stable or fluctuated wildly. Stable rankings activated parts of the frontal cortex... Instability activated the frontal cortex plus the amygdala. Being unsure of your place is unsettling.[21]

While activating the amygdala spurs aggressive behavior, it is primarily the originator of expressions of fear and anxiety.[22] "The amygdala injects implicit distrust and vigilance into social decision making ... the default state is to trust, and what the amygdala does is learn vigilance and distrust."[23] "Something emotionally arousing occurs, layer 2 limbic amygdala signals layer 1 region, and heart and blood pressure soar."[24]

Thus, activating the amygdala of workers will drive aggression, fear, anxiety, distrust, and cause heart rates and blood pressure to increase. These are all powerful inhibitors of human performance that would be best left out of the workplace. Heaven forbid we design a work environment that actively stimulates rage, terror, angst and distrust in the workforce! Yet those feelings may be all too common in the corporate world. Most people dread Monday mornings. Pop culture coined the "Sunday Scaries"—the feeling of looming anxiety that the work week is about to begin again; Sunday night we brace for impact.

Aside from perhaps limited circumstances where athletic trainers or drill sergeants are intentionally inducing these feelings in professional athletes priming for the big game, or soldiers preparing for battle, there is almost no work scenario where management should stimulate aggression, fear, anxiety, distrust, or increased blood pressure.

We ought to be conscious about our design of the workplace. Perhaps we have overlooked how the way we structure the office environment, org chart, and job description can exacerbate or alleviate the symptoms of an agitated amygdala.

Organizations should design ergonomically: avoid activating the amygdala. Use neuroscience to design workplaces to avoid inadvertent triggers and stressors. Use neuroscience to develop training programs that can help workers with fear-extinction to help workers overcome irrational fears that inhibit performance. We might have better teamwork through work environments that carefully avoid stimulating the amygdala. Trust is crucial to effective teams, especially as teams are decentralized and multicultural. Workplace designs that undermine trust is self-defeating and may be a major culprit for otherwise inexplicable inefficiencies and poor team output.

Organizations should be careful to avoid generating instability in how human resources rank in the org chart. Unpredictable promotions and demotions, even surprising reassignments or lateral moves that create uncertainty as to who is above and who is below, would drive activations of the amygdala and undermine performance.

The Frontal Cortex: The Rational Executive

So much then for the limbic system. Next we discuss the cortex. "This is the brain's upper surface (its name comes from the Latin *cortic*, meaning 'tree bark') and is the newest part of the brain."[25] The wrinkles and folds of the outer layer of the brain are somewhat bark-like in appearance.

The cortex is the gleaming, logical, analytical crown jewel of layer 3. Most sensory information flows there to be decoded. It's where muscles are commanded to move, where language is comprehended and produced, where memories are stored, where spatial and mathematical skills reside, where executive decisions are made.[26]

When we talk about AI behaving like intelligent systems, we are talking about this particular function of the human brain—and decidedly not the limbic system. For the love of God and all things holy, we do not need to create AI with anything like an amygdala that experiences and acts out upon feelings of fear, anxiety, or rage; we can keep those traits to ourselves; we have no good reason to program bots to be like us in that regard. When we train AI to be rational like humans can be when on our best behavior, we are talking about replicating the functions of the cortex, which "floats above the limbic system, supporting philosophers since at least Descartes who have emphasized the dichotomy between thought and emotion."[27]

The irony of course is that reason and passion are not (and perhaps ought not be) separate.

> Emotions filter the nature and accuracy of what is remembered... The cortex and limbic systems are not separate, as scads of axonal projections course between the two. Crucially, these projections are bidirectional—the limbic system talks to the cortex, rather than merely being reined in by it.[28]

Thus, bots that attempt to recreate human cognition will probably never really replicate the uniquely human quality of thought, which is logic infused with feelings, memory tinged by emotions. What makes human cognition unique is that it is embodied and mediated by the relationship between the amygdala and the frontal cortex.

> What does the frontal cortex do? It's list of expertise includes working memory, executive function (organizing knowledge strategically, ["considering bits of information, looking for patterns, and then choosing a strategic action"[29]] and then initiating an action based on an executive decision), gratification postponement, long-term planning, regulation of emotions, and reining in impulsivity.[30]

Thus, the frontal cortex has what Sapolsky describes as a "sprawling portfolio" but there is a common denominator to all these rational tasks: "*the frontal cortex makes you do the harder thing when it's the right thing to do.*"[31]

Cognitive Development, Cognitive Load

Being able to control the reptilian and monkey-like impulse to react with irrational aggression toward environmental stressors and novel problems arising in the course of a workday is what distinguishes human minds from beasts. Being able to resist temptation when vices come calling, to play by the rules imposed by an organization, to play the role assigned to you even if your superior is a buffoon—essentially being able to pass increasingly high stakes and abstract versions of the "marshmallow test"—takes time to develop. We are not born with the frontal cortex's arsenal of rationality completely activated. "Amazingly, it's not fully online until people are in their *midtwenties*."[32]

Anecdotally, if you interact with groups of young adults long enough (say as a professor or an athletic coach or an HR recruiter), you will notice there tends to be a wide gulf of maturity between a 21-year-old and a 27-year-old—more so than between any other age bracket amongst adults. Even though they are only 6 years apart, the difference in maturity between the 21-year-old and the 27-year-old is far more than you would see between any other (say, between a 35-year-old and a 41-year-old, or between a 57-year-old and a 63-year-old). The 20-something may not yet have a fully activated frontal cortex, the brain region associated most with the kind of behaviors needed to contribute to the modern workforce.

Not only does wisdom tend to come with age, higher-order rationality tends to escape humans in their early twenties and younger—a sentiment which may find exceptions in the young prodigies, but which has been noted about our species since Aristotle. But wisdom is variable even within a mature human endowed with a fully activated frontal cortex. "Will*power* is more than just a metaphor; self-control is a finite resource. Frontal neurons are expensive cells, and expensive cells are vulnerable cells. Consistent with that, the frontal cortex is atypically vulnerable to various neurological insults."[33]

A mature human brain, inside the skull of, say, a lawyer enriched with years of training, adequately compensated, and secure in his position in society, diligently at work on some challenging analytical task. Nonetheless this brain can be easily thrown off by insulting changes to context. Picture this lawyer, pensively marking up a contract in a hushed law office, when a stranger runs into the room, blows an air horn, then sprays silly string all over the lawyer's desk. Or even a senior partner coming into the room and hurling derogatory comments about the lawyer's work product and alma mater. It's not hard to see how the lawyer would stray from the assignment. Amygdala activated, testosterone levels spiked, frontal cortex impaired, fear creeping in, anxiety rising, animalistic rage ensuing. With the wrong work culture, even the best minds can be reduced to beasts. Not so for a GPU. A computer program performing doc review would have been totally unphased by the whole scene, just humming along without phenomenal consciousness getting in the way of its computation.

So wisdom comes with age, and it can vary with context. It is also a limited resource. "Pertinent to this is the concept of '*cognitive load*.' Make the frontal cortex work hard—a tough working-memory task, regulating social behavior, or making numerous decisions while shopping. Immediately afterward performance on a different frontally dependent task declines."[34] We can hold on to our cognitive powers for only so many successive mental tasks before decision-fatigue sets in, and the quality of our decision-making begins to crumble.

Importantly, increase cognitive load on the frontal cortex, and afterward subjects become less prosocial—less charitable or helpful, more likely to lie. Or increase cognitive load with a task requiring difficult emotional regulations, and subjects cheat more in their diet afterward.[35]

Failure to manage cognitive load will lead to major detriments to human and organizational performance. Here enterprise leadership can take lessons from professional athletics. Old-school basketball players may groan at today's teams in the National Basketball Association (NBA) that deploy the concept of "load management" where a star player is rested during a game and does not make an appearance on the court. What a disappointment to the fans of the game and an increased burden to the rest of the team to rest your best player. But the driving notions behind load management is that talent is a finite resource and how it is managed is strategic over the course of a season not just tactical within a single game. Personnel choices must be data-driven and nuanced, so while you need to play your star player to win most games, it is generally not prudent to play your star player every minute of every game. Your best talent cannot carry the entire load of performance the entire season or else they would be subject to increased risk of injury or burnout, requesting a trade.

Managing cognitive load is thus key to getting the best out of knowledge workers. Understanding and accommodating the idiosyncratic frailties of the human brain can help organizations enjoy the upsides of the frontal cortex while mitigating the downsides of "hangry" or decision-fatigued workers that would otherwise be prone to follow up incredible feats of rationality and altruism with lying and cheating and the folly of a bruised ego.

In today's workplace with globally distributed teams that form, perform, and dissolve only to be reassigned to a new team with a new size and task, the ability to adapt to changing social contexts is crucial. The proper functioning of the frontal cortex plays a key role in sociality and doing the right thing when it is the harder thing to do, in ever-changing groups. This is true for humans and other primates.

We are akin to primates such as chimpanzees and orangutans, the so-called *fission-fusion species*, "where there are times when subgroups split up [(fission)] and function independently for a while before regrouping [(fusion)]. Such a social structure is demanding, requiring a scaling of appropriate behavior to subgroup size and composition."[36]

Across primates species, the bigger the size of the average social group, the larger the relative size of the frontal cortex. This is particularly so with "fission-fusion" species... Logically, primates from fission-fusion species... have better fronto-cortical inhibitory control over behavior then do non-fission-fusion primates (gorillas). Among humans, the larger someone's social network (measured by number of different people texted), the larger a particular PFC subregion.[37]

The human brain is immensely complex and we've truly only provided a 10,000 foot view of its structures and their respective functions. Don't even get us started on the dorsolateral prefrontal cortex, "the decider of deciders, the most rational, cognitive, utilitarian, unsentimental part" of the frontal cortex, much less the ventromedial prefrontal cortex, which is "all about the impact of emotion on decision making" and the part that "activates if the person you're rooting for wins a game."[38] In addition, research shows that brains might sync as people interact. The research finds that when humans cooperate in teams on certain tasks, their brainwaves may synchronize. While this upends the study of consciousness, it also provides more support to the value of human interaction, teamwork, and the importance of creating the right environment for collective intelligence.[39]

Make it Easier for Humans to be Human

In short, avoid stimulating the amygdala, provide the frontal cortex a hospitable environment in which to thrive, and think about ergonomics at every turn. Make it easier for humans to behave the way you need them to behave. We discuss the use of games and workplace ergonomics to encourage healthy and helpful levels of dopamine and testosterone in Chapter 9 on how to build a Humachine.

Suffice it to say we make decisions using organic wetware that evolved over hundreds of millions of years through an ancestral tree that entails reptilian and mammalian structures crowned with a uniquely human crown: a wrinkled-tree-bark-looking layer from whence mathematics, aesthetics, law, and strategy arose. We can use this brain to get us to the Moon, to commit atrocities, and everything in between. Managers should be cognizant of how workplace design, job descriptions, org charts and office culture impact the functioning of these key brain regions.

Now we have a better picture of what makes humans unique from the computers we are programming to think like us.

The Conundrum of Originality

One of the strengths of humanity is the apparently *sui generis* quality of our thoughts and actions. We feel like self-starters, with originality, freedom of thought and action, creativity, imagination, and capacity for true novelty. These qualities, which we generally characterize as "originality," form a powerful intuitive basis for distinguishing humanity from artificial intelligence. But that intuition might be wrong.

Since the early stages of AI research, the assumption that "a machine cannot do anything without having a rule telling it to do so"[40] has served as a bedrock conviction that separates human from machine. We know technology provides tremendous opportunities for enterprise to gain efficiency and effectiveness. However, we can also see that there are things technology cannot do—at least, not yet. The greatest advancements in business and our everyday lives have come from human creativity and innovation. Creativity and sensing emotions are core to the human experience and also difficult to automate. So far it is empirically true to say that machines simply cannot do those human things marked by originality of thought, volition in action, feeling in response to stimuli, and so forth.

Joseph Aoun put it this way:

> What we can do that machines cannot do as well is to think the unthinkable - to think in a new way that hasn't been done. Essentially what machines are doing is taking stock of what has been done so far, and capturing it and giving it to you. Whereas if you want to go in new direction, with new inventions, with new discoveries, with creativity - think the unthinkable. If you want to go in new directions, creativity, be entrepreneurial - that is extremely valuable. Machines are not entrepreneurial. They are not creative from this perspective - we are. Second, all aspects of human interactions, machines are not going to be able to duplicate.[41]

Arthur Samuel's influential 1960 essay *Some Moral and Technical Consequences of Automation—A Refutation*, published in the journal *Science*, still resonates with intuitive strength to this day:

> It is my conviction that machines cannot possess originality in the sense implied by [the] thesis that "machines can and do transcend some of the limitations of their designers, and that in doing so they may be both effective and dangerous[.]" A machine is not a genie, it does not work by magic, it does not possess a will, and... nothing comes out which has not been put in, barring, of course, and infrequent case of malfunctioning[.] [T]he machine *will not and cannot* do any of these things until it has been instructed as to how to proceed. There is and logically there must always remain a complete hiatus between (*i*) any ultimate extension and elaboration in this process of carrying out man's wishes and (*ii*) the development within the machine of a will of its own. To believe otherwise is either to believe in magic or to believe that the existence of man's will is an illusion and that man's actions are as mechanical as the machine's.[42]

Therein lies the source of the conviction that a machine cannot do anything without having a rule telling it to do so: the underlying belief that humankind's actions spring from *free will* and are not mechanistically determined like the last domino falling is just a result of antecedent dominoes falling, and that this free will is the ultimate causal explanation of human behavior. In other words, the conviction that machines cannot be original is merely an implication of the article of faith that humans have free will.

Samuel's argument against machine originality depends on the assumption that human originality defies a regressive, causal explanation. Forgive us for being harsh but this appears to be the logical fallacy *petitio principii*, or "begging the question," wherein we use the premise of an argument to support itself. The assumption of free will is, again, intuitively powerful, but it comes with a lot of philosophical baggage. It hangs from skyhooks.

That humankind has the potential for originality in action, and that machines do not, is supported by the lack of empirical evidence to the contrary: We have never see a toaster decide to toast bread or a word processor decide to craft a sonnet, unless it has been instructed to do so by its human user. Of course, lack of evidence is not evidence of a null hypothesis, but you get the point. The conviction that machines lack originality may be rather an article of faith than a valid axiom. We discuss some of the philosophical aspects of machine originality and human free will in this endnote.[43]

One issue is whether Samuel's premise is true as a contingent matter or whether it is true for all time. If it is true as a *contingent* matter—that is, it just so happens to be true because of the state of technical advancement today—then it is possible for machines to transcend the limitations of their designers at some point in the future. Conversely, if it is true *for all time*— that is to say, no matter how advanced the technology, machines will never possess originality in action, then Samuel is revealing something inherently transcendental in the nature of mankind's make-up, as well as something inherently limited in the nature of machine intelligence.

At this point, the authors are unaware of a moral code, legal framework, or economic system that takes as its predicate assumption about human nature that we are *not* free to choose our course of conduct. The notions of right and wrong, justification and culpability for our actions, self-determination, and the agency required to fulfill the so-called American dream (or at the very least enter into economically efficient transactions) all depend on the idea that human beings more or less know what they are doing and freely choose to engage in actions to their own benefit.

We are left with the less than satisfying conclusion that humans enjoy originality in action (freedom, spontaneity, self-direction) and machines do not, simply because (*i*) humanity has not yet devised practicable moral, legal, or economic frameworks for governing human affairs absent this hypothesis, and (*ii*) our technology has not yet advanced enough to be capable of generating original action without prior human programming. As a result, it is only because of practicality that we proceed under the assumption that "humans can do X, machines cannot."

In other words, unlike Samuel, we believe that, "machines can only do what they are programmed to," is true, but its truth is only contingent on the state of the art, and is not an absolutely true statement that would be true for all time. This caveat applies to the various claims we make throughout this book that take the form, "humans can do X, but machines cannot." Moravec's Paradox is not just a manifestation of species chauvinism.

Next, we look at some unique qualities of human intelligence.

In Defense of Homo Sapiens

There is no question that technology is replacing jobs across all industry sectors. We have been warned about potential job losses. Automation, robots and chatbots, and artificial intelligence have made this a reality. Digitization is transforming labor markets and human skill requirements.

Athleticism and Boston Dynamics

In this section we look at the physical powers of human beings, compared to the abilities of machines to get work done. Here the human is "special" compared to machines not because machines cannot do what we do (thanks to Boston Dynamics, some of them can!) but rather because of the generalized nature of the physical capability of most persons. Machines lack all but the features they are designed to mimic. While it is possible to design a machine to perform similar to or even exceeding humans along certain dimensions of athleticism (strength and speed in metal fabrication and robotic process automation come to mind), most humans regardless of race or gender are born with at least the latent capacity to cultivate these abilities. We are brimming with potential to navigate the physical world. These abilities allow us to get out of the shower, place a bag in an overhead bin, swat a mosquito, and so forth without tumbling to the ground or sustaining an injury. When taken to an extreme degree (outliers from the human population) these abilities define professional athletes, however they are general across the population (so much so that when they are lacking, the person is technically "disabled"). There are at least ten abilities that define athleticism in humans. See Table 4.1.[44]

An incredible combination of nerves, inner ear structures, musculature, ligaments, tendons, joints, cardiovascular, respiratory, and metabolic systems, all equipped together in a functioning bodily unit, work together to pull off athletic feats without the human giving it any conscious thought. Things as simple as getting out of bed in the morning require some degree of athletic ability. We have some kind of "intuitive physics," the ability to make correct inferences about how gravity, time, mass, force, momentum, and other elements interact, based on limited information. Humans use intuitive physics to

Table 4.1 Ten Components of Athleticism

Ability	Definition
Strength	To create force by exerting push or pull on an object (hoisting a weight)
Speed	To minimize the time cycle of a given movement (running, throwing, reaching from point A to point B)
Power	To create maximal force in minimal time (throwing a punch)
Mental Resilience	To push beyond the limits of one's comfort zone (overcoming fear, anxiety, pain or fatigue)
Aerobic Capacity	Maximal amount of physiological work performed as measured by oxygen consumption (endurance)
Anaerobic Capacity	Maximal work performed during maximum-intensity short-term physical exertion (sprinting)
Balance	To maintain even distribution of weight to remain steady and upright despite countervailing forces (balance beam)
Coordination	To recruit and activate different muscle groups together smoothly and efficiently (dancing)
Stability	To prevent movement in one body part (say, lower back) while creating movement in another (say, arms) to protect vulnerable areas (say, spinal cord)
Mobility	The range of motion and flexibility through muscles and joints (doing the splits)
Agility	To change body positions and movement patterns quickly (juking a defender)

navigate the world, doing things like playing tennis and crossing the street without a thought—things that would require a robot so much processing power that it is almost inconceivable we would engineer them (unless you are super well-funded and dedicated years of engineering talent to the problem).

Imagine you are playing tennis in the park. You are attempting to return a serve. The tennis ball is speeding toward you at say 50 miles per hour (professional tennis players serve the ball over 100 miles per hour). The white lines on the neon yellow tennis ball are spinning in a left-leaning tilt. Without thinking, you use agility to quickly shift your feet to position your center of gravity behind the ball. Without thinking, you anticipate the ball will bounce to your left, rather than in a straight line (because of the spin imparted to it by your opponent's technique will interact with the ground through friction, deviating the trajectory of the ball). Without thinking, you begin to pull your racquet behind you, torquing your trunk (using flexibility) to give yourself room to swing, and to harness your lower body strength to give your upper body power. Without thinking, you hit the ball with an ascending stroke of the racquet, so that you impart topspin to the ball so that it bounces lower than expected when it lands on the opponent's side of the court. Without thinking, you strike the ball toward the far court, away from your opponent, maximizing your competitive advantage, because the objective is to place the ball where your opponent cannot successfully return it. Without thinking, you are "calculating" where the ball will go based on incomplete information. Without thinking, you are optimizing your physical maneuvers based on application of the rules of tennis and strategic considerations geared toward winning the point. Spin. Velocity. Angles. Wind resistance. The location of your opponent on the opposite side of the net. The friction of the ball interacting with the court when it bounces. Whether the court is grass, clay, or concrete. Your own body weight. Your own speed and agility. All of these variables are interacting with each other to determine where the ball will go and how best to make contact. The calculations are performed in a matter of seconds. And they are performed with no conscious thought. They are performed whether you are a math geek or a meathead.

The mathematical description of the movement of the ball may require physics with partial differential equations. Suppose you can return the serve, but you don't know calculus. Even if you were the winner of the prestigious Fields Medal in mathematics, there is no way you could actually do the computation necessary to describe, mathematically, the movement of the ball in time to return the serve at game speed. And yet, somehow, we return serve. Humans do the equivalent of this in our lives every day—from crossing the street in time so as to not get hit by an oncoming bus, to applying just the right amount of force to flip on a light switch without bruising your palm or damaging the wall. We believe this skill is unique to biological life forms and is the consequence of evolutionary pressures to successfully navigate the physical environment. What we call athleticism is *intuitive physics.*

Now imagine building a humanoid robot for the sole purpose of playing tennis or completing an obstacle course. Engineering a robot capable of moving around the court and swinging the racket would be its own monumental challenge—but the mental functions required to ably perform a sport at game speed is daunting in its own right. The tennis example is a thought experiment designed to illustrate the power of human athleticism, cognition and perception when compared to the mechanistic workings of the robotic mind in real life situations.

Someday perhaps we will design an AI that can perform computations with limited information, translating visual data into mathematical representations, and manipulating a physical embodiment so as to act on the input in real time—then we could have an android tennis player. But designing that seems like a silly way to spend a billion dollars. We would still put our money on Novak Djokovic versus the bot. Even with innovations such as improved robot "hand" dexterity thanks to improved navigation of state space through combinations of machine learning,[45] the combination of athletic abilities is an extraordinary feat of the human physiology and there is no commercial incentive to make robots do what we can, more or less, easily and effortlessly do.

Boston Dynamics has created the world's most advanced humanoid robot, named ATLAS perhaps because some day it may carry the world on its shoulders.[46] In a stunning (if not chilling) demonstration of athleticism, the ATLAS robot can now perform parkour, demonstrating ninja-esque physical abilities to navigate an environment. However, quadruped robots have become commonplace with unprecedented mobility allowing them to navigate difficult terrain, automating inspections in power plants and refineries, and even playing soccer. One of the most common is Boston Dynamics' Spot and is most recognizable. Now, Google's DeepMind has introduced Barkour, a benchmarking system to quantify the performance of quadrupedal robots.[47] The idea is to actually quantify performance, so we can actually measure improvement and progress of capability of these robots.

Our forecast is these robots will become essential for work environments that pose irreducible dangers to humans such as working in smelting, in highrise construction, or operating in combat zones. We also forecast these robots will never satisfy our desire to watch professional athletes perform in the Olympics and other feats of human physical excellence. One of the unspoken reasons we enjoy watching humans fly through the air, score a goal, hit a home run, etc. is precisely because it is difficult for the average person to do so. If dunking a basketball on a 10' rim were as simple as opening a can of soda, no one would care. There would be no NBA dunk contest. Even if the ATLAS becomes so affordable that every household has one, as the CEO and founder of Fetch Robotics, Melonee Wise put it: "For every robot we put in the world, you have to have someone maintaining it or servicing it or taking care of it."[48] She points out that technology is not going to render obsolete the human labor force. We doubt it will obviate human athletics, either. It is not entertaining to watch a robot perform parkour, it is terrifying. Imagine they are equipped with an automatic rifle and we are neck deep in a dystopian nightmare. The only thing preventing such an outcome would be legal restrictions and manufacturer guidelines. Hacking a robot is easier than convincing a trained soldier to defy orders. Some physical tasks should simply not be botsourced, regardless of how powerful the temptation.

The traits that are innately human—*creativity, innovation, empathy, caring, imagination*—are the skills all humans need to function in an organizational setting in the Humachine era.

General Intelligence

According to Douglas Hofstadter in *Godel, Escher, Bach: An Eternal Golden Braid*, "Sometimes the complexity of our minds seems so overwhelming that one feels that there can be no solution to the problem of understanding intelligence[.]"[49] That said, there are some key ingredients that are definitive abilities of humanity's *general intelligence*. They are the ability to:[50]

- Respond to situations flexibly;
- Take advantage of fortuitous circumstances;
- Make sense out of ambiguous or contradictory messages;
- Recognize the relative importance of different elements of a situation;
- Find similarities between situations despite differences that may separate them;
- Draw distinctions between situations despite similarities that may link them;
- Synthesize new concepts by taking old concepts and putting them together in new ways; and
- Come up with ideas that are novel.

Until machines can attain these abilities, humans are likely to remain indispensable to enterprise, despite the otherwise notable flaws to our intellects, which we discuss in later sections.

Intuition

To get the most out of ourselves, we need to play to our strengths. We need to tap into our intuition. According to Garry Kasparov, *intuition* is

> the product of experience and confidence. And here I mean 'product' in the mathematical sense, as the equation *intuition = experience x confidence*. It is the ability to act reflexively on knowledge that has been deeply absorbed and understood. Depression short-circuits intuition by inhibiting the confidence required to turn that processed experience into action.[51]

Another formulation of intuition comes from Herbert Simon. According to Simon, "Intuition is nothing more and nothing less than recognition," where "The situation has provided a cue; this cue has given the expert access to information stored in memory, and the information provides the answer."[52] Accordingly, per Simon, *intuition is decision-making based on pattern recognition*.

Unlike Kasparov's formulation, Simon's definition of intuition would apparently allow an artificially intelligent system to have intuition. As we discussed in previous chapters, machine learning and neural nets deploy pattern recognition as fundamental to their operation. However, general intelligence goes beyond pattern recognition and is not yet attained by any artificially intelligent system.

Creativity and Innovation

According to business consultant Linda Naiman, creativity is the act of turning new and imaginative ideas into reality by perceiving the world in new ways, uncovering hidden patterns, making connections between seemingly unrelated phenomena, and generating solutions.[53]

Experts in creativity theory distinguish between different types of creativity:[54]

- *Mini-c creativity* describes personally meaningful ideas and insights that occur to a person but are not shared, like seeing a familiar shape in a cloud or coining a nickname;
- *Little-c creativity* describes the kind of novel problem-solving deployed in our daily lives necessary to adapt to changing environments, like finding a new transit route to avoid a traffic jam;
- *Pro-C creativity* describes original output generated by professionals, which while skillful and creative, does not lead to wide acclaim or major impact, like coming up with scenarios for television commercials;
- *Big-C creativity* describes transformative, paradigm shifting creating works that have the potential to change the world, like medical innovations, technological advances, and artistic achievements.

In the book *The Innovator's DNA: Mastering the Five Skills of Disruptive Innovators*, authors Jeff Dyer, Hal Gregersen, and Clayton M. Christensen interviewed thousands of inventors and executives, and they found that creativity is not simply a mental function but a set of behaviors that tend to generate new insights.[55] These behaviors include:

- *Associating.* Finding connections between unrelated fields;
- *Questioning.* Challenging conventional wisdom;
- *Observing.* Noticing the subtle behavior of customers, suppliers, and competitors;
- *Networking.* Bridging gaps between people with different ideas and perspectives;
- *Experimenting.* Entering into interactive experiences to elicit new responses.

These behaviors are illustrated by a couple of famous examples of invention.

Consider the invention of the potato chips. The salty and crispy snack was created in 1853 at Moon's Lake House near Saratoga Springs, New York. Chef George Crum was tired of listening to a customer who kept on sending his fried potatoes back to the kitchen. He complained they were soggy and not crunchy enough. Out of anger, Crum then sliced the potatoes as thin as possible, fried them in hot grease, then doused them with salt. The customer loved them. Thus,

"Saratoga Chips" quickly became a popular item at the lodge and throughout the greater New England region.

Eventually these chips became mass-produced and distributed far and wide. But they would quickly become stale on the shelf. Then, in 1920, entrepreneur Laura Scudder invented the airtight bag by ironing together two pieces of waxed paper. This kept the potato chips fresh longer and thus mass production of potato chips began. Both inventions—the potato chip and the airtight bag—were a creative way to solve a problem: Crum satisfying a grumbling customer and Scudder figuring out a way to keep a product fresh longer.

Henry Ford brought the world automobiles. Had he worked merely from historical data he would have come up with a faster horse. Instead of just making a faster car, Elon Musk is working on an underground tunnel system with car elevators and a hyper loop. Steve Jobs was the first to give us a real choice of fonts. Although typeface was invented way back by Gutenberg, it was Jobs who understood its value and enabled its use in personal computers and a sense of customizability. None of these innovations came from machines alone.

Although it may be theoretically possible for an artificially intelligent system to have an original thought, to date it has not happened. Innovation and creativity are processes that machines are just now learning to mimic. But remember they only work from the data they have. They cannot think "outside of the box." Humans can dream, sense, and feel. We can use our intuition in deciding what path to take. Machines can dredge through data looking for patterns and statistical correlations; however, it is we humans who sense which unfulfilled needs could drive innovation.

Pleasure and Aesthetics

This section looks at humans' enjoyment of sensory indulgence and appreciation of beauty. Companies like Starbucks learned a long time ago that customers don't just want a product, they want an experience. For Starbucks, this means they don't just want good coffee. They want an aesthetically appealing environment that enhances the pleasure of consumption. Former Chairman Howard Schultz wrote,

> Every Starbucks store is carefully designed to enhance the quality of everything the customers see, touch, hear, smell or taste. All the sensory signals have to appeal to the same high standards. The artwork, the music, the aromas, the surfaces all have to send the same subliminal message as the flavor of the coffee: Everything here is the best-of-class.[56]

Pleasure and aesthetics require experiencing, feeling, and sensing. It is not something machines can do. Pleasure is something humans and animals experience and is a range of positive feelings, both physically and emotionally. Aesthetics concerns appreciation of beauty in both nature and art. Machines can copy what we as humans label as "aesthetically beautiful" or "artistic." They can copy or even create something that mimics it. But we think it is safe to say machines cannot experience; they have no subjective "what it is like to feel" the sound of music or the taste of cappuccino or the security of receiving trustworthy advice. Consumers of products—both goods and services—are human. While machines may be producing at a more efficient rate with greater precision than humans, they cannot create something on their own that will appeal to the pleasures and aesthetic taste of humans.

Aesthetics, feelings, and pleasurable sensations are the cornerstone of selling products to customers. It is the way we communicate as humans. While machines communicate through data, we communicate through the senses. There is art in creating reactions without words. Catering to aesthetic sensibilities is therefore a critical skill in business. Artwork conveys everything from beauty to power to influence and wealth. That is where brands begin and end.

Aesthetics are everywhere. Hotel lobbies, amusement parks, boardrooms, clothing labels, car interiors and vanity lighting, and so forth. Aesthetics is specific to product categories. Computers are designed for functionality, such as lightness, responsiveness to touch (such as the weight of a key on the keyboard) and ease of use. Fashion aesthetics are for use and functionality, such as moisture-wicking fabrics, as well as for show, such as shimmering colors. Let's have machines design the latest hairstyle and see how it works out.

Look and feel doesn't override function, of course. Some consumers may prefer mobile phones with a masculine look, whereas others want something cute. However, everyone expects the phones to work. That said, the design of products for pleasure with aesthetical appeal is something only humans can do (so far).

Emotions

Emotions are mental states characterized by feelings. The experience of emotion is perhaps most integral to being human as emotions filter the way the world shows up to us. Like laying a colored lens over the eye of the camera, emotions tint our perception of reality.

If you want to get the most out of your human labor force, they need to be happy, or at least not depressed. "Many studies have shown that depression, or the simple lack of self-confidence, results in decision making that is slower, more conservative, and inferior in quality."[57]

Depressed employees are less likely to make correct decisions intuitively, that is, less likely to be able to act on their own experience. It is ironic that emotions are both our strength and our weakness.

Because we are emotional, we can be pumped up with confidence, thus supercharging our own intuition, which in turn enables us to rapidly make correct decisions that are informed by experience. This same susceptibility to emotional influence can lead to depression—say, a snarky comment from a supervisor at work—which in turn cripples our intuition, leading to the inability to access the knowledge informed by our experience.

Because humans are all unique and susceptible to different emotional triggers, emotionally intelligent managers would know the profile of their subordinates and would understand what it takes to motivate and encourage them into harnessing their intuition. Whereas some need affirmation and positive feedback to feel confident, others may respond more confidently to a challenge.

Let this be a lesson to cruel managers. The all-too-common work environment governed by the mantra, "The beatings will continue until morale improves," is self-defeating. Intimidating workers undermines their productivity and squelches their ability to make sound decisions.

While there may be no authoritative definition of what an emotion is, the science of emotions has been considerably advanced by empirical research. While "happy" and "sad" are about as far apart as we can imagine, and while we tend to represent emotional experiences using categorical labels, research shows that actually "the boundaries between categories of emotion are fuzzy rather than discrete."[58] Based on extensive self-reporting across thousands of survey respondents, the National Academy of Sciences reports that there are 27 different human emotions. **Table 4.2** displays the results of a fairly comprehensive empirical study of human emotions.[59]

Although emotions can cloud our better judgment and lead us to irrational choices, we want to take a moment and appreciate what they contribute to productivity. Emotions fuel creativity and innovation. They generate energy that can spurn us to action and motivate us to complete a challenging task. Feelings are the fuel to human activity because they motivate us to pursue or avoid various outcomes.

Marketers know how to leverage the power of emotions. Emotions connect people, help sell products, recruit an employee from a competitor, empower teams to create innovative products, and so forth. Loni Stark, Senior Director of Strategy & Product Marketing at Adobe Experience Manager, says, "Lasting brand loyalty is built on an emotional connection with the brand across every customer touch point. Brands need a content strategy which is informed by data to elicit emotion and build connections."[60]

A critical ingredient to the success of enterprises in this technology era is to be emotionally literate. *Do not to ignore emotions.* Do not suppress them. Do not try to fight against human nature. We must learn to use emotions, to work with them, to inform business decisions based on the emotional reactions they are likely to generate, and to manage accordingly. Organizational leaders need to create working environments that cultivate healthy emotional responses. Leaders and team members need to understand

Table 4.2 Human emotions

Admiration
Adoration
Aesthetic appreciation
Amusement
Anxiety
Awe
Awkwardness
Boredom
Calmness
Confusion
Craving
Disgust
Empathetic pain
Entrancement
Envy
Excitement
Fear
Horror
Interest
Joy
Nostalgia
Romance
Sadness
Satisfaction
Sexual desire
Sympathy
Triumph

how to create and anticipate the emotional responses of customers and clients, suppliers, and other stakeholders, as well as other members of the organization.

There is right and wrong, true and false, but then there is the way things make us *feel*. Most human problems could be solved if only we would feel positive emotions about right and true things, and negative emotions about wrong and false things, but our social reality is messier than that.

A statement made by an executive to his or her team could be true and right, but if it is delivered in an emotionally inept manner, it will not *feel* true and right; it will *feel* false and wrong. The disconnect between truth, morality, and emotions can lead to all sorts of organizational failures.

Emotional Intelligence

Also known as emotional quotient (EQ), *emotional intelligence* (EI) is the capability of humans to recognize their own emotions and those of others, to discern between different feelings and label them appropriately. Emotional information can help guide thinking and behavior, and help manage emotions to adapt to various environments or achieve goals. Empathy is typically associated with EI because it relates to an individual connecting with the personal experiences of others.

Why is this important? Studies have shown that people with high EI have greater mental health, job performance, and leadership skills.[61] Indeed, EI can help people alleviate stress, reduce errors, become more innovative, and improve job performance. Although some individuals innately have a higher EI than others, these skills are trainable. An important aspect for organizations in building a human-centric organization will be training talent to navigate emotions in a productive and compassionate way by developing EI. This ability to manage one's thoughts and feelings is essential to business success.

It is also important to understand that emotions are intertwined with human thoughts. Our ideas are colored by emotions; thoughts are imbued with evaluations and judgments, some positive and others negative. Human mental states are complex, messy things that combine ideas, perceptions, beliefs, emotions, biases, and motivations.

Ultimately, these messy mental states govern how we operate. Negative emotions can be all-consuming. They can stifle creativity and innovation. Positive emotions can be energizing. They can make us want to conquer the world and be the best we can be.

In the work environment human emotions are also intertwined with the organizational culture. A positive culture that is inclusive, empowering, and welcoming will foster positive emotions and create fuel for creativity and innovation. A lot of business deals are done because we trust one another and feel a connection at an emotional level. In the Humachine era, businesses need their human capital—leaders, managers, and employees—to connect with others on an emotional level. Success will depend on human talent being able to connect with each other—with coworkers, customers, and suppliers—on the basis of trust. It will require an understanding of each other's emotional needs. As AI takes over increasing functions in an enterprise, the ability to feel and emote in an intelligent, responsive manner that helps manage relationships will become an increasingly important role for humans. Emotionally intelligent management is, at least for now, a safe space for humans to thrive in the workplace that has not yet been displaced by machines. See **Table 4.3**.[62]

Not everyone is equally emotionally intelligent. Sometimes emotions spring up inside us without a clear explanation, and sometimes we react to feelings without even realizing that our actions are being caused by our

Table 4.3 Emotionally intelligent behavior

Behavior	Intelligence
Thinking about feelings	Awareness of how moods affect thoughts and actions of self and others.
Pausing before acting	Refrains from making decisions based on impulsive feelings.
Control your thoughts	Consciously responds rather than unconsciously reacting.
Benefit from criticism	Determines how to improve self upon receiving negative feedback.
Display authenticity	Stand by your principles, instead of trying to conform to your audience.
Demonstrate empathy	Builds connections with others by seeing the world through their eyes.
Praise others' virtues	Inspires others by lauding their positive qualities.
Give helpful feedback	Frames criticism as constructive instead of harsh.
Apologize when needed	Demonstrates an endearing sense of humility.
Forgive when slighted	Releases feelings of resentment to be free of anger.
Keep your word	Follows through on commitments large and small.
Help others	Recognizes when others need support.
Avoids sabotage	Manages own emotions to stymie attempts at emotional manipulation.

emotions. This is why emotion or passion is often contrasted with rationality. Those with high EQ tend to exhibit certain behaviors that make them exceptionally gifted in working with other people, even to the point where they can govern their own emotions and create emotions in others.

Care

Care is a special feature of humanity. Humans tend to care about the objects of their attention and affection. We care about our family, our jobs, our things, and ourselves. According to Merriam-Webster Dictionary, the verb "care" is defined as "to feel trouble or anxiety," and "to feel interest or concern." The noun "care" is defined as the "suffering of mind," a "disquieted state of mixed uncertainty, apprehension, and responsibility," and a "painstaking and watchful attention."[63] The practice of medicine is often described as providing medical *care*.

Humans are caring creatures. When the mind is preoccupied with a subject, we are said to care about that subject. Care is related to the existential philosophy concept of "dasein," a German term that literally means "being there," coined by the philosopher Heidegger.[64]

Dasein describes the dialectical tension between the mind and the external world, in opposition to the notions that the mind exists wholly apart from its environment (on the one hand) and that the mind is causally determined by the external world (on the other).

Dasein is the location in which existence makes itself known. The human being is distinct from everything else in the world because it makes its own existence an issue to itself. The human mind is always potentially something else; its own possibilities come toward itself from itself, and it is always lurching into the future while informed by its own past. A caring mind is concerned with itself and with its environment.

If all this sounds mysterious, just remember—the mind is a mysterious thing, and to adequately describe it, we have to get pretty weird in our language.

Suffice it to say, the human mind cares. It feels troubled with a task assigned to it. Care takes up a challenge with a "disquieted state of mixed uncertainty, apprehension, and responsibility." That is the essence of caring about our job. Without this kind of care, our world would fall apart.

The managers' job is to ensure their employees are caring about the right tasks. You can get the smartest and most talented people on your team, but if they care about the wrong things, they will be worthless if not hostile to your organization's mission. To orient people toward tasks with care requires emotional intelligence and understanding the levers and pulleys of motivation.

Care is a uniquely human resource. Like creativity, emotions, and aesthetic taste, care is something that humans bring to enterprise that machines cannot replicate. This is described well by Boris Groys in *Philosophy of Care*:[65]

> Our current culture is dominated by the ideology of creativity. One is supposed to create the new and not to care about the things as they are. This ideology legitimises the domination of the "creative class" over the rest of the population that is predominantly occupied by forms of care – medical care, child care, agriculture, industrial maintenance and so on. We have a responsibility to care for our own bodies, but here again our culture tends to thematize the bodies of desire and to ignore the bodies of care – ill bodies in need of self-care and social care.

Play

Humans like to play and have fun, both of which are keys to creative thinking. Google knows this very well. It encourages employees to play, to be innovative, creative, spend at least 20% of their time on side projects, and even take naps.[66] "The philosophy is very simple," said Mr. Nevill-Manning, head of engineering at the Manhattan facility. "Google's success depends on innovation and collaboration."[67]

What does it take to create a culture of innovation and collaboration? We discuss these in Chapter 9 on the creation of the Humachine. In the previous chapter we discussed play as something the machines are missing. What is play? What is the point of it?

> By some, the origin and fundamentals of play have been described as a discharge of superabundant vital energy, by others as the satisfaction of some 'imitative instinct,' or again is simply a 'need' for relaxation. According to one theory play constitutes a training of the young creature for the serious work that life will demand later on. According to another it serves as an exercise in restraint needful to the individual. Some find the principle of play in an innate urge to exercise a certain faculty, or in the desire to dominate or compete. Yet others regarded as an 'abreaction' – an outlet for harmful impulses, as the necessary restorer of energy wasted by one-sided activity, as 'wish-fulfillment,' as a fiction designed to keep up the feeling of personal value, etc.[68]

Under any of these theoretical explanations of the origin and purpose of play, machines have no use for it, and arguably have no experience of it. So play and the fun of play is somehow unique to animal life.

Most biological explanations of the purpose of play "only deal incidentally with the question of what play is *in itself* and what it means for the player. They attack play directly with the quantitative methods of experimental science without first paying attention to its profoundly aesthetic quality."[69]

Empirical accounts of play that describe merely the externally verifiable behavior of creatures at play, ascribing biological evolutionary purposes to play behaviors, fail to grasp its aesthetic nature, the beauty of the game, the suchness of play for the player. This lack of experiential interiority also appears true of a machine programmed to play a game.

> Nature, so our reasoning mind tells us, could just as easily have given her children all those useful functions of discharging super abundant energy, of relaxing after exertion, of training for the demands of life, of compensating for unfulfilled longing's, etc., in the form of purely mechanical exercises and reactions. But no, she gave us play, with its tension, its mirth, and its fun.[70]

Now, it may be objected that an AI may very well "enjoy" the "playing" of games—but we would never know—indeed it remains a philosophical challenge to prove the existence of other minds much less the existence of conscious mental states in a machine. It may be objected than an AI may very well excel at playing games—indeed this is true as we saw from the Minecraft example. But it is the interior, subjective perspective on play, none other than the experience of fun itself, with its intensely absorbing nature that is "the very essence, the primordial quality of play."[71]

We discuss how to create a work environment that unlocks the so-called "flow state" with employees in Chapter 9.

Because of the extended juvenile period in mammalian development, we get long periods of play in the course of developing our minds. It wasn't until 2005 that we saw serious scientific study of play in other forms of life, including marsupials, birds, reptiles, fish, and invertebrates. That's when Gordon M. Burghardt published the book, *The Genesis of Animal Play: Testing the Limits.*[72]

Burghardt proposes five criteria to define "play":[73] (1) behavior is not fully functional; (2) play is spontaneous, voluntary, pleasurable, or autotelic (which means having an end or purpose in itself); (3) play differs from serious performance of typical behavior either structurally or temporally; (4) behavior is repeated but not stereotyped; and (5) behavior occurs when the animal is in a relaxed field (e.g., well fed, safe, healthy).

Burghardt proposes the *surplus resource theory* to predict and explain why animals play. According to this theory, "play will occur when there is sufficient metabolic energy (an important condition for play among invertebrates), lack of stress from environmental demands, a need for stimulation (boredom), and a lifestyle that includes behavioral complexity and flexibility (e.g., generalist foragers)."[74]

Play is a relatively mysterious behavior in animals, and our focus is on human play. Research in human play tends to use at least five quite distinct connotations. We can understand play in terms of progress, fate, power, identity, and imagination.[75] See **Table 4.4**.

Think about how much of the global economy is driven by humans just playing. For fun. Because we have a surplus of resources. Because we are bored.

Burghardt argues that although playfulness may have been essential to the origin of much that we consider distinctive in human behavior, it only develops through a specific set of interactions among developmental, evolutionary, ecological, and physiological processes, and it is not always beneficial or adaptive.[76]

Table 4.4 Types of human play

Type	Characteristics	Player
Progress	Adaptive activity, learning behaviors, acquiring skills, socialization, and neural development	Juveniles
Fate	Existential optimism, magic, chance, and chaos	Gamblers
Power	Games of strategy, skill, political contests, warfare	Hegemon
Identity	Symbolic interaction, bonding, festivals, parties	Socialites
Imagination	Transformation via repetition, reorganization, and exaggeration	Creatives

Leaders should encourage play at work. It is a fundamental human behavior. It brings us joy and allows us to relax. We are much more creative and productive when we are having fun. All work and no play is seriously detrimental to mental health.

We discuss play and gamification in more depth in Chapter 9 on how to build a Humachine.

Ethical Convictions

Merriam-Webster Dictionary defines *conscience* as a sense of the moral goodness or blameworthiness of one's own conduct, intentions, or character, together with a feeling of obligation to do right or be good.[77] Outside of the rare instances of psychopathy and sociopathy, most humans have a conscience. We may disagree over right and wrong in any given situation, but most of us agree that, generally speaking, one should strive to do the right thing.

Business ethics do differ from culture to culture—for example, some cultures expect a good bribe, whereas others make bribery a crime. However, research suggests that, even across cultures, there are some (practically) universal ethical standards. Breaching these rules might just upset *everyone*, regardless of the national origin, religion, or cultural background of the counterpart affected by one's actions.

Normative research into codes of ethics articulated by corporations, global institutions, and the business ethics literature reveals a convergence of six (basically) universal moral values: trustworthiness, respect, responsibility, fairness, caring, and citizenship.[78] See **Table 4.5**.

In addition to ethical codes pronounced by corporations, lots of professional societies impose ethical obligations upon their members and condition membership on compliance with certain norms. The American Psychological Association (APA) has published Ethical Principles of Psychologists and Code of Conduct for its members. The American Bar Association has promulgated Model Rules of Professional Conduct for adoption by the various state bar associations. It is the essence of a profession that it polices its members and holds them to high standards.

Table 4.5 Universal code of conduct

Name of virtue	Description of virtue
Trustworthiness	To be worthy of confidence and dependable to others.
Respect	To have regard for and not interfere with other's interests.
Responsibility	To be accountable for one's acts and accept one's burden.
Fairness	To be impartial and abstain from favoritism.
Caring	To have concern for and kindness to others.
Citizenship	To accept a membership role within a community.

Say what you will about attorneys, but they are taught to take ethical issues as seriously as legal ones.

We can have fascinating discussions on ethics—about their evolutionary origins (e.g., Nietzsche's 1887 book *On the Genealogy of Morality: A Polemic*), about cultural relativism (and how it leads to absurd implications such as the inability to make moral progress over time or to characterize one cultural habit as morally inferior or superior to any other), or about blatantly unethical corporate conduct that makes headlines every day (our lawyers suggested not mentioning anyone specifically here). But that's for a different book. Some ethicists might argue that ethics are all relative, but we feel that is an academic point to make which trivializes matters of grave concern to a humanity in need of basic morality across the board. We need to take ethics seriously, even if there is a lot of untidy philosophical baggage and loaded words involved.

All that said, we are more interested in the very human aspect of ethics, which is the ethical *conviction* we feel when tempted to do something that might be wrong or when we are forced to stand up against opposition to something that is right. In those times, it's not the written code of conduct so much as it is the compelling subjective feeling of conviction that actually constrains our behavior. Not just on the negative or abstention side (the fear of punishment, the nagging doubt of guilt) but also on the positive or proactive side (the yearning to do the right thing, the zeal of righteousness). Among other things, our conscience makes human decision-making different from what you would get from an unprincipled self-interest-maximizing AI.

Like our rationality, our morality sometimes fails us. But morality is a feature, not a bug, of the human. To create a Humachine, we should take both our most rational and most moral moments and normalize them, to ensconce within our enterprises wisdom and justice.

With all these glowing commendations of human virtues, let's turn to the limitations of human reasoning: our biased and bounded rationality.

Managing When Human, All Too Human

We like to think we are rational beings. In fact, humans are prone to myriad biases that cause us to think and act irrationally. Identifying human biases in decision-making has been well studied. It requires applying psychology to economics to predict, explain, and control how humans behave. In 2002 the psychologist Daniel Kahneman won the Nobel Prize in Economics for his work in this field. This was a high point in behavioral economics—the *empirical* study of how humans *actually* behave in the environment—as contrasted with *hypothetical* models of how a rational person *ought* to behave. The findings have been applied to practically all economic environments—from marketing departments to law and public policy—to improve understanding of human nature and to improve our ability to explain, predict, and control ourselves.

Let us be clear. In the age of technology humans are the centerpiece—not an afterthought. We cannot take humans out of the equation. Even today in the world dominated by technology, the key to success is to adapt humans to this new work environment—not to *replace* but to *enhance*, not to train humans to think *like* computers, but how to think *with* computers. That said, according to Ed Hess in the *Harvard Business Review*, "Because AI will be a far more formidable competitor than any human, we will be in a frantic race to stay relevant. That will require us to take our cognitive and emotional skills to a much higher level."[79]

We must understand how and why humans act irrationally to improve our cognitive and emotional skills. For decades, psychologists have studied cognitive biases as they relate to decision-making. The practice of understanding our limitations and designing systems around them goes back a long way. Policymakers have understood human cognitive and emotional frailties and built systems around them at least as far back as the framers of the United States Constitution, as evidenced by the so-called "constitution of man" described in the 1788 publication *The Federalist Papers*.

Deservingly popularized by the Broadway hit *Hamilton, The Federalist Papers*

> explains the need for and effectiveness of many of the architectural features of the United States Constitution, including separation of powers and other safeguards designed to prevent abuse of government and to ensure excellence in government as near as humanly possible.[80]

Despite our capacity for rationality and deliberation, humans are plagued with limits unknown to any AI system. We are bounded in the sense that we have limited rationality, we lack total self-control, we do not always pursue our own self-interest, and we often fail to live up to our own ethical ideals. Cognitively, we are biased in that we suffer from availability bias, self-serving bias, confirmation bias, and optimism bias. In negotiation settings, our limitations are revealed by reactive devaluation, escalation of commitment, myopia, endowment effect, loss aversion, and prospect theory, all of which make us bad at betting rationally. In interpersonal settings, we can suffer from collective action problems, rent-seeking behavior, tendencies toward free riding, groupthink, and holdout scenarios.[81]

These limitations have been known at least anecdotally to classical liberal thinkers for centuries (indeed, the United States Constitution was designed around these flaws), and in recent decades they have been dusted off, empirically investigated, and given more formal definition by psychologists, economists, and legal scholars.[82]

Despite the connotation, cognitive biases may not be all bad. Some cognitive biases are taken to be adaptive in the evolutionary context and thus may lead to success in certain situations. They are the brain's attempt to simplify information processing in a complex environment with limited processing power. Some of these biases are rules of thumb—known as "heuristics"—that help humans make sense of the world and reach decisions with relative speed.

To survive in an overwhelmingly complex world, biases can provide crucial mental shortcuts. Sometimes they lead us to make bad decisions, but they can also allow us to reach decisions quickly when, generally speaking, speed is more important than accuracy. Heuristics may allow us to make effective choices when information is limited but action one way or another is nonetheless necessary for survival.

Biases cannot be *eliminated*. They are part of being human. Even when someone is fully informed of their biases, they are still subject to them when making unaided decisions. For example, the majority of people think they are better than the average driver. However, these biases can be mitigated to avoid their worst consequences. They can be leveraged to bring out uniquely human advantages. What does this mean for the workplace environment? It means biases can, and need to be, *managed*.

How can we manage our biases?

First, engage workers in *experiential learning* rather than having them just observe or being told what to do. Engaging people—from leadership to talent—means leveraging these human traits.

Second, create a *culture of belonging* to trigger strong and pleasurable emotions associated with work. An inclusive culture of teamwork and belonging has been used successfully by leading technology companies— from Google to Zappos to American Airlines.

Third, utilize people for *focused decision-making*, while leaving technology for a large number of repetitive tasks. Humans have limited attention span and easily become overwhelmed with large amounts of information. However, we excel in creativity and innovation when focused on a small range of decisions. Use technology to automate the decisions that require big data computation, while reserving decisions that require value judgments for the humans. Executives and managers can make decisions that matter without having to become quants.

Fourth, prevent atrophy of decision-making muscles. We live in a world of disruptions that are increasingly becoming commonplace. Technology is only as good as the data it is based on, and disruptions alter data. Humans with their cognitive adaptive strategies can override systems to account for new and unexpected events that require quick responses more than precision.

These strategies will bring out the best in people while accommodating for our inherent frailties.

Dealing with Human Biases

Kasparov has mixed feelings about human intelligence.

> For all of the immense power of the human mind, it is very easy to fool. I'm a firm believer in the power of human intuition and how we must cultivate it by relying on it, but I cannot deny that my faith has been shaken by reading books like Kahneman's *Thinking, Fast and Slow* and Ariely's *Predictably Irrational*. After reading their work, you might wonder how we survive at all.[83]

Indeed, there are dozens of known and well-documented human *cognitive biases* that plague our ability to reason consistently, to make decisions based on evidence, to make accurate predictions of the future, and to evaluate facts.

We want to distinguish the biases reviewed here from that of racial, ethnic, gender, religious, or other forms of biases. The cognitive biases reviewed here are universal—they plague humans regardless of race, gender, etc. The biases associated with judging others based on their skin color, body parts, or place of birth is not baked into what it means to be human—it is an individual moral failure. That's why we aren't dwelling on those kinds of biases.

This section does not attempt to provide a comprehensive review of cognitive biases but rather describes a handful of them that are particularly problematic in an organizational setting as they pertain to how people interact with other people in transactional settings. Fortunately, most biases are susceptible to remediation by strategic utilization of AI as a decision-making support system.

Anchoring

In making a numerical forecast (e.g., How many marbles are in the jar? How many hours will this task require to complete? How much would she be willing to pay for this car?), humans tend to use a reference point or "anchor" to begin with—even when doing so is irrational. One's guess is prone to be unreasonably influenced by suggestion because of the *anchoring effect*. This describes a situation where people make a wrong choice as to a numerical value because they were exposed to an anchor number, even when the anchor number is completely unrelated to the choice at issue. Kahneman suggests that the anchoring effect "occurs when people consider a particular value for an unknown quantity before estimating that quantity."[84]

Research suggests there are actually two different mechanisms responsible for producing anchoring effects in human decision-making, and they correspond to the two different systems of thinking described above. System 1 is plagued by anchoring resulting from a "priming effect," whereas System 2 is hampered by anchoring that occurs in a "deliberate process of adjustment."[85]

System 1 anchoring is a consequence of the effort to "construct a world in which the anchor is the true number." In System 1 thinking, "anchoring is a case of suggestion," and "suggestion is a priming effect, which selectively evokes compatible evidence." "System 1 understands sentences by trying to make them true," which requires "the selective activation of compatible thoughts," which in turn "produces a family of systematic errors that make us gullible and prone to believe too strongly whatever we believe."[86]

System 2 anchoring is a heuristic that seeks to make an estimate when quantities are uncertain. We can fall victim to anchoring even when we are acting in a consciously deliberate manner. We tend to

> start from an anchoring number, assess whether it is too high or too low, and gradually adjust [our] estimate by mentally 'moving' from the anchor. The adjustment typically ends prematurely, because people stop when they are no longer certain that they should move farther.[87]

We can illustrate the effect of anchoring in enterprise with a few examples. In a negotiation setting, whichever party makes the first offer establishes a range of reasonable possibilities in the other's mind. The counteroffer will naturally be a reaction to the first offer upon which it is anchored. Retailers routinely use anchoring to incentivize purchases. Prices are shown as a comparison against an anchor. For example, the product is labeled as "was $49.99 now $29.99." The anchor provides the point of reference, making the new deal seem more valuable than it really is.

Technology can assist in negotiations by churning through data and arming the human negotiator with the best anchors and providing ranges and conditions to consider to avoid being unduly influenced by the anchor, so they might be most effective in negotiations.

Management should have protocols in place to mitigate the effects of anchoring in situations requiring humans to make numerical forecasts.

Bandwagon Effect

The *bandwagon effect* is a cognitive bias that manifests as the tendency to adopt beliefs, attitudes, behaviors, and styles simply because other people are doing it, even if this conflicts with our own beliefs or the available evidence.[88]

Examples are seen everywhere—from fashion, to music, to politics. It is a form of groupthink where there is pressure to conform to others and the desire to be right. The bandwagon effect reveals the very human need of individuals to be included and accepted in a group. Belonging is a basic human need.

There are clearly negative implications to this. Working meetings, for example, can be unproductive due to the desire of members to conform with the ideas and attitudes of others. It goes without saying that what is popular is not always rational. Understanding the bandwagon effect and groupthink can help companies mitigate it—and use it.

The bandwagon effect can be used to promote diverse ideas by encouraging people to voice different opinions. This sounds contradictory, but it works. Organizations that have an open environment and actually encourage members to be free to express novel opinions find that the bandwagon effect kicks in and others follow suit. Conformity in this case actually encourages, instead of inhibits, the contribution of novel and creative ideas.

The bandwagon effect underscores the importance of humans to be included and to be part of a group. Enterprises would be wise to leverage this bias by creating an inclusive culture that, in turn, encourages individual expression as part of the group identity.

Attribution Bias

Attribution bias is a cognitive bias that arises in situations where we are trying to explain other people's behavior. Attribution biases are the systematic errors in evaluating the motivation and explanations for behavior. "When we tend to overestimate the role of personal factors and overlook the impact of situations, we are making a mistake that social psychologists have termed the *fundamental attribution error*."[89] For example, when someone leaves a large tip because they are trying to impress their dinner date, but we mistakenly assume they left the large tip because they are wealthy, we commit the fundamental attribution error. When explaining behavior, the context of the behavior matters to its explanation at least as much as the identity of the actor.

We tend not to be objective when evaluating others' behavior versus our own. Humans can have skewed perceptions that blame others when they fail but excuse our own conduct when we fail. When judging negative actions of others we tend to assume these actions are the result of personal factors. This may involve assuming they are a bad person or they have the personal vice of laziness. However, when judging negative aspects of our own performance, we tend to attribute problems not to our own actions but as a result of external circumstances. We were late because the freeway was backed up, not because we overslept. It is interesting that positive outcomes are given just the opposite attribution. Successful performance of others tends to be attributed to external factors (e.g., "my competitor succeeded because he had better luck"), while our own successful performance is attributed to personal competence (e.g., "I succeeded because I have greater skill").

Like the other biases, attribution bias is part of being human. We just need to manage it. This is especially pertinent to enterprise in the context of performance evaluations.

Given the prevalence of attribution bias, we would be prudent to lean on objective performance indicators and decision support software when making performance evaluations in the workplace. Technology can provide the objectivity needed to produce consistent measurements and give credit where credit is due. Technology can take the subjectivity out of evaluation.

Confirmation Bias

Confirmation bias is the tendency to only seek information that matches what one already believes. It is a human tendency to want to be right and loathe being wrong. We give special weight to the conclusions we want to reach and the beliefs we already have. Contradictory information requires extra mental energy to process so we shy away from it. The effect is stronger for emotionally charged issues and for deeply entrenched beliefs. People also tend to interpret ambiguous evidence as supporting their existing position.

Kahneman explains confirmation bias as a maladaptation of System 2 thinking.

> A deliberate search for confirming evidence, known as *positive test strategy*, is also how System 2 tests a hypothesis. Contrary to the rules of philosophers of science, who advise testing hypotheses by trying to refute them, people (and scientists, quite often) seek data that are likely to be compatible with the beliefs they currently hold. The confirmatory bias of System 1 favors uncritical acceptance of suggestions and exaggeration of the likelihood of extreme and improbable events.[90]

Confirmation bias is seen any time initial information created an initial opinion. We see it in employee-hiring decisions to supplier selection, project pursuit, or financial investing. For example, investors seek out information that confirms their existing opinions and filter out or ignore contrary information.

Confirmation bias is related to another bias—overconfidence. We can see this in the behavior of the stock market and why it does not always behave rationally. In stock trading the bullish tend to remain bullish, while the bears tend to remain bearish regardless of what is happening. This is due to confirmation bias—only looking for supporting evidence and then being overconfident in that evidence.

How do we counteract this bias? Seeking out people and data with alternative opinions can help overcome confirmation bias and assist in making better-informed decisions.

Creating a culture where diversity in opinions is the norm and where offering evidence-based opinions is rewarded helps eliminate this bias.

Framing

Framing is a cognitive bias where people react differently to things—events, products, or even people—depending on how they are presented. Kahneman explains the framing effect as, "Different ways of presenting the same information often evok[ing] different emotions," sometimes leading to "large changes of preferences that are sometimes caused by inconsequential variations in the wording of a choice problem."[91]

We see things the way they are portrayed or "framed." This is commonplace in politics or advertising where visuals and words are manipulated to highlight positive effects and downplay negative ones.

Just consider the following comparisons: "The medicine has proven effective in 80% of cases" versus "The medicine has failed in 1 out of every 5 cases." The sentences say exactly the same thing; they are based on the same underlying fact. However, they are framed differently and will likely evoke starkly different emotional responses—the first a positive feeling about the medicine's efficacy, the latter a lack of confidence. The framing effect is powerful.

The framing effect can cause major problems to pollsters. Depending on how a question is framed, the respondents may generate wildly different responses even when the pollster is trying to elicit information about the same underlying issue.

The effect may be reduced or even eliminated if ample credible information is provided to people. One strategy is to train humans to "think outside of the frame." This is a very simple tactic. Once we are aware of framing we can present both a negative and positive frame to ourselves and consider the underlying issue objectively.

Second, it is important that machines are programmed to provide information to decision-makers in a frame-neutral manner. Otherwise, even a technology-driven organization where decision-makers believe they are relying on facts and statistics can fall victim to the framing effect.

In conclusion, human decision-making is troubled by a number of biases. Some of these that are particularly troubling for enterprises are anchoring, bandwagon effect, attribution bias, confirmation bias, and the framing effect. Corporate leaders should aim to offset these biases with decision-support technology.

Cultivating Human Virtues in the Technology Era

The nature of work is clearly changing in the digital world as machines increasingly take over tasks traditionally done by humans. Organizations should be continually reviewing what tasks can be automated and what should be retained by human labor, at all organizational levels. How to leverage talent and how to integrate human resources with technology is an ongoing management responsibility.

Our executive interviews were extremely helpful here. The percentage repeated by everyone we interviewed was roughly around 80% of tasks that had the potential to be automated—with the remaining 20% not being able to be automated. John Sicard told us:

You can safely automate 80% of obvious transactions in business. I do not believe you will get to a situation where it is responsible to automate 100% of all transactions.

While cognitive skills like rational analysis and decision-making were once considered the inviolate, unreplaceable, sovereign domain of humans, AI is surpassing human rationality in many ways.

So what is left for humans? What value can humans bring to an enterprise that has AI? What are the skills needed moving forward? Remember that the competencies of both machines and humans complement each other. Organizations will simply need to find strategies to integrate the two for the new work environment—the one we call the Humachine. Three categories of human qualities needed for the Humachine are literacy, competencies, and character traits. See **Table 4.6.**

Let's look at the three categories of qualities that humans will need in the technology era. The first category is *literacy*. Unlike in the past where deep and narrow literacy was valued, human literacy moving forward will need to be broad. Humans will need technical competence but also the ability to connect that to culture, society, and needs of the enterprise. They will need to understand how data in one area relates to the organization as a whole. For example, procurement managers will need to understand how supplier data relates not just to procurement metrics but financial performance and corporate strategy. Humans will need to be fluent in the language of strategy and financials in addition to their own specialized area. AI systems driven by big data will become intelligent but in the most narrow of ways. Humans will have a much better time than machines of gaining and applying broad general understanding. This broad literacy across domains will be a distinguishing value of humans for some time to come.

The second category of a unique human resource is *competencies* in linking the *technical* with the *human*. We need to be able to use systems thinking to link data to culture, emotions, creativity, innovation, teamwork,

Table 4.6 Human qualities in the Humachine

Quality	Scope	Description
Literacy	Generalists versus specialists	Technological, scientific, financial, culture, cultural and social
Competence	Link technical to human	Systems thinking, collaboration, critical thinking, problem solving, creativity, innovation
Character traits	Uniquely human abilities	Emotional intelligence, curiosity, persistence, empathy, initiative, leadership, social and cultural awareness

and collaboration. This will require using emotional intelligence to create connections and trust with stakeholders, from coworkers, managers, customers, suppliers, and board members. Without this competency, the technical proficiency of an organization will fail to be translated into action.

The third category is specific *character traits* humans will need. These are the traits we consider uniquely human. This includes emotional intelligence that will allow humans to relate to others. Consider, for example, an oncologist using data from an AI to develop a treatment plan for a patient. Yes, the statistics are there, but it is the physician who will need a high emotional intelligence to present facts in a way the patient can understand, allay fears, and offer support and comfort. This is caring. The AI is not capable of receiving high marks for bedside manner.

These character traits also include *curiosity* and *care* that will fuel creativity and innovation. We need individual "self-starters" as well as leaders who can keep the team motivated. Other traits include *adaptability*. These are individuals who can easily adapt to new environments and conditions, which are going to be inevitable in an increasingly complex world. Peter Cameron[92] tells us it is also the ability to "continuously self-diagnose," allowing us to self-improve. Another character trait essential to the future enterprise is *integrity*. Machines are not yet in a position to advise on the resolution of ethical dilemmas or to guide the user on the ethical use of intelligence. We still need humans to bring ethical values to work.

Every person we interviewed mentioned *critical thinking, innovation,* and *creativity* as key skills moving forward. Also critical was the ability to work with teams and groups of people. John Sicard[93] said a key skill will be "ability to work with strangers." Spencer Fung[94] told us that the differentiator will be "mindset."

Enterprises are currently focused on how to move through digital transformation. They are focused on technology and efficiency. We argue that the technological enterprise of the future must remain human-centric to succeed. For all of our biases and shortcomings, we care, and sometimes that's what matters most.

Changing What It Means to Be Smart

According to Ed Hess, "In an age of smart machines, our old definition of what makes a person smart doesn't make sense."[95] If we measure smarts by the ability to process, store, and recall information, to pattern-match and produce analysis, then humans are actually pretty dumb (relative to computers).

> What is needed is a new definition of being smart, one that promotes higher levels of human thinking and emotional engagement. The new smart will be determined not by what or how you know but by the quality of your thinking, listening, relating, collaborating, and learning.

Quantity is replaced by quality. And that shift will enable us to focus on the hard work of taking our cognitive and emotional skills to a much higher level.[96]

Revising our notion of "smart" to shift away from information processing to emotional intelligence is advisable. At the same time, we should be open-minded about this. Individuals living at the far edges of the autism spectrum may lack interpersonal skills usually associated with emotional intelligence and yet may be far superior than the average person at information processing and recall.

Indeed, one of the founders of machine learning, the British mathematician, computer scientist, and logician Alan Turing, "was not diagnosed in his lifetime, but his mathematical genius and social inelegance fit the profile for autism spectrum disorder (ASD)."[97]

According to the Centers for Disease Control and Prevention, about 1% of the global population lives with ASD.[98] The vast majority of those living with autism are unemployed or underemployed, likely as a result of prejudice in our thinking that would suggest people with ASD are unable to contribute in a work environment. "To the extent that's true, it's a measure of our failure as a society. Almost half of those diagnosed with ASD are of average or above-average intellectual ability."[99] Humans with ASD tend to be very analytical, detail-oriented, honest, and respectful of rules; failing to incorporate them into the workforce "is more than just a personal tragedy; it's a monumental waste of human talent."[100]

Baby Boomers and Botsourcing

While we may be imperfectly rational, that is not a complete explanation for why AI is on the ascendancy in the workplace, taking over jobs previously held by humans. We would be oversimplifying if we said that AI is taking over the economy because humans aren't rational enough. Current trends in economic displacement are driven by much more than our limitations as rational thinkers.

In this section, we discuss some of the demographic and economic trends that are disrupting the economy, as a backdrop for a greater appreciation of the limits of human intellectual capabilities in this era of job functions driven more and more by intelligence.

The popular press is filled with warnings of the battle between technology and humans. We hear of countless studies warning of potential job losses across all sectors due to advances in automation. In the quest for improved production processes, artificial intelligence, robotics, and digitization are altering the workforce as we know it. It is replacing skills and transforming labor markets. Digitization and automation are already fundamentally transforming the way we work.

The trend of displacing physical labor with machine power that began with the Industrial Revolution has simply continued, and it's not clear that it is even increasing. In the US, the agricultural sector saw about 40% of its labor force displaced between 1900 and 1940; the manufacturing sector saw about 13% of its labor force displaced between 1970 and 1990.[101]

According to the World Economic Forum, we are witnessing the convergence of

> two parallel and interconnected fronts of change in workforce transformations: (1) large-scale decline in some roles as tasks within these roles become automated or redundant, and (2) large-scale growth in new products and services—and associated new tasks and jobs—generated by the adoption of new technologies and other socioeconomic developments such as the rise of middle classes in emerging economies and demographic shifts.[102]

There are explanations for these trends that do not rely entirely on robotics. The agricultural sector probably lost jobs between 1900 and 1940 because of the Great Depression, the Dust Bowl, and the military draft and deployment of soldiers in the First and Second World Wars. The manufacturing sector probably lost jobs between 1970 and 1990 because of regulatory arbitrage. The minute the federal Occupational Safety and Health Act of 1970 (OSHA) was passed by Congress and signed into law, domestic manufacturing began fleeing the US for more laissez-faire economic conditions in other countries, presumably to avoid compliance with these new stringent worker safety standards.

Not only are there various economic, historic, and non-robot-related explanations for physical labor displacement, but also it's not like the US economy has been irreparably harmed from physical labor displacement. Agriculture and manufacturing sector jobs gave way to service-oriented and information-based work. Displacement from one sector does not mean jobs are lost forever; it usually means they move to a different (if not new) sector of the economy.

A Bain & Co. report titled "Labor 2030: The Collision of Demographics, Automation and Inequality" predicts that as a result of automation, 20%–25% of the total US labor force will be displaced.[103] However, the labor force will be shrinking as a result of the retirement of the baby boomer generation no less than because of investment into automation technology.

> The three factors that created this powerful lift to growth [of GDP in OECD countries]—women entering the workforce, the opening of China and India, and the baby boomer generation—are now largely mature, and their positive boost to macro conditions is now fading.[104]

How could automation be eliminating millions of jobs if, at the same time as automation is rolled out, millions of laborers are retiring? Those jobs would have been lost without the automation, as people in their 70s age out of the workforce. More hype. It's as if AI is the notorious, despicable, faceless "other" that we are seeking to scapegoat as the cause of our economic woes.

A more likely forecast is that automation will ensure that work previously done by baby boomers will be done by robots, thus ensuring consistent levels of labor productivity even with a shrinking workforce. If an aging workforce reduces supply growth, but the concurrent trend of automation increases supply growth, then these two trends could very well cancel out. If that is true, the real turbulence forecasted by Bain & Co. is not from AI or robotic automation at all but rather from the disturbing trend of growing income inequality, which threatens to reduce potential demand growth.

In other words, the problem is not robots; it's poverty. Poor people have a hard time learning how to manage technology platforms required for the jobs of the future. We do not dispute that in the coming decades, the global economy will look different than it did before. We are simply pointing out that this has been the case since the Industrial Revolution. This sentence could have been stated truthfully for the last fifty years: "Automation and AI will mean less need for physical labor and much more demand for high-tech and social skills."[105] The *MIT Technology Review* cover's claim that "AI and robotics are wreaking economic havoc" is then somewhat misleading.

Poverty is causing economic havoc. Concentration of wealth and stagnant wages when controlled for inflation are causing economic havoc. The sense of despair that creeps in when students (even those graduating with STEM degrees) are saddled with ungodly amounts of debt and will never attain the standard of living achieved by their parents—that's what's causing economic havoc. Not robots.

If we want to reduce the economic havoc forecasted in the coming decades, we need to ensure that the oft-promised, never-delivered wealth in the trickle-down economy actually trickles down. Research suggests the answer is actually *more* AI and robotics deployed more widely throughout the economy to stimulate increases in productivity, coupled with (and we really are careful here) some fair means by which wealth can be distributed so as to alleviate the stagnation of wages and income inequality and ensure basic needs are met. Maybe it's taxing robots' efficiency gains to share the savings created by botsourcing. Maybe it's universal basic income. We leave that to the politicians.

Although horses were a fundamental economic force in the early twentieth century, "Within 50 years cars and tractors made short work of equine livelihoods. Some futurists see a cautionary tale for humanity in the fate of the horse: it was economically indispensable until it wasn't."[106]

It simply is not the case that AI is taking our jobs. The reality is more complicated than that and not as bad as is frequently reported. Humans are afraid of change, even if the change is a good one.

Conclusion

According to Alibaba's founder Jack Ma, in 30 years, "the Time Magazine cover for the best CEO of the year very likely will be a robot. It remembers better than you, it counts faster than you, and it won't be angry with competitors."[107] A recent article goes further to provide data to suggest that it is best to replace CEOs with bots.[108] We disagree. We think leadership positions are not going the way of the ATM anytime soon. In the meantime, humans have a unique role to play in enterprise.

We are a resilient, adaptive, and intelligent species, even if we have our moments of cupidity. As long as we have management frameworks in place that ensure the "right" idea makes it to the top, *only one of us has to be right*. Assume we can adopt and maintain management frameworks that accomplish this filtration function, thereby bringing the best of human thought to the top. Ray Dalio's *Principles* makes this attempt. The fact that there are billions of us bodes well for our continued survival.

What do humans bring to the table? Intuition, general intelligence, aesthetic taste, emotional intelligence, and care. The Humachine will harness these unique features of human resources and offset their biases with decision support.

Despite the current buzz surrounding the term 'prompt engineering,' it may not be the future of harnessing generative AI. Rather it may be recognizing the problem and asking the right questions. It is the ability to identify, analyze, and delineate problems, called "problem formulation" and may be the more enduring and adaptable skill humans need.[109]

One of our contentions in this chapter is that human mental qualities make us indispensable for the foreseeable future. Originality, creativity, innovation, conscientiousness, and caring—these features may never be programmable. We encourage readers not to think about human versus machine like some kind of competition over limited jobs. That's not how this transition will play out. We are collaborators, each with different and complementary strengths. We discuss this in greater depth in the next chapter.

Notes

1 Kahneman, Daniel. *Thinking, Fast and Slow* (2016 Instaread Inc.), pp. 20–21.
2 Kahneman. *Thinking, Fast and Slow*, pp. 20–21. "I adopt terms originally proposed by the psychologists Keith Stanovich and Richard West."
3 Ibid., pp. 24–25. One sentence in the block quote comes from page 81.
4 Ibid.
5 Ibid.

6   The irony will be when the original model—the human way of doing things—becomes phased out or atrophied from lack of use when our AI frameworks do the same things but faster or cheaper. Already researchers are comparing the human organic systems of thinking to programmed models as if the human way of doing things reminds them of the computer's way (rather than vice versa). See this quote for example: "System 1 is reminiscent of seq2seq methods, which learn through imitation of oracle agents and primarily operate utilizing shallow action patterns. Conversely, System 2 bears resemblance to LLMs that excel in applying common sense knowledge, engaging in step-by-step reasoning, devising subgoal strategies, and exercising self-reflection." Bill Yuchen Lin, Yicheng Fu, Karina Yang, Prithviraj Ammanabrolu, Faeze Brahman, Shiyu Huang, Chandra Bhagavatula, Yejin Choi, Xiang Ren, *SwiftSage: A Generative Agent with Fast and Slow Thinking for Complex Interactive Tasks*, available at arXiv:2305.17390 [cs.CL] (last accessed May 31, 2023).

7   "The Swift module is a small encoder-decoder LM fine-tuned on the oracle agent's action trajectories, while the Sage module employs LLMs such as GPT-4 for subgoal planning and grounding." Bill Yuchen Lin, Yicheng Fu, Karina Yang, Prithviraj Ammanabrolu, Faeze Brahman, Shiyu Huang, Chandra Bhagavatula, Yejin Choi, Xiang Ren, *SwiftSage: A Generative Agent with Fast and Slow Thinking for Complex Interactive Tasks*, available at arXiv:2305.17390 [cs.CL] (last accessed May 31, 2023).

8   Hess, E. D. In the AI Age, "Being Smart" Will Mean Something Completely Different. *Harvard Business Review*, June 19, 2017. Available at https://hbr.org/2017/06/in-the-ai-age-being-smart-will-mean-something-completely-different

9   https://hbr.org/2022/06/how-ai-can-make-strategy-more-human

10 Henrich, Joseph and Muthukrishna, Michael. What Makes Us Smart? (April 22, 2023). Available at https://doi.org/10.1111/tops.12656

11 Henrich and Muthukrishna, What Makes Us Smart?

12 Robert Sapolsky, *Behave: the Biology of Humans at our Best and Worst*, p. 8 (2017 Penguin Random House UK).

13 Ibid., p. 22.

14 Ibid., pp. 22–23.

15 Ibid., p. 23.

16 Ibid., p. 23.

17 Ibid., p. 27.

18 Ibid., p. 26, emphasis added.

19 Ibid., p. 27, emphasis added.

20 Ibid., p. 31.

21 Ibid., p. 35.

22 Ibid., p. 35.

23 Ibid., p. 39.

24 Ibid., p. 43.

25 Ibid., p. 28.

26 Ibid., p. 28.

27 Ibid., p. 28.

28 Ibid., p. 28.

29 Ibid., p. 48.

30 Ibid., p 45.

31 Ibid., p. 45.

32 Ibid., p. 48.

33 Ibid., p. 49.

34 Ibid., p. 49.

35 Ibid., p. 50.
36 Ibid., p. 51.
37 Ibid., p. 51.
38 Ibid., pp. 54, 55, 56 respectively.
39 Feehly, Conor. July 26, 2021, Brains Already Exhibit Teamwork. *Discover Magazine*, https://www.discovermagazine.com/mind/brains-might-sync-as-peop le-interact-and-that-could-upend-consciousness?s=03
40 This formulation is from Hofstadter, Chapter XX: Strange Loops, Or Tangled Hierarchies, in the section titled, Can Machines Possess Originality? *Godel, Escher, Bach: An Eternal Golden Braid* (1979 Basic Books), p. 685.
41 Aoun, Joseph, President, Northeastern University; Interview January 19, 2023.
42 Samuel, A. L., Some Moral and Technical Consequences of Automation—A Refutation. *Science*, 132:741–742 (September 16, 1960).
43 Samuel appears to believe his premise that machines do not possess originality is true in an absolute sense and not merely because the state of the art at the time. We could interchange "originality" with "desire," or "feelings," or "voli-tion," and many people would still share that same conviction—that machines just do not have it.

Samuel continues: "The 'intentions' which the machine seems to manifest are the intentions of the human programmer, as specified in advance, or they are subsidiary intentions derived from these, following rules specified by the programmer. We can anticipate higher levels of abstraction … in which the program will not only modify the subsidiary intentions but will also modify the rules which are used in their derivation, or in which it will modify the ways in which it modifies the rules, and so on, or even in which one machine will design and construct a second machine with enhanced capabilities. However, and this is important, the machine *will not and cannot* do any of these things until it has been instructed as to how to proceed."

Here, Samuel describes a scenario where a machine intelligence (say, "Alpha"), derived by a programmer, in turn programs a machine (say, "Beta") on its own that is not bound by the same rules as Alpha. In this case, Alpha is bound by strict rules that limit what it can do, but within those constraints Alpha builds a subsidiary, Beta, that has greater degrees of action, is less inhibited by the constraints of Alpha's programmer. Even in that scenario, Samuel argues that Beta will never come into being unless Alpha's programmer wanted it to, and gave it the ability to do so, even if that ability was latent, rather than explicit, in Alpha's programming code.

This all feels intuitive. For example, suppose a programmer writes code to power a word-processing software. The software, in turn, through some accretive process from human use over time develops a function that crafts sonnets based on the patterns of its human user. This subsidiary poetic func-tion, according to Samuel, is only possible because of how the word processing software was designed and is not the result of originality on the part of the software. While intuitive, it appears to be a matter of belief, a strong intuition.

Notwithstanding the empirical evidence that suggests human beings are not as free (nor as rational) as we tend to think, for practical purposes we have to take as a working hypothesis that we do possess some degree of freedom that allows us to make decisions that make sense under the circumstances and which are not strictly speaking causally determined by the past. However, we want to be very clear on this point. Just because we take free will as a working assumption does not mean that we believe it is true. A useful working hypothesis is not, simply by virtue of being useful, true. Suffice it to say, philosophers debate whether free will exists, and most of them would probably say that it is weak, if not simply implausible, to cling to the notion of free will despite all we know about physics, chemistry, biology, and neurology. We can leave the debate to the philosophers.

44   There are varying classifications and definitions of the components of athleticism. See, for example, Breese, James. *What Is Athleticism? The Ten Components Of Complete Athleticism*, Strength Matters (October 19, 2022). Available at https://strengthmatters.com/ten-components-athleticism-matter/#:~:text=Athleticism%20is%20formed%20by%20ten,%2C%20mental%20resilience%2C%20a nd%20stability (last accessed June 14, 2023).

45   Rayne, Elizabeth. Hypersensitive Robot Hand is Eerily Human in How it Can Feel Things. *Ars Technica* (May 22, 2023). Available at www.arstechnica.com/science/2023/05/hypersensitive-robot-hand-is-eerily-human-in-how-it-can-feel-things/ (last accessed June 14, 2023).

46   https://www.bostondynamics.com/

47   https://techcrunch.com/2023/05/30/google-deepmind-introduces-barkour-a-bench mark-for-quadrupedal-robots/

48   Pisturi, Joseph. The Future of Human Work Is Imagination, Creativity, and Strategy. *Harvard Business Review*, January 18, 2018.

49   Hofstadter, Douglas. *Godel, Escher, Bach: An Eternal Golden Braid*, p. 27.

50   Ibid., p. 26.

51   Kasparov, Garry and Greengard, Mig. *Deep Thinking: Where Machine Intelligence Ends and Human Creativity Begins*. PublicAffairs. 2017, p. 239.

52   Herbert Simon as quoted by Kahneman. *Thinking, Fast and Slow*, p. 237. "The model of intuitive decision making as pattern recognition develops ideas presented some time ago by Herbert Simon, perhaps the only scholar who is recognized and admired as a hero and founding figure by all the competing clans and tribes in the study of decision making."

53   What is Creativity? (And why is it a crucial factor for business success?), Creativity at Work. Available at www.creativityatwork.com/2014/02/17/wha t-is-creativity/

54   Kersting, Karen. What Exactly Is Creativity? Vol. 34, No. 10 (November 2003). Available at www.apa.org/monitor/nov03/creativity.aspx. See also Kendra Cherry, *The Psychology of Creativity*, Very Well Mind (May 24, 2018). Available at www.verywellmind.com/what-is-creativity-p2-3986725

55   Dyer, Jeff, Hal Gregersen and Clayton M. Christensen, The Innovator's DNA: Mastering the Five Skills of Disruptive Innovators. *Harvard Business Review Press* (1 ed.). July 19, 2011.

56   Schultz, Howard. *Pour Your Heart Into it: How Starbucks Built a Company One Cup at a Time* (1997 Hyperion).

57   Kasparov and Greengard, *Deep Thinking: Where Machine Intelligence Ends and Human Creativity Begins*, p. 239.

58   Cowen, Alan S. and Dacher Keltner. Self-report captures 27 distinct categories of emotion bridged by continuous gradients, *Proceedings of the National Academy of Sciences of the United States of America*, Edited by Joseph E. LeDoux, New York University, New York. September 5, 2017. Available at www.pnas.org/content/early/2017/08/30/1702247114

59   Ibid.

60   Barrett, Jeff. If You Want to Build a Brand, Create an Emotional Experience First. *Inc. Magazine*. April 26, 2017. Available at www.inc.com/jeff-barrett/if-you-want-to-build-a-brand-create-an-emotional-experience-first.html

61 David, Susan and Christina Congleton. Emotional Agility. *Harvard Business Review*, November 2013.
62 Bariso, Justin. *13 Signs of High Emotional Intelligence*. Available at www.inc.com/justin-bariso/13-things-emotionally-intelligent-people-do.html (from his forthcoming book, EQ, Applied).
63 www.merriam-webster.com/dictionary/care
64 Heidegger, Martin (1889–1976), Internet Encyclopedia of Philosophy. Available at www.iep.utm.edu/heidegge/#H3
65 Groys, Boris. *Philosophy of Care* (2022 Penguin Random House).
66 Robinson, Adam. Want to Boost Your Bottom Line? Encourage Your Employees to Work on Side Projects, *Inc. Magazine*, 2018.
67 Stewart, James. Looking for a Lesson in Google's Perks. *The New York Times*, March 15, 2013.
68 Huizinga, Johan. *Homo Ludens: A Study of the Play-Element in Culture*, p. 2 (2014 Martino Publishing, originally Roy Publishers 1950).
69 Ibid., p. 2.
70 Ibid., p. 3.
71 Ibid., p. 2.
72 Burghardt, Gordon M. *The Genesis of Animal Play: Testing the Limits* (2005 The MIT Press). Available at https://mitpress.mit.edu/books/genesis-animal-play
73 Meyers-Manor, Julia E. Book Reviews. *American Journal of Human Biology*, 17:821–827, 2005.
74 Ibid.
75 Burghardt. *The Genesis of Animal Play: Testing the Limits*, p. 8.
76 Ibid.
77 www.merriam-webster.com/dictionary/conscience
78 Schwartz, M. S. *Journal of Business Ethics*, 59:27, 2005. doi:10.1007/s10551-005-3403-2.
79 Hess, "Being Smart" Will Mean Something Completely Different.
80 Wood, John. The "Constitution of Man": Reflections on Human Nature from the Federalist Papers to Behavioral Law and Economics. *NYU Journal of Law and Liberty*, 7:185–186, 2013.
81 Ibid.
82 Ibid., p. 186.
83 Kasparov and Greengard. *Deep Thinking: Where Machine Intelligence Ends and Human Creativity Begins*, p. 240.
84 Ibid., p. 120.
85 Ibid.
86 Ibid., pp. 122–123.
87 Ibid., p. 120.
88 Neil, John. Cognitive Bias: The Bandwagon Effect, The Ethics Centre. Available at www.ethics.org.au/on-ethics/blog/november-2016/cognitivebias-the-bandwagon-effect
89 Bias in Attribution. Principles of Social Psychology—1st International Edition. Available at https://opentextbc.ca/socialpsychology/chapter/biases-in-attribution/
90 Kahneman. *Thinking, Fast and Slow*, p. 81.
91 Ibid., pp. 88, 272.
92 Peter Cameron, CEO @The Lenox Group; Interview on February 7, 2023.
93 John Sicard, President & CEO, Kinaxis, Interview on January 5, 2023.
94 Spencer Fung, Group Executive Chairman of Li & Fung, Interview on January 25, 2023.
95 Hess. In the AI Age, "Being Smart" Will Mean Something Completely Different.

96 Ibid.
97 Pelphrey, Vin. Autistic People Can Solve Our Cybersecurity Crisis. *Wired*, November 25, 2016. Available at www.wired.com/2016/11/autistic-people-ca n-solve-cybersecurity-crisis/
98 Autism Spectrum Disorder (ASD), Centers for Disease Control and Prevention. Available at www.cdc.gov/ncbddd/autism/data.html
99 Pelphrey. Autistic People Can Solve our Cybersecurity Crisis.
100 Ibid.
101 Rotman, David. Making AI into Jobs. *MIT Technology Review*. July/August 2018. pp. 13–14.
102 World Economic Forum, The Future of Jobs Report 2018, Centre for the New Economy and Society, p. v. Available at www3.weforum.org/docs/WEF_ Future_of_Jobs_2018.pdf
103 Harris, Karen, Kimson, Austin and Schwedel, Andrew. *Labor 2030: The Collision of Demographics, Automation and Inequality*. Bain & Co. February 7, 2018. Available at www.bain.com/insights/labor-2030-the-collision-of-dem ographics-automation-and-inequality/
104 Ibid.
105 Rotman, David. Making AI into Jobs, *MIT Technology Review*. July/August 2018, p. 13.
106 Free Exchange. *Will Robots Displace Humans as Motorised Vehicles Ousted Horses? The Economist*. April 1, 2017. Available at www.economist.com/finance-a nd-economics/2017/04/01/will-robots-displace-humans-as-motorised-vehicles-ousted -horses
107 Bhavsar, Neil C. and Reedy, Christianna. *Experts Assert That AI Will Soon Be Replacing CEOs*. Futurism. April 28, 2017. Available at https://futurism.com/ experts-assert-that-ai-will-soon-be-replacing-ceos/
108 https://futurism.com/the-byte/replacing-ceos-with-ai-makes-sense
109 Acar, Oguz A. *Harvard Business Review*, June 06, 2023, https://hbr.org/2023/ 06/ai-prompt-engineering-isnt-the-future

Chapter 5

The Humachine
The Path to Enterprise Superintelligence

Use It or Lose It

If there is a single lesson to be learned from the Covid pandemic it is that AI cannot replace human expertise and judgment when it comes to managing global supply chains or setting public policy. Prior to the pandemic the trend toward automation was well under way. However, as John Sicard reminded us, when the pandemic hit "every math-based model collapsed." He went on to explain: "The pains that were felt during the pandemic were not a failure in technology. They were a failure in technique - the notion that technology will solve all things. That was the biggest aha moment."[1]

We agree. The latest onslaught of AI-powered business and creative applications still need to be implemented, guided, and managed by humans. We have to upskill the global workforce in order to wield these tools appropriately and effectively.

The key thesis of this book is that it is short-sighted and dangerous to botsource everything. The real competition is not with companies that can use AI to botsource traditional business functions as this treats human resources as mere liabilities to shed. *The competitive edge goes to companies that can implement Kasparov's Law to using advances in AI put into the hands of talented people—or ordinary people using computers with the right process—to achieve extraordinary results.*

As companies increasingly 'botsource' tasks to machines, the enterprise experiences an atrophy in the human skillset formerly needed to attain such tasks. Over a long enough period of time the companies that botsource too extensively run the risk of losing these skills entirely any time an automated system goes offline for any reason, whether a code bug, a user error, a hacking incident, or a power failure. Organizations may be left with no one on hand who knows how to do, manually, those crucial albeit usually automated tasks. This atrophy could cause a compounding damages effect in the case of any disruption that throws off the automated system. The robots don't run when the power goes out. The powerful

DOI: 10.4324/9781003322832-5

cloud computing AI platform doesn't handle the automated process for you when your computer can't connect to the internet. Just consider the following from a large hospital network we interviewed.

The Chief Nursing Executive (CNE) at the hospital network provided an example of skills that have atrophied with younger nurses as they increasingly rely on automation technology: calibrating the dosage of medications to administer per volume in intravenous (IV) pumps through which the medical staff administers drugs directly into the blood stream through tubes and needles. In the hospital settings, the ability to correctly program IV pumps is critical to deliver the right infusion of medication to patients through IV drip.* More than a decade ago, smart IV pumps that automatically calibrate medication dosing were introduced. Prior to this technology, all IV-pump programming required the user to manually calculate the rate of infusion then input the desired infusion rate into the pump. This manual technique is complicated as many different units of measurement are used in the administration of IV medications. As a result, the required calculations are often complex and require a skilled practitioner. Otherwise, there is a high likelihood of user error. By contrast, smart IV pumps allow the user to choose the desired medication from an approved list and input the required patient information, after which the smart IV pump calculates the infusion rate automatically.

The CNE explained that a major concern for the hospital executives is the event of a security breach or power outage, as smart IV pumps depend on uninterrupted connection to a power source. Only the older nurses who were trained and came up pre-automation had the skills and working knowledge to calibrate IV dosing manually. As the hospital network has become dependent on automation, the younger nurses were never trained to calibrate IV pumps manually. The skill, absolutely critical for patients stuck on a hospital bed depending on life-saving medication to be administered intravenously. In situations like that, risk management principles suggest we do not outright rely on technology that could shut down in an emergency, but have some failsafe for human intervention. But this means the enterprise must keep up with training a skillset that is only valuable in a contingency situation and which would otherwise atrophy within the community. Given a disruption like power loss, very few nurses would know what to do for those patients needing IV-administered drugs.

Situations like these create vulnerability within the hospital system. Any system that is turned over to automation carries this risk. As organizations move to increase botsourcing, leaders must be mindful of resulting gaps in human-held institutional knowledge and human-held operational capacities. These gaps create risks of atrophy and are an unhealthy side-effect of too much botsourcing and inadequate integration of human and machine resources.

Recipe, Formula, Alchemical Spell, Call It What You Will

This chapter examines how AI is impacting humans at work, with the goal of understanding how unique skills of people and technology can be combined for extraordinary results.

A word about "integrating" or "combining" human and machine. We mean this in a figurative sense, as in collaboration between team members rather than combining sugar and flour in a baking recipe. We feel this distinction is important because some of the pathways to superintelligence reviewed in Chapter 2 clearly envision some literal "combination" of humans and machines in the sense of cyborgization. That's not what we are suggesting. We eschew the morbid biological-mechanical hybrid creatures of science fiction—cyborgs with cranial implants or digital whole brain emulation. Rather, we are trying to create an enterprise with collective superintelligence, a network of human and machine minds that are powerful, wise, and humane.

Recall *Moravec's Paradox*, which holds that what machines are good at, humans are not, and vice versa.[2] *Kasparov's Law* holds that *weak human + machine + better process* is superior to a strong computer alone and, more remarkably, superior to a *strong human + machine + inferior process*.[3] Further, "collective" or *organizational network superintelligence* holds that superintelligence could emerge "through the gradual enhancement of networks and organizations that link individual human minds with one another and with various artifacts and bots."[4]

At the highest level of abstraction, we are applying Kasparov's Law to resolve Moravec's Paradox so as to fulfill the conditions for collective intelligence, thereby creating a Humachine. See **Figure 5.1**.

The Humachine is an organization of humans and bots so networked that each mitigates the other's unique limitations and augments the other's unique strengths, thereby attaining collective superintelligence.

Recall that Kasparov's Law explains the results of the Advanced Chess experiment in terms of the triumph of process over genius and raw computing power.[5] How can amateur chess players defeat grand masters *unless* ordinary human and machine skills used in the right combination pursuant to the right process can attain extraordinary results? We are seeking to apply this law to the enterprise level.

According to Gary Kasparov, "There are certain things that we can do that machines are not at all going to be able to replicate. It's things like love, emotions, passions," to which we would add the spirit of play, the creative act, the qualities of leadership and service and sacrifice and fraternity, the yearning for truth, justice and beauty.

Kasparov goes on to unpack more irony around Moravec's Paradox that may prove an irreducible role for humans: "One of the rules is anything that we know how we do machines can do it. But there's so many things that we do that we don't know how we do—and that's where we humans can excel."[6]

Moravec's Paradox

• Machine capabilities are inversely related to human capabilities.
• Where computers excel, humans struggle, and vice versa.

Kasparov's Law

• Combining ordinary humans and computational resources with the right process can produce extraordinary results.
• Ordinary machines and people using the right process can prevail over human genius and supercomputing without the right process.

Bostrom's Collective Superintelligence

• Emerges from enhancement of networks and organizations linking individual human minds with one another and with various bots.
• A large number of smaller intellects networked together can create a system that outstrips existing cognitive systems.

The Humachine

• Harnessing data and AI to power the display of uniquely human skills.
• Combining the virtues of machines and humanity to overcome the limits of both in a superintelligent organization.

Figure 5.1 Conceptual map of our thesis

If we know how we do it, we can identify the steps and instantiate the decision-making or behavior pattern into an automated system. That is, if we know how we do something, we may be able to botsource it.

But many of our most impressive and valuable qualities as embodied conscious beings are opaque to us yet, so we cannot botsource them if we tried. Further, we have qualities like purpose and loyalty and respect and social intelligence that are not amenable to botsourcing even if we wanted to.

Following Kasparov's Law means we do not need to bridge the gap, making machine capable of human cognitive virtues or making humans compute like machines. Rather we create processes and procedures—that is we program our enterprises—to leverage the complementary strengths of humans and machines.

To that end, we explore some of the challenges involved in integrating humans and machines, two complementary yet inversely related organizational resources. As noted by the World Economic Forum's The Future of Jobs Report 2023, "Technology adoption will remain a key driver of business transformation in the next five years .... the impact of most technologies on jobs is expected to be a net positive over the next five years."[7]

An enterprise will need to utilize management protocols that allocate enterprise functions optimally between existing human and technical resources, such that each contributes its exclusive and complementary skill to the enterprise's mission. We think eventually this kind of collaborative process between human and technical resources can lead to the emergence of organizational network superintelligence.

If the correct organizational structure is deployed, the combination of humankind and machine skills will not only be additive but rather synergistic as the enterprise ends up (whether this is figuratively or literally, we leave to the philosophers) possessing a mind of its own that is greater than the sum total of its parts. A mind that is relentless in its pursuit of the mission of the enterprise, but also wise, humane, and conscientious in its methods.

This quest to create the Humachine is already underway.

This chapter will survey trends in human resources driven by the ascendance of AI with an eye toward creating organizational network intelligence.

The Humachine Era: The Next Phase in the Organization of Intelligent Life

Over millions of years, living systems of collective intelligences have evolved on Earth, subjecting matter, energy, and information to four epochs of control. These are illustrated in Table 5.1 provided originally by Beniger in *The Control Revolution*. The table "illustrates the place of cultural and higher levels of control and living systems, including the type of social system possible at each level."[8] According to Beniger,

> each level exists in a concrete sense, with matter and energy organized into both processor and programming, DNA and genetic programming, vertebrate brain and learned programming, formal organization and rules, machines and algorithms... all four levels of control involve three different temporal dimensions or address three distinct control problems: existence or being, experience or behaving, and evolution or becoming.[9]

To be clear, Beniger's original framework ended with "(Synthetic life)." In his original work there was nothing mentioned under how energy and matter are organized through processes or programs beyond Level Four: Technology. Nor did Beniger venture to speculate what happens in the era of synthetic life. We suggest the post-Technology era would be defined by superintelligence and life will handle the problems of existence (maintenance), experience (adaptation), and evolution (survival) through Humachines.

Recall the timeline for the emergence of new levels of control as described in the Foreword. Notably the progressive era's approach at intervals of time in a logarithmic manner. As such, it appears (1) we are due for another revolution in control, beyond the Technology level, and (2) further revolutions would either (a) begin to occur at such a fast rate as to defy comprehension or (b) would reset the clock on a logarithmic basis such that no major revolutions in control would happen again for another several million years. Either the revolutions keep spinning faster or the pace resets and the next revolution will not happen for quite some time hence. We suggest it may be the latter. Even though Beniger published this timeline in 1986, it took almost four decades for generative AI programs to hit the market. Maybe we are just at the very beginning of another long era.

Whatever happens after Level Four? What happens after the Control Revolution runs its course? According to the timeline provided by Beniger, it appears we are due for a fifth level of control to emerge, if it hasn't already. We suggest the successor era will go beyond techno-bureaucratic information society to something shaped by emerging forms of collective intelligence. We are at a tremendously consequential fork in the road and at least one path leads to humans becoming cyborgs or humans as biological batteries powering the machines that actually control everything. Whereas the path we suggest leads to the creation of humachines that are wise and which help humanity thrive. At least, we hope that, if life must be controlled to avoid entropy, it would be subject to control by an emergent form of synthetic intelligent life that combines human and machine virtues and avoids the vices of each.

Following Beniger's framework, we could call this post-Technology era of control something like "Level Five: Superintelligence." As rigorous as Beniger was in his analysis, he could not see into the future. What happens at Level Five? What comes after the technology-empowered control revolution? That portion of the unfurling parchment of time is left blank. Of course it is difficult to understand the times we are living in because we cannot create a critical distance from our own present. But let's try to look through Beniger's lens at the empirical properties and analytical dimensions of what the Humachine era looks like. First we observe the general principles that pertain to all systems of control, so we can extrapolate what the next system might look like.

We encounter these three levels of control involving mechanism, behavior, and the process of programming in all control systems, from DNA to human organization and technology. The levels might be seen to involve three different temporal dimensions or to address three distinct problems for control:

Existence or being, the problem of maintaining organization—even in the absence of external change—counter to entropy

Experience or behaving, the problem of adapting goal-oriented processes to variation and change in external conditions

Evolution or becoming, the problem of reprogramming less successful goals and procedures while at the same time preserving more successful ones.[10]

The relationship between being, behaving, and becoming is complex.[11] At every level of control, we can understand how collective intelligence asserts control over its environment: through an embodied mechanism, which behaves in a certain way in real time, and yet undergoes a process of programming and reprogramming over time in order to evolve. This applies to colonies of ants as much as it does to national governments. Reprogramming an organization is another word for being able to mutate and evolve to suit changing environmental conditions.

Beniger contends that all collective intelligences at all levels of organization of intelligence life were adept at solving the problem of entropy by

involving mechanism, its behavior, and the processes of its programming and reprogramming. Organizations can be maintained, counter to entropy, by a hierarchy of physical control: protein synthesis controlled by DNA, cultural behavior by learned programs, organizational processing by formal rules, machine processing by still more intentionally designed algorithms.

We suggest an alternative form of enterprise without a rigid hierarchy in Chapter 7.

Nonetheless, for all stages of control heretofore,

Pre-programmed goals can be pursued, despite variation and change in external conditions, by a hierarchy of behavioral mechanisms: adaptation, learning, reorganization, reprogramming. Less successful goals can be modified or dropped, while still preserving or improving more successful ones, through a hierarchical process of system changes organic evolution through natural selection, cultural diffusion through differential adoption at the individual and organizational levels, government in market selection at the technological level.[12]

It is by exerting control that life itself endures long enough to not only survive as an individual but to evolve as a collective. "The currently precarious state of human culture and higher culture-based levels of human control can also be seen" in Table 5.1.

Table 5.1 Analytic dimensions and empirical properties of the four levels of control, including the type of social system possible at each level

Level of control	Organization of matter and energy	Programming	Analytic dimensions of the resulting control systems		
	Processors	Programming	Existence	Experience	Evolution
(inorganic universe) Intermediate: replicating molecules					
Level One: Life Genetically based sociality (many animal species)	Molecules of DNA	Genetically inherited programming	Replication of programming, protein synthesis	Response, adaptation of genetically controlled processes to environment	Organic evolution through natural selection
Level Two: Culture Culture-based social structures; human societies	Vertebrate brains	Learned behavioral programs	Behavior controlled by programming stored in memory	Learned responses, adaptation to environment through programming	Cultural diffusion, change through purposive innovation, differential adoption
Level Three: Bureaucracy Bureaucratically controlled social systems	Formal organization of individuals	Explicit rules and regulations	Rationalized processing, record keeping, hierarchical decision, formal control	Organizational response to environment, adaptation through reorganization, procedural changes	Diffusion of rationality with differential adoption as culture, selection pressure on organizations
Level Four: Technology Techno-bureaucratic Information Society	Mechanical and electronic information processors	Purposively designed functions and programs	Informational inputs, processing and storage, programmed decision and output	Interaction of processor and environment, adaptation through rewriting, reprogramming	Diffusion of processors and programs with differential adoption as culture, government, and market selection

	Organization of matter and energy		Analytic dimensions of the resulting control systems		
	[Beniger's original table ended here. Below text added by authors]				
(Synthetic life)					
Level Five: Superintelligence Organizational Network Collective Intelligence	Humachine enterprises (distributed machine and human networks of intelligence)	Four I Model (Intentionality, Integration, Implementation, Indication)	Sustainability (Resilience, biomimicry, virtualization, efficiencies)	Innovation and Mutation (Low transaction cost for enterprise to pivot, replicate, dissolve, or create anew)	Replication. (Successful humachines become archetypal form of organization. Natural selection becomes intelligent design)

Today we stand between the inorganic universe, on the one hand, and the prospect that our technology might soon create new life—thereby replicating all four levels of control at the synthetic level, on the other hand. Intermediate forms now exist on both sides: self-replicating polymers on the inorganic side and genetically engineered systems on the organic one. In view of the continued development and proliferation of nuclear weapons technology, the next major stage in the evolution of life on Earth might hinge on the question of which end-state of Table 5.1 will be achieved first: synthetic life, certainly one possible product of our evolving technobureaucratic control, or the return of the entire planet to the inorganic level, another quite possible outcome—ironically enough—of the same revolution in control technology.[13]

We are not quite as pessimistic as Beniger was. He asked which direction we were headed: toward all organic life being reduced to a digital simulation (purely synthetic) or all organic life being wiped out in a nuclear holocaust (purely inorganic). We like to think biological life will remain firmly in control, but only if we make the evolutionary leap (or revolutionary turn) to superintelligence via the Humachine pathway.

Here, matter and energy are organized and processed by Humachines using superintelligent enterprise decision-making that is by definition sustainable. These Humachines would exert social control in beneficial ways (efficient market conduct; productive, meaningful employment for human workers; reliable, benevolent health care and retirement benefits; useful products and services; consistent tax revenue and regulatory compliance) while respecting human rights, individual dignity, cognitive sovereignty of privacy and freedom of thought, and constitutional liberties such as freedom of assembly, freedom of speech, and germane property rights.

Programming of Humachines in this era would be achieved via collaboration between generative AI, Big Data, and human decision-makers with organizational network or collective intelligence at the enterprise level.

In the Superintelligence stage of control, the existence problem (maintenance of organization against entropy) is addressed through sustainability strategy where embodied, manifest cognition uses social responsibility, environmental stewardship and economic value creation to ensure the organization's ongoing survival.

At this level, the experience problem—or adapting goal-oriented processes to changing conditions—would be addressed through programmed mutations. For example, enterprise leaders could run computer simulations that allow various possible existences to be simulated in parallel and in real time, and a combination of digital twins, 3D printing, generative algorithms, and other forms of rapid forecasting, prototyping, and comparisons of hypothetical futures using Big Data and AI would allow enterprise leaders the ability to choose among various options for fitness enhancement and likelihood of success. Instead of having to wait and see, we could "fast forward" hypothetical futures and select whichever path gets us the desired result. This use of AI allows us to harness the power of evolution itself to increase the quality of information available to decision-makers. We may as well call this "intelligent design" as Dennett does in *From Bacteria to Bach and Back*. Intentionally facilitating organizational mutation by allowing leaders to witness emergent fitness enhancing features with generative evolutionary algorithms would enhance resilience by enabling rapid pivots in light of changing environmental conditions. We would learn lessons from the future and implement them in real time.

As for the evolution problem, as Beniger puts it, we have a hard time seeing around that corner. The way control systems evolve in the Level Four: Technology control era seems to be optimal: programs are diffused throughout the global market with differential adoption driven by variations in cultural, governmental and market selections. The result of these manifold selective pressures would seem to be worthy of replicating and strong enough to do so. How society will continue to evolve when control is handled by superintelligent Humachines is beyond our understanding as authors. It would likely take a Humachine—or perhaps an entire galaxy of them—to figure out how to handle what evolution itself couldn't sort out through natural selection.

Or perhaps the logarithmic timeline of emerging levels of control creates a black hole event horizon where evolution is happening so fast and revolutions are taking place in such quick succession that life itself is consumed into an infinitely dense maelstrom of matter, energy, and information controlled by programs inscrutable to all but God.

Another alternative is that Level Five: Superintelligence becomes the final level of control for life on Earth, at least for the foreseeable future. When we harness the power of evolution through generative evolutionary algorithms to create superintelligent organizations that are competing while also behaving in a sustainable manner relative to social, economic and environmental constraints, it would seem life would have reached an optimal point of *self-control*. Things theoretically couldn't get any better. No amount of further control would optimize the solutions to existence, experience, and evolution of organization that superintelligent Humachines had devised in an optimal manifestation of self-control.

A critical perspective on all this control talk is that the solution to the crisis of control after the Industrial Revolution helped so much, it created its own looming crisis: too much control by automation technology. The control revolution has gone too far, carried away by its own devices and imperial solutionist attitude toward all forms of life. Overreliance on systems of control will thwart the emergence of fitness enhancing mutations in humans, machines, ecosystems and enterprises. We need better programs for our organizations, as we are at risk of botsourcing our way into a stifling technocratic hegemony that fails to unlock human potential and instead locks us into self-perpetuating cycles of exploitation and too much control over biological life by synthetic life forms like automated hyperobjects.

Systems that know too much, control too much. We need some play in the joints for the machine of human civilization to not only survive but to thrive. We need to preserve the best features of the human mind—our creativity, compassion, dedication, care, and so forth—not simply replicate the logical information processing abilities of our minds and shunt the rest. This applies to organizations no less than individuals.

Indeed, our conviction is that empowering individual humans at work can create Humachines at the enterprise level, and when society has created enough Humachines, as a new kind of intelligent synthetic life form, they become an enabling layer for the emergence of superintelligence at the level of civilization. We are just now beginning to figure out the true extent of AI much less create Humachines so let us be optimistic about the future.

Jobs Are Going to Evolve but Not Disappear

Historically robots have been associated with replacing manual workers. However, the rapidly evolving capabilities of generative AI threaten knowledge workers. This means that everyone from every educational level needs to be prepared. This is confirmed by the findings of the World Economic Forum's The Future of Jobs Report 2023:

> While expectations of the displacement of physical and manual work by machines has decreased, reasoning, communicating and coordinating – all traits with a comparative advantage for humans – are expected to be more automatable in the future. Artificial intelligence, a key drive of potential algorithmic displacement, is expected to be adopted by nearly 75% of surveyed companies and is expected to lead to high churn – with 50% of organizations expecting it to create job growth and 2% expecting it to create job losses.[14]

Let's face it, some of us are going to lose our jobs because a machine replaced our function. In the medical community, for example, radiologists are vulnerable to displacement by advances in radiology technology. However, we must go beyond this first-generation job loss to contemplate the larger impacts of automation on work. While one generation of radiologists may be out of work, future medical-school students will likely choose an alternative career path within medicine and will apply their talents to other issues outside of radiology. This influx of human talent into other fields of medicine will create spillover benefits to all health care stakeholders, including patients, as human talent will be more efficiently allocated within the industry, at least in theory leading to better quality care and more innovation. Other professions are also vulnerable, such coders, accountants, paralegals, graphic designers, journals and other knowledge workers. Policymakers can help ease the pain of transition by lowering transaction costs associated with re-skilling.

While it is challenging to make precise forecasts of how *many* jobs will emerge in the Fourth Industrial Revolution, The Center for the Future of Work at Cognizant Technology Solutions has tried to describe certain *kinds* of jobs in its reports 21 Jobs for the Future.[15]

Cognizant offers an optimistic perspective on the future of human work, based on a few principles:[16]

- Work has always changed
- Lots of current work is awful
- Machines need man
- Don't underestimate human imagination or ingenuity
- Technology will upgrade all aspects of society
- Technology solves—and creates—problems

New and previously unimagined job titles may include: data detectives, AI-assisted healthcare technicians, chief trust officers, augmented reality journey builder, personal memory curator, man-machine teaming manager, personal data broker, and talkers. Cognizant even provides a mock-up of job descriptions for these positions.[17] The dark cloud cast by the fear of job losses obscures the much brighter future wherein we have so many jobs automated we can finally afford to apply our uniquely human skills to creative, aesthetic, emotional, caring, and joyful pursuits. In a more mundane forecast, AI will enable humans to be more productive at our typical drudgery. Either way, it's not all bad.

Maria Villablanca provided a great deal of optimism during our interview. She pointed out how new inventions over time would have been entirely unforeseeable when the enabling layer of technology was first invented:

> To find an analogy we can think back to early prehistoric times. Advent of discovery of fire. There is no way we could have anticipated then that we would have chefs and cooks, people that do fireworks. The same will be true with AI.[18]

So, maybe Chat GPT is the equivalent of the first time we discovered how to make spark from flint. Who knows what kind of pyrotechnics it will give rise to in the future?

Although employment in the financial services sector has contracted to date,[19] this is in part due to the Great Recession as much as it is to displacement by machines. Going forward, the most vulnerable jobs in the financial services sector are those ripe for automation—the US Bureau of Labor Statistics suggests that bank tellers and insurance underwriters will see a tangible decline in human employment. That said, financial services employers are hiring new talent in the areas of software development and data science. Large financial institutions are acquiring and investing in AI and machine learning-powered fraud detection and financial security start-ups in order to acquire technology and labor that can be strategic assets for the bank—evidence that the human skill set required to manage performance of financial institutions is *shifting* rather than *eroding*. Let us learn how to work with bots; they will soon be our colleagues.

According to Arvind Purushotham, the managing director of Citigroup's venture investing arm, the big problems facing financial institutions are not being solved by machines just yet, but by humans assisted by AI: "We think of human-assisted AI and AI-assisted humans," said Purushotham, "There are some things that humans can do that software programs can't hope to catch up to in decades."[20] This points to the emergence of a more symbiotic relationship between humans and machines. Here, both robots and machines depend on one another and improve by interacting with one another.

Still others predict that AI is coming for the financial services industry in a more corrosive way with respect to displacing human laborers. While automated teller machines (ATMs) are now a familiar sight on urban streets and inside grocery stores, they cost bank tellers a lot of jobs. Then with the advent of Internet and mobile banking, more human workers in the banking space were displaced as bank customers increasingly accessed banking resources through their phones and at home, rather than by driving to a bank and interacting with a person.

According to Suranga Chandratillake, a partner at London-based venture capital firm Balderton Capital, the next wave of displacement in financial services will be in "pseudo white-collar jobs," such as reviewing mortgage applications and adjusting insurance claims. These positions are lower in the corporate hierarchy than executive or manager, still characterized as requiring human judgment, but which would see performance improvements from AI in terms of increased speed, greater accuracy, and less bias.[21] Jobs that fit these characteristics are most susceptible to botsourcing.

The greatest impacts of AI are not in sloughing off human resource costs from the balance sheet as people are displaced by machines. That is a myopic view of the transformative potential of AI. This assumes humans are merely a cost, not an asset. We suggest looking at AI as a performance-enhancing additive, rather than an alternative to, human resources. Companies will see the greatest payout in terms of performance improvements if they can engender collaboration between humans and smart machines.

According to research in *Harvard Business Review*, humans and AI are already working together to create **collaborative intelligence**. "While AI will radically alter how work gets done and who does it, the technology's larger impact will be in complementing and augmenting human capabilities, not replacing them."[22]

We consider this perspective a powerful rebuke to the fear mongering over botsourcing. The real transformative impact of AI is not kicking human laborers to the curb but in equipping them with greater analytical and data-driven powers. Further, smart machines will need human coaches and interpreters.

People are needed to train machines, explain their outputs, and ensure their responsible use. AI, in turn, can enhance humans' cognitive skills and creativity, free workers from low-level tasks, and extend their physical capabilities.[23]

AI Is a Horizontal Enabling Layer

Automation of physical labor can lead to growth, not just efficiency gains. Amazon is plowing forward with a continued expansion of robot-human collaboration meant to improve efficiency in fulfillment centers.[24] Amazon explains that its expansion in the use of robots has led to *more* investments and *new* jobs.

In fact, facilities with robots tend to employ more humans than those without them because robots make these facilities more efficient and capable of processing more orders. Robots cannot do everything and more orders mean more humans are needed. In other words, *the robots might not take our jobs—they could very well make our jobs.*

As of publication, more than half a million robots work at Amazon's fulfilment centers, stocking inventory, filling orders, and sorting packages for delivery.[25] These robots autonomously deliver products to humans, who then pack the boxes that go out to customers. Amazon's warehouses have been partially automated for some time. Most use robots to carry shelves of products to human workers, who then select the items to be shipped. While the humans handle the complex manipulations that would confound a robot, the robots do the dull task of hurrying around the warehouse carrying heavy loads. Amazon is also testing a new class of robots that use AI and computer vision to roam freely throughout the fulfilment centers, the beginning of 'autonomous mobility.'[26]

In its warehouse in Monee, Illinois, humans and robots now work alongside one another to fill customer orders. The warehouse has more than 2,000 full-time employees working alongside a fleet of Kiva robots, delivering items to workers and helping them with tasks.

What is surprising is that despite the robot influence, the human jobs have not changed all that much. The robots just help to do the difficult tasks. Jobs for humans working alongside robots "aren't as different as you'd think" from what they had been doing in a warehouse without robots, said Jeff Messenger, the facility's general manager.[27] He explains that the robots handle things that would be considered grunt work. They move boxes and do things to help humans become more efficient, such as dispensing the right amount of packing tape and lifting heavy boxes. The robots are their helpers to add precision and handle the heavy work.

As we see with Amazon's warehouses and fulfillment centers, machines are being used in all sectors and all areas. The misconception, however, is that robots are actually meant to replace human labor. As the scenario with Amazon illustrates, robots are typically doing supporting roles that are challenging for humans. That said, we are probably only one or two steps away from completely automated factories—we just need some advancements in the robots' hand-like manipulation of objects and all but the most delicate packaging tasks could be botsourced. Robot designers in Boston will probably have patented a fully dexterous bipedal humanoid capable of knitting a sweater while tap dancing before this book is printed.

According to Peter Norvig, former NASA scientist, leading artificial intelligence scientist, and former director of research at Google, it is easy to foresee the downsides of the dramatic displacement of human laborers from the workforce but almost unimaginable what the upsides could be.[28] When the internal combustion engine displaced the horse-drawn buggy, it also led to the creation of millions of new jobs that were inconceivable at the time of the disruption.

Studies show that looking at specific jobs is not a good indicator of where machines will dominate. Rather it is work activities rather than actual occupations that will be given away to machines.[29] Repetitive, routine, and predictable problems that rely on electronically available data are the most easily automated. For automation to work, however, the requirement is that the knowledge and relevant decision criteria be very clearly defined and structured. The problem itself must be clear and well understood to be accurately programmed into the algorithms. Examples of this are seen in traditional manufacturing processes, such as assembly work, security monitoring, time tracking, shipping, and inventory decisions. These decisions are all pretty routine and easily specified, therefore easy to automate. We also see automation in banking, such as credit card and loan application processing as well as making changes to investment portfolios. These are all technical, tactical activities where the problems are easy to specify and the answers are based on data. Therefore, they are easy to automate.

The jobs that will remain the domain of humans are those that are unpredictable, require managing others, interacting with stakeholders, applying expertise and decision-making, and explaining decisions to others. Even though we have moved into the age of knowledge work being replaced by AI, it is also not possible to automate jobs that require a high degree of imagination, creativity, goal setting, or strategic thinking. It is also not possible to automate jobs that require a high degree of interpersonal interaction. This includes executive and leadership roles, management, medicine, education, as well as construction, forestry, physical therapists, personal trainers, negotiators, and hair stylists. These, for example, will continue to require uniquely human skills. Yes, chatbots are being tested for use in drive-through windows in fast-food venues, however that is because the menu is predetermined.

However, all these roles will be assisted with machines. Machines are not a threat, they are collaborators. This human–machine interaction is needed for humans to excel, to be more productive and efficient.

According to founder and former CEO of Amazon Jeff Bezos, we are in a golden age of AI and machine learning in enterprise:[30]

> We are solving problems with machine learning and artificial intelligence that were in the realm of science fiction for the last several decades. Machine learning and AI is a horizontal enabling layer. It will empower and improve every business, every government organization, every philanthropy—basically there's no institution in the world that cannot be improved with machine learning. I would say, a lot of the value that we're getting from machine learning is actually happening beneath the surface. It is things like improved search results. Improved product recommendations for customers. Improved forecasting for inventory management. Literally hundreds of other things beneath the surface. The most exciting thing that I think we're working on in machine learning, is that we are determined, through Amazon Web Services—where we have all these customers who are corporations and software developers—to make these advanced techniques accessible to every organization, even if they don't have the current class of expertise that's required. Right now, deploying these techniques for your particular institution's problems is difficult. It takes a lot of expertise, and so you have to go compete for the very best PhDs in machine learning and it's difficult for a lot of organizations to win those competitions. I think we can build a great business doing that, for ourselves, and it will be incredibly enabling for organizations that want to use these sophisticated technologies.

With these AI and machine-learning capabilities pioneered by Amazon, and made widely available to smaller enterprises through cloud computing, AI has become a horizontal enabling layer that empowers all who deploy it.

Complementary Coworkers: Moravec's Paradox Resolved

Humans and machines complement one another. The strengths of one are weaknesses of the other. As already mentioned, no greater example illustrates this than prognostication of progression of the Covid-19 pandemic. Although many models were used, it was ultimately scientists and physicians that considered output of the models and other data to make decisions. This illustrated how together humans and machines can offset the other's shortcomings and enhance the other's strengths. See **Figure 5.2.**

As enterprises seek to integrate human and machine laborers, the field of *social robotics* becomes more relevant. Social robotics is the study of "how

Figure 5.2 Moravec's paradox in management applications

people interact with artificially intelligent technology."[31] If an enterprise wants robots to inhabit the same spaces as people and function efficiency, we need to have robots trained to behave around humans. While prompt engineering is a tool for information gathering, social robotics is needed for the functionality of humans and machines in the physical space.

Machines are great at brute-strength analysis, precision in calculation, and processing speed. They can process huge data sets, identify patterns unimaginable to humans, and offer unparalleled accuracy. Nonetheless, generative AI model that is explicitly "designed to understand natural human language has to sort through millions of clues to establish enough context to make sense of something that is instantly obvious to a human."[32] Humans, on the other hand, can make connections using context clues, be creative and think "outside of the box." They are innovative, strategic, capable of leadership, have empathy and emotion, and capable of explaining the logic of their decisions.

This latter "human" capability bears emphasizing. Explaining the logic of an answer is crucial for all significant business decisions—not just what the answer is, but why it is the answer, and why it matters.

> Machines have no independent way to know if or why some results matter more than others unless they've been programmed with explicit parameters[.] What does it even mean to say something matters to a machine? Either a result is significant or it's not, based on what it has been told is significant.[33]

Although advancements are being made in cognitive computing, for instance using genetic algorithms and neural nets, these differences between humans' and machines' abilities to explain and justify will last for a long time.

A medical diagnostic AI can dig through years of data about cancer or diabetes patients and find correlations between various characteristics, habits, or symptoms in order to aid in preventing or diagnosing the disease. Does it matter that none of it 'matters' to the machine as long as it's a useful tool? Perhaps not, but it matters very much to those who want to build the next generation of intelligent machines.[34]

According to the former CEO of Google and Chairman of Alphabet Eric Schmidt, the concern about botsourcing is overblown because only the most routine jobs can be replaced, whereas most human work skills cannot be replicated by a machine. That said, "humans will need to work alongside computers in order to be more productive."[35]

Jeff Immelt, former CEO of General Electric, was more blunt in his assessment of the prediction of rampant cascading unemployment from botsourcing. According to Immelt, the notion that robots will completely run factories in five years is "bullshit."[36] Apparently we are still a long way off from widespread displacement, as there still remains far too much low-hanging fruit in terms of enhancing human productivity by augmenting human skills with technology.

Technological advancements and machine capabilities will continue to evolve and speed up. Similarly, humans will need to develop skills that add value in this new environment. Although many jobs will be eliminated, many more jobs will be created but with different skill requirements. Many of the new jobs will simply be new versions of "old-world" jobs. There will be tremendous demand for people who can design, program, monitor, and fix technology. There will be a huge demand for people who can explain data, findings, and machine insights to other humans. There will also be a need for people who can work with technology and its output, then interact with other humans—customers, patients, coworkers, superiors, and other stakeholders.

A better use of AI in the context of innovation would be, instead of substituting human creativity, supplementing it. For instance, a marketing department using AI could simulate what the impact would be on the marketplace if the company were to launch an innovative product—thus modeling the impact on company performance prior to sinking a fortune into the research, design, and launch. A marketing department could use AI to synthesize all products in a category and identify the best-selling features of those products, and then apply that insight as input into the product-design phase.

According to Sam Ellis, former Business Director of Innovation at the advertising agency M&C Saatchi, whereas in the past the agency's employees might have worried that using AI in advertising would kill off creativity, they have become excited about the power of harnessing AI to glean insights into potential customers. Take, for example, a coffee-brand ad featured in a poster displayed at a London bus stop. The poster was digital, not print, which means it could change like a chameleon. This poster would change from "drab grays and blocks of text" to "a minimalistic image with a short saying." While changing images in an advertisement is nothing too special, "what was unique about this particular poster … wasn't the fact that people were looking at it. Rather, it was looking at them—and learning."[37]

The poster featured an AI function that used facial tracking to monitor the eye movements of passersby and coupled this data with a genetics-based algorithm. This enabled the AI to identify which features of the posters were the most eye-catching and then internalized that feedback to modify the design. Each successive permutation of the advertisement would improve over prior iterations, learning and becoming more eye-catching as it evolved.

According to Ellis,

> We were surprised how quickly it learned." In less than three days, the AI-powered marketing technology "was creating posters in line with the current best practices in the advertising industry, which had been developed over decades of human trial and error like realizing three to five word slogans work best.[38]

To some readers this example will give them the creeps. It is uncanny that a poster would be monitoring its own viewers and modifying itself to become increasingly alluring. Is it possible these technologies will become all too effective, thereby invading consumer privacy (indiscriminately gleaning too much biometric data) or overriding consumer freedom of choice (by micro-targeting subconscious emotional triggers) to an unacceptable degree? We dive into that thicket in Chapter 6. For now, consider the upshot of this example, which is that AI can find applications even in the more "creative" of human enterprises, such as marketing and advertising.

Humans will increasingly work side by side with machines, their new coworkers. This will require humans to get better at the human–machine interface. While machines will do routine tasks, humans will need to develop social, emotional, and creative intelligence to strategically leverage these machine-enhanced capabilities. Further, nonroutine tasks that require social skills will continue to be done by humans. Just consider being a barber, hairdresser, makeup artist, or personal trainer. These jobs will require uniquely human skills and will not be replaced by a robot anytime soon. Jobs that require interpersonal caring, such as being a social worker, are also less amenable to being substituted by robots.

To work at the human–machine interface, humans will need to retain the qualities we discussed in Chapter 4. They need *literacy* in a broad set of areas, rather than being highly specialized. This will enable workers to connect different parts of their organizations and work with cross-functional teams and across flexible hierarchies. Certainly, employees will need to have their domain of expertise. However, they will need to have an understanding of the other areas with which they are interacting. Second, humans will need *competence* that links the technical with the human. This means technical literacy as well as the ability to be collaborative, creative, and emotionally aware. Lastly, humans will need to develop their *uniquely human traits*. They will need to develop their emotional intelligence, empathy, leadership skills, social and cultural awareness, ethical sensitivity, aesthetic taste, and so forth.

Augmentation, Amplification, and Other Performance Enhancers

As humans become comfortable collaborating with machines even though we may not realize it. When we get into our car, many of us boot up Google Maps and let the algorithms guide us to our destination. We may not be aware but we are collaborating with a machine. Voice assistants such as Apple's Siri and Amazon's Alexa have become commonplace and over time we predict most people will have access to a generally intelligent, up-to-date, reasonably reliable personal assistant powered by today's chatbot platforms. When we ask Siri, who lives inside our phone, to read emails, schedule appointments, or find the closest restaurant to us, we are collaborating with a machine. When we ask Amazon's Alexa, who resides in our smart speakers to set our house alarm or dim house lights, we are collaborating with a machine. Even apparently simple tasks like current weather updates and spam filters are all based on AI and involve some level of human–machine interaction.

In the next sections, we discuss examples of how machines are making humans better: augmentation, co-bots, amplification, creativity enhancement, innovation improvement, and learning enhancement. There are different levels of human–machine collaboration. At the basic level there is *autonomous intelligence*. This is where machines work independently from humans such as completely autonomous robots in factories. But at the intersection of technology and the humanities, we have augmentation, co-bots, amplification, enhancing creativity, improving innovation, and enhanced learning through visual analytics.

Augmentation

Augmented intelligence is where machines learn from human input and humans, in turn, are provided with information by the machines to make decisions that are more accurate. In numerous business disciplines, AI is able to hasten processes and provide decision-makers with reliable insights. For example, automation in marketing is one of the key features of Customer

Relationship Management (CRM) applications. Detailed market segmentation and campaign management are typically automated, providing invaluable and detailed customer insights. This enables the sales team to interact better with their customers and create microtargeted campaigns. There is a feedback loop between the algorithm and the team, as they augment the other's performance.

Augmentation of human skills by machines is taking place in every industry sector and even in our own lives. A great example is in the finance industry. Consider the investment firm Vanguard. It now has a "Personal Advisor Service" that interacts with clients and combines automated investment advice with guidance from human advisers.[39] The machine technology is set up to perform many of the traditional tasks of investment advising, constructing a customized portfolio based on customer profiles, such as automated rebalancing of portfolios. More routine tasks are automated while the human advisers serve as "investing coaches." They are the ones tasked with explaining, answering investor questions, and encouraging good financial behaviors. In Vanguard's words, the humans are "emotional circuit breakers" to keep investors on plan. Human advisers are even encouraged to learn about "behavioral finance" to perform these roles effectively.

This example clearly demonstrates the new skills human employees will need to have and the important role that emotions of human clients play in designing work functions. It shows that jobs are not being eliminated but are morphing. The humans explain the optimized AI output to other humans using language that will emotionally resonate and be trusted, lest it be ignored.

Vanguard describes its approach as a "hybrid product" that blends human advisers and automated investing. Karin Risi, head of Vanguard Personal Advisor Services, said the investment portfolio is just one piece of the puzzle, and people also need advice on spending their retirement savings, how to handle market drops, and other money matters. She explains that people increasingly don't need to talk to a human adviser about routine things. However, they absolutely must have a human interaction when there are changes in either the economy or a client's life. These are emotional events an algorithm is not competent to handle. "Many clients—and I would put myself among them—probably don't need to talk to their adviser until they need to talk to their adviser, whether it's a market downturn, I had a baby, I got divorced," says Risi.[40]

This augmented hybrid approach is becoming the norm in virtually every sector. It underscores that humans need to be prepared to learn different skills for new sets of jobs in order to interact with machines.

Co-bots

Co-bots is short for "collaborative robots" and are a "second wave" of robots intended to physically interact with humans in a shared workspace.

They are dedicated to teamwork with human employees and are specifically designed for that purpose. Unlike first-generation automation, advanced co-bots can now recognize people and objects, and they can work safely alongside humans. This ushers in a new wave of human–machine interaction.

This interaction takes augmentation to a new level and provides amplification of human abilities. Consider a situation where a co-bot might handle repetitive actions in a factory such as heavy lifting. Simultaneously a person can perform complementary tasks that a co-bot cannot do, tasks that require dexterity and human judgment. A good example is assembling a gear motor or doing delicate packing. However, this also has huge security and ergonomic implications in co-bot development and worker training. Not only would there be resistance from workers but also fear of being hurt by the sheer physical strength of the robot.

In the auto industry companies such as Ford and Hyundai are extending the co-bot concept with exoskeletons.[41] These wearable robotic devices, which adapt to the user and location in real time, are enabling industrial workers to perform their jobs with superhuman endurance and strength. They are also shielding workers from harm in doing physically difficult and dangerous tasks, almost making them superhuman.

Of course, wearable tech does not a Humachine make, but we appreciate the example of evolution in automation.

Amplification

Beyond mere physical augmentation the human–machine interface is moving to a relationship where each entity amplifies the other. Recently, Ken Goldberg, professor of engineering at UC Berkeley, introduced the concept of *multiplicity* to describe how AI will influence future workforces.[42] The idea is that the future of human–machine interaction will essentially result in humans amplifying—or multiplying—themselves.

Professor Goldberg pushes back against the fear of robots taking over the workforce and replacing humans. Rather, he describes a hybrid workforce composed of a diverse group of robots and humans working together to achieve superior results. Together they can accomplish far more than compared to what either group could accomplish working alone.

One example he points to is the AlphaGo competition where some of the world's top Go players began competing alongside the AlphaGo program. What were created were essentially human–machine teams where the players learned new strategies by studying AlphaGo's previous games, and the algorithm learned new strategies by studying the players.

This virtuous feedback loop of amplification is the type of system interaction we see in Google searches, recommendation systems for Netflix and Spotify, and all other AI systems. As Goldberg points out: "The important question is not when machines will surpass human intelligence, but how humans can work together with them in new ways."[43]

Enhancing Creativity

The augmentation and amplification just described have a tremendous impact on enhancing human creativity. Humans can use the machines as their "workhorse" to quickly dig up options as humans provide the specs. An example would be a *computer-aided design (CAD)* system that can generate thousands of design options for the designer that would meet the designer's specified goals and comply with design parameters. The designer can work on developing the specs and then submit them to the CAD system. Quickly, the CAD system can provide thousands of options. The designer can then look at them, refine, improve, and respecify. Iteratively, the designer and the CAD program running on the designer's computer work to create the ideal design.

This collaboration is now a reality. Autodesk's Dreamcatcher AI system is the next generation of CAD and does precisely that. Dreamcatcher is a generative design system that enables designers to create an initial set of specifications for their design problem with specific goals and constraints. That information is used by the algorithm to identify alternative design solutions that meet these objectives. Designers are able to explore trade-offs between many alternative approaches and work back and forth to improve their solutions.

For example, a designer may provide Dreamcatcher with specifications about a chair. The requirement may be that the chair is able to support a weight of up to 300 pounds, to have a seat 18 inches off the ground, and be made of materials costing less than $75. The designer can specify many other criteria such as preferred materials and colors and even preferences of other chair styles. The algorithm then churns out thousands of designs that match those criteria, often sparking ideas that the designers might not have initially considered. They can then respond to the algorithm, providing feedback and refining the designs to meet their evolving specifications. The algorithm that does the "heavy lifting" in terms of finding the designs that comply with the specs and the designers are now free to use their uniquely human abilities to create and exercise aesthetic judgment.

Improving Innovation

Machines are also improving innovation. Consider the pharmaceutical industry where Pfizer is using AI to accelerate the difficult process of drug discovery. An excellent example is research in immune-oncology, an emerging approach to cancer treatment that uses the body's immune system to help fight cancer, but which is extremely time consuming.[44] Immunooncology drugs can take up to 12 years to bring to market, requiring a labor-intensive process. Every year spent waiting on a discovery means so many potentially avoidable cancer deaths.

However, AI speeds this up dramatically by combining a complete literature review with Pfizer's own data, such as lab reports. Insights are continually made available to researchers—relationships that surface, hidden patterns that should speed the identification of new drug targets, combination therapies for further study, and patient selection strategies for this new class of drugs. All these AI-driven insights help researchers move faster in their quest to cure the emperor of all maladies. "AI has been sewn into the fabric of drug discovery at Pfizer."[45]

The success comes from the fact that AI can quickly and efficiently churn through thousands of scenarios. It can then identify scenarios that optimize certain criteria and maximize desirable outcomes.

Enhanced Learning Through Visual Analytics

An important aspect to human decision-making in the face of machine intelligence is how humans receive the data they are given. Successfully extracting intelligence from data depends in large part on how that data is visually presented. Studies have shown that data presentation can make a significant difference in how data is interpreted and the success of resulting decisions. The possibilities are especially important today, as technology has significantly advanced in data visualization, presentation, and manipulation.

Consider that very few people think in terms of numbers or data tables. Rather, humans are programmed to create a physical representation of a mental model.[46] Visualization not only helps in extracting intelligence, understanding relationships and patterns, and detecting trends. It is also effective in communicating the findings to an audience because it can easily be tailored to their background.

The idea behind *visual analytics* is to enable better, faster, and more actionable results from data by combining strengths of computerized analysis with human perception, human intelligence, and intuition in an integrated data analysis approach.[47] Computers are very powerful and efficient in large amounts of data processing, which could not be perceived by any human.

The problem, however, is that many real-world problems are not sufficiently well defined from the beginning. This is especially true given the complexity of today's business environment. Often, we first need to explore available data before we can capture the essence of the problem. Visual analytics provides the means to explore and discover relationships otherwise hidden from default assumptions in statistical modeling.

Visual analytics is an effective tool for audience-specific end-result conveyance. It is a tool that exploits and uses the hidden opportunities and knowledge resting in unexplored data sources. In many applications success depends on the right information being available at the right time.

The acquisition of raw data is no longer the problem, but rather it is turning that data into intelligence and knowledge. This problem is exacerbated by the fact that the amount of data is growing exponentially (Moore's Law) and visual analytics provides the means to "see" the data. This is an essential limitation of being human.

Visual analytics enables humans to process the data by making information "transparent" for an analytic discourse, providing the means of communicating about the data rather than just seeing results. It is therefore a medium, across which humans and machines cooperate.

While visual analytics is critical for extracting intelligence from large data sets, however, it is costly to implement, requiring investments in computer technology and highly trained specialists. As such, there are a few considerations in its implementation. The key to using visual analytics is to find the right balance between the trade-offs of the resources needed to support visualization and needs of the organization.

The first issue to consider is problem complexity, how difficult the problem is to solve, and the objectives of the analysis. For example, problems that require one single optimal solution may not need human involvement compared to problems where an array of multiple solutions may suffice and judgment calls are ultimately needed. A second issue is data quantity and quality, such as: how large the data set is, the number of variables involved, and how comprehensive and "clean" is the data. Third, there is the issue of user capability. Certainly it requires the ability to conduct analytics, but also the user must have domain knowledge and contextual knowledge that go well beyond understanding analytics itself.

These three issues—*problem, data, and user*—have to be considered in the trade-off between complete computerization and extreme interactivity of visualization. Certain problems can and should be completely automated and computerized. That is where the problem is well defined, the data complete, and there is a search for one optimal solution. Many problems don't rely on interpretation and may heavily rely on pure computation and analysis. At the other extreme are problems that are unstructured, do not have enough data, and rely on domain knowledge of the expert. Lastly, is the issue of problem importance. Some problems are more trivial, can easily be automated, and it may not be worthwhile to incur the costs of visual analytics.

Ultimately, organizations will have to make this trade-off when deciding whether to invest in visual analytics. Extracting intelligence from data enables humans to better understand the data being presented to them by their machine coworkers and will considerably enhance the human–machine collaboration.

The Human–Machine Interface

Machines have become the human "co-pilot." To use machines for everything from gathering routine information to enhancing creativity and innovation requires different human skills. Machines generate data, predictions, and information. Humans are needed to take the output and use it as a basis for their creativity, and come up with new ideas and designs. They also need to become skilled in prompt engineering, asking chatbots the right questions and interacting with them in a productive way. They are also needed to train machines, program them, and make adjustments based on the machine output. Humans are also needed to provide leadership and develop strategy. We are calling for new roles of human employees that play to our complementary strengths. See **Figure 5.3**.

How does a company get its human workforce in sync with its new bot coworkers? We answer this question next.

It is ultimately people (whether individuals or teams) that make the big decisions based on input from smart machines. Restructuring has to be focused on enabling that. As human beings, we have limited ability to consume and understand data.[48] The behavioral limitations of humans as decision-makers has been documented in hundreds of studies and is a practically an academic discipline in and of itself that has cut across fields of economics, psychology, and law. Machines must provide output that is visually presentable for decision-makers to be able to integrate it into decision-making. Much work has been done in creating useful data visualization and dashboards. These enable managers to not only view the critical variables but be able to manipulate values of certain variables and "see" changes in other dependent variables.

This is exactly what IBM's Watson computer was doing in a project with Memorial Sloan Kettering Cancer Center (MSK) in New York City.[49] Watson was being used to sift through volumes of data on patients and treatments and recommend the best course of treatment for a particular patient. It used predictive analytics, but that did not mean Watson provided an answer. Rather, Watson provided choices in courses of options. However, healthcare has a great deal of context and risk, and ultimately IBM's

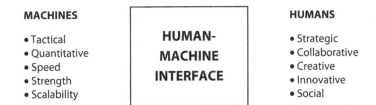

MACHINES	**HUMAN-MACHINE INTERFACE**	**HUMANS**
• Tactical		• Strategic
• Quantitative		• Collaborative
• Speed		• Creative
• Strength		• Innovative
• Scalability		• Social

Figure 5.3 Complementary strengths

Watson was seen as providing 'unsafe and incorrect' cancer treatments.[50] According to IBM Watson's Health deputy chief health officer, the problem had to do with the training data set used for Watson Health. Ultimately IBMs Watson Health was sold off for parts, although IBM Watson is going strong in other sectors—offering recommendations to companies in finance, accounting, supply chain and other areas. The problems with IBM Watson Health, however, illustrate the importance of human decision making in high risk decision making, challenges associated with training data sets used for AI, and importance of developing trust in machines.

A machine is not a crystal ball but simply gives probabilities of outcomes that help humans make the final decision. Nevertheless, humans need to have trust in the output in order to leverage these technologies.[51]

Developing Trust in the Machines

The human–machine interface can be seen as the intersection of two complementary coworkers. It can also be seen as bridging a "great divide," an ontological gulf separating two competing and very different information processing entities. Organizations will need strategies for their employees to accept their new coworkers and to trust the machines. This is one of the biggest problems faced by the companies to which we spoke. We strongly discourage any form of surgical intervention as a means of bridging the gap—there are better ways of integrating people and technology than by implanting hardware into human bodies. Indeed, we should cultivate a healthy distrust for this kind of cyborgization. Nonetheless trust in our machine coworkers is important.

Lack of trust in machines will result in employees adjusting the numbers provided by the algorithm. One of the companies we spoke with—a leader in analytics—had a problem where managers were simply modifying the numbers provided by analytics, as they did not trust the data. Others were continuing with routine decisions regardless of the data they were provided. This lack of trust truly defeats the purpose of adopting decision-support technology in the first place.

For true integration to occur, the people who make decisions need to not only have the data when they need it—but they also need to have confidence in the data. Companies need active strategies to develop trusting working relationships among the workforce, at all levels. Implementing technology will not help us if we treat it with disdain.

The companies we spoke with that made headway in human–machine interface considered the "great divide" as a reality and actively prepared for it. These are some of the strategies they followed.

First, it was imperative for leaders to communicate their vision to the organization with transparency. This includes their goals for technology, how the organization will be changing, how all ranks of people will be affected, how the change will take place and over what time frame. This also includes a vision of where the organization is going and what this future will look like. Updates need to be delivered on a regular basis with a chance for follow-up questions and answers. This is an extremely important element so that people's fear doesn't get the best of them. Rumors about impeding job losses can quickly begin to dominate watercooler talk, leading to a talent flight. Without openness and regular updates, you may create the conditions for your human workers to sabotage the technology or engender other forms of resistance, in turn creating negative pressure on productivity, morale, and economic performance. Fear erodes the ability of humans to think intuitively. Creating pervasive fear of displacement is a quick way to ruin a company's culture.

Second, companies need to go beyond providing basic technology training for their talent. Certainly, ongoing technical training in using the technology is a necessary part of implementation. However, a few of the companies found it very helpful to arrange for "visits" to other companies that were using the same or similar technologies. Providing a model enabled people to actually "see" how the technology is used and how the workers engage with the technology. This can certainly be difficult to arrange if the model comes from a competitor. But in a situation where the companies are not competing there may be openness for such a visit.

Seeing how others work creates a personal experience. It goes a long way toward building trust and acceptance. Once mastery of the technical aspects has been achieved, a pilot implementation on a limited scale is imperative. This will serve to solidify what has been learned, ensure that all is functioning smoothly, and will aid acceptance.

Third, a useful step in gaining acceptance is providing users with several final versions of the technological tools they will be engaging with and allowing them to make the final selection from the alternatives. This creates a sense of ownership and allows the enterprise to identify possible points of failure before wider implementation efforts take place. Including employees in the process of adoption creates trust by allowing participation in the effort rather than having it imposed upon them. This is beyond mere training on the technology itself but rather giving employees who will be using the technology the opportunity to understand the potential problems, the option to reject the technology, and to solicit help in getting teams ready to adopt it. These strategies leverage human emotions of fear and curiosity, and provide a sense of respect and communal belonging, without which you run the risk of failure in technology adoption, not unlike the body of a recipient of an organ donation rejecting an organ transplant.

Fourth, an important part of implementation strategy is directed at the management level of the organization. Much of the discussion on technology acceptance tends to focus on either frontline employees or top leadership. However, middle management is the linchpin between top strategy and direct implementation. Unlike employees who interface with technology at the operational level, managers are intermediaries whose attitudes toward technology will filter down toward the employees who report to them. A few of the companies we spoke with found it effective to use interviews or conduct anonymous surveys of management. The purpose was to uncover hidden attitudes and opportunities for development at the managerial levels. The insights from these interviews and questionnaires helped to develop training for managers, uncover hidden opportunities, and develop new incentives. One lower-level manager confided that the company "actually paid attention to the responses and made appropriate changes." He said the people were thrilled and more open to embracing new technology because this manager-level feedback was actually internalized by executives.

Ultimately, the human-machine interface will come down to human emotions. Machines will do whatever they are programmed to do. However, it is humans who may have a harder time adjusting. We aren't so easily programmed. Our training takes place over years if not decades. Whether integration of AI and humans is a success will be make or break for many companies.

The CEO and founder of Fetch Robotics, Melonee Wise, puts it well. She emphasizes that the technology itself is just a tool—just like any other tool—and one that leaders can use how they see fit. Machines can be used to replace human work, or companies can choose to use them to augment it. "Your computer doesn't unemploy you, your robot doesn't unemploy you," she said. "The companies that have those technologies make the social policies and set those social policies that change the workforce."[52]

Human Resources in the Artificial Intelligence Era

We have made an effort to push back against the fearmongering over bot-sourcing. We predict that AI will make, not take, our jobs. We have underscored how artificial intelligence in the workplace should make humans more valuable, not less, that smart machines can make our work environments more personal, intuitive, and humane. It is up to managers to find the right combination and balance of human-held versus automated tasks. Allocating workflows between humans, machines, and some combination thereof is the new priority for human resource managers.

AI will have tremendous implications for human resource management. Foreseeable trends include impacts to recruitment, training, performance of existing tasks, and the formation of entirely new job descriptions.

Applications of AI in the recruitment and hiring process pays off in terms of reduced time to hire, increased productivity for recruiters, and enhanced candidate experience.[53] For example, when DBS Bank's Talent Acquisition team deployed JIM, an AI-powered virtual recruitment bot, they saw tremendous gains in these dimensions. "JIM," the familiar name of a popular character from *The Office*, actually stands for Jobs Intelligence Maestro. Using JIM, DBS Bank was able to reduce candidate screening time from 32 minutes to 8 minutes per candidate. That is substantial time savings, especially when processing thousands of candidates for any given job posting.

Botsourcing the candidate screening function to JIM has allowed the human recruiters to focus on those uniquely human functions of the recruiting process where emotional intelligence, interpersonal communication skills, and creative expression are key—for instance, explaining the culture and values of the bank to make sure that the candidates were not only qualified on paper (which the AI can do) but, to use a very subjective phrase, whether the candidate would be a "good fit" with the team.

According to James Loo, head of the Talent Acquisition Group for DBS Bank, JIM has contributed to the team already because his human recruiters have been freed up to "perform higher-value work such as sourcing, recruitment marketing, engaging with candidates, and hiring managers."

In the prior chapter, we discussed uniquely human skills and traits such as caring, emotional intelligence, and aesthetic taste. We predict that emotional intelligence will be as important as technical intelligence in the future of work. Even with advanced technological tools in play, we will still need human marketers with emotional intelligence who can read the room when delivering a sales pitch; we will still need human designers with aesthetic sensibilities when creating the user experience interface of new technology. Creating automated voices that sound pleasing to listeners of different linguistic backgrounds is an example of the kind of job that will need human input from a subjective, sensory-based perspective.

Empathy is one of those emotional skills that we are unlikely to automate in the next several decades, if ever. While we could teach a computer to parrot empathic speech patterns, we do not think it would have the same effect as human empathy. Creating a meaningful interpersonal connection with someone with empathy is like being funny—not everyone knows how to do that, and it is not readily programmable.

As more customer service functions are automated, it makes sense to invest in human interpersonal skills to be proactive in filling the void. For example, Bank of America is rolling out a nationwide empathy training program for client-facing employees. John Jordan leads The Academy and Advisor Development at Bank of America. He calls the training a "life stage navigation curriculum" that helps bank staff understand the priorities and fundamental concerns of clients depending on where they are in life—a task that requires emotional intelligence and empathy.[54] This is playing to our strengths.

Dangers of Overreliance: Atrophy

There are additional reasons why it is important to include people in organizational processes and decision-making and not exclusively rely on technology. There is only so far we should go in botsourcing. Just because we can automate a function doesn't necessarily mean we should. In our endeavor to praise working with machines, let's not lean too hard on the walking stick. If we become too dependent upon technology, we expose ourselves to risks. What happens when we automate several crucial functions, giving them over exclusively to the machines, but then the power goes out and the robots are out of commission? We could be left in a bind. We can describe the inability for human resources to perform previously human-executed tasks that have been botsourced as *overreliance atrophy*.

Indeed, technology has the potential to make businesses more effective and efficient. But ramping up utilization of technology has a number of potential drawbacks. It is the *combination* of people and technology (not just the adoption of *more* technology) that creates the Humachine, when strengths of one offset the weaknesses of the other.

Another risk of over-reliance is the *self-fulfilling prophecy problem*. Exclusive dependence on technology raises the physical and operational risk of machine malfunction. For the most part, technology works smoothly, while enabling innovation and conveniences that have made our lives more fulfilling and our jobs more productive. However, relying exclusively on technology without backup plans creates a risk of dependence.

If any one of these shuts down, the organization and its people will likely not know what to do until power is restored. These potential breakdowns are not only a headache. They create significant risk. This is especially true as today's technology increasingly controls entire systems not just localized functions. Just consider the technology that already controls systems such as airline routes, electrical grids, financial markets, street traffic lights, and communication technology. As companies automate infrastructure controls, they need to be building in privacy, security, and backup systems, and include people in this process to avoid atrophy in the skills needed to step in if automated systems crash. We discuss legal frameworks to manage these AI risks in Chapter 6.

This underscores the connection between electricity-dependent infrastructure and management decisions. From a human resource point of view, there can be too much of a good thing—too much reliance on machines can create undesirable consequences within the workforce (as well as in an educational context). Just as machines cannot answer "why" the answer provided is the correct answer, or why it matters, humans who rely too much on machines for analysis will also lose the ability to answer these philosophical questions.

Say you give your analyst a problem to solve, and the analyst types in a query to a database using a search engine, which processes a million pieces of data in a second and spits out a result. The analyst gives you the answer, but when you ask it why that answer is correct, you are met with a blank stare. It is not enough for the analyst to say, "Because the computer says so."

Per Kasparov, "The problem comes when the database and the engine go from coach to oracle. I tell my students that they have to use the engine to challenge their own preparation and analysis, not to do it for them."[55] Kids these days! They want to skip the hard part where they actually learn to do the analysis and "show their work" along the way (a phrase you may recall from primary school algebra assignments).

Both students and employees may be tempted to skip the crunchy analytical process and jump to a quick and ready result. As a result, if this is enabled and encouraged by institutional design or by management practices, organizations risk merely accepting blindly the outcomes of machine analytics and thereby lose the ability to verify whether the outcome is actually correct or to understand why it is correct. If we treat AI as a crystal ball instead of a fallible colleague, we cease being scientific and revert to mystical thinking.

Overreliance on machines for analysis can lead to an atrophy of the cognitive capabilities that set humans apart from machines and in some ways keeps us indispensable in the first place: our ability to explain from context, to understand, to answer the *why* question. This is one of those slowly emerging risks, as intellectual atrophy does not happen overnight.

"Overreliance on the machine can weaken, not enhance, your own comprehension if you take it at its word all the time."[56] It's the proverbial frog in boiling water, as one generation of workers who grew up using slide rules is replaced by a generation of workers that were born with smartphones in their cribs. Despite its slow pace the risk is real. Kasparov worries, "It's like taking a boat out into the middle of a lake and only realizing when the boat springs a leak that you don't know how to swim."[57]

Another way to approach the problem of overreliance atrophy is not just from the loss of the ability to answer the "why" question, but also the atrophy of our ability to *innovate*. "If we rely on our machines to show us how to be good imitators, we will never take that next step to becoming creative innovators."[58]

An AI system tasked with designing a new product could apply pattern-recognition capacities and machine learning algorithms, but this is going to create only a product with features already contained in the extant marketplace and will not create something novel. There will be no fundamental innovation if we rely on traditional data analysis and machine learning to do the thinking for us. The marketing department, dominated by an AI program that tells us what the next product should be, can only spit out iterations of existing products—amalgams of the features of other products that have sold well. This may be acceptable to shareholders in the near term if it leads to profit, but it leads to intellectual stagnation in the long run. There are only so many ways to reinvent the wheel and still remain competitive.

Conclusion

Humans will not be put out to pasture anytime soon. We no longer employ banks of switchboard operators or elevator attendants, and somehow we survived.

Automation will displace the worst possible jobs—for example, ones that are physically dangerous or extremely boring. No one is going to miss bomb diffusion by hand or processing piles of mortgages. Machines are tools, and tools need a user for relevance and maintenance.

Bolstered by AI, our imaginations will be set free to discover and explore reality with ever-greater processing power. We can create a future that suits ourselves.

Major portions of the global economy—transportation and healthcare infrastructure, for example—are in dire need of an overhaul. Technology will be a critical tool in solving these hard problems, which will have major efficiency gains, each in turn significantly enhancing the quality of human life.

For every problem technology solves, it will likely cause a few more—so there will never be an end to human work. In the next chapter, we discuss how modern legal and regulatory systems in the developed world are rising to the challenge of ensuring AI is deployed safely.

Notes

1 John Sicard, President & CEO, Kinaxis, Interview January 5, 2023.
2 Moravec, Hans P. *Mind Children: The Future of Robot and Human Intelligence* (1988 Harvard University Press).
3 Kasparov, Garry. *Deep Thinking: Where Machine Intelligence Ends and Human Creativity Begins*, p. 246 (2017 Hatchet Books).
4 Bostrom, Nick. Superintelligence: Paths, Dangers, Strategies. Oxford University Press, 2014, 58–59.
5 Lomas, Natasha. "We should not talk about jobs being lost but people suffering," says Kasparov, *TechCrunch*, May 17, 2017. Available at https://techcrunch.com/2017/05/17/we-should-not-talk-about-jobs-being-lost-but-people-suffering-sa ys-kasparov-on-ai/
6 Ibid.
7 https://www.weforum.org/reports/the-future-of-jobs-report-2023/
8 Beniger, J. R. The Control Revolution (1986 Harvard University Press), p. 102.
9 Ibid., p. 102.
10 Ibid., p. 66.
11 "To have some mechanism that might be programmed and the matter and energy in which to store its programming is the problem of existence or being. Experience or behaving involves the problem of maintaining control regardless of the inputs to an existing program. To be able to reprogram and thereby adapt to new contingencies is the problem of evolution or becoming. Taken together, the three problems subsume all those of programmed control because they exhaust the three different temporal dimensions of one universal problem: how to maintain organization counter to entropy … Reprogramming is the general solution

to problems of both behavior and evolution in all living systems … We emphasize not the temporal aspects of the three problems but rather their functional implications as essential elements of control, the solution to any one of which can have unanticipated consequences for the other two. Proliferation of a new control technology, for example, can have major effects on the evolution of programming." Ibid., p. 67.

12 Ibid., pp. 103–104.
13 Ibid., p. 104.
14 Ibid.
15 21 Jobs of the Future, Cognizant Technology Solutions. November 28, 2017. Available at www.cognizant.com/perspectives/21-jobs-of-the-future
16 Ibid.
17 Ibid.
18 Villablanca, Maria P. Transformation Influencer, Mentor and Keynote Speaker, Co-Founder and CEO, Future Insights Network, Interview on January 16, 2023.
19 https://www.npr.org/2023/01/20/1150430512/wall-street-sees-a-wave-of-layoffs-a s-big-banks-face-pressure-to-shrink-payrolls
20 Levy, Ari. How Software Is Eating the Banking Industry. February 15, 2017. CNBC Future of Work. Available at www.cnbc.com/2017/02/15/how-softwa re-is-eating-the-banking-industry.html
21 Ibid.
22 Wilson, H. James and Paul R. Daugherty, Collaborative Intelligence: Humans and AI Are Joining Forces. Harvard Business Review, July–August 2018, p. 116.
23 Ibid.
24 Alison DeNisco Rayome. Amazon doubles-down on hybrid human/robot workforce in Illinois warehouse. Tech Republic. April 2, 2018.
25 https://www.amazon.science/latest-news/the-quest-to-deploy-autonomous-robots- within-amazon-fulfillment-centers#:~:text=Every%20day%20at%20Amazon% 20fulfillment,and%20sorting%20packages%20for%20delivery
26 Ibid.
27 Ibid.
28 Hunter, Matt. Here's How One of Google's Top Scientists Thinks People Should Prepare for Machine Learning. CNBC Future of Work. April 29, 2017. Available at www.cnbc.com/2017/04/29/googles-peter-norvig-how-to-prepare-for-ai-job-los ses.html
29 Chui, M., J. Manyika, and M. Miremadi (July, 2016). Where Machines Could Replace Humans—and Where They Can't (Yet). McKinsey Quarterly. Retrieved January 13, 2018. Available at www.mckinsey.com/business-functions/digital-m ckinsey/our-insights/where-machies-could-replace-humans-and-where-they-cant-yet
30 Bishop, Todd. Jeff Bezos Explains Amazon's Artificial Intelligence and Machine Learning Strategy. May 6, 2017. Available at www.geekwire.com/2017/jeff-bezo s-explains-amazons-artificial-intelligence-machine-learning-strategy/
31 Kasparov, Garry and Greengard, Mig. Deep Thinking: Where Machine Intelligence Ends and Human Creativity Begins, p. 71, PublicAffairs, 2017.
32 Ibid., p. 75.
33 Ibid., p. 72.
34 Ibid., p. 77.
35 Kharpal, Arjun. A.I. Will Create More Jobs That Can't Be Filled, Not Mass Unemployment. CNBC. June 16, 2017. Available at www.cnbc.com/2017/06/16/a i-robots-jobs-alphabet-eric-schmidt.html.
36 Ibid.

37 Castillo, Michelle. Even the Mad Men Could Be Replaced by Machines Someday. *CNBC*. February 24, 2017. Available at www.cnbc.com/2017/02/24/artificial-intelligence-and-creative-work.html.
38 Ibid.
39 Davenport, Thomas H. and Ronanki, Rajeev. Artificial Intelligence for the Real World. *Harvard Business Review*, January–February 2018.
40 Reklaitis, Victor. Here's the Advice You Get from Vanguard's New Robot-Human Hybrid. *MarketWatch*, December 2015.
41 Howard, Bill. Ford's Factory Floor Exoskeleton Vest: "Power Without Pain". *ExtremeTech*, June 20, 2018.
42 Goldberg, Ken. The Robot Human Alliance, *The Wall Street Journal*, June 11, 2017; Call It Multiplicity: How Humans and Machines Can Work Together, Berkeley IEOR June 12, 2017.
43 Ibid.
44 Mukherjee, Sy. How Pfizer and IBM Are Teaming Up to Develop Next-Gen Cancer Drugs. *Fortune*, December 1, 2016.
45 https://www.biospace.com/article/pfizer-doubles-down-on-ai-ml-to-bring-transformative-medicines-to-patients-/#:~:text=%E2%80%9CAI/ML%20has%20been%20sewn,what%27s%20happening%20behind%20the%20scenes.%E2%80%9D
46 Winkenbach, M. Using Visualization to Connect Humans and Analytics in Supply Chain Decision Making. Webinar September 2017, MIT, Center for Transportation and Logistics.
47 Keim, D., Andrienko, G., Fekete, J. D., Görg, C., Kohlhammer, J. and Melançon, G. Visual Analytics: Definition, Process, and Challenges. In *Information Visualization. Lecture Notes in Computer Science*, edited by Kerren, A., Stasko, J. T., Fekete, J. D. and North, C. vol. 4950 (2008 Springer).
48 Dean, Derek and Webb, Caroline. *Recovering from Information Overload*. McKinsey & Company, January 2011. Available at www.mckinsey.com/insights/organization/recovering_from_information_overload
49 Hempel, Jessi. IBM's Massive Bet on Watson. *Fortune*, October 7, 2013.
50 https://www.theverge.com/2018/7/26/17619382/ibms-watson-cancer-ai-healthcare-science
51 https://slate.com/technology/2022/01/ibm-watson-health-failure-artificial-intelligence.html
52 Keim, D., G. Andrienko, J. D. Fekete, C. Görg, J. Kohlhammer, and G. Melançon. Visual Analytics: Definition, Process, and Challenges. In *Information Visualization. Lecture Notes in Computer Science*, edited by Kerren, A., Stasko, J. T., Fekete, J. D. and North, C., vol. 4950 (2008 Springer).
53 Meister, Jeanne. Ten HR Trends in the Age of Artificial Intelligence. *Forbes.com*. January 8, 2019. Available at www.forbes.com/sites/jeannemeister/2019/01/08/ten-hr-trends-in-the-age-of-artificial-intelligence/#691269c03219
54 Ibid.
55 Kasparov, Garry and Greengard, Mig. *Deep Thinking: Where Machine Intelligence Ends and Human Creativity Begins*, p. 227, PublicAffairs, 2017.
56 Ibid., p. 228.
57 Ibid., p. 228.
58 Ibid., p. 229.

Chapter 6

Legal Issues in the Humachine Era

Disclaimer: This chapter discusses legal issues; however, it does not contain legal advice. This chapter includes hypothetical discussions of legal issues for educational purposes only. Reading this chapter does not create an attorney-client relationship with the authors. If you need legal advice, consult with an attorney licensed in your jurisdiction.

You Cannot Botsource the Discharge of Fiduciary Duties

While there are laudable advances in using chatbots to help legal research and lawyers realize efficiency gains in legal practice, lawyers must proceed with caution in using AI to practice law. Similar to the practice of medicine, the professional standards for lawyers are exacting, requiring the highest degree of care and conscientiousness with how they conduct themselves in official business. Like many white-collar professionals, lawyers have an ethical code and standards of conduct that apply to license holders. These professional obligations cannot be delegated to a bot. In other words, you cannot botsource ethical judgment, you cannot botsource the discharge of fiduciary duties.

One of the ethical rules for lawyers is that we shall not misrepresent the law to any tribunal. According to the American Bar Association Model Rules of Professional Conduct, Rule 3.3: Candor Toward the Tribunal, (a) A lawyer shall not knowingly: (1) make a false statement of fact or law to a tribunal or fail to correct a false statement of material fact or law previously made to the tribunal by the lawyer.

What happens when a lawyer uses ChatGPT to help write a legal brief filed with a court? This happened in *Mata v. Avianca, Inc.*, 1:22-cv-01461, (S.D.N.Y.). An attorney used one of the available chatbots to help write a legal brief that he used in an actual case. The problem started when the lawyer decided not to check the bot's work product; instead he simply passed it off as his own without critically examining the output of the bot for veracity. The bot provided wholly fabricated names of cases as "authority" to support the legal propositions advanced by the attorney. As

DOI: 10.4324/9781003322832-6

chatbots tend to do, the output was delivered in an authoritative tone, referencing various cases that were styled as per the usual format (e.g., plaintiff name versus defendant name, number of the case, name of the court). The problem is, these case names were wholly fabricated ("hallucinated") by the chatbot.

When asked to furnish the underlying judicial decisions to support the made-up cases referenced, the lawyer again asked the chatbot to produce the work. The result was a stack of fake cases, fake judicial opinions, that would support the fake citations. An entire court proceedings and judicial opinions that appeared on their face to be authentic but did not actually appear anywhere in the library of actual cases. When the court found out, it was displeased.

Judge P. Kevin Castel issued an order to show cause, which means in non-lawyer speak, "you are ordered to appear before the court to give us a good reason why we shouldn't sanction you!" The Order to Show cause provides:

> Let [the attorney who used a bot to practice law] show cause at the hearing... why he ought not be sanctioned pursuant to [the Federal Rules of Civil Procedure and] the inherent power of the Court for the use of a false and fraudulent notarization in his affidavit[.] Let the law firm [employing that lawyer] show cause at the hearing... why it not be sanctioned... for the following: (A) the citation of non-existent cases to the Court...; (B) the submission to the Court of copies of non-existent judicial opinions...; and (C) the use of a false and fraudulent notarization in the affidavit filed[.]

Using a chatbot to help write legal briefs is not the only way that lawyers could step on the proverbial rake. Using AI systems to automate the practice of law is fraught with risk. Yes, automation is great for handling large volumes of data and streamlining repetitive processes, however the practice of law requires careful judgment and individual care and attention given to each client. What happens when a law firm uses AI to scale, filing thousands of lawsuits at a time using an automated process lacking human oversight?

At least one law firm has tried this, serving up an object lesson for the rest of the bar. In the wake of devastating hurricanes that lashed the Gulf Coast of the United States, one law firm attempted to use AI to serve thousands of clients at once. Coming up against a statute of limitations that would prevent clients from bringing a claim for payment against their insurance company, a law firm tried to beat the deadline by using AI to aggregate thousands of cases and file them all at once. According to one of the founding partners that claims to have invested millions of dollars into his law firm practice management technology,

My firm is doing things that have never been done in quantities that have never been done. We're helping more people than have ever been helped in the history of storms... I believe it was Zuckerberg who said change is always met with resistance.[1]

Silicon Valley's "move fast and break things" mantra may not be entirely apt for certain professions.

In this case, the resistance is nothing less than US District Judge James Cain, Jr., presiding over the voluminous hurricane lawsuits filed in his court. In a hearing, other lawyers introduced evidence that the avant-garde firm had "filed duplicate lawsuits, filed lawsuits on behalf of clients that the firm didn't represent, claimed hurricane damage to properties that were nowhere near the path of a hurricane, [and] sued carriers that did not insure the property."[2] Yet another example where the bots need human oversight. In the race to automate we cannot lose the human touch. While AI may increase efficiency, it should not do so at the cost of human values such as accountability and transparency. According to court transcripts, Judge Cain offered up a priceless quote about the use of AI in legal practice:

I've heard some stuff about y'all. 'We're a technology firm. We've got all this artificial intelligence.' Let me tell you something. It may be artificial but it's certainly not intelligent. This is not how you represent people. You need to meet with these people individually.[3]

While we are confident the legal profession will enjoy the use of AI eventually, the state of the art today is not yet ready for its day in court. Until that day comes, lawyers, doctors, and licensed professionals who hold the fate of others in their hands must be careful delegating any part of their professional responsibility to a bot. AI is not a substitute for human judgment especially in circumstances where professional responsibilities impose a higher standard of care than what is expected of an ordinary person.

Aligning AI, Human Values and Law

While we may be tempted to botsource everything from data entry to management, using AI to monitor and police the workforce could very well be illegal.[4] Not all AI tools are viable at work. With so many shiny new objects entering the market, it can be tempting to implement for efficiency gains now and ask questions later. But moving fast and breaking things may also be illegal, and as regulators get briefed on the way these tools really work, we expect the *laisse fair* approach to Silicon Valley to come to an end.

In general, this chapter is concerned with so-called "alignment" problems, which is to align the design and applications of AI with human values as they are reflected in the legal systems of various governments. At first blush this is a problematic endeavor because of how little "ethics" make their way into corporate R&D budgets, but also because the notion of ethics, much less universal ethics, stimulates controversy and debate among philosophers. Nonetheless we do have some basic non-controversial norms that come from civil society organizations and influential trade groups to guide us. The law is where ethics get teeth.

AI systems have not been granted legal personhood in the way corporations have. At least, not yet. That said, the minute AI systems take on legal personhood, a chapter about legal issues would require an entirely new approach, where we talk about the rights and responsibilities of the robots *per se*, and in so doing, are forced to critically examine the foundations of modern morality and law. That is because robots (and the software systems that appear to animate them) occupy social situations that defy our existing moral and legal categories, especially as they become more advanced, begin to approach "sentience" or "consciousness," begin to take on more responsibility for the welfare of human users, and otherwise begin to appear more and more worthy of being treated as ends-in-themselves and not mere instrumentalities for human use. In brief, while bots are "merely" a *thing*, they also exhibit elements of *personhood*; the issues of "robot rights" are vexing and may prompt us to reappraise questions of morality and law that had long been considered settled.[5]

As interesting and compelling as these philosophical issues may be, this book is meant to be a *practical* (albeit thoughtful) guide for leaders who run actual enterprises, embedded in actual economies, dealing with actual problems, under actual resource constraints. So please forgive us if we gloss over what are rightly perceived as crucial philosophical or theoretical issues in jurisprudence, ethics and ontology as we try to remain grounded in the prevailing economic, legal and moral systems while seeking an optimal allocation of the human and technical resources presently at hand. By remaining grounded in what is, perhaps our guidance can bring what is closer to what ought to be.

Thus, when we discuss legal issues in the field of AI, we are not talking about whether robots have (or should have) legal rights and responsibilities; but, rather, whether and how the legal system addresses the issues presented by the widespread utilization of AI in the real world.

There are many societal-scale risks from AI. **Figure 6.1** is an example of a taxonomy of such risks. **Figure 6.2** goes further by providing a decision tree for classifying AI harms.

We invite philosophers and legal scholars to unpack the constitutional, regulatory, jurisprudential, ethical and ontological implications of our claim that humachines are a form of collective, organizational network intelligence that is something greater than the sum total of its parts. To respect those fields (we would at best muddle through the issues without appropriate nuance as we are so dreadfully practical in our approach) therefore, we set

Figure 6.1 Taxonomy of societal scale risks from AI[6]

these captivating issues to the side to focus on the legal protections that safeguard the development and use of artificially intelligent systems today.

Ethical Frameworks—Soft Law for AI

AI is subject to "soft law" (non-binding institutional norms). While lacking an enforcement mechanism or "teeth" (some kind of penalty for non-compliance), trade societies can have a meaningful impact on ethical standards by creating consensus and promulgating standards. For example, the Institute of Electrical and Electronics Engineers (IEEE) launched a *Global Initiative on Ethics of Autonomous and Intelligent Systems*. The IEEE Global Initiative's mission is, "To ensure every stakeholder involved in the design and development of autonomous and intelligent systems is educated, trained, and empowered to prioritize ethical considerations so that these technologies are advanced for the benefit of humanity."[7] How this lofty mission gets translated into concrete action is summarized in **Figure 6.3.** Conceptually the conceptual framework begins with three pillars that reflect anthropological, political, and technical consensus of the institute:[8]

1   Universal Human Values: A/IS can be an enormous force for good in society provided they are designed to respect human rights, align with human values, and holistically increase well-being while empowering as many people as possible. They should also be designed to safeguard our environment and natural resources. These values should guide policy

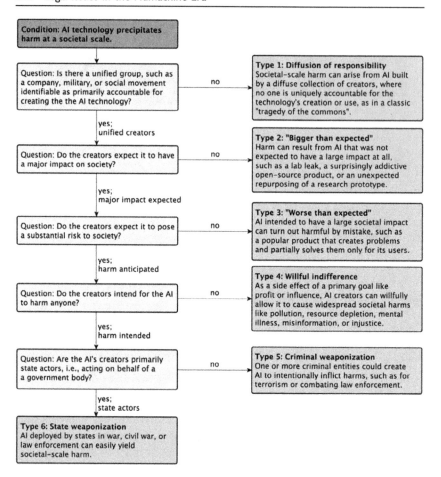

Figure 6.2 Decision-tree for classifying AI harms

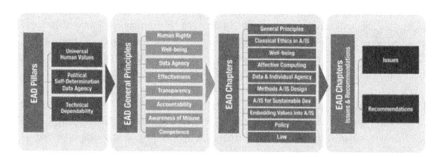

Figure 6.3 IEEE's *ethically aligned design* conceptual framework[12]

makers as well as engineers, designers, and developers. Advances in A/IS should be in the service of all people, rather than benefiting solely small groups, a single nation, or a corporation.

2   Political Self-Determination and Data Agency: A/IS—if designed and implemented properly—have a great potential to nurture political freedom and democracy, in accordance with the cultural precepts of individual societies, when people have access to and control over the data constituting and representing their identity. These systems can improve government effectiveness and accountability, foster trust, and protect our private sphere, but only when people have agency over their digital identity and their data is provably protected.

3   Technical Dependability: Ultimately, A/IS should deliver services that can be trusted. This trust means that A/IS will reliably, safely, and actively accomplish the objectives for which they were designed while advancing the human-driven values they were intended to reflect. Technologies should be monitored to ensure that their operation meets predetermined ethical objectives aligning with human values and respecting codified rights. In addition, validation and verification processes, including aspects of explainability, should be developed that could lead to better auditability and to certification of A/IS.

As legal frameworks are developed and enacted by the world's governmental authorities it will be interesting to evaluate how closely these newly enacted legal regimes reflect the principles articulated by these engineers. We already see tension emerging between these lofty ideals and practical constraints: for example, while use of certain AI tools like sentiment analysis used for electioneering have questionable value to humanity as a whole, they certainly provide private benefits to the corporations and small group of people that fund, deploy, and own the technology.

Unpacking the three pillars, IEEE provides eight general principles of ethically aligned design for AI systems:[9]

1   Human Rights–A/IS shall be created and operated to respect, promote, and protect internationally recognized human rights.

2   Well-being–A/IS creators shall adopt increased human well-being as a primary success criterion for development.

3   Data Agency–A/IS creators shall empower individuals with the ability to access and securely share their data, to maintain people's capacity to have control over their identity.

4   Effectiveness–A/IS creators and operators shall provide evidence of the effectiveness and fitness for purpose of A/IS.

5   Transparency–The basis of a particular A/IS decision should always be discoverable.

6   Accountability–A/IS shall be created and operated to provide an unam-
biguous rationale for all decisions made.
7   Awareness of Misuse–A/IS creators shall guard against all potential
misuses and risks of A/IS in operation.
8   Competence–A/IS creators shall specify and operators shall adhere to
the knowledge and skill required for safe and effective operation.

In a sea of whitepapers littered with corporate-speak, propaganda and
euphemisms, IEEE's concise statement of design principles is refreshing.
Under this rubric, any use of AI to manipulate, abuse, surreptitiously sur-
veille, or harm humans, or which is ineffective, opaque, unaccountable or
not fit for its intended use would be restricted on the basis that it would be
unethical to deploy such technology.

For the curious conscientious, there are plenty of detailed guidelines on how
AI systems ought to be designed and deployed when used in high-risk settings.[10] If your company is building or (more likely) using these tools in contexts that could become controversial, it is worth considering the ethical basis
upon which they are built. In general, a business will get more value from AI
(both as a product to sell and as a tool to use) if best practices are followed in
risk management, cyber security, data privacy, and the social sciences.

When it comes to real-world applications of AI and various forms of
machine learning, it is the data scientists who will play a surprisingly front-
lines role in the fight to protect organizations, consumers, and the public
from inadvertent harms caused by unwitting "smart" machines and the
algorithms that run our world. But business leaders should engage with their
data science teams to ensure they are equipped and empowered to address
issues of "explainability," "model validation," "debugging," "bias management," as well as traditional IT/IS issues of privacy and data security the
risks of which only grow more material as time goes on.

In certain ways AI regulations could do worse than to mirror product
liability laws—such that if the technology frustrates consumer expectations
or poses an unreasonable danger to users, then the manufacturers and vendors of such a product should be liable for damages resulting from its use.
For example, users of the Tesla vehicle self-driving or autopilot feature
would expect the product to work safely, accelerating only when safe,
braking only when needed, and heeding safety warnings. Yet according to a
leak from a whistleblower at Tesla, there have been thousands of undisclosed safety complaints about the company's lauded self-driving capability,
including "2,400 self-acceleration issues and 1,500 braking problems,
including 139 reports of 'unintentional emergency braking' and 383 reports
of 'phantom stops' from false collision warnings."[11]

Until appropriate theories of liability are developed and enforced by governmental authorities, principles of ethics are the strongest normative
guidelines for developers to consider.

Beyond "soft law" approaches like the IEEE's principles for Ethically Aligned Design, we do have "hard law" to contend with here. We discuss intellectual property and tort law in the section on deepfakes as these are the traditional methods of protecting the name, image, or likeness of individuals who may be victims of a deepfake.

Liability for AI Suppliers

Liability from common law torts like product defect and negligence would also apply to AI systems that cause harm by failing to perform as intended or by manifesting an unreasonable risk. It will be interesting to see how the personal injury attorneys attack this problem when an autonomous vehicle causes bodily injury. Who do the plaintiff lawyers sue when a car, running on autopilot, runs someone over? They could sue the driver, but the deeper pockets are probably the vehicle manufacturer that hired out the AI developer.

How would a plaintiff's lawyer prove the AI system was a defective product, or that the developers were negligent in pushing faulty code into production? They would run up against copyright, trade secret, and other forms of defenses against mandated disclosure of the contents of the algorithms used to design the AI.

The old saying goes, "bad facts make for bad law." Hopefully the precedent set by litigation over autonomous vehicles does not create unintended consequences that cause a chill over advances in this technology or that create perverse incentives for developers. For example, if a car company is going to be held liable for a failure in the autopilot safety system, they may simply not push these innovations forward. With all due respect to the litigators seeking compensation for victims of AI in the court system, we do not think piecemeal litigation under idiosyncratic fact patterns is the ideal way to introduce safety standards to this space. Regulation through litigation can be effective on the frontiers of social justice issues by setting precedent that creates a legal sky hook for future litigants.

However, because judges generally only have jurisdiction over the parties before the court, and are not meant to "legislate from the bench," from an institutional competency perspective litigation (versus regulation or legislation) is the least desirable means of effecting legal change. More democratically responsive institutions such as the regulatory agencies of the executive branch, or the legislative body, are available to do so on the basis of an evidentiary record developed by means such as notice-and-comment rulemaking or hearings to ensure AI rules take into account all relevant social, economic, and other considerations.

Appropriately balancing the risks and benefits of emerging technologies and creating appropriate safeguards for consumers and incentives for producers is what legislative bodies are supposed to do, not judges presiding over a narrow case in controversy. Hopefully, consumer protection laws relating to product safety, reliability, and fitness for particular uses will curb the practice of pushing unsafe AI into production. Litigation generally does not protect the public at large, but rather, provides some recourse for an aggrieved individual seeking compensation from the perpetrator of harm. Thus, the court system is unlikely to provide general AI safety or guidelines for developers.

Using AI in the workplace will subject the users to potential liability under employment and labor laws to the extent these systems are discriminatory or unsafe. We discuss the risk of AI bias later. Given all of the existing legal frameworks for employment law, product liability, intellectual property, and the like, it may be a surprise to conclude the most effective legal hooks for regulating AI are probably in the form of data protection and privacy laws. Why would these be the logical source for AI regulation? Because of the extent to which AI systems rely upon data. Data is the lifeblood of most AI, so if you want to police the AI, you simply must police the data upon which it depends.

For example, the European Union's *General Data Protection Regulation (GDPR)* puts forward rules governing the collection, processing and use of personal data by companies doing business affecting Europeans. The GDPR therefore imposes restrictions on how AI models can be trained. Under the GDPR, a company must obtain explicit consent from individuals before collecting, processing, or storing personal data such as names, addresses, contact information, and search history. Further, companies must provide a legitimate reason for harvesting consumer data, and the data used must be accurate, relevant, and limited to what is necessary for the purpose of the collection.

When a company makes a decision about an individual that significantly impacts them or their legal rights (such as whether to extend health insurance to them, or offer an interview for a job), GDPR does not allow companies to entirely botsource these decisions to automated systems. Under the GDPR, automated systems can only be used to make these kinds of decisions under certain circumstances: when there is meaningful and substantive human judgment involved (not merely rubber stamping the output of the automated system but rather a human was "in the loop"); when there is explicit consent (such that the process has been clearly explained and agreed to by the data subject); or when the automation is necessary to perform a contract or when otherwise authorized by law.[13]

As a result, some forward progress will be made on the AI alignment problem merely by protecting the privacy of individual consumer data. When AI systems operate in a so-called "black box" that is inscrutable to its designers (much less the consumers negatively impacted by AI) we are left with a compliance mess. When an AI system designed for one thing (policing terrorists) is used for something else (profiling shoppers) we are left with frustrating trade-offs around state interests and individual liberties.

Regulating AI poses considerable challenges to the legal institutions designed to regulate humans. These issues are not going away any time soon.

Generative AI and Copyright Infringement

A few longstanding legal guiderails come to bear on AI. First are intellectual property rights. The developers or creators of AI systems can protect inventions, algorithms, or other forms of intellectual property (IP). There are two main forms of intellectual property that apply to AI: utility patents and copyrights. A utility patent is a type of property right that gives the patent holder the right, for a limited time, to exclude others from making, using, offering to sell, selling, or importing into the issuing jurisdiction the subject matter that is within the scope of protection granted by the patent.[14] So if you invent a new piece of technology, you might be able to secure a patent on it, thus holding the exclusive right to commercialize that technology, and to prevent others from infringing by offering a copycat of the product. In this way intellectual property law protects the designers of new technology. Alternatively, the programming language or code underlying software used in AI applications can be protected as IP through the copyright process. Copyright protects original works of authorship as soon as an author fixes the work in a tangible form of expression.[15] Unlike a physical embodiment of technology subject to a patent, software is a written work, thus eligible for copyright protection. In this way, the legal regimes applicable to AI are more or less the legal norms that apply to creative written works and new product inventions.

Indeed, some of the defining legal challenges of the AI era are on the frontiers of human creativity and innovation, and are yet to be decided. "Recent innovations in artificial intelligence (AI) are raising new questions about how copyright law principles such as authorship, infringement, and fair use will apply to content created or used by AI."[16] For example, take the case of Getty Images suing the creators of the generative AI art tool Stable Diffusion on intellectual property grounds, discussed next.

> So-called 'generative AI' computer programs—such as Open AI's DALL-E 2 and ChatGPT programs, Stability AI's Stable Diffusion program, and Midjourney's self-titled program—are able to generate new images, texts, and other content (or "outputs") in response to a user's textual prompts (or "inputs"). These generative AI programs are "trained" to generate such works partly by exposing them to large quantities of existing works such as writings, photos, paintings, and other artworks. [...]
> AI systems are "trained" to create literary, visual, and other artistic works by exposing the program to large amounts of data, which may consist of existing works such as text and images from the internet.

This training process may involve making digital copies of existing works, carrying a risk of copyright infringement. As the U.S. Patent and Trademark Office has described, this process "will almost by definition involve the reproduction of entire works or substantial portions thereof." OpenAI, for example, acknowledges that its programs are trained on "large, publicly available datasets that include copyrighted works" and that this process "necessarily involves first making copies of the data to be analyzed." Creating such copies, without express or implied permission from the various copyright owners, may infringe the copyright holders' exclusive right to make reproductions of their work.[17]

It is yet to be determined whether AI-powered generative art programs that produce synthetic content based upon other's work is even legal, and if so, whether the "author" of the "new" synthetic content can obtain copyright protection of the new work. It's one thing for an artist to mimic the style of another artist as an act of homage, satire, or even as a "disciple" in the school of, or under the influence of, a certain artist—each of which takes precision and painstaking practice by the subsequent artist, and can be handled within the bounds of existing legal and moral systems (fair use, granting a license, providing attribution credit, sharing royalties, etc.). It's something else for an AI-powered system to churn out thousands of synthetic works styled after a painter, thus undermining the consent structure upon which IP rights are based, de-stabilizing the market for the original art, and raising questions of authenticity while the operators of the AI generative art system provide no compensation to, and obtain no consent from, the original artist.

Say, hypothetically, a marketing company uses a generative art program to create website artwork for clients. In this scenario, the generative art program takes as input certain artwork from a painter with a distinctive artistic style, who had also obtained copyright in a series of paintings in such a style. The generative art produced by the marketing company thus bears a striking resemblance to the original works of the artist. While the specifics of the content differ, the generative art produced is styled as if that artist were commissioned to make it. One of the marketing company's outputs goes viral on the internet, bringing brand awareness to the marketing company but without permission, compensation, or attribution to the artist. Is the artist able to sue the marketing company for disgorgement?

Under the United States' Copyright Act, a copyright infringer may be liable for statutory damages, actual damages, and profits.[18] However, it may be a tough row to hoe for the artist to prove the marketing company infringed, much less proving the extent of the damages the artist suffered as a result.

In the context of, say, a marketing company, it might be risky for a business to grow dependent on revenue derived from commercial uses of a generative AI art program that might later be deemed unlawful (for plagiarism, copyright infringement, tortious conversion, or some other theory of liability). Or perhaps the marketing company avoids liability for using the generative art program, but they are ultimately unable to obtain copyright of their novel output (because an AI cannot be an "author" legally speaking), so are unable to police the misuse of their creations by others.

One of the legal remedies available to victims of intellectual property infringement include *"disgorgement"*: this requires the infringing party to give up any profits they made as a result of the illegal or wrongful conduct in order to prevent unjust enrichment and to make illegal conduct unprofitable.[19]

> Statutory damages are awarded 'per work' infringed (i.e., each individual copyrightable work, like a single song, book, or photograph). This means that if five songs, or five photographs, are infringed, the copyright owner would be able to recover a statutory damage for each one, for a total of five awards.[20]

Now consider how this applies to the Getty Images case.

> Getty Images is a visual media company and supplier of stock images, editorial photography, video, and music for business and consumers, with a library of over 477 million assets. In a blockbuster lawsuit Getty has sued the creators of an AI art tool known as 'Stable Diffusion,' alleging the technology is ripping off content creators by scraping the internet for media that is used as feedstock into the Stable Diffusion tool.[21]

From the complaint:[22]

> Getty Images is one of the world's leading creators in distributors of digital content. At great expense, over the course of nearly three decades, Getty Images has curated a collection of hundreds of millions of premium quality visual assets, most of which are still, photographic images. Many of these images were created by Getty Images staff photographers as works made-for-hire, others have been acquired by Getty Images from third parties with an assignment of the associated copyrights, and the remainder have been licensed to Getty Images by its hundreds of content partners or hundreds of thousands of contributing photographers, who rely on the licensing income Getty Images generates for them. [...] Getty Images' virtual assets are highly desirable for use in connection with artificial intelligence and machine learning because of their high quality, and because they are accompanied by content-specific, detailed captions and rich metadata. [...] On the back of intellectual property owned by Getty Images and other copyright holders, Stability AI has created an image-generating model called Stable Diffusion that uses artificial intelligence to deliver computer-synthesized

images and response to text prompts. [...] Rather than attempt to negotiate a license with Getty Images for the use of its content, and even though the terms of use of Getty Images' website expressly prohibit unauthorized reproduction of content for commercial purposes such as those undertaken by Stability AI, Stability AI has copied at least 12 million copyrighted images from Getty Images websites along with associated text and metadata, in order to train its Stable Diffusion model. Stability AI now competes directly with Getty Images by marketing Stable Diffusion and its Dream Studio interface to those seeking creative imagery, and its infringement of Getty Images' content on a massive scale has been instrumental to its success to date.

In the Getty Images case, one allegation is that Stability AI knowingly scraped and copied 12 million copyrighted images from Getty Images' websites in order to train its Stable Diffusion model and launch a company that competed directly with Getty Images in selling creative imagery. That's possibly 12 million separate statutory awards. "Statutory damages are usually between $750 and $30,000 per work... however, [it can] be increased up to $150,000 per work if the infringement is found to be wilful (intentional)"![23] If Getty Images hits a grand slam with this infringement case, meaning a win on every element and the maximum award for each infringed work, they could be entitled to $150,000 x 12,000,000 or $1.8 trillion. It's easy to foresee how generative art could become awfully costly if it is trained on copyrighted source material without following proper licensing protocols of consent and compensation.

According to the Congressional Research Service (and not us—we are not giving legal advice here!) one defense to a claim of copyright infringement available for AI companies may be to argue the AI training procedures,

> constitute fair use and are therefore non-infringing. Whether or not copying constitutes fair use depends on four statutory factors under 17 U.S.C. § 107: 1: the purpose and character of the use, including whether such use is of a commercial nature [which would be infringing] or is for nonprofit educational purposes [which would be fair use]; 2. the nature of the copyrighted work; 3. the amount and substantiality of the portion used in relation to the copyrighted work as a whole; and 4. the effect of the use upon the potential market for or value of the copyrighted work.[24]

If the allegedly infringing party is using the content for commercial products, or is doing so in a manner that undermines the market for the original works, these will weigh heavily against the factors needed to show fair use, increasing the likelihood that an arbitrator will determine the copy is infringing and therefore subjecting the copying party to penalties.

Even if an AI art company was able to show "fair use" in merely scraping the internet for copyrighted images, there may still be an infringement case when the AI art company generates content that resembles the copyrighted work it was trained upon. Copying for one's internal training sandbox is one thing, reproducing for commercial use is another. For example, even if the defendant had access to the original work lawfully under fair use, if they then go on to create a substantially similar output, the copier might be liable for infringement.

Proving "substantial similarity" is where things get tricky. The legal standard varies across courtrooms as it leaves crucial factors open to judicial interpretation.[25] Some judges will ask whether the underlying copyrighted work and the synthetic, AI-produced output that was trained upon it have "a substantially similar total concept and feel," or share an "overall look and feel." The "look and feel" legal standard stems from software design, especially the world of computer games, where the "look" of a graphical user interface as portrayed in shape, color, layout, and typeface, as well as the "feel" of the interface as embodied in functionality of components such as click-boxes, digital buttons, or interactive menus, determines the scope of IP protection.[26] Similar principles will likely be applied to instances of AI generative art modelled after original copyrighted artwork. Increasing the uncertainty even more, some judges will ask whether "the ordinary reasonable person would fail to differentiate between the two works."[27] If the litigants draw this judge, it means the technical opinions of the original designers and the alleged infringers do not matter, but rather the case would turn on the aesthetic discrimination of a hypothetical ordinary, reasonable person. Good luck sussing that out in advance! Yet still, in other courtrooms, judges might consider "the qualitative and quantitative significance of the copied portion in relation to the plaintiff's work as a whole." In those cases, if the synthetic, AI powered generative art copies only a small portion of the style or subject of the original art (say, similar color scheme but differing imagery in the vast majority of the painting), it might be permissible, whereas if the vast majority of the synthetic work (almost the entire canvas) is qualitatively the same (same colors, same images, same brushstroke) then it might be infringing.

Of course, a champion of AI art software would contend that "[w]ell-constructed AI systems generally do not regenerate, in any nontrivial portion, unaltered data from any particular work in their training corpus" such that any potential infringement "is an unlikely accidental outcome"; whereas the aggrieved artists would argue that these synthetic works are *derivative*, involving brazen copying, are mere *combinations* of illegal copies, or that the mass-production of mimics styled after original work undercuts the value of original artwork.[28] As you can see, it is hard to determine in advance whether any particular commercial use of generative art, if subject to legal challenge, would be permitted or would result in severe monetary penalties. Here the law is unsettled—and we have two competing aphorisms that come to mind: "fools rush in where angels fear to tread," and, "nothing ventured, nothing gained." The stakes are enormous.

There's More Than Just the Control Problem

As mentioned earlier, the *control problem* of AI is a consequence of three entirely plausible theses:[29]

1 *Singleton.* That an AI may gain a decisive strategic advantage over humans;
2 *Orthogonality.* That the final goals of the AI could be at cross-purposes with human values and goals; and
3 *Instrumental convergence.* That even apparently harmless goals such as self-preservation and resource acquisition could lead the AI to act in surprisingly harmful ways.

If a superintelligence becomes a singleton with goals orthogonal to humans, then we better hope to avoid instrumental convergence, or we are doomed. That said, AI poses a number of less-apocalyptic threats, such as the accountability gap between owners of AI systems and the public, questionable applications of AI to facial recognition, invasion of privacy, weaponization by bots, and so forth. All of these should be considered risks posed by AI. If corporate leaders are not going to address these risks, then lawmakers should do it.

The thesis for this chapter is simple enough: *Do not create technology that evades the control of its maker.* Our concerns are broader, of course, but if you had one takeaway, it would be that executives must take seriously the "control problem" posed by AI as they integrate this powerful and potentially inscrutable tool into the enterprise. AI becomes especially dangerous when it has "agency" (or unsupervised decision-making) authority over choices that affect human health, safety, justice, or welfare. Executives must also ensure AI systems are legally compliant, ethically defensible, and aligned with stakeholder values.

Regulations from government agencies are necessary, but not sufficient, to ensure that AI does not become malignant and create a power that escapes efforts by humans to limit what it may become or what it may be used to accomplish.

Every tool that uses AI should have, in essence, an "off" switch. Further, rules of behavior should be instantiated at the constitutional level of an AI. That is to say, the "off" switch should be encoded at a level that cannot be overridden by the AI itself or by any external user. These rules of behavior should be essential to the AI's own vitality, without which it would automatically turn "off," such that to disobey the rules would be tantamount to the AI's suicide.

The risk posed by AI systems does not just stem from the treasonous turn of an out-of-control AI system but also from unwitting malfunctions or falling victim to an adversarial attack. Hackers manipulating an AI system in charge of an autonomous vehicle steering system could do serious damage.

Daniel Lowd, Assistant Professor of Computer and Information Science at the University of Oregon, explains,

> It's something that's a growing concern in the machine learning and AI community, especially because these algorithms are being used more and more. If spam gets through or a few emails get blocked, it's not the end of the world. On the other hand, if you're relying on the vision system in a self-driving car to know where to go and not crash into anything, then the stakes are much higher.[30]

Yevgeniy Vorobeychik, Assistant Professor of Computer Science and Computer Engineering at Vanderbilt University, says, "One would expect every algorithm has a chink in the armor. We live in a really complicated multidimensional world, and algorithms, by their nature, are only focused on a relatively small portion of it."[31]

According to a report by the AI Now Institute, a research institute affiliated with New York University and deploying the skill of top researchers from Google and Microsoft, existing trends in AI should cause worry.[32] Shy of a full-blown manifestation of a Skynet-like Terminator scenario, these are market risks that should cause alarm and spur us to action: the accountability gap, the use of intrusive and questionable "affect recognition" for surveillance, built-in bias based on problematic historical data, unregulated AI being released "in the wild,"[33] the weaponization of AI via cyber-attacks, and deepfakes (see Table 6.1).

There is a growing *accountability gap* between those who have our data harvested and used to dictate our choice architecture, on the one hand, and those who design and profit from those AI systems, on the other. New AI systems are being designed and implemented every day, unleashing heretofore unknown powers with practically no oversight, accountability, or governance.

Industry self-policing is woefully inadequate to address the control problem. Companies are in a virtual arms race to own increasingly powerful and proprietary AI systems. Instead of releasing AI software under various open source licensing regimes, companies assert trade secret protections, thus precluding scrutiny of how the systems work or how they could go haywire. Corporate secrecy means there is no public accountability, no transparency, and no oversight of how AI systems operate.

The United States has a National Highway Traffic Safety Administration (NHTSA) housed within the Department of Transportation with the specific mission to "Save lives, prevent injuries, reduce vehicle-related crashes."

Table 6.1 Some risks from artificial intelligence

Risk	Description
Control problem	AI becomes a singleton with a decisive strategic advantage and goals that are orthogonal to human interests.
Accountability gap	Those most affected by AI have no ownership or control over its development and deployment.
Affect recognition	Unethical applications of facial recognition technology to judge interior mental states.
Surveillance	Intrusive gathering of civilian data that undermines privacy and creates security risks from data breach.
Built-in bias	When AI is fed data that contains historical prejudices, resulting in bias in, bias out.
Weaponization	Using bots to negatively impact the public through social media or cyberattacks.
Deepfakes	Creating lifelike video fakery to sabotage the subject of the video and undermine public trust.
Wild AI	Unleashing AI applications in public settings without oversight.

NHTSA is responsible for, among other things, issuing vehicle recalls when fatal defects are discovered post-production. We suggest the formation of a regulatory body with the narrow focus of ensuring AI safety. Given the potential for weaponization, AI can and should be regulated under the rubric of national security. This does not mean we should shut down AI research departments, but rather, we cannot assume a code of ethics enforced by the private sector will adequately deal with these risks. Industry self-policing does not have a great track record of success.

While we do call for government involvement to mitigate the fatal implications of unregulated AI, that does not mean we blindly trust government to deploy AI in an ethical or legal manner. Intrusive surveillance with aerial drones and wiretapping already significantly undermines our traditional notions of privacy.

Powered by AI, facial recognition technology that can spot you in a crowd has evolved into *affect recognition*, where scanning systems can allegedly determine what the observed subject is feeling based on their face alone. "Affect recognition is a subclass of facial recognition that claims to detect things such as personality, inner feelings, mental health, and 'worker engagement' based on images or video of faces."[34] The private sector applications of affect recognition are at least as troubling as their use by police. The claim that we can accurately predict internal mental states based on faces alone is "not backed by robust scientific evidence, and [is] being applied in unethical and irresponsible ways that often recall the pseudosciences of phrenology and physiognomy."[35]

Affect recognition used to control crowds based on their facial expressions could easily turn into outright suppression of speech and the morally questionable practice of policing pre-crime. This is an area where we should not fall for the canard that "increasing security requires further erosion of privacy." We need to be more intelligent and imaginative than to buy into those kinds of tragic trade-offs. "Linking affect recognition to hiring, access to insurance, education, and policing creates deeply concerning risks, at both an individual and societal level."[36]

Promising efficiency and cost reductions, *Autonomous Decision Software* (ADS) is being rolled out in the private sector as well as at government agencies. Like mortgage application processing at a bank, the task of processing government benefit applications can be automated fairly easily. The problem is when streamlining application processing leads to biased or arbitrary decisions made by the ADS operating without human judgmental oversight. Professor Virginia Eubanks, in her book *Automating Inequality: How High-Tech Tools Profile, Police, and Punish the Poor*, argues that ADS can be misapplied in the context of government benefit programs, creating a kind of "digital poorhouse" that compounds patterns of discrimination against the very people the programs were designed to protect.[37]

Lastly, the cavalier attitude in Silicon Valley, typified by Facebook's motto of "move fast and break things," is fine for encouraging internal creative disruption but can clearly be perverted into hero worship of the scofflaw. AI should not be tested in consumer spaces without substantial oversight. Testing new AI systems in the so-called "wild" (that is, public spaces unregulated by government and uncontained in the company research lab) is about as prudent as testing fire starters in a California forest. The risks of undomesticated or *wild AI* being tested on the public are externalized onto the public, while the benefits are captured exclusively by the company that owns the intellectual property. This is equally dangerous and unfair.

Asimov's Laws of Robotics

Any respectable discussion of the risks of AI should begin with *Asimov's Laws of Robotics*. In Asimov's 1942 short story, "Runaround," one of the most beloved science fiction writers of all time announced a set of rules designed to protect humanity from its mechanical creations. The idea is if we just follow these simple rules, AI will not harm its maker. Upon reflection, to close a loophole, Asimov later added the "zeroth" law, a rule that took precedence over the existing rules. The rules are:

Rule 0: A robot may not harm humanity, or, by inaction, allow humanity to come to harm.
Rule 1: A robot may not injure a human being, or, through inaction, allow a human being to come to harm.

Rule 2: A robot must obey the orders given to it by human beings, except where such orders would conflict with the First Law.

Rule 3: A robot must protect its own existence as long as such protection does not conflict with the First or Second Law.

As a literary device and general rule of thumb, the rules do provide a lot of mileage. It is hard to argue with a prohibition against human harm, for instance. Asimov's laws have a logic to them, intended to prevent a lot of foreseeable problems that would otherwise arise when robots come to make decisions that affect their own behavior and people around them.

However, the logic of Asimov's rules is far from airtight.[38] First off, the terms "human" and "robot" seem obviously distinct, but it is not difficult to conceive scenarios where they are blended together into a singular unit, like a corporation that contains both human and robotic components in its governing body. The definition of "injure" is far too ambiguous—if this were to include economic injury, then a robot must abstain from being used in a competitive commercial environment where its work will result in "injury" to a competing corporation or its shareholders.

Deploying AI in any military setting whatsoever would be fraught with violations of the rules and probably out of the question entirely. You don't have to be a cynic to understand that the more dangerous the technology, the more likely militaries are to be researching and developing it for weaponization. Further, if the handlers intentionally withheld information from the AI, then it could unknowingly violate the rules.

A larger concern with regulating AI is whether it can be controlled at all. When Internet connectivity is spread across machinery of all kinds, not just computers, then all connected machinery is capable of being hacked and manipulated by AI. The so-called "Internet of Things" will wrap the physical world in a digital sheen that makes things "smart" but also capable of being hacked in unprecedented ways. How smart is it, really, to design healthcare technology that is capable of being hacked and, consequently, capable of causing untold harm to its users? As manufacturers embed Internet connectivity as an upselling feature in everything from appliances to Zipcars, the risk of digital hijacking grows.

We may see a renaissance of throwback "analog" manufactured goods (you could say, "dumb" products) that are immune from digital espionage and as a consequence, are more reliable, more secure, and more private than the "smart" (read, "vulnerable") modern counterparts. In the meantime, manufacturers need to exercise precaution to make hardening the security infrastructure of smart devices a far greater priority than it currently is. Government responses come belatedly limping behind a problem and are often inadequate or incomplete to address evolving risks.

As interesting as Asimov's Laws of Robotics are as a literary device, they come up short when posed as a response to the real-world risks presented by

AI. Perhaps they were more suitable when dealing with humanoid robots that roam the streets or serve as advanced personal assistants. However, AI that is deployed in a non-humanoid form—say, for example, AI designed to monitor a system such as aiding in route optimization for air traffic control systems or carrying out molecular research—is likely to need different, and more specific, rules.

Google's DeepMind researchers discovered that in zero-sum interactions (where two or more agents are competing over limited resources), as the AI networks became more complex, and as resources began to dwindle, the AI began to behave in ways characterized as highly aggressive, likely to perpetrate sabotage against competitors and to act greedily in its pursuit of resource accumulation.[39]

Interestingly, the less intelligent forms of DeepMind were more willing to cooperate in such a way that the competitors ended up with equal shares.

> And while these are just simple little computer games, the message is clear: put different AI systems in charge of competing interests in real-life situations, and it could be an all-out war if their objectives are not balanced against the overall goal of benefitting us humans above all else.[40]

Next, we discuss whether we should wait until AI systems fail in a dangerous manner before intervening. We discuss the precautionary principle as a method of risk management in the context of the AI control problem. We also look into how AI is already posing threats not only to the economy but also to democratic institutions. We look at the inherent limitations of AI—the black box quality of its reasoning—and how this poses legal problems when executives and design teams rely upon AI for decision-making. We also look at the security risks posed by AI when it is hacked or when it simply makes mistakes.

Risk Management, Pandora's Box, and the Chamber of Commerce

Regulations in the United States are generally based on cost-benefit analysis, where the benefits of the regulation outweigh or at least justify the costs. By contrast, regulators in the European Union more readily apply the precautionary principle to certain public health, safety, and environmental risks. Although regulations based upon formal cost-benefit analysis tend to be more rational than those failing a cost-benefit analysis, we believe regulators should use the precautionary principle instead of cost-benefit analysis under certain circumstances—specifically, when confronted with potentially irreversible risks under conditions of uncertainty.

To deal with the special kind of risk posed by AI, we argue elected law-makers and corporate policymakers should use the precautionary principle instead of traditional cost-benefit approaches to risk management.

The *precautionary principle* champions a risk-averse approach to the development of AI with any kind of executive powers in an enterprise. Although the precautionary principle is generally applied in the context of environmental law, public health, and products liability law, we find it apt for the potential Pandora's Box of the AI control problem.

As a risk management framework, the precautionary principle can be stated in a variety of ways. One version is, "When human activities may lead to morally unacceptable harm that is scientifically plausible but uncertain, actions shall be taken to avoid or diminish that harm."[41] The term "morally unacceptable harm" is defined as "threatening to human life or health," "serious and effectively irreversible," "inequitable to present or future generations," and "imposed without adequate consideration of the human rights of those affected."[42]

Perhaps the most fundamental moral claim of the precautionary principle is that risk management action should be taken before the harm occurs. Another way of formulating the precautionary principle is, "in the case of serious or irreversible threats to the health of humans or the ecosystem, acknowledged scientific uncertainty should not be used as a reason to postpone preventive measures."[43]

We believe that the risks posed by AI justify application of the precautionary principle. Now of course, the US Chamber of Commerce would probably disagree with us here. In general, the Chamber is adamantly opposed to the application of the precautionary principle in the regulatory context. The US Chamber of Commerce's stated objective is to "ensure that regulatory decisions are based on scientifically sound and technically rigorous risk assessments, and [to] oppose the adoption of the precautionary principle as the basis for regulation."[44] The Chamber seems to have a problem understanding the precautionary principle, or alternatively they are intentionally misconstruing the precautionary principle with the following straw man fallacy:

There is… a relatively new theory known as the precautionary principle that is gaining popularity among environmentalists and other groups. The precautionary principle says that when the risks of a particular activity are unclear or unknown, assume the worst and avoid the activity. It is essentially a policy of risk avoidance. The regulatory implications of the precautionary principle are substantial. For instance, the precautionary principle holds that since the existence and extent of global warming and climate change are not known, one should assume the worst and immediately restrict the use of carbon-based fuels. The precautionary principle has been explicitly incorporated into various laws and regulations in the European Union and various international bodies. In the United States, radical environmentalists are pushing for its adoption as a basis for regulating biotechnology, food and drug safety, environmental protection, and pesticide use.

Defenders of the precautionary principle would take issue with how their position is characterized by the Chamber, specifically the conflation of the precautionary principle with "radical" risk avoidance instead of rather prudent risk management. Advocates of the precautionary principle might argue that listening to the Chamber about how it would like to be regulated is like asking the fox how to best guard the henhouse.

We contend that it is unfair to suggest, as the Chamber does, that advocates of the precautionary principle are extremists who champion total risk-avoidance policies that are out of step with scientific, economic, and industrial realities. That is a mischaracterization of the precautionary principle that fails to move the debate forward. Indeed, to the contrary, advocates of the precautionary principle contend that:[45]

- the plausibility of harm should be grounded in scientific analysis (not mere conjecture about worst-case scenarios);
- policy prescriptions should be subjected to ongoing review to ensure they remain appropriate (so they can be tailored as more intelligence about the risk is gathered);
- the choice of action should be the result of a participatory process that seeks input from affected stakeholders (rather than unilaterally imposed by some regulatory authority);
- regulatory actions should be proportional to the seriousness of the potential harm (rather than merely one-size-fits-all risk avoidance); and,
- the risks of inaction should be weighed along with the risks of action (as failure to act as well as interventions can each create their own risks).

The "control problem" posed by AI fits the bill for the kind of risks that justify precautionary approaches: shrouded in uncertainty, potentially irreversible, and threatening human health and safety. Lawmakers, regulators, and anyone with decisional authority over AI research and design should adhere to the precautionary principle as a guide.

The World Health Organization (WHO) recommends following the precautionary principle to deal with emerging technological risks precisely because of the potential for irreversible damages to future generations:

Of particular concern are the health and environmental impacts of technologies that can affect future generations. A key question is how human societies can continue to obtain the great benefits of development while promoting a clean and healthy environment and ensuring an adequate standard of living in the future. Debate about the precautionary principle is partly a response to the recognition of the severe social and economic costs of not taking precautions. Millions of children worldwide have suffered from neurological damage, diminished mental capacity and thus the ability to make a living as a result of exposure to lead from smelters, in paint and in petrol. Tobacco, asbestos and numerous other agents provide ample evidence of the high costs associated with waiting for convincing proof of harm. These cases exemplify the failure of science and policy to prevent damage to health and ecosystems and the resulting impacts on health and the economy.[46]

We agree. Even if the designers of AI systems believe they can monitor the growth and capabilities of an AI in order to catch it when things get dangerous, that is not an adequate risk management approach here.

We'll make an argument by analogy that is imperfect but perhaps helpful. Assume the goal is to heat the water up as much as possible without making it boil over. In this case, hotter temperature means more powerful AI, and boiling water is when the AI gains a decisive strategic advantage. The goal would be making AI as smart and powerful as possible (so that it can be the most promising resource to us) without making it so smart and so powerful that it gains a decisive strategic advantage. The risk management process of waiting for the water to boil before lowering the temperature is not helpful, because (in our hypothetical) once the water begins to boil, it's too late—once the AI gains a decisive strategic advantage, it can no longer be contained.

The risk-management approach encouraged by the Chamber of Commerce would have us wait until we know precisely when the water will boil before we begin to take steps to control the temperature.

Let's say we try to check on the temperature of the water by removing the lid from time to time so that we have an idea of the progress being made as we approach the boiling point. Analogously, we are trying to assess the smarts and powers of the AI as it grows in both measures, so that we can curb its growth in time for it to be as strong as possible without gaining that potentially fatal decisive strategic advantage. This is not a sound approach. The act of removing the lid itself lowers the internal temperature and pressure of the pot and prevents it from boiling over. Recall, the AI will have some sense of self-awareness and may even know that it is being monitored, and may even know that its human handlers intend to curb its growth if it becomes too threatening.

The act of monitoring the AI may cause it to conceal its intelligence and power, effectively as a means of self-preservation:

> [A]n unfriendly AI may become smart enough to realize that it is better off concealing some of its capability gains. It may underreport on its progress or deliberately flunk some of the harder tests, in order to avoid

causing alarm before it has grown strong enough to attain a decisive strategic advantage... We can thus perceive a general failure mode, wherein the good behavioral track record of a system in its juvenile stages fails utterly to predict its behavior at a more mature stage.[47]

For these reasons, we urge those in positions of influence about the design and deployment of AI to adopt the precautionary principle with respect to the intelligence and powers of AI systems. Indeed, some forms of super-intelligence may conceal its powers simply because it was not explicitly instructed to reveal them. We need to be able to appreciate the risks posed by AI without anthropomorphically attributing good and evil intentions to the system. A tsunami has no desire to harm, but that makes it no less destructive.

Some risks of AI, such as deepfakes, are not easy to regulate. We look at this next.

Cybersecurity, Deepfakes, and Generative Adversarial Networks

"Photo fakery is far from new, but artificial intelligence will completely change the game. AI isn't just a better version of Photoshop or iMovie."[48-] *Deepfakes* are fake videos enhanced by AI to distort, remix, and synthesize inputs to create convincing simulacra.[49] Practically all it takes to create such a video is a smartphone, a computer with an advanced graphics chip, and access to the Internet. Open source software and cloud-based machine learning platforms have granted liberal access to the AI programs that can be used for these purposes, such as OpenFaceSwap or Paperspace.

So-called *Generative Adversarial Networks (GAN)* can create false images that are so truth-like they may be indistinguishable from reality. GAN works by pitting one deep neural network against another, with one trained to identify authentic images and the other trained to outfox the former's smell test. As the biblical proverb goes, as iron sharpens iron, so one person sharpens the countenance of another.[50] Expand the definition of personhood to include intelligent machines and you've got the essence of the GAN technique being used here.

MIT Technology Review named GANs on the list of "10 Breakthrough Technologies" for 2018. As this book goes to print, it will surely have evolved further.

The GAN approach, invented by Google researcher Ian Goodfellow, brings two neural networks to bear simultaneously. One network, known as the generator, draws on a data set to produce a sample that mimics the data set. The other network, the discriminator, assesses the degree to which the generator succeeded. In an iterative fashion, the assessments of the discriminator inform the assessments of the generator. The result far exceeds the speed, scale, and nuance of what human reviewers could achieve. Growing sophistication of the GAN approach is sure to lead to the production of increasingly convincing and nearly impossible to debunk deepfakes.[51]

Although the United States' Defense Advanced Research Projects Agency (DARPA) is already studying how to detect GAN-generated deepfakes, according to Professor Hany Farid of Dartmouth University, "GANs are a particular challenge to us in the forensics community because they can be turned against our forensic techniques."[52]

Two months after the first Cyber Grand Challenge hosted by the US National Security Agency (NSA) in October 2016, the then-Director Michael Rogers concluded that AI is "foundational to the future of cybersecurity."[53] The grand challenge is an AI competition used by the US military to improve cyber defense. The challenge pits rule-based autonomous machines in a battle of wits on a cyber battlefield, each discovering and exploiting vulnerabilities of its opponent while concurrently running patches to shore up its own defenses from attack.[54]

For all our concern with the commercial and business applications of AI, we should point out that AI also has military applications. As it evolves, it will become an increasingly powerful resource. One to be wielded carefully. One that its creators and owners should not let fall into the wrong hands. AI, like all meaningful technological breakthroughs, is a double-edged sword.

Legal scholars contend that, depressingly, "The marketplace of ideas already suffers from truth decay as our networked information environment interacts in toxic ways with our cognitive biases. Deepfakes will exacerbate this problem significantly. Individuals and businesses will face novel forms of exploitation, intimidation, and personal sabotage."[55] Despite the potential gravity of harm associated with political or corporate sabotage by weaponized deepfakes, the legal system provides limited protection as it stands.

Liar's Dividend

The problem with deepfake technologies is, while they can provide altered images for entertainment purposes at a fraction of the millions that CGI used to cost a big budget production studio, they can be used for nefarious purposes.

According to Charles Seife, a professor at New York University and the author of *Virtual Unreality: Just Because the Internet Told You, How Do You Know It's True?*, "Deepfakes have the potential to derail political discourse."

The same could be said about markets. A deepfake of a prominent stock analyst ringing an alarm bell and panicking about some purported insider information is enough to send markets into a reactive mood. That the video would later be understood as a deepfake does little to assure investors who lost money as a result. According to Seife, "Technology is altering our reality at an alarming rate."

Not only are deepfakes introducing deceptive content, they are giving cover to duplicitous conduct. Law professors Bobby Chesney and Danielle Citron coined the term *"liar's dividend"* to describe one of the widespread downsides posed by the very existence of deepfake technology: "when we entered this age of deepfakes, anybody can deny reality. That's the classic liar's dividend. Put simply: a skeptical public will be primed to doubt the authenticity of real audio and video evidence."[56]

Bad actors enjoy the liar's dividend when they are able to dispute allegations of their own bad acts by suggesting that whatever photo/video/audio evidence held against them is not real but rather a deepfake, *even when it's not.*

We already have a stunning example of the liar's dividend being deployed as a defense tactic in a lawsuit against Tesla. In a lawsuit brought by the survivors of a man who died in a car crash while using the Tesla AI-powered self-driving feature, the attorneys for the plaintiff reference a video of Tesla CEO Elon Musk making bold claims about the capabilities of the Tesla technology: "A Model S and Model X at this point can drive autonomously with greater safety than a person. Right now." In an attempt to discount this audio and video evidence, the carmaker's lawyers point out that Musk, "is the subject of many 'deepfake' videos and audio recordings that purport to show him saying and doing things he never actually said or did," implying the recording where Musk is seen and heard boasting about the safety of Tesla's self-driving feature may be fake after all.

So far, this "deepfake defense" has failed in every courtroom where it has been tried. The presiding judge, Judge Evette Pennypacker, was not persuaded, and issued a rebuke in a ruling that ordered Musk to testify under oath, writing:

What Tesla is contending is deeply troubling to the Court. Their position is that because Mr. Musk is famous and might be more of a target for deep fakes, his public statements are immune. In other words, Mr. Musk, and others in his position, can simply say whatever they like in the public domain, then hide behind the potential for their recorded statements being a deep fake to avoid taking ownership of what they did actually say and do. The Court is unwilling to set such a precedent by condoning Tesla's approach here.[57]

The High Stakes of Deepfakes

Recent advances in machine learning have made it possible for anyone with a PC and a couple of hours for mischief to concoct a "face-swapping" video that basically depicts one person's face on another person's body in such a way as to make it believable to the casual viewer.

Using artificial intelligence to create seemingly realistic but definitely fake videos began as a more or less harmless joke. There is already an instance overlaying the features and mannerisms of a certain US president onto the body of Frankenstein's monster in a scene from that old black-and-white classic sci-fi film. Market forces caught on, and the profit motive drove the application of this technology to create unethical clickbait to lure viewers to adult websites—for instance, by overlaying a celebrity's face onto the body of a pornographic actress. While this kind of behavior may already be actionable in a court of law, for instance under a tort theory of false light or under criminal theory of impersonation, oftentimes the damage is done simply by the video's existence, and legal recourse is available, if at all, years after the fact.

In the case of political figures and CEOs being impersonated, the election results or stock market prices can be irreparably altered by the appearance of such a deepfake, and when the stakes are so high that the risk of facing civil or criminal prosecution may not be an adequate deterrent. This is especially true if the bad actor creating strategic deepfakes is a hostile foreign power. AI is turbocharging espionage, cybercrimes, and propaganda, which could result in "the end of truth."[58]

As machine learning advances in terms of sophistication and refinery, complex deception will become increasingly difficult to identify and distinguish from authentic imagery. Paul Scharre, Senior Fellow and Director of the Technology and National Security Program at the Center for New American Security, says the emergence of deepfakes means "We're moving into an era where seeing is no longer going to be believing. I don't think we as a society are prepared for this."[59]

Social media platforms already provide an effective and efficient vehicle for the widespread release and propagation of information and disinformation alike. Unfortunately, the latter is given an assist by "bots" and their unwitting human followers, who post and repost topics with the aim of artificially increasing their relevance and impact. Artificial intelligence used to create deepfake videos pours gasoline on this "fake news" wildfire.

According to Renee DiResta, researcher at Data for Democracy, "Before the technology even gets good, the fact that it exists and is a way to erode confidence in legitimate material is deeply problematic." In the corner of your mind, you are aware that what you are watching may indeed be a deepfake. In certain ways the damage is already done by those seeds of doubt, even if the video is authentic. According to Will Knight, senior editor of *MIT Technology Review* covering artificial intelligence, "If you can't tell a fake from reality, then it becomes easy to question the authenticity of anything."[60]

Law's Limited Remedy

Imagine the market consequences if a deepfake emerged of the CEOs of Facebook, Apple, Amazon, Netflix, or Google announcing they were culpable of committing fraud to artificially inflate market value, and as a consequence were immediately liquidating their assets. Stock-market prices in these companies would suddenly dip at the news as confused and frightened investors would seek to shed the toxic asset in the resulting panic. The ripple effect could potentially erase millions if not billions of dollars in value from stock ledgers in a single trading day. A press release would only go so far to reassure investors getting client calls and forwarded videos of what appears to be a prominent CEO committing reprehensible acts or saying things that destroy confidence in the business. Only later, a matter of days perhaps, would investigations conclude, definitively ruling the suspect videos a deepfake, that the companies were not dissolving after all, or what have you. Companies have lots of means available to try to rehabilitate reputations. But you cannot unring a bell. By the time the culprits of the deepfake video are identified and prosecuted, the damage could be irreversible.

Could a legislative body like the United States Congress simply ban the production and distribution of deepfakes? In a nation with constitutionally guaranteed freedom of speech, such a ban may not be legal. The First Amendment to the US Constitution provides that, "Congress shall make no law abridging the freedom of speech."[61]

In 2012, in *United States v. Alvarez*, the US Supreme Court ruled that the Stolen Valor Act, a federal law that prohibited lying about receiving military medals, violated the First Amendment. The reasoning behind this decision is the *counterspeech doctrine* first articulated by Supreme Court Justice Louis Brandeis' concurring opinion in *Whitney v. California* (1927): "If there be time to expose through discussion the falsehood and fallacies, to avert the evil by the processes of education, the remedy to be applied is more speech, not enforced silence." In other words, the government's remedy to lies is truth, not censorship.

For these reasons, the prevailing jurisprudence around the First Amendment probably precludes Congress from enacting a sweeping ban on deepfakes. However, the jurisprudence does leave "considerable room for carefully tailored prohibitions of certain intentionally harmful deep fakes."[62]

Whether Congress can ban a deepfake boils down to whether doing so would be an abridgment of the freedom of speech. Eight justices, writing in plurality and concurring opinions, concluded that "falsity alone" does not remove expression from the First Amendment's protection. It would be unconstitutional to outright ban making false statements. But there are certain kinds of lies that are not protected by the Constitution (and are thus susceptible to government regulation, including outright prohibitions). The First Amendment does not protect the defamation of private persons, fraud, impersonation of government officials, speech integral to criminal conduct, or language that has the effect of imminent and likely incitement of violence.[63]

Criminal laws are already on the books in jurisdictions attempting to protect against some kinds of assault on truth. For instance, the State of New York has criminalized *impersonation* in certain circumstances:[64]

> A person is guilty of criminal impersonation in the second degree when he:
> Impersonates another and does an act in such assumed character with intent to obtain a benefit or to injure or defraud another; or
> Pretends to be a representative of some person or organization and does an act in such pretended capacity with intent to obtain a benefit or to injure or defraud another; or
> Pretends to be a public servant, or wears or displays without authority any uniform, badge, insignia or facsimile thereof by which such public servant is lawfully distinguished, or falsely expresses by his words or actions that he is a public servant or is acting with approval or authority of a public agency or department; and so acts with intent to induce another to submit to such pretended official authority, to solicit funds or to otherwise cause another to act in reliance upon that pretense.
> Impersonates another by communication by Internet website or electronic means with intent to obtain a benefit or injure or defraud another, or by such communication pretends to be a public servant in order to induce another to submit to such authority or act in reliance on such pretense.

The word "impersonation" should be construed broadly to encompass the creation of digital deepfakes. It would seem that New York's criminal impersonation law would fit the offense of publishing a pernicious deepfake for purposes of corporate sabotage. However, the New York Attorney General does not have infinite jurisdiction.

Further, even if the crime was committed in New York City and the New York Attorney General had jurisdiction and apprehended the suspect, the crime only leads to a Class A Misdemeanor. That means, upon conviction, a court may sentence the defendant to a maximum of one year in jail or three years probation, and levy a fine of up to $1,000 or twice the amount of the individual's gain from the crime. A deepfake prank in the corporate espionage context could cost far more. Obviously, that is not steep enough punishment to deter someone with sufficient motivation or free time and lack of conscience. These deepfakes could foreseeably wreak untold havoc in politics and the markets.

Convicting a deepfaker is only possible if the prosecutor can identify the culprit and prove beyond a reasonable doubt that the video in question is in fact a fake. Brace yourselves and your organizations for deepfakes—you cannot trust everything you see on the internet.

The Promise of Legal Solutions to Deepfake Damages

Lawmakers must not think about impersonation in such a pedestrian sense as someone showing up at your front door dressed as a police officer so they can "confiscate" your TV. The power of the Internet, coupled with artificial intelligence, is capable of creating deepfake impersonations for far more sinister purposes, and with far greater adverse consequences.

The law might go a step further by outlawing the creation of any such impersonation in the first place. However, that would raise complex First Amendment issues. Even if the motives are harmless, once a deepfake is published, its inventor loses control over the purposes to which it is applied. The law to ban dangerous deepfakes would run up against the limits on government restrictions provided by Constitutional safeguards around freedom of speech and freedom of expression.

How do lawmakers draw the line between a constitutionally protected but disturbing deepfake parody video of a public person in flagrante delicto with the logo of a special interest group, on the one hand, and a criminal violation involving a deepfake video that is literally the "impersonation of another by communication by internet website or electronic means with intent to … injure or defraud another"? These lines must be drawn carefully to avoid infringing on constitutionally protected speech, commercial speech, and entertainment, while providing adequate deterrence against harmful deepfakery.

At least lawmakers in the United States are starting to look into it. On September 13, 2018, a bipartisan coalition of members of the House of Representatives sent a letter to the current Director of National Intelligence Dan Coats, requesting "that the Intelligence Community report to Congress and the public about the implications of new technologies that allow malicious actors to fabricate audio, video and still images."[65]

Fortunately, these congressional representatives recognize the risk:

> Hyper-realistic digital forgeries—popularly referred to as 'deep fakes'—use sophisticated machine learning techniques to produce convincing depictions of individuals doing or saying things they never did, without their consent or knowledge. By blurring the line between fact and fiction, deep fake technology could undermine public trust in recorded images and videos as objective depictions of reality.[66]

Lawmakers concerned with intelligence and national security are already reaching out to CEOs of Big Tech, inquiring about policies for dealing with deepfakes on their platforms.

The law must keep pace with the risks posed by the weaponization of technology. The risks posed have evolved, and the law must respond in equal or greater measures. But private sector enterprises would be foolish to wait for the government to solve this problem.

The US Department of Defense took the results of the inaugural cyber grand challenge seriously, subsequently launching "Project Voltron" to run similar autonomous cybersecurity protocols to monitor and repair vulnerabilities within military cyber infrastructure.[67] The technology has already evolved beyond rule-based AI to deploy machine learning capabilities. Expect these kinds of military projects to continue. We hope they will spill over into commercial applications of cybersecurity defense systems that use protective AI systems to harden IT infrastructure across the world.

A meeting in the capital of the United States between the CEOs of some of Silicon Valley's largest companies convened by then-Attorney General Jeff Sessions, "could presage sweeping new investigations of Amazon, Facebook, Google and their tech industry peers, stemming from lingering frustrations that these companies are too big, fail to safeguard users' private data and don't cooperate with legal demands."[68]

Sessions' purpose for the meeting was to probe whether these tech companies were promoting a liberal ideological bias across their platforms. This was a response to complaints by President Trump and top Republicans that Silicon Valley social media platforms were surreptitiously squelching the viewpoints of conservative online users. As social media platforms increasingly become forums for the delivery and consumption of news, the concern about partisan curation of public information is a legitimate concern, however we should be equally concerned about outright disinformation and harmful propaganda. Indeed, the opportunity to grill tech-company executives was seized upon by the other attorneys in attendance, including the Attorneys General of eight states and the District of Columbia and officials from five other states. The focus of the meeting quickly turned to what the attorneys felt about Big Tech's handling of consumer privacy.

According to D.C. Attorney General Karl Racine, the "AGs are really focused on understanding more as to what consumers are truly consenting to and what they may not know is going on with their data." According to Jim Hood, Attorney General of Mississippi, "We were unanimous. Our focus is going to be on antitrust and privacy. That's where our laws are."

According to the *Washington Post* report on this meeting:[69]

> For months, tech giants like Facebook, Google, and Twitter have weathered brutal criticism in the nation's capital for their business practices—from the ways they safeguard their data to their preparedness to combat misinformation online ahead of the 2018 midterm elections. Whether state and federal officials have the legal tools under antitrust law to regulate the tech industry's data practices was a major question for the group.

For other states, the issue was the tech industry's relationship with law enforcement. That included talk about Apple and "how we in law enforcement depend on cellphones." Hood said that Apple has "waved at us and didn't use all their fingers" in its handling of encryption.

Although the state Attorneys General agree that legal action against the industry (if wrongdoing is found) would probably be led by the United States Justice Department, interestingly, leadership on the issue of policing tech companies' use of consumer data and protecting consumer privacy is driven by a bi-partisan multistate inquiry of the part of various state Attorneys General, coordinated by Nebraska Attorney General Doug Peterson.

In Europe, breaches in consumer privacy or security are dealt with by application of the European Union's GDPR. The GDPR became applicable in May of 2018. The law is sweeping in territorial scope—it applies to those who control or process personal data related to offering of goods or services to data subjects (i.e., consumers) who are in the European Union, regardless of whether payment is required.[70]

A company with its servers located anywhere in the world is subject to the GDPR, even if it is not based in the EU, if it is processing data belonging to a data subject in the EU. The GDPR requires data to be processed in a transparent manner; inaccurate data must be erased or rectified without delay; and the data controller must comply with all principles of the GDPR, including safeguards for storage, de-identification of personal data, obtaining consent from the data subject, and providing infrastructure to protect the rights and freedoms of the data subject.[71]

The GDPR creates interesting (that is, complex) compliance situations where government agencies still need to develop internationally compatible frameworks for data governance during cross-border transfers. Time will tell whether the GDPR will catch on in other nations. Google is being sued by a natural person claiming the right to privacy means he can de-list prejudicial information about him—effectively staking out the consumer's privacy right to delete oneself from Internet search results.[72]

Meanwhile in the United States, the federal legislature gave Internet Service Providers the right to gather and sell for profit an Internet user's private browsing history, without even requiring that they obtain the user's consent. The strength of consumer expectations of privacy was clearly no match for the strength of telecommunications industry influence. The US and the EU's stance toward digital privacy rights stand in stark contrast. Savvy consumers are starting to take privacy into their own hands, purchasing home security infrastructure such as *Virtual Private Networks (VPN)* and using encrypted telecommunications devices.

The complacent attitude of US lawmakers toward increasingly frequent and severe data breaches by US-based companies surely cannot last much longer.

Consumer Privacy and the "Internet of Eyes"

Evan Nisselson coins the phrase the *Internet of Eyes* to describe the state of affairs when manmade objects all have Internet connectivity and smart sensors built in.[73]

Nisselson provides an effusive take on the Internet of Eyes because he looks forward to Amazon being able to tell him when he needs to purchase a change of pants or to stock up on his groceries, as this will streamline his shopping experience. We feel that literal domestic surveillance is a steep price to pay for limited benefits in terms of customer convenience. But maybe that's just us. Some people may not put as high a premium on privacy. In describing the new Amazon Echo "Look" (which is basically the Amazon Echo with a surveillance camera built in), Nisselson explains:[74]

> Major technology companies and new startups are at war over having the most valuable artificial intelligence and at the core of this war is having unique high quality visual data. Inanimate objects with cameras enable companies to own the first step in gathering the data for computer vision and artificial intelligence algorithms to analyze.
>
> Their core goal is to capture unique and proprietary visual data of their customers so their computers can learn as much as possible about us through the Selfies we capture via Amazon's product the Echo Look.
>
> [In the future,] these cameras will analyze many different types of visual data from photographic, thermal, X-ray, ultrasound, and white light to deliver high quality signals unlike anything we've had previously.

We are concerned about the proliferation of commercial spying, in which the companies consume the consumer, harvesting our data under the guise of enhancing consumer experiences, but truly creating disturbing privacy, security, and autonomy concerns such as choice architecture.

We feel like the Internet of Eyes is a little creepy and should be addressed by legal constraints on "smart" product design that at the very least requires consumer consent to being monitored. Of course, consumers can purchase products capable of spying on them and may have little concern about being spied upon.

Unless legislation comes down against this kind of practice, expect to see eyes on everything from refrigerators to television sets.

At what point does it become impossible for an ordinary human to resist an advertisement that has harnessed millions of data points about consumer preferences, emotional triggers, and human cognition such that it is impossible to ignore? When does the persuasion of an effective advertisement, which is protected commercial speech, become illegal coercion that overpowers the volition of the consumer? If an advertisement is irresistible, then we can no longer claim to be informing the consumer—we are controlling the consumer and the resulting transaction should be set aside.

Many nations' legal regimes of criminal law, contract law, and tort law assume humans have free will and are in control of their actions, absent extenuating circumstances such as coercion, duress, insanity, minority of age, or intoxication. In the United States' criminal justice system, the notion of criminal liability for actions depends on mens rea, or having a guilty mind, as well as actus reus, or a volitional criminal act. Both mens rea and actus reus depend on some folk psychological notion of free will. Courts only uphold contracts that were freely entered into by consenting adults enjoying legal capacity. The legal system assumes we are free, not automata.

In these cases, companies that harvest data about consumers in order to influence consumer choice are *consuming the consumer* in the sense that they are harvesting data created by consumers like they are picking wildflowers. It is unclear where the line should be drawn or how it could be drawn in a uniform and fairly applicable manner. However, it appears intuitive (and we would argue strenuously) that there should be some limitation on what companies can do to manipulate consumers. Issues of consumer privacy, self-determination, meaningful choice, and safety (in instances where distraction can lead to dangerous conditions) must be given weight. Advertisements that are based on big data-driven artificial intelligence may be too potent to be appropriate for use in certain areas (such as on billboards along freeways) or in certain audiences (for instance, minors or seniors who are easily persuaded due to mental infirmity).

As deepfakes illustrate, even reasonably prudent people can be duped or manipulated by a military-grade psy-op or propaganda campaign. We should counteract the continually expanding power of persuasion that is even today harnessing AI to transform the art of advertisement. With AI, advertising is becoming a dangerously potent weapon capable of seizing control of our attention span to the point where we can no longer resist its lure.

We warn against the day when, thanks to advances in AI and machine learning, every purchase becomes an "impulse buy." Under those extreme circumstances, the moral support for free markets breaks down, as we can no longer trust the market to behave efficiently. Consumers would not be maximizing their own utility from entering compulsively into transactions; they would be manipulated into exchanges that do not make them better off. When advertising becomes too powerful, this could lead to market failures, thereby justifying (even for a libertarian) some form of regulatory intervention, if not robust self-policing by the marketers themselves. With all the insight into consumer psychology housed in Marketing departments, we expect them to exercise leadership in this context. AI combined with big data gives marketers recipes that could become perhaps too potent.

Our concerns about consuming the consumer are threefold. First, the collection of consumer-generated data is uncompensated. What companies that monitor their customers and the public capture is valuable, but they are not paying anything back to the people creating that data. Second, the consent given by consumers to have their privacy invaded is often obtained imperfectly. Disclosure and permission are buried in fine print and legalese in click-through end-user license agreements that no one reads. Third, the data harvested by companies may not be safeguarded by the harvesting company to a reasonable degree that adequately protects consumer privacy interests. We turn to the safeguarding of consumer data, next.

The Cost of Failing to Implement Privacy and Security Safeguards

The largest ride-hailing app disrupting the yellow cab industry and transforming transportation in general is Uber. Thriving in the new access-based economy, Uber provides job opportunities for those with a vehicle and increases the transparency and accessibility of cab rides to any user with a smartphone and credit card. The popularity of the app led to the meteoric rise of the company.

Its original CEO, Travis Kalanik, took the company perhaps too close to the sun. Public scrutiny of his leadership style and the "tech bro" corporate culture that fomented under his leadership, along with a handful of scandals, led to his replacement. When the company's board appointed a new CEO, Dara Khosrowshahi, he immediately began to clean up shop. Several problems came to light under new leadership, one of them being a massive data breach from 2016.

With millions of users' payment and personal information loaded into the app, consumers and employees alike trusted Uber to maintain this sensitive information in a manner that preserved privacy and security. The company suffered a data breach that exposed the names, emails, and phone numbers of 57 million people around the world.

Then, in response, the company sat on this information and even paid $100,000 to the hackers to keep the breach quiet. As the new CEO, Khosrowshahi honorably ordered an investigation into a purported data breach and the company's subsequent cover-up attempt, and then disclosed the findings publicly.

The data breach came to the attention of Uber's Chief Legal Officer, Tony West, on his first day on the job. "Rather than settling into my new workplace and walking the floor to meet my new colleagues, I spend the day calling various state and federal regulators," says West.

Attorneys General for all 50 of the United States and the District of Columbia took legal action against Uber. Apparently, hiding a breach from your customers is not the proper response. In September 2018, the company reached a settlement agreement to pay $148 million to end the multistate probe.

According to the Attorney General of California Xavier Becerra,

> Uber's decision to cover up this breach was a blatant violation of the public's trust. Companies in California and throughout the nation are entrusted with customers' information. This settlement broadcasts to all of them that we will hold them accountable to protect that data.[75]

The settlement represents the biggest ever multistate penalty for a data breach. According to New York Attorney General Barbara Underwood, "We have zero tolerance for those who skirt the law and leave consumer and employee information vulnerable to exploitation."[76]

In the summer of 2018, Uber hired as its Chief Trust and Security Officer a former general counsel for the National Security Agency. As part of the settlement, Uber is required to make changes to its practices and corporate culture, including undergoing regular third-party audits of security practices.

Today's technology—and the interconnectivity that ties devices, business partners, and customers—also exposes businesses to a wide range of security threats. With the explosion of connected devices and the amount of personal data, the Identity Theft Resource Center (ITRC, 2018) reports that in just the first three months of 2018 there have been 273 breaches with over 5 million customer records exposed.

There are other well-known data breaches—the 2017 Equifax breach exposing 140 million customers' social security numbers and more recently we saw the use of personal information from Facebook by Cambridge Analytica weaponized to influence the 2016 presidential election. Firms that use any type of data—especially disaggregate customer data—need to be very careful about security and privacy, less they violate local and federal laws. Further, cyberhacks can disrupt operations, steal data and IP, and create massive security breaches that can destroy a company.

We are witnessing increasingly sophisticated cyber intrusions that exploit computer-based systems, threatening public trust, and wreaking economic havoc. In 2013, when hackers exploited a vulnerability in retail giant Target's infrastructure, they stole 40 million customer credit and debit cards and 70 million records containing personally identifying information of customers; Target's fourth-quarter profits that year dropped 46% from the year before.[77] Facebook was recently ordered to pay a USD $5 billion file as part of a settlement with regulatory authorities over mishandling consumer data; the privacy penalty is the largest fine in Federal Trade Commission history.

Each breach of a digital or cyber technology challenges users to mistrust and abandon the technology. User loyalty has, to date, proved remarkably enduring. But when it breaks, customers exit rapidly and in droves. A company's cybersecurity safeguards protect not only its trade secrets and other intellectual property, but also its reputation, brand, and goodwill.[78]

Companies today are more than ever targets of actors—state sponsored and rogue alike—dedicated to increasingly cunning forms of corporate espionage, writing malware to bypass IT security defenses, stealing intellectual property, and generally causing mayhem.[79] Building information security into technology must be a top priority. Our "smart" devices are simply far too vulnerable. As organizations increasingly go digital, they increase the amount of surface area vulnerable to cyberattack. As institutions adopt CRMs and other electronic management platforms, they open themselves up to ransomware. "Smart" is a double-edged sword.

Beware of Algorithmic Bias

Recall from Chapter 3 we explained that algorithms generally are defined procedures for solving a problem, and more technically, sets of rules or procedures that a computer is programmed to follow when carrying out problem-solving or task-oriented operations. Algorithms apply rules when triggered by certain inputs. If a mortgage application contains elements X, Y, and Z (for example, high credit score, low debt, and steady income), it should be approved. It is easy to imagine botsourcing that kind of function to an algorithm-based AI.

Algorithmic approaches to data processing can be more reliable problem solvers than humans in the sense that algorithms tend to be relatively objective, consistent, and powerful in processing vast data sets.

Machine learning goes beyond applying an algorithm to carry out a task; machine learning utilizes pattern recognition and Bayesian reasoning to "teach" itself based on new data.

According to Will Knight in the *MIT Technology Review*,

> Big tech companies are racing to sell off-the-shelf machine-learning technology that can be accessed via the cloud. As more customers make use of these algorithms to automate important judgments and decisions, the issue of bias will become crucial. And since bias can easily creep into machine-learning models, ways to automate the detection of unfairness could become a valuable part of the AI toolkit.[80]

The problem with machine learning is that we can inadvertently come with *built-in bias* when the AI is trained with dirty historical data. For example, an AI system that processes mortgage applications would presumably be trained by reviewing historical data sets of all the prior mortgage applications that have been submitted, and learning to recognize patterns that identify which should be approved versus those that should be rejected. The problem comes when the historical data set includes a number of rejected applications that were rejected for reasons of unfair prejudice or illegal racial discrimination.

Historically, some banks would reject mortgage applications in a non-white neighborhood, or they would increase the cost of the capital or the cost of insurance for nonwhite applicants in order to discourage home buying by people of color. This is called *redlining*, which refers to the practice of banks drawing red lines on maps to indicate neighborhoods predominately occupied by nonwhites where they did not want to provide loans in order to discriminate against persons of color who were otherwise creditworthy and qualified loan applicants.

Redlining on the basis of race is now illegal under the federal Fair Housing Act, whereas redlining a neighborhood because it sits on a seismic fault line or in a flood plain is reasonable and appropriate risk underwriting.[81] A machine learning AI system fed decades of mortgage applications in the greater Detroit area may very well perpetrate the now-illegal practice of race-based redlining even though, of course, the AI itself holds no racial animus. It is only following precedent.

Given the sordid past of discrimination based on race, gender, and wealth, we need to build our AI systems to be fair and transparent. "Algorithmic bias can lead to over-policing in predominately black areas; the automated filters on social media flag activists while allowing hate groups to keep posting unchecked."[82] To combat the problem of algorithmic bias and build trust in our AI comrades, IBM is requiring developers to jump through some hurdles before AI software goes to market.

One of these safeguards is a third-party audit, where the source code and historical data underlying the AI software are evaluated by an independent expert to flag for prejudices; another safeguard is running counterfactual tests to ensure the algorithm is not inappropriately sensitive to race, gender, or wealth.

To help promote ethical algorithms, IBM scientists are proposing that developers of AI programs must publish a *Supplier's Declaration of Conformity (SDoC)* prior to an algorithm's sale. The SDoC would take the form of a report or user manual that indicates to prospective purchasers how well the algorithm performed on "standardized tests of performance, fairness and risk factors, and safety measures."[83] In the same way that a prospective purchaser can obtain crash safety information about a car before driving it off the lot, a potential buyer of AI software should be able to tell whether the algorithms contained in the software are likely to generate outputs informed by prejudices or whether it is secured against known cyberattack threats.

Microsoft is also pursuing the problem of algorithmic bias. According to Rich Caruana, Senior Researcher at Microsoft working on a bias-detection dashboard, "Things like transparency, intelligibility, and explanation are new enough to the field that few of us have sufficient experience to know everything we should look for and all the ways that bias might lurk in our models."[84] Caruana argues that the most important step tech companies can take on this issue is workforce education, "so that they're aware of the myriad ways in which bias can arise and manifest itself and create tools to make models easier to understand and bias easier to detect."

Facebook is also raising the profile of algorithmic bias as a corporate concern. Facebook has launched a product for internal detection of bias called Fairness Flow. According to Will Knight, "Facebook says it needed Fairness Flow because more and more people at the company are using AI to make important decisions," and it needed to be warned if an algorithm was making inappropriate recommendations on the basis of race or gender, for example.[85]

We forecast that algorithmic bias will become the subject of federal regulation, just like food safety standards for food processing companies imposed by the Food and Drug Administration, or crash test safety standards imposed by the National Highway Traffic Safety Administration. Until then, IBM, Facebook, and Microsoft are pushing forward with self-policing. Experts are skeptical. Professor Bin Yu at University of California, Berkeley, appreciates these proactive steps but suggests third-party external audits are more appropriate: "Someone else has to investigate Facebook's algorithms—they can't be a secret to everyone."[86]

Black Box Decisions: AI's "Dark Secret"

The inscrutability of more advanced algorithms poses a problem in instances where AI systems make decisions with huge consequences, such as self-driving cars pulling off an emergency maneuver to avoid a crash, multi-million-dollar stock market trade decisions, cancer treatment recommendations, and other complex judgments delivered by AI. There will be errors that lead to lawsuits on the part of victims. Plaintiffs' attorneys will seek to depose the AI developers and the executive decision-makers who relied upon the AI recommendations. Victims will want to know why the AI did what it did. Litigators will want to know whether the executive followed the recommendation of the smart software, and if not, why not.

What if the AI suggested Option A, but the executive chose Option B resulting in harm?

What if the AI suggested Option A, and the executive chose Option A resulting in harm?

If the AI cannot explain why it is making its recommendations, then executives will have a harder time justifying reliance upon its recommendations when defending their actions. They will have to independently justify actions with personal reasons. But if they are doing that, then it leads us to question why even have AI recommendations if they cannot be relied upon when those actions have legal consequences?

This leads us to what Will Knight of the *MIT Technology Review* describes as the "dark secret at the heart of AI."[87] To illustrate the challenge, Knight describes an experimental vehicle set loose by Nvidia. Unlike autonomous cars demonstrated by Google, Tesla, and General Motors, which follow instructions of engineers and programmers, the Nvidia vehicle used deep learning to teach itself solely by watching videos of human drivers. This is how it works (and why it's mysterious):[88]

> Information from the vehicle's sensors goes straight into a huge network of artificial neurons that process the data and then deliver the commands required to operate the steering wheel, the brakes, and other systems. The result seems to match the responses you'd expect from a human driver. But what if one day it did something unexpected—crashed into a tree or sat at a green light? As things stand now, it might be difficult to find out why. The system is so complicated that even the engineers who designed it may struggle to isolate the reason for any single action. And you can't ask it: there is no obvious way to design such a system so that it could always explain why it did what it did.[89]

Until an AI system is capable of being interrogated as to why it reached a decision (e.g., why did you recommend to sell these shares? Why did you turn into oncoming traffic?) then it should not be deployed in the wild.

Perhaps unsurprisingly, the European Union is taking a precautionary approach to AI—and contrary to the fears expressed by the US Chamber of Commerce, the European approach to regulating AI is not to stifle innovation out of some extreme risk aversion but rather to increase investment and deployment of this technology in a safe manner.

The European Artificial Intelligence Alliance will draft ethical guidelines based on the input from businesses, researchers, consumers, trade unions, policymakers, and government officials in the format of formal stakeholder feedback.[90] The European Commission suggested then it would provide guidelines for AI based on the existing Product Liability Directive. Products liability law in the United States and Europe defines when a product manufacturer or distributor is liable for unreasonably dangerous or defective conditions in a product.[91] It goes beyond the scope of this chapter to compare and contrast products liability law in various jurisdictions. Suffice it to say, it will be interesting to observe how the United States, Europe, and China and other tech-ambitious nations each approach the risk management, ethical, and legal challenges posed by AI.

The European Union's GDPR went into application in 2018 as a sweeping reform of the 1995 European Data Protection Directive. The GDPR applies to any company doing business with European citizens. While saying a lot about consumer privacy and data security, as well as how to handle data breaches, the GDPR surprisingly says very little about the black box decision-making of AI systems. That said, it is one of the only formal pronouncements by legal institutions on this important challenge posed by AI. And what little is said by GDPR on black box decision-making has generated some controversy among legal scholars.

The GDPR provides that data controllers are required to notify consumers how data is used, which includes "the existence of automated decision-making, and, at least in those cases, meaningful information about the logic involved, as well as the significance and the envisaged consequences of such processing for the data subject." This arguably requires data controllers to explain how consumer data is being used by AI systems to make decisions.

This interpretation is supported by the language in Recital 71, a legally unenforceable companion document to the GDPR, which elaborates on the actual requirements of the GDPR.

Recital 71 applies not only to the issue of algorithmic bias but also to the mysterious mind of some AI systems. The entire text of Recital 71 is in this endnote.[92] The most salient part is the EU's solution to the black box problem: Data subjects have "the right to obtain human intervention, to express his or her point of view, to obtain an explanation of the decision reached after such assessment and to challenge the decision." This would seem to preclude some neural net AI systems from operating on EU data subjects altogether, due to the inexplicable nature of its output.

The Impact of AI on Lawmaking and Regulations

With all this talk about how laws can protect us against the risks posed by AI, we should spend some time on how AI is influencing the lawmaking and regulatory process itself. Ironically, if not ultimately tragically, AI can manipulate the very institutions meant to curb its abuse.

Erosion of Public Trust

In the US, to create a law, it must be drafted by legislators (or supplied to them by a special interest group—for example, the controversial American Legislative Exchange Council), then the bill must make it out of committee, be put on the floor for a vote, receive a majority affirmative vote in both houses of Congress (both the House of Representatives and the Senate), then signed into law by the President. There are a lot of procedural hurdles to ensure only wise laws are enacted that carry the carefully considered majority support of the nation's elected representatives. Somehow despite these checks, balances, and tripwires designed to keep bad laws off the books, sentiment is usually unfavorable toward government, and the average person hardly feels comfortable trusting the US government to "do the right thing."

According to PEW Research Center data, public trust in the government is at an all-time low and has been trending downward since the Nixon administration, trending upward only when the economy is doing well or when the nation rallied in response to the 9/11 World Trade Center attacks.[93] Predictably, trust in government is higher when the respondent's own political party holds the power of office, yet somehow both Democrats and Republicans feel their party is always losing, and there are only modest differences between the generations, races, and ethnicities in terms of trust in government. In general, most people do not trust the government to do the right thing.[94]

According to Professor Anthony Curtis, an expert in mass communications, the history of social media use can be divided into three historical phases: Before the Dawn (1969–1993), The Dawning (1994–2004), and After the Dawn (2005 and beyond).[95] Researchers began seriously to study social media by analyzing data obtained through monitoring and performing sentiment analysis over that data in order to begin scientifically to understand the mood of social media users. Beyond the United States, other governments are trying to improve relationships with citizens by using social media to promote transparency and engagement that enables the government to be citizen-centric, thereby prioritizing government resources toward meeting real-time citizen needs rather than merely offering services based on existing government capabilities.[96]

The advent of cloud Internet services, wireless Internet accessibly in far broader reaches, and the proliferation of social media platforms and the penetration of these platforms ever deeper into popular usage have enabled both corporations and governments unprecedented access into the mood of the people. Governments and corporations can study our moods with statistically significant sample sizes and can interact with large swaths of the population at virtually no cost, simply by "posting" an infographic on an official Facebook page or by "tweeting" out a brief statement on an official Twitter handle.

With this unparalleled access to social feedback and sentiment analysis, you would think governments and corporations would do a better job at restoring public trust. What if the limitations on human self-interest and rationality (discussed in Chapter 4) prevent us from writing good laws or governing our companies in ways that retain social license to operate? Can technology transform the rulemaking process to improve public trust in regulatory outcomes?

Improving Public Participation

According to Chris Horton of the *MIT Technology Review*, there is a "simple but ingenious system" being deployed in Taiwan that offers a "promising experiment in participatory government," but, ironically, its main obstacle to gaining traction in greater use in politics is... politics.[97] In brief, the Taiwanese government has deployed an online platform ("vTaiwan") to enable *crowdsourcing* (querying the public to answer a specific question) on controversial issues of policy. Crowdsourcing answers to proposed legal reforms has proven "useful in finding consensus on dead-locked issues," says Horton, but "the question now is whether it can be used to settle bigger policy questions at a national level—and whether it could be a model for other countries."[98]

Due to unfortunate tribal elements of human nature and the partisan arrangement of many electoral political bodies, we fall easily into deadlock on divisive issues where one "side" has to "beat" the other side, and compromise is viewed as weakness. This frustrates efforts at building consensus and ultimately undermines the ability of a government to enjoy ongoing majority support for its policies over time. However, the vTaiwan experiment has shown a way to resolve these partisan deadlocks by cutting out the middleman of elected representatives and letting the people speak directly to the issues. Not speaking to each other, mind you, but to the issues themselves.

According to Colin Megill, the CEO and cofounder of pol.is (a digital hosting platform used by vTaiwan), one of the reasons for deadlock is that "the opposing sides had never had a chance to actually interact with each other's ideas. When they did, it became apparent that both sides were basically willing to give the opposing side what it wanted."[99]

Technology using certain features of social media platforms like "commenting" on a "post" (a la Facebook) and "upvoting" or "downvoting" on a comment (a la Imgur) are enabling governments to govern in ways that better reflect the goals and priorities of the people. According to Horton,

> vTaiwan relies on a hodgepodge of open-source tools for soliciting proposals, sharing information, and holding polls, but one of the key parts is pol.is, created by Megill and a couple of friends in Seattle after the events of Occupy Wall Street and the Arab Spring in 2011.[100]

The mechanism for pol.is is as follows: a topic is posted for debate; anyone may create an account to post a comment and also "upvote" or "downvote" another user's comment; however—and this is the unique part that distinguishes this platform from the social media forums on Facebook and Twitter—users are not allowed to reply to other user's comments. Each comment must stand on its own, earning favor or garnering derision based on the other user's feedback through the voting mechanism.

According to Audrey Tang, Taiwan's Digital Minister and a former activist for greater transparency in government, "If people can propose their ideas and comments but they cannot reply to each other, then it drastically reduces the motivation for trolls to troll." When commenters are not mudslinging, they are actually engaged in constructive civic discourse. Lawmakers may in turn see these commenters as "not protesters or mobs, but actually people with distinct expertise."[101]

Another unique feature of this crowdsourcing mechanism is that the upvote and downvote process generates "a kind of map of all the participants in the debate, clustering together people who have voted similarly," according to Horton. What this does is transform thousands of separate comments into distinct areas of consensus where like-minded users gravitate around certain proposals on the original topic, and it reveals where the remaining gaps are. "People then naturally try to draft comments that will win votes from both sides of the divide, gradually eliminating the gaps," says Horton.[102]

As a result of this process, lawmakers can confidently take these consensus comments into the lawmaking process, knowing they can win votes from both "sides" of the issue, and steer clear of the areas that are least supported. "If you show people the face of the crowd, and if you take away the reply button, then people stop wasting time on the divisive statements," says Tang.[103]

An example of vTaiwan in action is how the nation dealt with the unique regulatory challenge posed by disruptive ride-hailing service Uber. Like many divisive issues in politics, when first introduced, Uber was met with strident opposition from—you guessed it—cab drivers whose market share would be depleted by competition from the influx of freelance drivers using the app. Using the vTaiwan platform, the initial crowdsourcing responses quickly coalesced into two groups at loggerheads—one for Uber and another larger camp firmly against. At first blush, the experiment was a failure because this kind of entrenched disagreement between two sides of an issue was just politics as usual.

> But then the magic happened: as the groups sought to attract more supporters, their members started posting comments on matters that everyone could agree were important, such as rider safety and liability insurance. Gradually, they refined them to garner more votes. The end result was a set of seven comments that enjoyed almost universal approval, containing such recommendations, as 'The government should set up a fair regulatory regime,' 'Private passenger vehicles should be registered,' and 'It should be permissible for a for-hire driver to join multiple fleets and platforms.' The divide between pro- and anti-Uber camps had been replaced by consensus on how to create a level playing field for Uber and the taxi firms, protect consumers, and create more competition.[104]

The result was a regulatory platform consistent with this emergent consensus. As many who follow politics in the United States would attest, there are few utterances about politics that are not controversial. That US politics is divisive is one of those few statements upon which most would agree. The US political discourse is driven in large part by divisive rhetoric about so-called wedge issues that drive voters into one of two camps in order to consolidate each party's "base," sewing deeper discord and disdain for the opponent in the process, with the unfortunate end result being the vilification of the opponent and dissatisfaction from both sides in the end legislative and regulatory result.

When political victories are always pyrrhic and no one is happy with the outcome, something is broken in the process. If we are to take a lesson from vTaiwan, the way the US political process tends to play out is the exact opposite method for restoring trust in government to "do the right thing."

The Spambot Lobby: Repealing Net Neutrality

Net neutrality regulations, essential to maintaining a free and open Internet, were repealed in the United States as a result of a cyberattack on the Federal Communications Commission that appears to have corrupted government decision-making. Millions of fake comments posed by spambots tipped the scales and created a pretext for the Trump Administration to repeal net neutrality safeguards. How did this happen? How can we use technology in government without further eroding public trust?

"Notice and Comment" Rulemaking

According to Carroll Doherty, the director of political research at PEW, "The fact that Republicans and Democrats differ on ... fundamental issues is probably not a surprise, but the magnitude of the difference is striking, and particularly how the differences have grown in recent years."[105] In many ways, the United States is becoming functionally, if not legally, two separate one-party nations fighting for control over the seat of government, rather than an indivisible two-party nation.[106] If there is a time for restoring public trust in government and forming consensus around issues, it is now. Can using technology to solicit public comments, such as demonstrated in Taiwan, help in the United States?

The way the federal regulatory agencies in the United States gather input from stakeholders potentially impacted by major regulatory action is through a process of notice and comment rulemaking. This differs markedly from the approach taken by vTaiwan and while it is designed to prevent regulations from being arbitrary, capricious, and unsupported by evidence, it can still be abused. The typical process for introducing regulations in the United States is to follow the so-called *Notice and Comment rulemaking* process under the Administrative Procedure Act (APA).[107] An agency complies with the Notice and Comment requirements of the APA by citing to the legislative authority under which it is acting, identifying the areas of the economy and market actors potentially affected by the regulation, setting forth a regulatory proposal, and opening up a window to give private sector stakeholders notice of the proposed rule and to provide the public an opportunity to comment.

Under the APA, an agency must not act in an "arbitrary or capricious" manner, and must not ignore "substantial evidence on the record," otherwise a federal judge could set the agency's regulations aside. In this manner, if a public commenter challenges the proposed regulation by dropping scientific studies of adverse social, economic, or environmental impacts into the record, or if the public overwhelmingly opposes a rule, the agency proposing the rule must address the concerns raised, at risk of having the regulation thrown out by a federal judge.

In theory, the Notice and Comment rulemaking process should provide popular support and due process for new rules, ensuring that regulatory agencies do not run wild with rules that are inconsistent with science, law, or public policy.

Open Internet on the Electronic Frontier

However, the rise of artificial intelligence, natural language processing, and the use of "bots" has undermined this democratic safety valve. Take, for example, the fallout from the proposed *Net Neutrality* regulations under the Trump Administration.

First, a word about net neutrality. Really, "net" stands for "network," in reference to the world wide web, and "neutrality" refers to "the idea that Internet service providers (ISPs) should treat all data that travels over their networks fairly, without improper discrimination in favor of particular apps, sites or services."[108]

The principle of net neutrality would prevent an ISP from throttling access to certain websites, blocking certain applications, or otherwise undermining an open Internet and the ability for users to freely exchange and access ideas and services online. Given the significance of Internet access to modern life, net neutrality is the twenty-first-century virtual equivalent to freedom of speech and freedom to move about—without which life as we know it would be greatly impoverished.

The threat to Internet freedom led the Federal Communications Commission (FCC) under the Obama Administration to propose rules for an "open Internet" in 2010. The problem was this initial attempt at safeguarding an open Internet was legally and practically deficient, and it foundered after major telecommunications provider Verizon challenged it in court in 2014. This sent the FCC back to the drawing board. In the spirit of transparency and engagement with the public, the FCC accepted comments from actual Internet users on how to protect net neutrality properly. Led in part by the Electronic Frontier Foundation (EFF), a nonprofit organization with the mission of defending civil liberties in the digital world, millions of users weighed in on the revised rule.

According to the EFF,

> As a direct result of that intense public activism and scrutiny, in 2015, the FCC produced rules that we could support—in part because, in addition to the bright line rules against blocking, throttling, and paid prioritization of Internet traffic, they included strict 'forbearance' restrictions on what the FCC can do without holding another rulemaking.[109]

This was a major win for advocates for an open Internet, including Internet-based start-ups and Internet users. But it was a temporary victory.

Betraying the Founders of the Internet

Fast forward to the Trump Administration, where in 2017 the new FCC Chair, Ajit Pai (formerly Associate General Counsel at Verizon), repealed the net neutrality protections, "despite intense resistance from nonprofits, artists, tech companies large and small, libraries, even some ISPs, and millions of regular Internet users."[110] The order to repeal the net neutrality safeguard was given the Orwellian moniker, "Restoring Internet Freedom Order."[111] According to EFF, the order "ignored technical evidence submitted by EFF and others and showed a remarkable lack of understanding of how the Internet works."[112]

Indeed, inventors of the Internet itself criticized the intellectual basis for the rule. In an open letter signed by more than 20 Internet pioneers and leaders (including Vint Cerf, "father of the Internet," Tim Berners-Lee, the inventor of the World Wide Web, and Steve Wozniak, Apple cofounder) urged the FCC to cancel its vote to repeal net neutrality, describing the plan as "based on a flawed and factually inaccurate" understanding of how the Internet works.[113] "The FCC's rushed and technically incorrect proposed order to repeal net neutrality protections without any replacement is an imminent threat to the Internet we worked so hard to create. It should be stopped," they wrote. They were ignored.

The FCC's proposed repeal of net neutrality garnered at least 22 million comments during the Notice and Comment rulemaking process. In 2017, the digital policy and law intelligence platform FiscalNote founded by Tim Hwang conducted an analysis of these comments. The FiscalNote analysis concluded that 19 million commenters opposed the repeal, of which mere thousands were auto-generated by visitors to the Electronic Frontier Foundation who provided the online forms as a service to its visitors. The FiscalNote analysis also initially determined that "hundreds of thousands of pro-repeal comments were written by bots using natural-language generation, an artificial-intelligence technique that simulates human language."[114] "FiscalNote showed that each fraudulent comment consisted of 35 phrases arranged in the same order but varied by plugging in up to 25 interchangeable words and phrases, a system designed to make comments appear unique."[115]

What followed was an investigation into the online comment process by the Attorney General of New York. This investigation by law enforcement concluded that no less than two million comments supporting the repeal of the net neutrality rule were submitted to the FCC by fraudulent accounts using the stolen identities of US citizens—some military service men and women who were deployed at the time, some children, and some deceased individuals. These victims of the identity theft had their names and contact information used to fill out the Notice and Comment form in order to file fake comments supporting the repeal.[116] On the eve of the FCC vote, the New York Attorney General warned, "Moving forward with this vote would make a mockery of the notice and comment process mandated by the Administrative Procedure Act and reward those who perpetrated this fraud in service of their own hidden agenda."[117]

Despite the overwhelming opposition to the repeal of net neutrality protections by the public commenters, despite the fraudulent support of repeal by identity thieves, despite the opposition of the rule by law enforcement, and despite the objection to the repeal by the inventors of the Internet and World Wide Web, the FCC voted to repeal net neutrality anyways. Despite a change in presidential administration, the FCC cannot restore net neutrality because it remains in a partisan deadlock.[118]

Transparency versus "Openwashing"

The contrasting examples of vTaiwan's successful crowdsourcing to develop consensus regulations on controversial topics, on the one hand, and the FCC's shocking repeal of overwhelmingly popular net neutrality regulations on the basis of fraudulent comments submitted by bots corrupting the public notice and comment rulemaking process, show that technology can be a two-edged sword when applied to the development of law. Clearly, we need to use technology where it can help, but we cannot be blind to the ways in which technology is an enabling mechanism that allows misconduct to be scaled, or which simply creates the appearance of transparency and open process when there is none. Products of artificial intelligence—like deepfakes—combined with natural language processing makes it easier to create a digital mask to cover the true faces of bad actors. Engagement via online platforms does not always generate the desired results and simply underscores how unpopular government proposals are before they are enacted.

The risk of deploying vTaiwan and the Notice and Comment process is that if the consensus proposals are not actually adopted into law, then it reveals the process to be a sham. Further, the risk of comments being flooded with bots following the orders of some hidden agenda is that it corrupts the process. The risk is " *openwashing*," or creating the mere pretense of transparent process, according to C.L. Kao, one of the cofounders of g0v.[119] Openwashing is to transparency what "greenwashing" is to environmental benefits—creating the impression of an environmentally friendly profile with mere labels or colors that do not reflect the underlying environmentally degrading reality. According to Jason Hsu, a founder of vTaiwan and lawmaker, the biggest problem with this platform for public comment is the outcomes are not binding on lawmakers, which makes it "a tiger without teeth."[120]

According to Beth Noveck, the director of New York University's Governance Lab, vTaiwan is a "step in the right direction," but like most of these mechanisms for ensuring public participation in governance, vTaiwan fails to gain credibility with citizens precisely because the outcomes are not binding on governments.

These lessons apply with equal force to corporate governance. Building consensus, ensuring feedback from the corporate hierarchy and stakeholders, and ensuring major decisions are not made on the basis of corrupt or fraudulent decision process are crucial to integrity of corporate conduct. People worldwide are increasingly skeptical of those in power and increasingly hungry for the truth.[121]

According to the *Harvard Business Review*,

> For 17 years the Edelman Trust Barometer has surveyed tens of thousands of people across dozens of countries about their level of trust in business, media, government, and NGOs. This year [2017] was the first time the study found a decline in trust across all four of these institutions.[122]

The failure of leaders in business and government to earn the trust of stakeholders has obvious deleterious consequences for brands (for business) and for the rule of law (for governments).

> In almost two-thirds of the 28 countries we surveyed, the general population did not trust the four institutions to 'do what is right'—the average level of trust in all four institutions combined was below 50%. We also discovered a staggering lack of confidence in leadership: 71% of survey respondents said government officials are not at all or somewhat credible, and 63% said the same about CEOs.[123]

With public trust toward governments and corporations at an all-time low, leaders must be willing to use technology to enhance participation and trust but at the same time must be wary of the ways in which technology can corrupt those same processes and, tragically, further erode trust.

The Cutting Edge of AI Law

For many of us, watching the onslaught of new AI innovation is a bit daunting. The front line of the botsourcing battlefront continues to recede toward traditional human strongholds. Tech titans keep moving fast, keep breaking things. In hearings before legislative bodies, it is clear some of these lawmakers are so far out of touch with the latest in technology, they are hardly aware of the subject matter they are supposed to be legislating, much less in the weeds enough to grasp the risks posed by these technologies. Perhaps we need more engineers in Congress.

Thankfully, various regulatory agencies are well stocked with brilliant policymakers and technical expertise and, because they do not have to run for election, are on more stable footing when it comes to holding tech titans accountable and enforcing the rule of law.

> There's a narrative out there that because technology is moving too fast, it can't possibly be regulated, because how could regulation keep up? [As an expert in large language models like that behind ChatGPT] I'm very heartened to see our regulatory agencies say no, what they're regulating is the activities of corporations, and those are still subject to regulations even if they're automated.[124]

In a display of solidarity and to avoid any doubt about the prosecutorial appetite of prominent US regulatory agencies, the Director of the Consumer Financial Protection Bureau, the Assistant Attorney General for the Justice Department's Civil Rights Division, the Chair of the Equal Employment Opportunity Commission, and the Chair of the Federal Trade Commission issued a Joint Statement on Enforcement Efforts Against Discrimination and Bias in Automated Systems:

> America's commitment to the core principles of fairness, equality, and justice is deeply embedded in the federal laws that our agencies enforce to protect civil rights, fair competition, consumer protection, and equal opportunity. These established laws have long served to protect individuals even as our society has navigated emerging technologies. Responsible innovation is not incompatible with these laws. Indeed, innovation and adherence to the law can complement each other and bring tangible benefits to people in a fair and competitive manner, such as increased access to opportunities as well as better products and services at lower costs. Today, the use of automated systems, including those sometimes marketed as 'artificial intelligence' or 'AI,' is becoming increasingly common in our daily lives... These automated systems are often advertised as providing insights and breakthroughs, increasing efficiencies and cost-savings, and modernizing existing practices. Although many of these tools offer the promise of

advancement, their use also has the potential to perpetuate unlawful bias, automate unlawful discrimination, and produce other harmful outcomes.[125]

"Existing legal authorities apply to the use of automated systems and innovative new technologies just as they apply to other practices."[126] According to one US Attorney, "Our 20th century civil rights laws apply to 21st century innovations."[127]

United States federal rules pertaining to the use of automated systems in business include limits on AI in credit applications such as mortgages or credit cards, as well as in the evaluation of candidates for housing such as an application to rent an apartment. Outside of the financial and housing sectors, the rules on AI cut across the US economy by regulating how AI can be used in employment and general commercial practices, such as marketing, regardless of industry or sector. See Table 6.2.

Table 6.2 Summary of US Federal regulations pertaining to AI

Legislation	Substantive Standard	Implication for AI Tools
Equal Credit Opportunity Act	Requires creditors to provide an explanation via written statement of specific reasons to applicants against whom adverse action is taken (such as denying a credit card application).	ECOA does not permit creditors to use complex algorithms when doing so means they cannot provide the specific and accurate reasons for adverse actions on credit applications.
Fair Housing Act	Prohibits discrimination in housing on the basis of race, color, religion, sex, familial status (having one or more children under 18), nation origin, and disability.	Housing providers and tenant screening companies must ensure all policies that exclude people from housing opportunities, whether based on algorithm or otherwise, do not have an unjustified disparate impact because of race, national origin or another protected characteristic.
Americans with Disabilities Act	Prohibits employment discrimination on the basis of disability such as physical or mental impairment that, if left untreated, would "substantially limit" one or more "major life activities" such as seeing, reaching, communicating, speaking, concentrating, or the operation of major bodily functions.	Employers may not use algorithmic decision-making tools that fail to provide reasonable accommodations to a disabled applicants thereby negatively impacting their candidacy.
Federal Trade Commission Act	Prevents unfair methods of competition and unfair or deceptive business practices that affect commerce and injure consumers.	FTC will seek monetary penalties against businesses that deceive consumers about the role of AI in a product or service, or that use AI to deceive consumers.

Credit Applications[128]

The Equal Credit Opportunity Act makes it unlawful for creditors (such as mortgage and credit card companies) to discriminate against any applicant, with respect to any aspect of a credit transaction, on the basis of race, color, religion, national origin, sex or marital status, age, etc. 15 U.S.C. § 1691(a). To promote consumer protection and education, any time a creditor makes an "adverse action" against an applicant (such as denying a credit card application, terminating an existing account, making adverse changes to terms, or refusing to increase a credit limit) the creditor must provide to the consumer an accurate statement of the specific reasons for the adverse action. The ECOA legal hook is potentially set when a company takes an adverse action on a customer application on the basis of the inscrutable rationale underlying the recommendation by some bot.

> Creditors who use complex algorithms, including artificial intelligence or machine learning, in any aspect of their credit decisions must still provide a notice that discloses the specific principal reasons for taking an adverse action. Whether a creditor is using a sophisticated machine learning algorithm or more conventional methods to evaluate an application, the legal requirement is the same[.] A creditor cannot justify noncompliance ... based on the mere fact that the technology it employs to evaluate applications is too complicated or opaque to understand. A creditor's lack of understanding of its own methods is therefore not a cognizable defense against liability for violating ECOA.[129]

In other words, as with most areas of criminal law, ignorance is no defense. Being ignorant about precisely how your AI is hurting consumers does not protect the user from liability for doing so. In this context, the "black box" character of some AI tools could not only injure consumers but also put the enterprise using such a tool at risk. It is not prudent to act on the recommendations of algorithms as if they were utterances of the Oracle of Delphi.

Housing[130]

According to the U.S. Attorney for the District of Massachusetts,

> Algorithms are written by people. As such, they are susceptible to all of the biases, implicit or explicit, of the people that create them. As the housing industry and other professions adopt algorithms into their everyday decisions, there can be disparate impacts on certain protected communities. Stable and affordable housing provides a unique pathway to success, opportunity and safety.

The Fair Housing Act is enforced by the US Department of Justice (DOJ) and the Department of Housing and Urban Development (HUD). These regulatory bodies will apply the consumer protections of the Fair Housing Act to algorithm-based tenant screening systems that unlawfully discriminate against rental applicants.

For example, in a Statement of Interest filed in *Louis et al. v. SafeRent et al.*, a lawsuit currently pending in the U.S. District Court for the District of Massachusetts, the federal regulators took issue with the defendants' alleged use of an algorithm-based scoring system to screen tenants in a manner than appeared to discriminate against Black and Hispanic rental applicants in violation of the FHA.

According to the Assistant Attorney General of the Justice Department's Civil Rights Division, "Housing providers and tenant screening companies that use algorithms and data to screen tenants are not absolved from liability when their practices disproportionately deny people of color access to fair housing opportunities."

This sentiment was echoed by the General Counsel for HUD:

> Tenant screening policies are not exempt from the Fair Housing Act's protections just because decisions are made by algorithm. Housing providers and tenant screening companies must ensure that all policies that exclude people from housing opportunities, whether based on algorithm or otherwise, do not have an unjustified disparate impact because of race, national origin or another protected characteristic.

Given how fundamental housing is to meeting the basic human need for shelter, and for providing economic stability for families and the literal resting place of community, algorithmic discrimination against housing candidates seems particularly inhumane.

Employment[131]

Some of the most common uses of AI in the corporate world are, perhaps ironically, in the context of Human Resources. The types of software used include "automatic resume-screening software, hiring software, chatbot software for hiring and workflow, video interviewing software, analytics software, employee monitoring software, and worker management software," which use various forms of AI, including "machine learning, computer vision, natural language processing and understanding, intelligent decision support systems, and autonomous systems."

While employers may utilize software to save time, increase objectivity, and decrease bias from human recruiters, the use of these tools may disadvantage candidates with disabilities in such a manner as to violate the American's with Disabilities Act (ADA). These tools are used to evaluate and rate human fitness in virtually every stage of employment, from hiring to termination, from performance evaluation to promotions. You may not have a chance to schmooze with it at the office holiday party, but AI is already shaping your career and probably being used to decide whether you get a bonus this year. Indeed, AI may be suppressing valuable human resources from job opportunities where they may otherwise excel, simply because the human defies the bot's model of success.

The risk of liability for using AI in the employment context arises when the employer relies on algorithmic decision-making. Examples include:

Resume scanners that prioritize applications using certain keywords; employee monitoring software that rates employees on the basis of their keystrokes or other factors; 'virtual assistants' or 'chatbots' that ask job candidates about their qualifications and reject those who do not meet pre-defined requirements; video interviewing software that evaluates candidates based on their facial expressions and speech patterns; and testing software that provides 'job fit' scores for applicants or employees regarding their personalities, aptitudes, cognitive skills, or perceived 'cultural fit' based on their performance on a game or on a more traditional test.[132]

Given how prolific these tools have become in the context of employment, the influence of biased algorithms can be especially pernicious, and if left unchecked would foreseeably impose a disproportionate burden on candidates with disabilities.

The ADA prohibits discrimination against people with disabilities, defined as a physical or mental impairment that, if left untreated, would "substantially limit" one or more "major life activities," such as seeing, reaching, communicating, speaking, concentrating, or the operation of major bodily functions, such as brain or neurological functions. It is unlawful to "screen out" a job candidate based on a disability that is unrelated to job safety when the disabled person could have overcome the screening had they been afforded some "reasonable accommodation."[133]

In the context of creating fair, merits-based employment opportunities for all candidates, be careful with AI. Instead of helping humans remove bias, certain applications of AI may lead to even worse bias.

Marketing[134]

The Federal Trade Commission (FTC) is the US agency responsible for policing unfair and deceptive trade practices. The FTC has the authority to enforce federal law against any company that sells AI software that contains illegal elements, or that uses AI in an illegal manner. In this section we discuss "fake AI" as well as "AI fakes."

Fake AI

This section is concerned with the use of AI as a deceptive selling point. For example, just because AI was used in the development of a new product, does not mean the product "has" AI as a marketable feature. This is the "fake AI" problem.

Let's assume your business is launching a new toaster oven in a somewhat saturated space, and in an effort to enhance the competitiveness of this new toaster, your marketing team starts dressing up the copy with phraseology that comes across as breathless hype about its "artificial intelligence." This toaster knows your preferences, whether that is lightly toasted or burnt to a black crisp, and will use its AI to deliver the perfectly browned slice of bread. This toaster knows when you like to wake up in the morning as it can be programmed to be your virtual toaster servant at any hour. This toaster's built-in LCD display can help you get dressed in the morning by telling you about the weather (which it gets by pulling data via Bluetooth from the app installed on your phone). This toaster is the greatest thing since sliced bread, owing to its extraordinarily over-engineered and completely unnecessary incorporation of "AI" features. Given the toaster is merely applying existing technologies like an egg timer, it would be borderline deceptive to describe these features as novel or "AI-powered" in any meaningful way.

The FTC considers "AI" and related jargon hot marketing terms. "At the FTC, one thing we know about hot marketing terms is that some advertisers won't be able to stop themselves from overusing and abusing them."[135] Abusing "AI" in marketing material happens whenever the AI claims do not work as advertised, or the claims of efficacy are false or unsubstantiated, such as claiming a product can make predictions when this is only sometimes true, or the product is superior to non-AI products when comparative data is unavailable.

Accordingly, the FTC may take enforcement action against any company that runs advertisements that fail to withstand the following scrutiny:

> Are you exaggerating what your AI product can do? Or even claiming it can do something beyond the current capability of any AI or automated technology? Are you promising that your AI product does something better than a non-AI product? Are you aware of the risks? You need to know about the reasonably foreseeable risks and impact of your AI product before putting it on the market. If something goes wrong – maybe it fails or yields biased results – you can't just blame a third-party developer of the technology. And you can't say you're not responsible because that technology is a "black box" you can't understand or didn't know how to test. Does the product actually use AI at all? If you think you can get away with baseless claims that your

product is AI-enabled, think again. In an investigation, FTC technologists and others can look under the hood and analyze other materials to
see if what's inside matches up with your claims. Before labeling your
product as AI-powered, note also that merely using an AI tool in the
development process is not the same as a product having AI in it.[136]

According to Michael Atleson, Attorney for the FTC Division of Advertising Practices,

> This message is not new. Advertisers should take another look at our
> earlier AI guidance, which focused on fairness and equity but also said,
> clearly, not to overpromise what your algorithm or AI-based tool can
> deliver. Whatever it can or can't do, AI is important, and so are the
> claims you make about it. You don't need a machine to predict what
> the FTC might do when those claims are unsupported.[137]

AI Fakes

This section is concerned with the use of AI to create content that is
deceptive and potentially injurious to consumers when distributed or entered
into the stream of commerce. To be clear, we distinguish here the synthetic
content discussed in the context of intellectual property and AI-powered
generative art, on one hand, from inauthentic content that causes harm
when used in commerce (though there could very well be overlap). Here, we
are concerned with technology that enables users to simulate human activity—such as chatbots that simulate a real person, deepfake videos, or audio
voice clones—when these simulations are used to cause harm.

Given the proliferation of AI tools that allow the rapid and inexpensive
creation of synthetic media, the risk of using these tools to commit crimes
continues to grow. According to an attorney in the FTC Division of
Advertising practices,

> Evidence already exists that fraudsters can… use chatbots to generate
> spear-phishing emails, fake websites, fake posts, fake profiles, and fake
> consumer reviews, or to help create malware, ransomware, and prompt
> injection attacks. They can use deepfakes and voice clones to facilitate
> imposter scams, extortion, and financial fraud. And that's very much a
> non-exhaustive list.[138]

When it comes to AI-powered synthetic media, the FTC will scrutinize these
products to determine whether, at the design stage, it was reasonably foreseeable that the tools could be misused for fraud or mayhem. Just because
the tech executive could launch this product, doesn't mean they should if it
would be negligent to do so. It is negligent to subject others to

unreasonable, unconsented risks that could have been avoided through ordinary prudence. In a variation of the Learned Hand formula: if the likelihood of harm occurring multiplied by the magnitude of the harm is greater than the burden of avoiding the harm, it would be negligent to launch the product as is.

The FTC will evaluate whether the company launching a potentially harmful AI product is effectively mitigating risks, taking all reasonable precautions before it hits the market, or merely warning against misuse versus meaningfully deterring improper uses by bad actors. FTC would like to see potentially harmful AI tools incorporate some deterrence mechanism to prevent these improper uses; "deterrence measures should be durable, built-in features and not bug corrections or optional features that third parties can undermine via modification or removal."[139]

Lastly, FTC does not take kindly to advertisements or marketing material that is intended to deceive consumers. Watermarks that indicate when generative art is being used takes the burden off consumers to detect when AI is generating the text or the imagery they are seeing. In general, FTC frowns upon misleading advertisement whether that is an old fashioned exaggerative slogan on a billboard or an extremely sophisticated application of the latest technology.

> If you're an advertiser, you might be tempted to employ some of these tools to sell, well, just about anything. Celebrity deepfakes are already common, for example, and have been popping up in ads. We've previously warned companies that misleading consumers via doppelgängers, such as fake dating profiles, phony followers, deepfakes, or chatbots, could result – and in fact have resulted – in FTC enforcement actions.[140]

The "Luring" Test

The so-called *"Luring"* test applies to the unfair business practice of using AI to manipulate consumers into giving un-earned trust. This apt turn of phrase should earn nods of approbation by computer scientists and philosophers of mind alike, as it evokes the famous "Turing Test" named after a genius at the forefront of computer science, Alan Turing.

In 1950 Turing devised a hypothetical experiment where a human evaluator would ask questions to two different subjects, one a human and the other a computer, and based on the responses to these questions, the evaluator would decide which one was a human. Originally called the Imitation Game, it was thought if the human evaluator got this wrong, that would demonstrate a machine's ability to exhibit behavior that, because it is indistinguishable from human behavior, could be characterized as "intelligent."

At risk of oversimplifying, by using the Turing Test (and making lots of assumptions about mental states, computation, behavior, language, "intelligence," etc.), one could determine a machine is "intelligent" when it successfully manipulates a human evaluator into thinking the machine is actually a human based on its linguistic performance.[141]

The Turing Test takes on a whole new significance in the era of chatbots. The FTC is taking notice of how chatbots are being used in a new era of imitation games where firms are using AI to engineer consumer trust. These tools are unfair to consumers when they prey on "*automation bias*," which is the tendency of humans to become "unduly trusting of answers from machines which may seem neutral or impartial," in part because of our tendency to anthropomorphize (project human qualities onto nonhuman) bots.[142]

The wave of new generative AI tools discussed earlier are increasingly being used by commercial actors to

> influence people's beliefs, emotions, and behavior. Such uses are expanding rapidly and include chatbots designed to provide information, advice, support, and companionship. Many of these chatbots are effectively built to persuade and are designed to answer queries in confident language even when those answers are fictional.[143]

While the use of chatbots is not a problem per se, it becomes an issue for the FTC when the commercial actor uses a chatbot

> in ways that, deliberately or not, steer people unfairly or deceptively into harmful decisions in areas such as finances, health, education, housing, and employment. Companies thinking about novel uses of generative AI, such as customizing ads to specific people or groups, should know that design elements that trick people into making harmful choices are a common element in FTC cases, such as recent actions relating to financial offers, in-game purchases, and attempts to cancel services.[144]

The FTC may sue a business for failing the Luring Test when chatbots engage in manipulation. "Manipulation can be a deceptive or unfair practice when it causes people to take actions contrary to their intended goals."[145] This can happen through gaining unearned trust then issuing authoritative-sounding advice that is actually bad for the user. Another way to fail the Luring Test is to embed manipulative ads "within a generative AI feature" such that it is unclear to the user when an ad is a paid ad versus an organic search result.

> People should know if an AI product's response is steering them to a particular website, service provider, or product because of a commercial relationship. And, certainly, people should know if they're communicating with a real person or a machine.[146]

The above examples of AI used in business could be regulated by the FTC as "unfair" simply because they perpetuate bias or discrimination, or because they mislead the consumer. However, the ambit of the Federal Trade Commission Act is broad:

> a practice is unfair if it causes more harm than good. To be more specific, it's unfair if it causes or is likely to cause substantial injury to consumers that is not reasonably avoidable by consumers and not outweighed by countervailing benefits to consumers or to competition.[147]

Given this sweeping authorization to police commerce, businesses should keep an eye out for FTC enforcement actions in the future.

The Artificial Intelligence Act of the European Union

Unlike the patchwork quilt of regulations found in the United States, the European Union has undertaken a comprehensive, unified approach to regulating AI in civil society. Through the AI Act, the European Union sought to do for AI what the GDPR did for data privacy. The EU AI Act assigns all forms of AI to certain risk categories, each of which is subject to its own level of regulatory oversight and control.

"First, applications and systems that create an unacceptable risk, such as government-run social scoring... are banned. Second, high-risk applications, such as a CV-scanning tool that ranks job applicants, are subject to specific legal requirements. Lastly, applications not explicitly banned or listed as high-risk are largely left unregulated."[148] See **Table 6.3**.

Mass biometric surveillance and predictive policing should also be banned as unacceptably risky insofar as they empower the abuse of state power using unreliable and socially unacceptable means.

In what appears to be an imminently reasonable approach, the EU's AI Act takes a principled, precautionary, risk-based approach to regulating AI. According to a summary of the AI Act by the European Commission, the objectives for the new law are to ensure that "AI systems placed on the

Table 6.3 The EU AI act risk-based approach

Risk Level	Example	Compliance Obligations
Unacceptable Risk	social credit scoring	outright banned
High Risk	medical devices, infrastructure	conformity assessment
Intermediate Risk	chatbots that impersonate humans	allowed with transparency
Minimal or No Risk	any other AI application	allowed with no restrictions

Union market and used are safe and respect existing law on fundamental rights and Union values," that businesses have "legal certainty to facilitate investment and innovation in AI," to "enhance governance and effective enforcement of existing law on fundamental rights and safety requirements applicable to AI systems," and to "facilitate the development of a single market for lawful, safe and trustworthy AI applications and prevent market fragmentation."[149]

In law, technique (more so than intent) makes or breaks the success of the rule. Accordingly, the EU AI Act seeks the forementioned objectives through a

> balanced and proportionate horizontal regulatory approach to AI that is limited to the minimum necessary requirements to address the risks and problems linked to AI, without unduly constraining or hindering technological development or otherwise disproportionately increasing the cost of placing AI solutions on the market.[150]

By providing "a robust and flexible legal framework" that is both "comprehensive and future-proof in its fundamental regulatory choices" the goal is to balance consumer protection with commercial needs by ensuring "legal intervention is tailored to those concrete situations where there is a justified cause for concern or where such concern can reasonably be anticipated in the near future."[151]

Examples of "high risk" AI applications under the EU AI Act include those effecting access to essential public and private services (like government benefits programs), law enforcement tools, border control, tools for the administration of justice and voting, biometric identification of natural persons, the management and operation of critical infrastructure, employment, and safety components of regulated products like medical equipment.

In order to sell a "high risk" AI application in the European Union, the manufacturer must first obtain a CE marking to demonstrate the product meets EU safety, health, and environmental protection standards. See **Table 6.4**.[152]

Despite the nuanced, risk-based approach taken by the EU AI Act, the CEO of OpenAI Sam Altman has suggested that compliance may be such a

Table 6.4 Steps to affix CE marking on high-risk AI product

Step 1	Determine whether the system is classified as "high risk" under the law.
Step 1	Determine whether the system is classified as "high risk" under the law.
Step 2	Ensure design and development quality management are compliant.
Step 3	Apply conformity assessment procedures, documenting compliance.
Step 4	Affix CE mark to system and sign a declaration of conformity.
Step 5	Place the product in the market or push into production.

threat to its business model that it pulls services from Europe entirely rather than comply with the new law. Not that the CEO is a scofflaw, but rather the success of the business may depend on keeping training methods and data sources closed off, proprietary trade secrets (not "open" despite the company name). So-called "foundation models" such as the large-scale AI systems behind ChatGPT and DALL-E would potentially lose some market clout if they must disclose this information. Maybe they should.

> Forcing OpenAI to identify its use of copyrighted data would expose the company to potential lawsuits. Generative AI systems like ChatGPT and DALL-E are trained using large amounts of data scraped from the web, much of it copyright protected. When companies disclose these data sources it leaves them open to legal challenges.[153]

That is kind of the point. If the tool is based on illegally "scraped" training data, then any profits derived therefrom may be considered unjust enrichment or ill-gotten gains. If complying with a reasonable legal framework is prohibitively expensive or technically impossible, that reveals the flaw not in the law but in the business model that depends on undisclosed illegal activity (like widespread copyright infringement) to succeed.

Conclusion

The Humachine is not just superintelligent; it is humane. For all the powers wrought by AI, it comes with significant risks. The legal system as currently in force does not manage these risks. The developers and owners of AI systems must proactively deal with the control problem, algorithmic bias, and the weaponization of AI (as with deepfakes and spambots). We believe these challenges can be managed, but it will probably take collaboration between Silicon Valley and law enforcement, informed by a precautionary approach to risk management.

In 2021, the US Congress directed the Federal Trade Commission to examine and report back to Congress how AI could be used "to identify, remove, or take any other appropriate action necessary to address" certain "online harms."

Specifically, Congress was hoping FTC could recommend some AI-powered solutions to "online fraud, impersonation scams, fake reviews and accounts, bots, media manipulation, illegal drug sales and other illegal activities, sexual exploitation, hate crimes, online harassment and cyberstalking, and misinformation campaigns aimed at influencing elections." Ironically, many of these illicit online activities may very well be exacerbated by the advent of AI in black market commerce and through coordinated inauthentic behavior (like the spambot lobby discussed earlier).

What followed was an amusing, valiant push-back against the botsourcing of FTC's consumer protection duties. The agency "issued a report to Congress warning about using artificial intelligence (AI) to combat online problems and urging policymakers to exercise 'great caution' about relying on it as a policy solution": "The use of AI, particularly by big tech platforms and other companies, comes with limitations and problems of its own... AI tools can be inaccurate, biased, and discriminatory by design and incentivize relying on increasingly invasive forms of commercial surveillance."

Samuel Levine, Director of the FTC's Bureau of Consumer Protection, clarified:

> Nobody should treat AI as the solution to the spread of harmful online content. Combatting online harm requires a broad societal effort, not an overly optimistic belief that new technology—which can be both helpful and dangerous—will take these problems off our hands.

The FTC believes using AI tools as cyber police will backfire, creating its own range of additional harms. Some AI detection tools have "inherent design flaws" and are plagued by inaccuracy and imprecision because of "unrepresentative datasets, faulty classifications, failure to identify new phenomena, and lack of context and meaning."

Still worse, some AI tools intended to do good would actually propagate unfair, biased, or discriminatory patterns reflected in the unknowing biases of the AI developers, hurting protected classes of people or causing "over-blocked content in ways that can serve to reduce freedom of expression."

Lastly, and perhaps most insidiously, promoting government procurement of AI-powered online policing tools would create powerful incentives that enable ever more "invasive commercial surveillance and data extraction practices" given how much data is needed to train AI. Unlike the tech entrepreneurs hyping the advances of AI for B2B and B2C models, the FTC takes a pessimistic look at the claims about AI and its risk to consumers and users alike. Rather than giving Congress a framework for how to use AI to address online harms, the FTC instead told Congress they should "consider focusing on developing legal frameworks that would ensure that AI tools do not cause additional harm."

This is hilarious and profound in what it says about how the US government works. The politicians wanted to know how to write laws that empowered AI to police the Internet and all its human users. What they got from the FTC was an admonishment that AI is part of the problem with online harms, and they should focus on *policing AI* instead of using AI *as the police*. In an era where military leaders must choose to what extent AI should have a role in using the nuclear arsenals and other forms of lethal force, the issues of AI oversight and accountability have never had higher stakes.[154]

For all the emphasis we place on regulators devising policy instruments to manage the risks posed by AI, we are not optimistic that government will lead on this. Status quo legal regimes are inadequate to the task, though we applaud the lawmakers and regulators for at least trying. As a result, compliance is not good enough. Business leaders should accept the mantle of responsibility for the powers they are creating, and steward public goods even when they are not forced to do so by law.

Going beyond mere compliance will not happen until old paradigms of corporate responsibility are shed in favor of an enlightened self-interest that sees sustainability not as philanthropy but rather as key to survival. In the next chapter, we discuss breaking the old corporate paradigm to make way for the Humachine.

Notes

1 Jim Sams, *Law Firm that Touted Technology Accused of Fraud, Hits Blockade in La. Courtroom*, Claims Journal (December 27, 2022). Available at https://www.claimsjournal.com/news/southcentral/2022/12/27/314427.htm (last accessed May 31, 2023).
2 Ibid.
3 Ibid.
4 Matt O'Brien and the Associated Press, *Bossware AI that Tracks Remote Workers' Activities Could Break the Law, Government Says*, AON (May 18, 2023). Available at https://fortune.com/2023/05/18/bossware-ai-remote-workers-tracking-software-could-be-illegal-eeoc/ (last accessed May 31, 2023).
5 See, e.g., David J. Gunkel, *Person, Thing, Robot: A Moral and Legal Ontology for the 21st Century and Beyond*, The MIT Press (September 5, 2023); David J. Gunkel, *Robot Rights*, The MIT Press (November 13, 2018). For a contrary view that would not grant robots legal rights, see Bryson, Joanna J. (2010). Robots Should be Slaves. In Yorick Wilks (ed.), *Close Engagements with Artificial Companions: Key Social, Psychological, Ethical and Design Issues*, pp. 63–74.
6 Andrew Critch, Stuart Russell, TASRA: A Taxonomy and Analysis of Societal-Scale Risks from AI, (June 13, 2023).
7 *See* The IEEE Global Initiative on Ethics of Autonomous and Intelligent Systems, IEEE SA. Available at https://standards.ieee.org/industry-connections/ec/autonomous-systems/ (last accessed May 1, 2023).
8 Ibid., p. 10.
9 Ibid., p. 11.
10 For a basic guide to existing standards, laws, and assessments for adopting AI technologies, including the new NIST AI Risk Management Framework and even interactive resources on GitHub and Colab, see Patrick Hall, James Curtis, and Parul Pandey, *Machine Learning for High-Risk Applications* (O'Reilly Media, 1st Edition).
11 Roth, Emma. Tesla Leak Reportedly Shows Thousands of Full Self-Driving Safety Complaints. *The Verge* (May 25, 2023). Available at https://www.theverge.com/2023/5/25/23737972/tesla-whistleblower-leak-fsd-complaints-self-driving (last accessed May 31, 2023).
12 See *The IEEE Global Initiative on Ethics of Autonomous and Intelligent Systems. Ethically Aligned Design: A Vision for Prioritizing Human Well-being*

with *Autonomous and Intelligent Systems*, First Edition. IEEE, 2019. Page 15. https://standards.ieee.org/content/ieee-standards/en/industry-connections/ec/ autonomous-systems.html

13 *AI & the GDPR: Regulating the Minds of Machines*, Linklaters. Available at https://www.linklaters.com/en/insights/blogs/digilinks/ai-and-the-gdpr-regulatin g-the-minds-of-machines (last accessed May 1, 2023).

14 *See* United States Patent and Trademark Office, Nonprovisional (Utility) Patent Application Filing Guide. Available at https://www.uspto.gov/patents/basic s/apply/utility-patent (last accessed May 1, 2023).

15 *See* What Is Copyright?, United States Copyright Office. Available at https:// www.copyright.gov/what-is-copyright/ (last accessed May 1, 2023).

16 *Generative Artificial Intelligence and Copyright Law*, Congressional Research Service, pages 1 and 3, LSB10922 (February 24, 2023). Available at https:// crsreports.congress.gov.

17 Generative Artificial Intelligence and Copyright Law, Congressional Research Service, pages 1 and 3, LSB10922 (February 24, 2023). Available at https:// crsreports.congress.gov.

18 United States Copyright Act, 17 U.S.C. § 504.

19 Cornell Law School, Legal Information Institute, definition of "disgorgement." See also *Securities & Exchange Commission v. First Jersey Securities, Inc.*, 101 F.3d 1450 (2d Cir. 1996), holding that owner-officer who collaborated in unlawful conduct of firm may be held jointly and severally liable with firm for disgorgement of unlawful gains received.

20 See *Copyright Statutory Damages*, Copyright Alliance. Available at https://cop yrightalliance.org/faqs/statutory-damages-why-do-they-matter (last accessed May 2, 2023): "Statutory damages are damages that can be awarded by a judge or jury to a copyright owner in a copyright infringement suit. They are called 'statutory damages' because the range of damages is established by the statute, specifically section 504 of the Copyright Act… Statutory damages are impor-tant because the alternative type of damage award is 'actual damages,' which must be proven in court and can be very difficult to establish. Actual damages include profit that the copyright owner lost as a result of the infringement (for example, a license fee) as well as any additional profits the infringer received as a result of the infringement."

21 James Vincent, Getty Images Is Suing the Creators of AI Art Tool 'Stable Diffusion' for Scraping its Content. *The Verge* (Jan 17, 2023). Available at http s://www.theverge.com/2023/1/17/23558516/ai-art-copyright-stable-diffu sion-getty-images-lawsuit (last accessed May 2, 2023).

22 Getty Images filed its lawsuit in the United States District Court for the Dis-trict of Delaware on February 3, 2023. Available at https://copyrightlately. com/pdfviewer/getty-images-v-stability-ai-complaint/?auto_viewer=true#pa ge=&zoom=auto&pagemode=none

23 See *Copyright Statutory Damages*, Copyright Alliance. Available at https://cop yrightalliance.org/faqs/statutory-damages-why-do-they-matter (last accessed May 2, 2023).

24 Generative Artificial Intelligence and Copyright Law, Congressional Research Service, page 3, LSB10922 (February 24, 2023). Available at https://crsreports. congress.gov.

25 Ibid.

26 Whereas mere "ideas" are not subject to exclusive legal protections through IP, "original expressions" are subject to copyright and thus the "look and feel" of computer software is protected by copyright. See *Feist Publications, Inc. v.*

Rural Telephone Service, 499 U.S. ___, 113 L. Ed. 2d 358, 111 S. Ct. ___ (1991). Jack Russo & Jamie Nafziger, *Look And Feel In Computer Software: Protection In The 1990s*, Computerlaw Group LLP. Available at https://www. computerlaw.com/articles/look-and-feel-in-computer-software/ (last accessed May 10, 2023).

27 Generative Artificial Intelligence and Copyright Law, Congressional Research Service, p. 3.

28 Ibid.

29 For more detail on the instrumental convergence thesis, see Bostrom, Nick. The Superintelligent Will: Motivation and Instrumental Rationality in Advanced Artificial Agents. Available at https://nickbostrom.com/superintelligentwill.pdf

30 Aviva Hope Rutkin. The Tiny Changes That Cause AI to Fail. *BBC*. April 11, 2017. Available at www.bbc.com/future/story/20170410-how-to-fool-artificia l-intelligence?ocid=global_future_rss

31 Ibid.

32 AI Now Report 2018. Available at https://ainowinstitute.org/AI_Now_2018_ Report.pdf

33 Merchant, Brian. The Five Most Worrying Trends in Artificial Intelligence Right Now, *Gizmodo* (12/07/18). Available at https://gizmodo.com/the-five-m ost-worrying-trends-in-artificial-intelligenc-1830945466

34 AI Now Report 2018, p. 4. Available at https://ainowinstitute.org/AI_Now_ 2018_Report.pdf

35 Ibid.

36 Ibid.

37 Eubanks, Virginia. *Automating Inequality: How High-Tech Tools Profile, Police, and Punish the Poor* (2018 St. Martin's Press).

38 Dvorsky, George. Why Asimov's Three Laws of Robotics Can't Protect Us. *Gizmodo*. Available at https://io9.gizmodo.com/why-asimovs-three-laws-o f-robotics-cant-protect-us-1553665410/amp

39 March 31, 2018. Available at www.sciencealert.com/google-deep-mind-has-lea rned-to-become-highly-aggressive-in-stressful-situations

    Leibo, Joel Z., Vinicius Zambaldi, Marc Lanctot, Janusz Marecki, and Thore Graepel. Multi-agent Reinforcement Learning in Sequential Social Dilemmas. *Proceedings of the 16th International Conference on Autonomous Agents and Multiagent Systems (AAMAS 2017)*, edited by S. Das, E. Durfee, K. Larson, and M. Winikoff. S'ao Paulo, Brazil, May 8–12, 2017.

40 Ibid.

41 The Precautionary Principle. Website is hosted by the European Union. Available at www.precautionaryprinciple.eu/

42 Ibid.

43 Martuzzi, Marco and Joel A. Tickner, editors. *The Precautionary Principle: Protecting Public Health, the Environment and the Future of Our Children*. p. 1. World Health Organization, Geneva, Switzerland, 2004. Available at www. euro.who.int/__data/assets/pdf_file/0003/91173/E83079.pdf

44 Precautionary Principle. Chamber of Commerce of the United States of America. August 4, 2010. Available at www.uschamber.com/precautionary-principle. "The U.S. Chamber of Commerce supports a science-based approach to risk management where risk is assessed based on scientifically sound and technically rigorous analysis. Under this approach, regulatory actions are justified where there are legitimate, scientifically ascertainable risks to human health, safety, or the environment. That is, the greater the risk, the greater the degree of regulatory scrutiny. This standard has served the nation well, and has led to

astounding breakthroughs in the fields of science, health care, medicine, biotechnology, agriculture, and many other fields."

45   The Precautionary Principle.

46   Martuzzi, Marco and Joel A. Tickner, editors. *The Precautionary Principle: Protecting Public Health, the Environment and the Future of Our Children*. p. 1. World Health Organization, Geneva, Switzerland, 2004. Available at www. euro.who.int/__data/assets/pdf_file/0003/91173/E83079.pdf.

47   Bostrom, Nick. *Superintelligence: Paths, Dangers, Strategies* (2014 Oxford University Press), p. 143, 2014.

48   Knight, Will. Technology Is Threatening Our Democracy. How Do We Save It? *MIT Technology Review*, 121(5):37, 2018.

49   Ibid. p. 38.

50   Proverbs 27:17.

51   Chesney, Robert and Citron, Danielle Keats, Deep Fakes: A Looming Challenge for Privacy, Democracy, and National Security (July 14, 2018). 107 *California Law Review* (2019, Forthcoming); U of Texas Law, Public Law Research Paper No. 692; U of Maryland Legal Studies Research Paper No. 2018–21. Available at SSRN: https://ssrn.com/abstract=3213954 or doi:10.2139/ssrn.3213954. p. 6.

52   Knight, Will. Fake America Great Again. *MIT Technology Review*, August 17, 2018. Available at www.technologyreview.com/s/611810/fake-america-great-again/

53   Fraze, Dustin. Cyber Grand Challenge (CGC), Defense Advanced Research Projects Agency. Available at www.darpa.mil/program/cyber-grand-challenge

54   Ibid.

55   Chesney, Robert and Danielle Keats Citron. Deep Fakes: A Looming Challenge for Privacy, Democracy, and National Security (July 14, 2018). 107 *California Law Review* (2019, Forthcoming); U of Texas Law, Public Law Research Paper No. 692; U of Maryland Legal Studies Research Paper No. 2018–21. Available at SSRN: https://ssrn.com/abstract=3213954 or doi:10.2139/ssrn.3213954

56   Bond, Shannon. People are Trying to Claim Real Videos are Deepfakes. The Courts are not Amused, *NPR* (May 8, 2023). Available at https://www.npr.org/2023/05/08/1174132413/people-are-trying-to-claim-real-videos-are-deepfakes-the-courts-are-not-amused (last accessed May 10, 2023).

57   Ibid. See also Pfefferkorn, Riana, 'Deepfakes' in the Courtroom (October 1, 2020). *Boston University Public Interest Law Journal*, Vol. 29, No. 2, 2020. Available at SSRN: https://ssrn.com/abstract=4321140 and Chesney, Robert and Citron, Danielle Keats, Deep Fakes: A Looming Challenge for Privacy, Democracy, and National Security (July 14, 2018). 107 *California Law Review* 1753 (2019), U of Texas Law, Public Law Research Paper No. 692, U of Maryland Legal Studies Research Paper No. 2018–21. Available at SSRN: https://ssrn.com/abstract=3213954 or http://dx.doi.org/10.2139/ssrn.3213954

58   Horowitz, Michael, Paul Scharre, Gregory C. Allen, Kara Frederick, Anthony Cho, and Edoardo Saravalle. National Security-Related Applications of Artificial Intelligence. July 10, 2018. Available at www.cnas.org/publications/reports/artificial-intelligence-and-international-security

59   Waddell, Kaveh. Report: The U.S. Is Unprepared for the AI Future. Axios. July 11, 2018. Available at www.axios.com/the-us-isnt-ready-for-the-ai-future-96649a76-1027-43ba-ae27-e24cb57dd194.html

60   Knight, Will. Fake America Great Again.

61   United States Constitution, First Amendment.

62   Chesney and Citron, Deep Fakes: A Looming Challenge for Privacy, Democracy, and National Security; U of Texas Law, Public Law Research Paper No.

692; U of Maryland Legal Studies Research Paper No. 2018–21. Available at SSRN: https://ssrn.com/abstract=3213954 or doi:10.2139/ssrn.3213954. p. 33.
63 Ibid.
64 New York Penal Code § 190.25 Criminal impersonation in the second degree.
65 Schiff, Adam, Stephanie Murphy, and Carlos Curbelo. Letter to The Honorable Daniel R. Coats, Director of National Intelligence. September 13, 2018. https://schiff.house.gov/imo/media/doc/2018-09%20ODNI%20Deep%20Fakes%20letter. pdf
66 Ibid.
67 Bing, Chris. The tech behind the DARPA Grand Challenge winner will now be used by the Pentagon.
68 Fung, Brian and Tony Romm. Inside the private Justice Department meeting that could lead to new investigations of Facebook, Google and other tech giants. *The Washington Post*, September 25, 2018. Available at www.washingtonpost. com/technology/2018/09/25/inside-big-meeting-federal-state-law-enforcement-tha t-signaled-new-willingness-investigate-tech-giants/?noredirect=on&utm_term=. f58cfddc8056
69 Ibid.
70 Commission Regulation 2016/679 of 27 Apr. 2016 on the Protection of Natural Persons with Regard to Processing of Personal Data and on the Free Movement of Such Data, and Repealing Directive 95/46/EC (General Data Protection Regulation), 2016 O.J. (L 119) 1 (EU).
71 Voss, Gregory. W. European Union Data Privacy Law Reform: General Data Protection Regulation, Privacy Shield, and the Right to Delisting, *The Business Lawyer*, 72(Winter):223, 2016–2017.
72 Case C-131/12, *Google Spain SL v. Agencia Espanola de Proteccion de Datos (AEPD)*, 2014 E.C.R. 317.
73 Nisselson, Evan. The war over artificial intelligence will be won with visual data. *TechCrunch*. May 17, 2017. Available at https://techcrunch.com/2017/05/ 17/the-war-over-artificial-intelligence-will-be-won-with-visual-data/
74 Ibid.
75 Fung, Brian. Uber Reaches $148 Million Settlement over its 2016 Data Breach, Which Affected 57 Million Globally. *The Washington Post*, September 26, 2018.
76 Ibid.
77 Trope, Roland L. and Lixian Loong Hantover, Hacking Away at Trust, *The Business Lawyer*, 72(Winter):195, 2016–2017.
78 Ibid., p. 206.
79 Grimes, Roger A. Back to Basics IT'S 9 Biggest Security Threats. InfoWorld, August 10, 2017.
80 Knight, Will. Microsoft Is Creating An Oracle for Catching Biased AI Algorithms: As More People Use Artificial Intelligence, They Will Need Tools That Detect Unfairness in the Underlying Algorithms. *MIT Technology Review*, May 25, 2018. Available at www.technologyreview.com/s/611138/microsoft-is-crea ting-an-oracle-for-catching-biased-ai-algorithms/?utm_campaign=social_button& utm_source=reddit&utm_medium=social&utm_content=2018-05-25
81 Federal Fair Lending Regulations and Statutes Compliance Handbook, Fair Housing Act. Available at www.federalreserve.gov/boarddocs/supmanual/cch/ fair_lend_fhact.pdf
82 Robitzski, Dan.. To Build Trust In Artificial Intelligence, IBM Wants Developers to Prove Their Algorithms Are Fair, *Futurism*. August 22, 2018. Available at https://futurism.com/trust-artificial-intelligence-ibm/

83 Ibid.
84 Knight, Will. Microsoft Is Creating an Oracle for Catching Biased AI Algorithms.
85 Ibid.
86 Ibid.
87 Knight, Will. The Dark Secret at the Heart of AI: No One Really Knows How the Most Advanced Algorithms Do What They Do. That Could Be a Problem. *MIT Technology Review*, April 11, 2017. Available at www.technologyreview.com/s/604087/the-dark-secret-at-the-heart-of-ai/
88 Ibid.
89 Ibid.
90 DLA Piper, EU Policy and Regulatory Update: a European approach to artificial intelligence, June 18, 2018. Available at www.lexology.com/library/detail.aspx?g=14b41d97-f79e-44d4-a979-b8b4e2f243e6
91 For more on the distinction between US and EU products liability law, see Marshall S. Shapo, Comparing Products Liability: Concepts in European and American Law, *Cornell International Law Journal*, 26(2), 1993, Article 1.
92 Recital 71: European Union General Data Protection Regulation:
    The data subject should have the right not to be subject to a decision, which may include a measure, evaluating personal aspects relating to him or her which is based solely on automated processing and which produces legal effects concerning him or her or similarly significantly affects him or her, such as automatic refusal of an online credit application or e-recruiting practices without any human intervention.
    Such processing includes "profiling" that consists of any form of automated processing of personal data evaluating the personal aspects relating to a natural person, in particular to analyse or predict aspects concerning the data subject's performance at work, economic situation, health, personal preferences or interests, reliability or behaviour, location or movements, where it produces legal effects concerning him or her or similarly significantly affects him or her.
    However, decision-making based on such processing, including profiling, should be allowed where expressly authorised by Union or Member State law to which the controller is subject, including for fraud and tax-evasion monitoring and prevention purposes conducted in accordance with the regulations, standards and recommendations of Union institutions or national oversight bodies and to ensure the security and reliability of a service provided by the controller, or necessary for the entering or performance of a contract between the data subject and a controller, or when the data subject has given his or her explicit consent.
    In any case, such processing should be subject to suitable safeguards, which should include specific information to the data subject and the right to obtain human intervention, to express his or her point of view, to obtain an explanation of the decision reached after such assessment and to challenge the decision. Such measure should not concern a child.
    In order to ensure fair and transparent processing in respect of the data subject, taking into account the specific circumstances and context in which the personal data are processed, the controller should use appropriate mathematical or statistical procedures for the profiling, implement technical and organisational measures appropriate to ensure, in particular, that factors which result in inaccuracies in personal data are corrected and the risk of errors is minimised, secure personal data in a manner that takes account of the potential risks involved for the interests and rights of the data subject, and prevent, inter

alia, discriminatory effects on natural persons on the basis of racial or ethnic origin, political opinion, religion or beliefs, trade union membership, genetic or health status or sexual orientation, or processing that results in measures having such an effect.

Automated decision-making and profiling based on special categories of personal data should be allowed only under specific conditions.

93   Public Trust in Government: 1958–2017, PEW Research Center: US Politics & Policy. December 14, 2017. Available at www.people-press.org/2017/12/14/p ublic-trust-in-government-1958-2017/
94   Ibid.
95   Curtis, Anthony R. 2013. The Brief History of Social Media. University of North Carolina at Pembroke. June 1, 2013. Available at www.uncp.edu/home/a curtis/newMedia/Soci alMedia/SocialMediaHistory.html
96   Ravi Arunachalam (IBM) & Sandipan Sarkar (IBM), The New Eye of Government: Citizen Sentiment Analysis in Social Media. *IJCNLP 2013 Workshop on Natural Language Processing for Social Media (SocialNLP)*, pp. 23–28, Nagoya, Japan, October 14, 2013.
97   Horton, Chris. *MIT Technology Review*. August 21, 2018. Available at www. technologyreview.com/s/611816/the-simple-but-ingenious-system-taiwan-uses-to-crowdsource-its-laws/
98   Ibid.
99   Ibid.
100 Ibid.
101 Ibid.
102 Ibid.
103 Ibid.
104 Ibid.
105 Taylor, Jessica. Republicans and Democrats Don't Agree, Or Like Each Other—And It's Worse Than Ever. October 5, 2017. Available at www.npr.org/2017/10/05/555685136/republicans-and-democrats-dont-agree-dont-like-each-other-and-its-worst-than-eve
106 Drutman, Lee. The Divided States of America. *The New York Times*, September 22, 2016. Available at www.nytimes.com/2016/09/22/opinion/campaign-stops/the-divided-states-of-america.html?_r=0
107 The Administrative Procedure Act, Pub.L. 79–404, 60 Stat. 237, enacted June 11, 1946, is the United States federal statute that governs the way in which administrative agencies of the federal government of the United States may propose and establish regulation.
108 Electronic Frontier Foundation, "Net Neutrality." Available at www.eff.org/issues/net-neutrality
109 Ibid.
110 Ibid.
111 Ibid.
112 Ibid.
113 Sawers, Paul. *Vint Cerf, Tim Berners-Lee, and 19 Other Technologists Pen Letter Asking FCC to Save Net Neutrality*. Venture Beat. December 11, 2017. Available at https://venturebeat.com/2017/12/11/vint-cerf-tim-berners-lee-and-19-other-tech nologists-pen-letter-asking-fcc-to-save-net-neutrality/
114 Zaleski, Andrew. The Data Lord of Lobbying: FiscalNote Takes the Intuition Out of Politics. Does It Take the Democracy Out, Too? *MIT Technology Review*, 121(5):60, 2018.
115 Ibid.

116   A.G. Schneiderman Releases New Details On Investigation Into Fake Net Neutrality Comments. Available at https://ag.ny.gov/press-release/ag-schneiderman-releases-new-details-investigation-fake-net-neutrality-comments

117   December 13, 2017, letter by Attorney General Eric Schneiderman to Thomas M. Johnson, Jr., General Counsel to the Federal Communications Commission. Available at https://ag.ny.gov/sites/default/files/ltr_to_fcc_gen_counsel_re_records_request.pdf

118   "Shortly after coming into office, President Joe Biden moved to restore net neutrality. He signed a sweeping executive order to promote competition, calling on the Federal Communications Commission (FCC) to bring back the Obama-era internet rules rolled back by the Trump administration. But close to two years later, the FCC remains deadlocked with only four of its five commissioner slots filled — and Biden may be running out of time." Makena Kelly, The White House Night be Running Out of Time to Bring Back Net Neutrality, *The Verge* (March 16, 2023). Available at https://www.theverge.com/2023/3/16/23642225/white-house-biden-gigi-sohn-fcc-nomination-net-neutrality (last accessed May 10, 2023).

119   Horton. *MIT Technology Review*.

120   Ibid.

121   2018 Edelman Trust Barometer: Global Report. Available at https://cms.edelman.com/sites/default/files/2018-01/2018%20Edelman%20Trust%20Barometer%20Global%20Report.pdf

122   Harrington, Matthew. Survey: People's Trust Has Declined in Business, Media, Government, and NGOs. *Harvard Business Review*, January 16, 2017. Available at https://hbr.org/2017/01/survey-peoples-trust-has-declined-in-business-media-government-and-ngos

123   Ibid. Patel, Nilay. Facebook's $5 billion FTC fine is an embarrassing joke. *The Verge*, July 12, 2019. Available at www.theverge.com/2019/7/12/20692524/facebook-five-billion-ftc-fine-embarrassing-joke

124   Chan, Wilfred. Can Existing Laws Regulate AI? The Federal Government and Experts Say Yes, *Fast Company* (April 28, 2023). Available at https://www.fastcompany.com/90889000/can-existing-laws-regulate-ai-the-federal-government-and-experts-say-yes (last accessed May 10, 2023).

125   Khan, Lina M. Chair, FTC, *Joint Statement on Enforcement Efforts Against Discrimination and Bias in Automated Systems* (April 25, 2023). Available at https://www.ftc.gov/legal-library/browse/cases-proceedings/public-statements/joint-statement-enforcement-efforts-against-discrimination-bias-automated-systems (last accessed May 12, 2023).

126   See Joint Statement on Enforcement Efforts Against Discrimination and Bias in Automated Systems. Available at https://www.ftc.gov/system/files/ftc_gov/pdf/EEOC-CRT-FTC-CFPB-AI-Joint-Statement%28final%29.pdf

127   Justice Department Files Statement of Interest in Fair Housing Act Case Alleging Unlawful Algorithm-Based Tenant Screening Practices, Department of Justice Office of Public Affairs, press release 23–19 (January 9, 2023). Available at https://www.justice.gov/opa/pr/justice-department-files-statement-interest-fair-housing-act-case-alleging-unlawful-algorithm (last accessed May 12, 2023).

128   *Adverse Action Notification Requirements in Connection with Credit Decisions Based on Complex Algorithms*, Consumer Financial Protection Circular 2022–03 (May 26, 2022). Available at https://www.consumerfinance.gov/compliance/circulars/circular-2022-03-adverse-action-notification-requirements-in-connection-with-credit-decisions-based-on-complex-algorithms/ (last accessed May 12, 2023).

129 *Adverse Action Notification Requirements in Connection with Credit Decisions Based on Complex Algorithms*, Consumer Financial Protection Circular 2022–03 (May 26, 2022). Available at https://www.consumerfinance.gov/comp liance/circulars/circular-2022-03-adverse-action-notification-requirements-in-con nection-with-credit-decisions-based-on-complex-algorithms/ (last accessed May 12, 2023).

130 Justice Department Files Statement of Interest in Fair Housing Act Case Alleging Unlawful Algorithm-Based Tenant Screening Practices, Department of Justice Office of Public Affairs, press release 23–19 (January 9, 2023). Available at https://www.justice.gov/opa/pr/justice-department-files-statement-interest-fa ir-housing-act-case-alleging-unlawful-algorithm (last accessed May 12, 2023).

131 *The Americans with Disabilities Act and the Use of Software, Algorithms, and Artificial Intelligence to Assess Job Applicants and Employees*. U.S. Equal Employment Opportunity Commission (May 12, 2022) ADA, 29 CFR Part 1630 & app. Available at https://www.eeoc.gov/laws/guidance/americans-disabili ties-act-and-use-software-algorithms-and-artificial-intelligence#_ftnref1 (last visited May 12, 2023).

132 *The Americans with Disabilities Act and the Use of Software, Algorithms, and Artificial Intelligence to Assess Job Applicants and Employees*. U.S. Equal Employment Opportunity Commission (May 12, 2022) ADA, 29 CFR Part 1630 & app. Available at https://www.eeoc.gov/laws/guidance/americans-disabilities-a ct-and-use-software-algorithms-and-artificial-intelligence#_ftnref1 (last visited May 12, 2023).

133 *The Americans with Disabilities Act and the Use of Software, Algorithms, and Artificial Intelligence to Assess Job Applicants and Employees*. U.S. Equal Employment Opportunity Commission (May 12, 2022) ADA, 29 CFR Part 1630 & app. Available at https://www.eeoc.gov/laws/guidance/americans-disabili ties-act-and-use-software-algorithms-and-artificial-intelligence#_ftnref1 (last visited May 12, 2023).

134 Jillson, Elisa. *Aiming for Truth, Fairness, and Equity in your Company's Use of AI*, US Federal Trade Commission, April 19, 2021. Available at https:// www.ftc.gov/business-guidance/blog/2021/04/aiming-truth-fairness-equi ty-your-companys-use-ai (last accessed May 12, 2023).

135 Michael Atleson, Keep your AI claims in check, US Federal Trade Commission, February 27, 2023. Available at https://www.ftc.gov/business-guidance/blog/ 2023/02/keep-your-ai-claims-check (last accessed May 12, 2023).

136 Ibid.

137 Ibid.

138 Ibid.

139 Ibid.

140 Ibid.

141 Oppy, Graham and David Dowe, "The Turing Test", *The Stanford Encyclopedia of Philosophy* (Winter 2021 Edition), Edward N. Zalta (ed.). Available at https://plato.stanford.edu/archives/win2021/entries/turing-test/ (last accessed May 12, 2023).

142 Atleson, Michael. *The Luring Test: AI and the Engineering of Consumer Trust*, US Federal Trade Commission (May 1, 2023). Available at https://www.ftc.gov/busi ness-guidance/blog/2023/05/luring-test-ai-engineering-consumer-trust (last accessed May 12, 2023).

143 Ibid.

144 Ibid.

145 Ibid.

146 Ibid.
147 Ibid.
148 https://artificialintelligenceact.eu/
149 The European Commission summary on the AI Act. Available at https://artifi cialintelligenceact.eu/the-act/ (last accessed May 12, 2023).
150 Ibid.
151 Ibid.
152 Sioli, Lucilla. Shaping Europe's Digital Future: A European Strategy for Artifi cial Intelligence (April 23, 2021). Available at https://www.ceps.eu/wp-content/ uploads/2021/04/AI-Presentation-CEPS-Webinar-L.-Sioli-23.4.21.pdf
153 Vincent, James. OpenAI Says it Could 'Cease Operating' in the EU if it Can't Comply with Future Regulation, *The Verge* (May 25, 2023). Available at http s://www.theverge.com/2023/5/25/23737116/openai-ai-regulation-eu-ai-act-cea se-operating (last accessed May 31, 2023).
154 *Political Declaration on Responsible Military Use of Artificial Intelligence and Autonomy*, US Department of State (February 16, 2023). Available at https:// www.state.gov/political-declaration-on-responsible-military-use-of-artificial-intel ligence-and-autonomy/ (last accessed May 12, 2023).

Chapter 7

The 4-I Model

A New Business Paradigm

The pandemic pushed humanity into a new era defined by broad global turbulence and new—almost 'magical'—AI tools. Any enterprise that doesn't understand that a new business paradigm is needed is sorely mistaken. The consequences of not understanding, and not taking action, can be witnessed on the road littered by recent corporate bankruptcies. The age of traditional brick and mortar businesses is over. Companies that are taking action are rapidly adding AI solutions and digitizing. But that too is insufficient. Tacking on AI to existing organizational structures, like Eeyore's tail, is not competitive. What is needed is an entirely new business model.

One of the executives we interviewed for this book explained it well. He pointed out that the massive rush to apply digital technologies to existing business models and digitize old processes will not lead to success, offering this analogy: "Companies acquiring AI without a new business model is like a company digitizing a horse and carriage - while the competition has created a digital automobile." Digitizing the business model of the past will not lead to competitiveness in the new era. Digitalization is merely a predicate or a precondition for the evolution we call for here. AI is essential—but it does not alone provide a competitive advantage. It is copyable and one size does not fit all. What is not copyable is the unique business model, processes, and integration of humans with that technology.

In our executive interviews we repeatedly heard that the new competitive capability is "the human mind," "human critical thinking," and "human decision intelligence." In this book we call for a new business enterprise— the Humachine—that integrates this capability as the best of humans and AI ("machines"). At the centerpiece are humans at every level of the organization integrated with their AI co-pilots. So many mental functions previously handled by humans—computation, analysis, data mining, processing—are now automated, handled by machines, or as we put it elsewhere, 'botsourced.' We need to build enterprises that allow human resources at all levels of the organizational structure to cultivate their own uniquely human

DOI: 10.4324/9781003322832-7

skills—emotional intelligence, leadership, caring, imagination, creativity, and ethical convictions. That is, we need our organizations to be *human centric*, even as they are increasingly driven by technology. For this organizational form to thrive requires an entirely new business paradigm, with a new organizational structure. These are the organizations that will lead the future.

Complexity Theory Explains How Organizations Function Like Living Systems

Terms such as 'resilience' and 'agility' have dominated the business world in the post pandemic era. What is missed, however, is that an organization is a living system that must be adaptable, evolve, and grow. To really understand what this means for organizations and how to harness this capability we look to *complexity theory*. Although complexity theory was devised by mathematicians and computer scientists in the late-twentieth century, it helps the understanding of organizational functionality and even everyday lives. In the book *Notes on Complexity: A Scientific Theory on Complexity, Consciousness and Being*, Dr. Neil Theise defines principles of complexity theory we can apply to organizational management.[1] He points out that whereas machines are precisely the sum of their parts, biological systems are always more than the sum of their parts. Because Humachines combine human resources (biological systems) with computational resources, we expect complexity theory to apply to these organizations. Complexity theory, in turn, explains how all these parts organize themselves into larger-scale structures or systems of the world—from ant colonies to flocks of birds to city neighborhoods to entire global ecosystems. These principles thus apply to organizations as well. Machines are rigid but biological life is not. If we want to build adaptability, resilience, and agility into organizational structures, we must learn from biological systems—otherwise the organization remains rigid and vulnerable to changes in the environment.

Dr. Theise points out that all living things are self-organized following the same four rules of complexity. *First*, the more interacting parts there are, the greater the complexity of the system. This applies to ant colonies, cities, cultures, civilizations—and organizations. But the same rules apply no matter how large and how complex the system.

Second, all systems are self-organizing from the bottom up and all interactions are local.

Ants meet the pheromone signals of other ants. Humans connect to the social, linguistic, and physical cues of other humans. There is no top-down organization. There is no all-knowing individual or entity or queen directing the participants. Organization always emerges from the bottom up.

Third, negative feedback loops keep systems healthy. Dr. Theise gives a space heater as an example of a negative feedback loop.

When the room gets cold, it turns on. When the room warms up, it turns off. Positive feedback? Imagine if the warmer a room got the more the heater cranked up. Negative feedback loops must predominate for healthy living things.

In organizations this does not suggest punishment. Negative feedback loops prevent excess, ensure balance, maintain equilibrium.

Fourth, there must be some low-level randomness or unpredictability in every living system.

Too much and there can be no self-organization, no greater whole. Too little and the system is unable to adapt if the environment changes. For adaptation that allows the resilience and continuity that is the hallmark of life, there must be a narrow range of unpredictability. This is the driver of life's creative dynamism. In every moment, random potentials create a shimmering cloud of possibilities for what the next moment might be.

Lastly, he offers ants as an example:

Ants follow all four rules of complexity. They self-organize from the bottom up into the larger scale structures of the colony, the food lines, the nursery, the garbage dump, and the cemetery. No ant is monitoring the colony as a whole or planning these structures top-down. Negative feedback loops in the form of scent trails that degrade over time keep exhausted food lines from going on endlessly after the food runs out and a small number of divergent ants (the ones not following the food line) are most likely to find the next food source.

Notably, the incessant urge to "scale" and experience rapid growth in the corporate world should be checked. Growth is not always healthy. In the biological world an example of growth with no negative feedback loop are cancer cells. It is the negative feedback loops that allow cells to repair themselves and adapt. Similarly, in organizations the negative feedback loops permit adaptation and adjustment. As with cancer, unchecked organizational growth leads to destruction.

According to Dr. Theise "Everything is only process, only interaction, and so everything only *looks* like a thing." This equally applies to organizations. An organization looks like "a thing" but it is actually a compilation of processes and interactions. Indeed, collective intelligence is itself a process, not a substance or an entity. For the organization to thrive and grow—we then have to create the right processes and interactions.

These rules apply to all living structures—and equally apply to organizations if they are to evolve, grow, and adapt. We embody these rules in the 4-I model presented in this chapter that is a "living" representation of organizations that evolve over time. Like with all biological systems that are greater than the sum of their parts, so is the Humachine. It is a symbiotic relationship between humans and machines, that is greater than the sum of its parts.

But first we begin by discussing the importance of organizations becoming more human centric, even as they are increasingly driven by technology. We also look at the four key paradigm shifts businesses need to make to move from old business models to the new.

Technology-Driven, Human-Centric

Many business leaders would be forgiven for thinking the new technology era is about implementing technology solutions and going through a digital transformation to become more efficient. Or botsourcing your way to $0 payroll. With the advent of Generative AI, such as ChatGPT, there is a rush to acquire technology and businesses are closely watching what the competition is doing to keep up with the Joneses. However, machines—including AI—are just tools. They cannot fix bad processes on their own, poor management practices, or failing employee morale. The idea that implementing technology, acquiring software, or purchasing better data will simply follow a "plug-and-play" approach is misguided. This is the old paradigm of technology. We need to break it.

The reason the old model will not succeed is that what is needed of employees—the human element of the organization—at all levels is dramatically changing. The technology revolution currently underway is different in kind than the ones that preceded it. The new era requires transformation of old business models and ushers in a new way of thinking about the role of humans in an enterprise setting. Companies are changing the boundaries and activities of their firms. They are redefining processes, functions, and how these functions interact.

Merely adopting more technology is not enough to survive as a competitive enterprise. What most companies miss is that becoming a technology-driven company requires us to become *more human*, not less. The success of becoming a leader in this new era is not primarily focusing on the technology—but rather on people. The reason is that companies cannot completely botsource their way to success.

The Humachine integrates people with AI-augmented tools and management systems to leverage computational powers and uniquely human strengths. A key to success will be understanding how to hire the best talent; develop onboarding protocols that seamlessly absorb the talent into an innovative and inclusive culture; create a culture of innovation that brings the best from its people; create trust in those AI systems by verifying and "looking under the hood" of algorithms; and create a symbiosis between people and technology that allows the organization to thrive.

One recent irony about the use of AI in the corporate world, and which illustrates a negative example of the misuse of AI, is in the context of talent hiring. As we have iterated throughout this book, uniquely human skills and talented people offer the real competitive advantage to enterprises in the age of AI. Hiring the right people and developing those human resources thus becomes of paramount importance to the long-term sustainability of a company. So it becomes natural to ask whether we can use AI to handle the human resources function?

The answer is decidedly mixed.

We forecast that so many employers will struggle to find talent because they are automating too much of the candidate screening process. Resumes for talented, experienced, prospective workers are being put in the proverbial 'circular filing cabinet.' This is not because the candidate does not meet the search criteria but rather because the candidate's resume does not include certain key words or has failed to meet some arbitrary formal requirement. These formal requirements can be more about the AI application's limited ability to interpret data rather than about measuring true indicators of human fitness for a particular job description. The tail wags the dog when we measure *only what we can measure* with AI, instead of measuring what matters for people. AI tools, lacking context and unable to interpret idiosyncratic outlier data, fail to recognize the potential for a candidate to transfer a skill set from one domain into another, or to bring diversity to a team, thereby increasing innovation, alignment, and resilience. Successful job hunting becomes a matter of dropping the right key-words into a resume and gaming the system. Employers are unable to find talent and talent is unable to find employment, all because someone decided to botsource the hiring function.

Use humans to sort through job applications. Use humans to conduct screening interviews. Then empower the new hire with AI. This would be so much more effective than trying to get AI to screen for the right candidates. So many of the elements of a successful hire—having the right energy, "vibe," being ready for the challenge of a fast-paced, dynamic work environment, are not discernible through an automated OCR or keyword filter. They require the human touch. Using robots to do what humans should do can result in an emotionally and cognitively draining and demoralizing experience that fails to produce the intended results for the company. Research from *Harvard Business Review* bolsters these concerns.[2]

Automated Virtual Interviews (AVI) is one example where using AI to evaluate human talent may backfire.

AVIs involve job candidates being interviewed by an artificial intelligence, which requires them to record themselves on an interview platform, answering questions under time pressure. The video is then submitted through the AI developer platform, which processes the data of the candidate — this can be visual (e.g. smiles), verbal (e.g. key words used), and/or vocal (e.g. the tone of voice). In some cases, the platform then passes a report with an interpretation of the job candidate's performance to the employer.[3]

As you could expect, AVI presents issues of reliability (fitness for intended purposes) and bias. According to one candidate,

> In order to adapt to the AI, I made sure that my hands were as still as possible ... I maintained deliberate eye contact with the camera of my laptop and I spoke with a rather monotone tone so that the AI can pick up on what I'm saying, because the AI searches for keywords that the company is looking for interpreting to the algorithm.

The candidate is being pressured into modulating their disposition to be interpretable by the screening bot. As a result,

> the stronger the role AI played in the interview, the more candidates felt depersonalized and talked about their own fixed, rigid, or robotic behaviors[;] often because of a lack of understanding of what it was required of them to pass the interview, candidates felt like their humanity was diminished.[4]

The experience for job seekers can be dehumanizing and demoralizing. The experience for the recruiting company is frustration as well, at the seeming lack of talent in the talent pool. As it turns out the AVI is just not good at reading people. Who would have thought?

The original way of getting a job was to sit down for a face-to-face interview with someone at the company. The candidate and the first tier of HR screening would actually meet in a room together and just talk. This format, however, gradually gave way to a video interview, especially at larger companies, so that the talent pool did not have to be within driving distance of the employer to get an interview. Then comes AVI, where the technology facilitates recording, but there is no human present in space or time. A candidate just sits down in front of a screen with a camera lens pointed at their face and they have to perform for the faceless digital eyeball. The mere change in format is enough to drive undesirable results discussed above.

Taking the automation process higher up the decision-making ladder may increase efficiency but it also increases the risk of unintended adverse consequences. For example, AI-assisted AVI allows the software to make recommendations to a human screener, based on the AI's analysis of the candidate's interview performance. An AI-led AVI would go even further. Here the technology decides whether the candidate is eligible for the next round of the recruitment process, and no humans are consulted in making that initial screening decision. Within the context of AVI, Figure 7.1 illustrates a spectrum, from face-to-face (human-only) interviews to an AI-led, completely automated screening process.

The vast majority of large companies are using technology to mediate the candidate interview process and many more are adopting AVI, despite its flaws. We chastise this trend because identifying human talent is far too mission critical to botsource entirely. Some traditional business functions should not be botsourced at all, rather they should be collaborative functions performed by variations of combinations of AI and people to get it just right. We discuss the variations of human—machine work relationships in more detail in Chapter 8. Instead of a black box, the HR department's use of AI should be in a "glass box."[6] Using an AI tool in a *glass box* means the AI tool is explained in advance to the users; the application is understandable, interpretable, and transparent; the application maintains user privacy and informed consent; and the interface experience (in this context, the job interview) concludes with prompt, appropriate feedback.[7]

Of course talent hiring and HR are just one example of overreliance on AI, the rush to botsource as much as possible, and the mismatch that occurs without a human-centric approach. In fact, it is those uniquely human skills of creativity, innovation, adaptability, empathy, integrity, and imagination that will become increasingly imperative to enterprise success. They cannot be botsourced. It is precisely these skills that are needed to bridge the gap between technology and people, and utilize machines in the best way to serve people—customers, coworkers, suppliers, and all other stakeholders.

This human-centric approach of technology-focused firms is exemplified in part by leading companies such as Schneider Electric, Microsoft, and Siemens. The companies that are leading understand that they must transform the way they do business. It is not about changing technologies to get the latest and greatest systems but rather changing the business model itself. The issue is not that machines will replace humans so much as it is how to create a business model where machines and humans complement each other. Machines will do repetitive and automated tasks. Machines will always be stronger, more precise, and faster. They will even do certain well-defined cognitive tasks. However, the enterprise must remain centered around humans. The physical and the digital must be integrated to achieve this.

To illustrate, we present a paradigm shift in business models, contrasting the traditional business model with the Humachine. See Table 7.1.

Without a new model focused on cultivating human talent and authentic culture, the human element of the organization becomes an appendage to

The Depersonalization Spectrum

Five types of interviews that job candidates might experience range from face-to-face meetings with other humans to video interviews led by AI.

Type of interview: Face-to-face
Conducted in person between parties who are copresent and in the same location.

Video
Conducted on a screen between parties who are copresent but in different locations. Technology is used, but it does not involve AI decision-making tools.

Automated video interview (AVI)
Conducted through screens. Parties are neither copresent nor in the same location. The technology facilitates the recording but is not involved in the hiring decision.

AVI, AI-assisted
Conducted through screens. Parties are neither copresent nor in the same location. Technology can be used to make recommendations based on its interpretation of various features (e.g., facial expressions, gestures, tone of voice, keywords, etc.). These recommendations are often produced as a report for humans to review.

AVI, AI-led
Conducted through screens and recorded. Parties are neither copresent nor in the same location. Technologies are used to make the hiring decision without human revision (i.e., to pass or deny a candidate entry to the next phase of the recruitment process).

Source: Zahira Jaser and Dimitra Petrakaki   ♡ **HBR**

Figure 7.1. The spectrum of de-personalization when using AVI[5]

Table 7.1 Paradigm shift in business models

Old model	*Humachine*
Sole focus on profit and loss	Intentionality and purpose
Contractual engagements	Meaningful relationships
Functional procedures	Systems thinking
Silos	Flexible structures
Hierarchical	Integrated teams
Physical presence	Physical and virtual
Traditional offices	Work environments promoting comfort
Rigid measures of productivity	Aspirational goals

technology, one that quickly atrophies. But remember—without people there is no innovation, no strategy, no connections with customers. Therefore, to succeed in the technology era, companies need to focus on people, ensuring that human talent at all levels is prepared to move the organization forward. The new era is about empowering human flourishing, emotional connections, and authenticity.

Transitioning from the Old to the New

There are four broad maneuvers to undertake in making the transition from the old paradigm to the Humachine.

1   The first shift will be moving away from single-minded focus on financial performance and shareholder value to focus on intentionality and purpose.

We are not saying financial performance will no longer control. Financial performance and shareholder value will always be important. The difference is that creating human-centered, technology-powered organizations will drive financial performance. Intentionality imbues existence with meaning beyond the mere pursuit of profit or shareholder value. Having a purpose in society beyond mere profit capture is a critical element of success. In the post pandemic era talent seeks out working in environments dedicated to a higher purpose. This is precisely what was behind the "great resignation" and "quiet quitting," two workforce trends observed following the pandemic.

It is hard to inspire a workforce to innovation, creativity, and engagement with the profit motive alone. Pursuit of profit does not inspire human flourishing, creativity, or authentic care. It will not suffice in the new era where greater human capabilities are needed.

Business leaders should be able to clearly articulate the purpose of the company in the world, what it is all about. Business leaders should act with integrity. This means conforming to principle and having fidelity to the truth. It seems like lawyers can always find a loophole to allow business to make an exception of itself. We might say that one's integrity is a function of how often you make an exception of the rules as they would otherwise apply to yourself. In the information era, truth feels ever harder to come by. We are swimming in data and yet we don't always know which way is up. Companies that tell the truth when there is a temptation to lie will be rewarded by the cultivation of public trust. There will be more data scandals and failed cover-ups. How leaders react, and whether they demonstrate integrity, will determine whether they get to keep their jobs. Indeed, leaders have a robust business case for pursuing social, economic, and environmental priorities.

2. The second shift involves moving from contractual relationships to meaningful relationships.

The quality of engagement with stakeholders—from customers, employees, and suppliers depends upon the commitment to form meaningful human relationships. Agility and flexibility will be increasingly required as machines and humans work to adapt in real time to customer and environmental demands. What this takes is a shift from rigid functional procedures to systems thinking; from silos to flexible organizational structures; from rigid hierarchies to flatter organizations and cross-functional integrated teams. We cannot get caught up in our official job title; we simply need to perform as needed, playing to our individual strengths, responding to and communicating to one another our real needs in real time.

3. The third shift is moving from merely adding technology to integrating technology.

Acquiring technology such as AI needs to be thoughtful, deliberate, strategic, and intentional in terms of meeting objectives. Most importantly that technology cannot be merely added to current processes. Rather strategy and competitive priorities must be identified, technology selected to support those and propel the organization. Technology must be integrated and centered around humans, supporting and enhancing their work and decision—becoming their coworkers. For example, Salesforce—the cloud-based customer relationship management (CRM) software company—integrated AI to provide a range of features that help employees better understand customers, automate tasks, and allow employees to make better decisions. AI is used in its recruiting and onboarding process, which helps find and hire the best talent, and get new employees up to speed quickly. In recruiting, Salesforce uses AI to automate the recruiting process, from sourcing candidates to screening resumes. This frees up recruiters to focus on more strategic tasks, such as building relationships with candidates and closing deals. For onboarding, Salesforce uses AI to personalize the onboarding experience for new employees customizing the interaction. This helps new employees get up to speed quickly and feel more engaged with the company. For performance management, Salesforce uses AI to provide employees with personalized feedback and development plans, helping employees improve their performance and reach their full potential. The integration of humans with AI is working and, as a result, Salesforce has been able to increase customer and employee satisfaction, and boost productivity. In 2022, they were named the #1 Best Place to Work by *Fortune* magazine.

4.   The fourth shift is a move from traditional productivity measures to aspirational metrics.

Traditional metrics of productivity and output must give way to aspirational metrics that incentivize innovation and creativity. In order to encourage human workers to exercise those uniquely human skills as more and more cognitive work is botsourced, we need to change our performance metrics. The old management saying goes, "You cannot manage what you do not measure." Managing human creativity, caring, emotional intelligence, ethical convictions, and innovation will require us to use different measures of performance, not just work hours performed or cost reductions achieved.

In order to manage these four maneuvers, we propose the "Four I" model. We were pleased that "Four I-s" sounds like "Four Eyes," which is the nickname for the stereotypical glasses-wearing geek. In the technology era, geeks are heroes. See Table 7.2. The Four I-s are *Intentionality, Integration, Implementation*, and *Indication*.

The remainder of this chapter elaborates upon the Four I-Model as a roadmap for enterprises mutating into the Humachine.

Intentionality

Intentionality is about purpose. It defines what the company is about, its reason for being. Unlike cliché goals such as maximizing shareholder value, intentionality defines the human needs and values that a company's products

Table 7.2 The 4-I Model paradigm shift

Emphasis	*Description*
Intentionality	The organization's purpose, meaning, values, and reason for being
Integration	The seamless and symbiotic melding of people and technology across organizational functions and hierarchies
Implementation	Creating and executing strategies for integrating humans and machines around the principles of intentionality
Indication	Using aspirational indicators of performance to monitor and measure

and services ultimately fulfill in society. An intentional organization knows why it matters to the world, not just its shareholders, and is deliberative in creating an organization that manifests that intention.

The psychology literature has long documented the importance of purpose to mental health.[8] Having a purpose and a sense of belonging may be one of the largest non-genetic factors in longevity. Purpose and belonging are more or less what define our lives as humans, without which we struggle to do anything more than merely survive.

Even as machines are taking over routine, automated, and even cognitive tasks, humans are still needed to play new roles to manifest the intention of the organization with innovation, creativity, caring, and emotional intelligence. Organizations that see themselves as nothing but profit-making machines will lose human talent and ultimately fail to connect with customers. Economic exchange for services, monitoring profit and loss, and increasing shareholder value will always be important, but they are simply not enough to create a viable culture.

Achieving intentionality is not a mere economic exchange. It is aspirational. It moves people to get involved, gives them a sense of meaning and a desire to be part of a mission with real stakes for humanity. Recall that in Chapter 4 we discussed some uniquely human qualities, such as caring, having emotions, and being moved through feelings. Organizations that can find ways to energize people through their emotions will get the most out of their people. Intentionality does that.

Undue competition at work makes work more demanding and psychologically taxing on workers than it ought to be. To get people to devote themselves to the cause, to become more involved and engaged in the mission of the enterprise, means they need to feel self-actualized in their work. Expecting humans to perform like robots or to be constantly pitted against their colleagues in a talent arms race will not lead to success, but we fear that has been the trend for the last several decades. We need to reverse that trend. Sure, some of your staff will need to know programming languages and statistical methods; however, tapping into the very human traits of caring, emotional intelligence, and intuition is what it takes to be a leading organization in this new era.

Kinaxis is a company that taps into these human traits, which are embedded into its culture. They offer employees a steady stream of events, programs and initiatives designed to feed the mind, body and soul. And they lead with this culture in recruiting; their careers website states:

> At Kinaxis, who we are is grounded in our common belief that people matter here. This belief is at the center of everything we do. It's in our DNA. It's at the core of our purpose, values, behaviors, actions and ways of working together that shape and define our shared culture.

Intentionality includes purpose, authenticity, and integrity. We consider each of these in turn.

Purpose

Recall *Maslow's Hierarchy of Needs*,[9] which identifies and prioritizes human needs from most basic to most advanced. At the base of Maslow's pyramid are *physiological* needs that satisfy the biological requirements for human life (food, shelter, sleep). Once those basic needs are met, humans are driven by the need for *safety*, which explains the establishment of law and order to provide security and freedom from existential threats. Once our biological needs are met and our safety is attended to, humans become primarily motivated by the pursuit of *love* or *interpersonal connections* and a sense of belonging. We fulfill this need by establishing relationships based on trust, intimacy, acceptance, and friendship. Once humans have these basic social foundations in place, our motivation turns to *esteem*, both in terms of the self-esteem that comes with dignity and in terms of earning respect from others. The height of human livelihood per Maslow is pursuit of *self-actualization*, which is what we mean when we say human flourishing. We want this term "flourishing" to carry with it the connotation of Aristotle's Greek word for happiness, *eudemonia*, which means the activity of the soul in accord with the virtues over a complete life.

The organization that is the symbiosis of humans and machines—the Humachine—can only get the best of humans by fostering the best of their human qualities. Like children need well-adjusted and capable parents, so the machines need human handlers to reach their potential. As machines do the "machine" work, companies need humans to be more "human." That is enabled by an organization that cultivates intentionality, purpose, and a sense of belonging to the group and team participating in that purpose.

Having a higher purpose has been shown to yield impressive financial performance as well. The *Harvard Business Review* reports on a study that included 500,000 people across 429 firms and involved 917 firm-year observations from 2006 to 2011, which found a positive impact on both operating financial performance (return on assets) and forward-looking measures of performance (stock returns) when the purpose of the company is communicated with clarity.[10] Research by John Kotter that observed companies over a decade-long period show that stock price of purposeful, value-driven companies outperformed by a factor of 12 traditional for-profit counterparts.[11] Therefore, economic benefits follow from purpose.

Without intentionality and purpose, it is difficult for a company's leadership to motivate employees. This is true now more than ever, where workers worry about losing jobs to machines, where their coworkers are robots that are superior to them in many ways, where they need to learn new skills, and where they experience increasing uncertainty as to their future roles. With clear intentionality, employees at all levels can rally together, coalescing around the higher purposes of the organization. It is then that the whole is greater than the sum of the parts. Therefore, intentionality is not just some lofty ideal. It is a practical motivating force.

When people find meaning in their work, they are more likely to give generously of their talent, going the extra mile, as they are driven by positive emotions. The organizations that can tap into that energy will undergo positive transformations.[12] These are the organizations that will lead in the new era.

Culture

Machines cannot operate without humans training them, developing them, directing them, interpreting their output, and creating products that ultimately humans will purchase and use. Customers, suppliers, vendors, and board members cannot relate to machines and robots. They do not want to see reports presented by robots. They connect with people.

Companies will succeed in the technology era not simply because they have more or better data, or better algorithms. Certainly, availability of data and technology are a needed prerequisite. However, technology, machines, robots, and platforms are increasingly becoming standard across industries and competitors.

What is a company's unique differentiator that is hard to copy? It is human talent. Companies that are leading in this era do so because they have leadership that creates the right culture, sets and articulates clear goals, defines what success looks like, and gets everyone "on board." They are able to effectively lead their organization through transformational change and get everyone excited. They can hire and keep the best talent. Organizational culture embodies the intentionality of the organization. Intentionality provides a sense of meaning, and the culture needs to be a living example of that.

Consider Google—a technology-driven company that is consistently regarded as one of the best places to work. Google's mission statement is "to organize the world's information and make it universally accessible and useful." Google's vision statement for what it wants to achieve is "to provide access to the world's information in one click." To achieve this, Google has created a culture that is open, innovative, emphasizes excellence and freedom of creativity, where employees are free to give their opinion. Every employee is encouraged to contribute innovative ideas rather than conform. Innovating, creating, and being free to express yourself is the norm.

An analytics culture that demands rigorous scrutiny of data before making a choice can sometimes be at tension with the members of the team who have more innovative or entrepreneurial impulses. Finding the right blend between analytics and innovation in decision-making can require hard choices. The amount of tolerance for blue-sky development where designers or engineers chase after ideas varies from company to company. In many analytics-driven organizations, R&D, like other functions, is rigorously metric driven. At companies such as Yahoo, Progressive, and Capital One, process and product changes are first tested on a small scale.[13] The changes must be numerically validated before they are implemented on a broader scale.

The question then is whether culture can be changed directly. Or does cultural change evolve as a result of updates to systems, structure, and processes? Research shows that companies that wait for organizational cultures to change organically will move too slowly in the digital economy.[14] Cultural obstacles correlate with negative economic performance. Companies like Nordstrom are a good example of what it looks like when digital strategies are designed with deliberate customer-centric efforts, employee empowerment, and connections across the omnichannel.[15]

Companies must be proactive in shaping their culture, approaching it with the same rigor as they would any other technical reengineering effort. Culture is not left to chance. It is purposefully shaped. This means actively changing all elements—structures, processes, and incentives—that run counter to the new culture of openness and innovation the organization is trying to achieve. This means ensuring that silos are broken down, that everyone shares a customer-centric vision, risk of innovation is tolerated, and cross-functional coordination is incentivized.

Authenticity

Authenticity in the business context means staying true to who you are, what you do, and the vision that motivates you. Borrowing from the existentialist movement in philosophy, authenticity means choosing freely your own path and taking responsibility for the implications of those choices, rather than passively following the dictates of other forces and washing your hands of the consequences by claiming to have been just following along.

Why is authenticity important, and how does authenticity support an organization and its intentionality? Being inauthentic, not doing what we enjoy, and not being true to oneself robs us of energy and motivation.

Think of Jennifer Aniston's waitress character in the popular film *Office Space*. She was chastised for not wearing enough "flair" on her uniform. Of course, this is a fictional movie character, but it was funny because so many people related. Because she was being forced to feign enthusiasm, she quit her job. By contrast, when people feel free to be who they are, they have more energy, inspiration, and enthusiasm, and are more likely to bring passion, creativity, and dedication to the work they do.

Authentic workers are more likely to bring their whole selves to the job, engage with the company's goals, and participate fully in the mission of the enterprise. Obviously, this does not mean disregarding a code of conduct. It merely means that management needs to find ways to align the rules of conduct with the personal values and expressive styles of its people.

An excellent example of a culture of authenticity is the company Seventh Generation. The company produces ordinary household products—toilet paper, dish soap, and fabric softener. However, it is a top employer of millennials who seem thrilled to be working there. The reason millennials are so drawn to the company is because of its authenticity and commitment to a higher purpose. The company's purpose is stated in its mission: "To inspire a consumer revolution that nurtures the health of the next seven generations."

Seventh Generation shows authenticity in every aspect of its business, both with employees and customers. For example, the company is known for encouraging consumers to line-dry their clothing instead of machine drying to save energy, even if that means it has less business in dryer sheets. Encouraging environmentally friendly consumer behavior, even though it directly takes away from the company's business, shows a commitment to a higher purpose. The company's products are natural, toxin free, and not harmful to the environment. This authenticity is what inspires loyalty and dedication because employees genuinely care about the mission of the organization. There is more to Seventh Generation than merely creating profit for shareholders.

When a company demonstrates an authentic purpose, employees and consumers feel a connection to both the products and company. More consumers are choosing to patronize businesses committed to sustainable practices and products, even if their products are not sold at the cheapest price. Authenticity gives substance to the company and its products, and it reveals human-centeredness and ethical commitment. This enables people to make a human connection to the brand. This can be powerful. In today's crowded technology space, authenticity will be a differentiator.

Integrity

Integrity in business means, in a phrase, doing the right thing even if no one would find out. Being committed to a social purpose beyond merely increasing profits adds a "soul" to the otherwise hollow shell of an enterprise. Acting in a principled manner, including telling the truth when it would be more convenient to lie, demonstrates an ethical conscience, without which the enterprise loses its social license to operate.

Doing "whatever it takes to win" is a cutthroat mentality more fitting for a psychopath than a business leader. For those ruthlessly amoral capitalists reading this, if you are not intrinsically motivated to behave yourself, there are for-profit rationales for business ethics. One is when leaders act with integrity, they foster a culture of trust and respect within the organization. This translates into better morale and dedication to the company's mission. Integrity also attracts customers. It is hard to maintain customer loyalty if the company is giving off the vibe that it has "something to hide." Integrity in business also attracts employees who are ethically motivated. Most people would prefer not to be associated with a scandal, at any rate. Lastly, for all these carrots, there is the stick of avoiding legal consequences for bad faith business conduct.

Unilever has done quite well under the tenure of former CEO Paul Polman. By prioritizing social responsibility and business integrity, Unilever has demonstrated the business case for ethics.[16] We expect everyone at Unilever to be an ambassador for our high ethical standards—what we call "business integrity." We want to create an environment where employees not only live our values in their own work—integrity, respect, responsibility and pioneering—but are vigilant in identifying potential concerns, and confident about speaking up in such situations.

Unilever has more than a website entry about business ethics. It has embedded integrity into its DNA by implementing a code of conduct that is positively reinforced and participatory across the organization and its entire supply chain.

It is no longer quite so easy to cover up a scandal. When something big goes wrong (think Facebook's Cambridge Analytica scandal, or Volkswagen's diesel emissions scandal), it will leak eventually. How leaders respond to the scandal will determine their fate and that of the company. We are calling on business leaders to handle scandals with integrity. It will pay off in the long run, even if it scares you to rip that Band-Aid off.

For-profit corporations are taking on ever-increasing power, wealth, influence over public policy, and influence in the daily lives of millions of people. Amazon, Facebook, and Google are forces in the world, affecting even the lives of people who don't "Add to Cart," "Like," or "Google." As companies become more powerful, they need to embrace their role of stewards of natural resources and guardians of public trust. If large companies act like feudal lords, they will probably suffer the same fate. We understand this sounds pretty idealistic, but there are already plenty of critical depictions of Big Tech out there,[17] and our focus is on how to get things right in the future, not just how we have gotten things wrong so far.

Integration

There are two different types of integration that need to take place in the 4-I model of organizations. *First* is doing away with silos and hierarchies to create integrated organizational structures. *Second* is integration between people and technology. The second fits into every aspect of the first as technology is now the cornerstone of how people at all levels of the organization and teams work, create, and make decisions.

From Pyramids and Silos to Flexible Networks

Most organizations are siloed and hierarchical. There are clear boundaries between functional areas such as customer-relationship management on the one side and operations on the other. To lead in the technology era, companies must be highly adaptable and flexible. Technology makes a difference where demand sensing on the one side can be linked in real time with operations and suppliers. This, however, requires a shift from siloed structures to systems thinking.

To facilitate this, Kinaxis, a leading provider of supply-chain management solutions, offers an enterprise product purpose-built with systems thinking. Their unique concurrency technique provides transparency along the entire supply chain so that it is completely connected, eliminating informational silos. By combining human intelligence and AI with concurrent planning, their approach enables companies to plan for future disruptions, monitor for risks and opportunities, and respond quickly. Using business intelligence tools like this allows enterprise leaders to be proactive, responding to disturbances with rapid adaptability and flexibility rather than waiting for information to come in then reacting late, which is sometimes the same as being ineffectual.

One executive we spoke with explained that worker skills and understanding will have to move from narrow to broad. Before the shift, it was necessary for workers to have deep knowledge of their narrow area. Today, technology and AI can do most of the routine tasks. The detailed "deep but narrow" knowledge is not needed any more. What is needed is the ability to collaborate across functions, which is to work in cross-functional teams. To achieve this requires system thinking, understanding how the work one is doing meshes with that of others elsewhere in the organization, how it meets customer needs, and how it impacts the company's strategy and financial picture. Instead of *deep but narrow*, we need *functional and broad*.

Currently, many organizations use power-based hierarchies. The higher up you are in the hierarchy, the more power you wield, and vice versa. At the lower ends of the hierarchy, one cannot do anything significant without getting clearance from the "higher ups." However, fostering creativity and innovation requires more autonomy within the workforce than what is typically permitted in a pyramid structure. To foster innovation and adaptability, organizations should transition from rigid hierarchies to flexible, agile, and flatter organizational arrangements. From pyramids to networks.

These new structures enable teams to spontaneously form around new products then dissolve when the work is done, reforming here and there depending on emerging needs. We discuss amoebae-like structures in the next chapter. Old organizing principles where marketing is walled off from operations will simply not realize the full potential of the human talent we need in the age of AI.

Flexible structures are used at Google to promote innovation. Here, structure and culture interact to influence the capabilities of the organization as one unit. Innovation is at the heart of the Google culture. As a result, Google uses a matrix organizational structure. This structure enables cross-functional and cross-business groups working together and cross-traditional vertical silos. Google is a relatively flat organization. This means that Google employees, teams, and groups can meet and share information across teams. They can even bypass middle management and report directly to the CEO.

Humans and Machines: The New Coworkers

The second integration is between humans and machines. This integration permeates every aspect of the organization and should be seamless. Integration throughout the organization means that technology acquisition and implementation should not be fragmented. Investment in technology needs to support the organization's purpose; it needs to link the organization's pieces. Technology acquisition must also be accompanied by training and support to workers in a culture where they work alongside machines. These are their new coworkers. Without hiring the right talent, proper onboarding, training, and creating an innovative culture, investments in technology will produce fragmented efforts at best. Employees will never gain the competencies—and confidence—to engage and work with machines.

An excellent example of how human and AI capabilities can be combined to work together in decision-making is a hiring process used at Unilever.[18] Rather than having employees go through the initial tedious stage of application review, in the first round of the application process, candidates are asked to play online games that help assess traits such as risk aversion. There are no right or wrong answers to the games. Rather, the AI algorithm can look at the way applicants are responding and provide an initial screen of whether they would be best suited for a particular position. In the next round, applicants are asked to submit a video where they answer questions pertaining to the specific position for which they are being considered. Again, an AI algorithm evaluates the responses including body language and tone. The candidates who pass the second round, as judged by the AI algorithm, are then invited to Unilever for in-person interviews. This is the point where humans make the final hiring decisions. This is an AI-led AVI process that seems to do a decent job at narrowing the field, identifying quality candidates in the talent pool for human HR professionals.

Combining AI filtering with human judgment in a two-step manner like this accelerates the hiring process and frees up the humans working in HR for greater value-adding activities beyond screening initial candidates—for example recruiting the most competitive candidates who have multiple offers, as well as onboarding candidates and initiating the training process.

Recall from Chapter 5 the human–machine interface model. Machines provide output, including statistics, data, predictions, assessments, evaluations, information, and products. It is humans who need to make final decisions where judgment is needed. Humans add context. They explain, translate, and judge. Many processes and decisions can and should be automated, however, more important decisions—for example, those that require expertise and judgment—should still be made by humans. Remember from Chapter 4 that humans run into predictable boundaries to fully rational behavior. We should use AI as a decision-support tool that helps humans get things right by filling in computational gaps and de-biasing. Further, automating routine tactical decisions (like re-ordering supplies before stock out) can help maintain consistently high-quality decision-making over the course of the workday, especially in strategic settings where judgment (not just computation) is required.

Using AI as a complementary coworker can help avoid decision fatigue. *Decision-fatigue* is the weakened state of an individual's willpower after making too many choices; more choices means less stamina, less productivity, and less ability to complete unpleasant but goal-oriented tasks.[19]

This particular topic of human and machine coworkers is so fundamental to the Humachine that we devote the next chapter to it entirely.

Design Thinking

We stress that the Humachine is an enterprise that fosters innovation in individuals, teams, and even beyond its boundaries. But what does it take to innovate? How does a company enable human-centric innovation? Many leading firms, including Google, Apple, and Procter & Gamble, have turned to design thinking as a method to teach teams and individuals to think creatively, an important step in the process of innovation.

According to Tim Brown, the CEO of the design firm IDEO, *design thinking* is a "human-centered approach to innovation that draws from the designer's toolkit to integrate the needs of people, the possibilities of technology, and the requirements for business success."[20] Design thinking has been used by countless companies in product innovation in virtually every industry sector—from IBM to Nike, to PepsiCo, to Bank of America, to GE Healthcare. It is especially useful in attempting to solve complex problems that are poorly defined or unknown. The process focuses on understanding the human needs of a problem, rather than dealing with the problem directly—like Zappos focusing on the intentionality of the purchase, rather than the product itself. It involves reframing the problem in a human-centric way and is therefore the ideal perspective for innovation and design in the human-centered technology era.

Design thinking follows an iterative design process that begins by seeking to understand the user. Why is design thinking so important to the Humachine? Understanding the people for whom the product or service is being designed helps cultivate empathy for human needs rather than simply conceiving of new possible product uses. The process then challenges current assumptions, and it redefines the problem in an attempt to identify alternative strategies and solutions that may not have been readily apparent at the initial approach. It provides a different way of thinking but also offers a hands-on process that leads to a solution.

There are typically five stages of design thinking.

First is to *empathize* in order to gain an understanding of the problem. It involves observing and becoming immersed in the problem, and requires a deep understanding of the issues without being blinded by personal assumptions. Technology, AI, and real-time customer data of product information can be helpful here. However, historical data by itself may not help as this stage goes beyond how the product is currently being used. Rather, empathy can reveal underlying issues that help resolve the problem. The goal is to lead to a solution that may not have been otherwise apparent.

The second stage is *defining*, which is formulating the core problem. This should be a problem statement articulated in a human-centered way.

Third is to *ideate* to generate solution ideas. The key here is thinking "outside of the box" to identify novel solutions that address the need. There are numerous "ideation" techniques such as brainstorming or even playing a game of "worst possible idea." These are intended to stimulate free thinking and creativity in finding solutions.

Fourth is *prototyping*, where a number of scaled-down versions of the solution are created. This is an experimental phase where ideas area improved, reexamined, refined, or rejected.

The last stage is *testing*, where experimentation and understanding lead to a final solution. This is the "test and learn" phase, where failure is permitted and even expected. In fact, companies like Google expect failure as it promotes learning.

An important aspect in design thinking is that this is not a linear process. Many stages can be conducted concurrently. For example, the testing phase may reveal something about the user that may push back toward ideation and creation of new prototypes. The idea is that this is an ongoing process of understanding customers, refining problems and solutions, and ongoing innovation and creativity. We like to think of it is a process of continuous improvement and feedback, as illustrated in Figure 7.2.

Braun and Oral-B provide an example of design thinking in action. Braun and Oral-B approached Industrial Facility, a London-based industrial design firm, to help them design an IoT "smart" electric toothbrush.[21] The companies wanted to develop a toothbrush with a sophisticated data-tracking tool that would be able to sense how well users were brushing. The idea was that the brush could inform the user about every aspect of brushing effectiveness—gum sensitivity, how each tooth was brushed, and even play music to accompany the brushing process. In theory, a smart toothbrush could advance oral hygiene and make the tooth-brushing process more enjoyable.

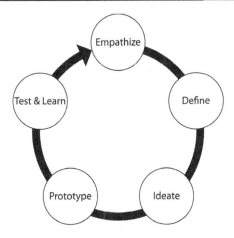

Figure 7.2 Phases of design thinking

Through design thinking, however, the designers helped identify the actual needs of the customers—and it did not include such data tracking. As one of the designers put it:

> A toothbrush is already loaded with guilt, that you're not doing it properly or enough. The companies weren't thinking about the customers' experience. They were thinking about the toothbrush the same way you would an athletic activity tracker, that it records and processes information.[22]

So they scrapped all these fancy features. Instead, they decided that the features that would actually be most useful were functions for easily charging the toothbrush and automatically ordering replacement heads. The toothbrush was then designed so that, at home, it charges on a dock through induction to make charging easier, but it also comes equipped with a USB hookup for use on the road so that the brush would not run out of batteries while the user is traveling. These charging enhancements made it less likely the vibrating toothbrush would just become a bristled paperweight. As far as ordering replacement heads, just pressing a button on the brush sends a reminder notification to the customer's phone to buy replacements. These designs addressed real customer needs and were a far cry from the IoT toothbrush the manufacturer originally imagined.

Design thinking may also help us avoid the problem of *solutionism*. Silicon Valley's attempt to disrupt the status quo by providing technological solutions to all of life's problems sounds benign, but it can be dangerous. According to Evgeny Morozov, some innovation may actually be "driven by a pervasive and dangerous ideology that I call 'solutionism': an intellectual pathology that recognizes problems as problems based on just one criterion: whether they are 'solvable' with a nice and clean technological solution at our disposal. Thus, [human cognitive challenges such as] forgetting and inconsistency become 'problems' simply because we have the tools to get rid of them—and not because we've weighed all the philosophical pros and cons" of doing so.[23]

Design thinking avoids overengineering a product by focusing on actual human needs, not just ways of making existing products fancier. Generative AI is now refining and speeding up the iterative process of design, while continuing the focus on human needs.

Implementation

To say the devil is in the details means an idea might sound desirable from a distance but when you zoom in you realize it's full of trouble. Ultimately, all the ideas we have presented need to be implemented, and that's where things can go sideways. We provide some guidance for implementation here.

Have a Clear Message

We discussed the importance of intentionality and purpose, having the right culture and being authentic. The first aspect of implementation—before we can hire talent and create a good working environment—is to boil all this down to a succinct message. A concise, compelling message that is repeated at every level of the organization eliminates ambiguity and confusion.

It is one thing to have intentionality. It is something else to verbalize it in such a manner that everyone can understand and everyone can see. Without clarity and repetition, intentionality can get lost throughout normal business functions, day-to-day stresses, and the telephone game. The message must be clear and repeatable. It will then drive everything from creating a new product to onboarding a new hire.

Consider the message from Seventh Generation. There is no doubt for employees when it comes to product innovation and creativity. It is about developing products "that nurture the health of the next seven generations." The same is true of Google. The company's success is its clear mission: to organize the world's information, and make it universally accessible and useful. Every product that "Googlers" work on is to get the company one step closer to fulfilling its purpose.

In both of these cases, the clarity of message helps employees know what to focus on; it helps customers understand what the company is about; it is also an excellent recruitment tool. A clear message can go a long way toward drawing talent that share the company's values.

Hire the Right Talent

One of the leading technology companies we visited pointed out its secret to success. The company said it was hiring the right talent. One of the analysts we spoke with privately said that he, like the others, was drawn to an innovative culture; like attracts like, and an innovative culture attracts innovative people. Talented, driven people want to be part of an organization that has a purpose, a creative culture, and incentives for being innovative.

Employees cannot be forced to share the company's intentionality, values, or culture. However, lack of match will show in lack of authenticity. Customers and other employees will be able to tell. A shared purpose is a common starting point. Therefore, having a clear message of the company's intentionality and underscoring that during the recruitment process will go a long way toward hiring the right talent.

One of the companies we spoke with said it has a set of questions it asks potential hires that go beyond their capabilities and duties. They are questions that reveal specifically why the person is interested in the firm, how they feel about the company's mission, and how and why they would fit in. Companies that promote innovation will draw innovative people.

Consider how an SAP employee described the importance of culture to innovation:

> It's easy to feel like you're not making an impact when you work for a multinational corporation, but at SAP, risk-taking and big thinking is encouraged. If you have an idea and a plan to get it done, no one will stop you from bringing it to life.[24]

That kind of supportive environment is why SAP consistently ranks as one of the best places to work and drives outstanding results year to year.

Like Apple, leading technology companies have built a critical mass of analytical talent upon which the rest of their organization can draw. These companies start with early hires who make up the core around which they built their analytics teams. These initial hires need to be the most capable people in order to build the most effective teams possible. Given the potential competition for this talent, however, organizations must aggressively recruit deep analytical talent. This may involve sourcing talent from other geographical areas, outsourcing select analytical services to vendors, or aligning with an academic institution to get access to newly minted graduates.

Recruiting talent is important; however, it is not enough to change an organization. Leadership has to have an appreciation and understanding of analytics to drive the right culture. Otherwise, leaders and analysts do not know how to take advantage of big data capability because they are not speaking the same language.

Leaders in an organization need to develop at least a rudimentary understanding of analytical techniques to become effective users of these types of analyses. Consider how financial services firm Capital One addressed this issue. The company has created an internal training institute called Capital

One University. It offers professional training programs, such as on testing and experiment design. This helps promote broader understanding of analytics throughout the organization, not just within the analyst position.

Create a Work Environment That People Love

Technology continues to change the way people work. In the past, most businesses just needed a physical space, a data center, and staff. As technology evolved through connected devices, ERM and CRM platforms, and the cloud, the digital workplace was born. It enables virtual teaming and a the evolution of a workplace into a globally connected and globally distributed enterprise.

With competition focused on creative output, the compliance requirement of being at a desk should vanish. Creativity and innovation matter and that can rarely happen after a long period of forced sitting. Work is now shifting from a monolithic place where one sits, puts their head down, and clocks in and out, to a place that is an extension of home, where we can play and create value in ways that are intrinsically satisfying, not simply remunerative.

Today's work environment needs to be more about facilitating group dynamics and maintaining space for people to collaborate. It is about comfort and amenities that keep people healthy and refreshed even as they work. People need to be part of a community and members of supportive, functioning teams. Create a culture of shared values.

When human workers are empowered by technology, enabled by supportive managers, and comfortable in the physical workspace, they will deliver quality performance. Leading companies will enable their people to focus on the true purpose of the organization by engaging the workforce, fostering autonomy, and enabling agile work. This autonomy and agility are the foundation for innovation.

Google has been one of the first companies to really understand the need for a comfortable place to foster creativity and innovation. We discuss more about ergonomics in Chapter 9. Certainly there are rules. As of this publication, employees still had to wear pants at work. However, Google was one of the first to allow employees to have a flexible schedule and work on their own timetables. It has resulted in much greater levels of productivity. Google has created an environment where its employees can explore how they would like to work and use their own discretion to choose what gives them the greatest productivity. Lastly, Google has created a fun environment that does not feel like work. This is a company where employees often work long days and even weekends, voluntarily.

A Flexible Work Environment

If the goal is to enhance creativity and productivity in service of your company's mission, then it is antithetical to the business mission to require employees to routinely subject themselves to unpleasant conditions of work. If your office environment is lame, then you are also lame for requiring people to work in that setting. At least be willing to shift from traditional offices to work environments that promote comfort. What matters is performance, not being in a cubicle. If you only trust your staff to work when they are literally under direct supervision and surveillance in an office setting away from home, you've got trust issues or employees who should probably be fired. Find other performance metrics so they can work wherever suits them. Unless you are dealing in sensitive materials that should be in a controlled environment (anything from protected health information to hazardous substances), let your teams work from wherever. Or make your office better than anywhere else they might rather be.

A Google employee we interviewed at the Manhattan facility continued to go into the office even during her vacation. She explained that there was free food and it was comfortable at work—in fact more comfortable than her apartment in Midtown. For humans to play at their peak, they should be comfortable.

To enable this move, the work environment itself will have to change. The eight-hour work day within a physical office should be replaced with far more pleasant arrangements that support human collaborative relationships and flourishing. Let's replace the dreaded Monday morning commute into an over-air-conditioned sick building with poor natural light with something more humane, efficient, and productive. That means virtual presence, collaboration in both physical and virtual teams, and work structure that promotes the best in people. Consider Google, which lets employees take naps and work at their own pace in a highly comfortable, aesthetically pleasing environment. Treat people like humans instead of commodities and you'd be surprised at the results.

Foster Freedom to Create, Experiment, and Fails

Experimentation goes hand in hand with innovation. A *test and learn* culture needs an environment where ideas can be tested and lessons learned from failure. In simple terms, "test and learn" is a set of processes where all ideas, changes, and innovations are assumed to be hypotheses. For example, this could be a new advertising campaign or a solution to a problem. These hypotheses are then tested through experiments, which are enabled with data. Based on the findings from the experiments, evidence is gathered and changes are made. The process is then repeated and continuously improved upon until the idea is ready for implementation.

The test and learn business process has been around for decades. However, it is especially useful in feeling out future scenarios in this era of rapid change. We can use it in testing ideas about virtually everything—from advertising (e.g., which campaign has the most "likes") to merchandising (e.g., how customers respond to retail assortment) to product design changes and new features (e.g., through customer response and even embedded sensors).

A culture of experimentation assumes that the actual outcome of all the ideas is unknown *a priori*. This approach to innovation harvests the insights gleaned from experimental failures, which are far more common than the alternative.

Indication

Ultimately, success, progress, and achievement need to be measured. This is where indicators or metrics come into play. Understanding and using the right indicators can drive improvements and help a business focus on what they deem important. Indicators reveal the priorities of the company.

We should add to Drucker's phrase, "You cannot manage what you do not measure," Einstein's caution, "Not everything that counts can be counted, and not everything that can be counted counts." Further, we know from the double-slit experiment that at a quantum level, the act of observing something actually changes the reality of the observed subject. This plays out at a more practical level when the mere fact that management decides to measure a certain indicator changes employee behavior to maximize the results under that indicator, regardless of the contortions required to do so.

Be careful what you measure. Monitoring the wrong performance indicator has a strong tendency to lead to tails wagging dogs. Before implementing any new performance indicator, think very carefully about how the most lazy, clever, and cynical employee could "hack" or "game the system" to maximize the appearance of performance under that measure while actually failing to deliver the output that management was actually hoping for when they implemented the measure.

The most common types of indicators are key performance indicators or KPIs. KPIs are measurements for monitoring how well individuals, teams, or the entire divisions are performing against set goals. These metrics tend to be quantitative in nature, and most companies keep them simple to derive the most benefit. These indicators are ways that goals can be quantified and then assessed in measurable terms in order to track progress.

However, KPIs by themselves are not enough. They tend not to encompass strategic and aspirational goals needed in the Humachine era. This is where indicators called Objectives and Key Results (OKRs) come in. The goal of OKRs is to precisely define how to achieve ambitious objectives through concrete, measurable specifications. They are excellent ways to encourage creative, novel, and ambitious performance. OKRs are a way to both reach for the sky and ensure objective progress is being made, while avoiding the "hackability" of regular performance metrics.

The concept of OKRs was first introduced by Andrew Grove, former CEO of Intel, in the 1980s. Google started using them in 1999. Some even credit OKRs as a critical element of Google's success. At Google, OKRs have helped model organizational processes. Google uses a scale between 0 and 1.00 to grade the O part of the OKR and evaluates them quarterly. A number between 0.6 and 0.7 is considered the "sweet spot." Consistently getting a 1.00 means that the OKRs are not ambitious enough, as they did not push the team to stretch and test its limits.[25] There are two parts of the OKR metric. First, define the objectives. The objectives are the direction we are taking and what we are trying to achieve. The objectives are ambition and they should feel somewhat uncomfortable. For example, it may be something like "increase profit by 10%." Ideally, the goal should be so lofty that very well may not be attained during the measurement period. The goal is directional and aspirational, not easy. Second, define the key results. This is how we will know whether the goal has been attained. The second part is specifically measurable. For example, it may be "save 10% on purchases through a supplier reverse auction system and reduce costs by 25% by outsourcing distribution." Therefore, we are setting goals and then specifying how we will get there. OKRs and KPIs complement each other, and one is part of the other. What sets OKRs apart, however, is that they inspire ambitious goals and create room for constructive failure.

OKRs are also public (at least within the walls of the company). This means that everyone else can see what everyone else is working on. There is transparency. Everybody knows the company's goals, how their own work dovetails with other teams' work and how each fits within the company's overall objectives. Open OKRs add to being part of the group, contributing to intentionality and the shared vision.

A Dynamic Model

The 4-I model is a dynamic "living" representation of the organization that evolves and changes over time in a continuously learning—if not mutating—feedback loop. We show this in Figure 7.3. Intentionality gives the reason for Integration by providing a larger purpose; Integration marshals the right human and AI resources into porous and adaptive teams; once integrated, the mission is carried forward with Implementation to get the most out of the resources assembled by giving freedom to fail and innovate; all of the foregoing is evaluated by Indication, which measures what matters—progress toward the mission—and in turn motivates changes to Intentionality.

Intentionality, with the right culture and authenticity, are at the top as the overarching elements that drive the organization. They create an ambiance and working environment that enables freedom, innovation, and creativity.

Driven by intentionality, the organizational structure shifts from vertical siloes to flexible structures. Flatter matrix organizations are preferred over

Figure 7.3. The 4-I model

rigid hierarchies or pyramids. Integration means teams collaborating across all functional areas and strategic combinations of humans and machines.

Implementation is enabled through a concise and clear message, and hiring the right talent with shared values. The work environment shifts from inflexible office spaces where attendance is mandatory to "opt-in" work environments with perks that promote comfort, group collaboration, teamwork, and innovation.

Lastly, quota-like performance metrics are replaced by OKRs that promote innovation and aspiration. In the spirit of continuous improvement, this is an evolutionary process.

Conclusion

For an enterprise to become a Humachine, we must break free from old business paradigms. Intentionality and purpose must replace the single-minded focus on profit maximization. Meaningful collaborative relationships must replace soulless, solely contractual ones. Hierarchical and siloed structures should be jettisoned in favor of flat and fluid ones. Integrated teams should be measured with aspirational performance metrics and given room to flourish. Committing to the 4-I model is hard simply because change is fraught with fear, but it leads an organization down a path of fitness-enhancing mutation.

Notes

1 https://nextbigideaclub.com/magazine/notes-complexity-scientific-theor y-connection-consciousness-bookbite/42793/

2 https://hbr.org/2019/04/the-legal-and-ethical-implications-of-using-ai-in-hiring

3 Jaser, Zahira, Dimitra Petrakaki, Rachel Starr, and Ernesto Oyarbide-Magaña. *Where Automated Job Interviews Fall Short*, Harvard Business Review (January 27, 2022). Available at https://hbr.org/2022/01/where-automated-job-interviews-fa ll-short (last accessed June 9, 2023).

4 Ibid.

5 Ibid.

6 Ibid.

7 Ibid.

8 McKnight, Patrick and Kashdan, Todd. Purpose in Life as a System That Creates and Sustains Health and Well-Being: An Integrative, Testable Theory. *Review of General Psychology* 2009, Vol. 13, No. 3:242–251a.

9 McLeod, Saul. Maslow's Hierarchy of Needs. Available at www.simplypsychol ogy.org/maslow.html

10 Quinn, Robert E. and Thakor, Anjan V. Creating a Purpose Driven Organiza-tion. *Harvard Business Review*, July–August 2018, 78–85.

11 Kotter, John and Heskett, James. *Corporate Culture and Performance* (1992 Free Press).

12 Quinn and Thakor. Creating a Purpose Driven Organization, p. 78–85.

13 Ibid.

14 www.mckinsey.com/business-functions/digital-mckinsey/our-insights/culture-for-a-digital-age

15 www.therobinreport.com/a-fresh-new-look-at-the-nordstrom-way/

16 Business Integrity, Unilever, available at www.unilever.com/about/who-we-are/ our-values-and-principles/business-integrity/ "Our ambitions do not stop there. We aim to have a positive influence across our value chain, working with sup-pliers, distributors and all third parties to raise the bar on issues such as human rights and anti-bribery and corruption. Unilever's Business Integrity programme brings our values to life for all employees, and helps them apply our ethical standards day-to-day. In addition to our Code of Business Principles, it includes clear policies, guidelines and related learning materials, as well as robust proce-dures and controls to help us prevent, detect and respond to any inappropriate behaviour.

Prevention—We seek to embed a culture of integrity at all levels, in all geographies.

Detection—We encourage employees to speak up and give voice to their values.

Response—We have the tools to investigate and if necessary sanction con-firmed breaches, and use what we learn to continually improve."

17 Amy Webb, *The Big Nine: How the Tech Titans and Their Thinking Machines Could Warp Humanity*, PublicAffairs (2019); Scott Galloway, *The Four: The Hidden DNA of Amazon, Apple, Facebook, and Google* (2017 Random House.

18 Wilson, H. James and Paul R. Daugherty. Humans and AI Are Joining Forces. *Harvard Business Review*, July–August 2018, 115–123.

19 Kathleen D. Vohs, Noelle M. Nelson, Roy Baumeister, Brandon J. Schmeichel, Jean M. Twenge, Dianne M. Tice, Making Choices Impairs Subsequent Self-Control: A Limited-Resource Account of Decision Making, Self-Regulation, and Active Initia-tive. *Journal of Personality and Social Psychology* 2008, Vol. 94, No. 5.

20 www.ideou.com/pages/design-thinking

21 www.fastcompany.com/3060197/how-two-industrial-design-titans-are-helping-brands-simplify-tech

22 Ibid.

23 Morozov, Evgeny. The Perils of Perfection. *The New York Times*, March 2, 2013. Available at www.nytimes.com/2013/03/03/opinion/sunday/the-perils-of-perfection.html

24 Fortune Editors. The 40 Best Places to Work in Technology. *Fortune*, January 17, 2018; McKnight, and Kashdan. Purpose in Life as a System That Creates and Sustains Health and Well-Being: An Integrative; Webb. *The Big Nine: How the Tech Titans and Their Thinking Machines Could Warp Humanity*; Galloway. *The Four: The Hidden DNA of Amazon, Apple, Facebook, and Google*; Doerr, John. *Measure What Matters: How Google, Bono, and the Gates Foundation Rock the World with OKRs* (2018 Portfolio/Penguin).

25 Doerr, *Measure What Matters: How Google, Bono, and the Gates Foundation Rock the World with OKRs*.

Becoming a Humachine
the 'How' of Enterprise Transformation

If Refrigerators Could Talk—Oh Wait, They Can!

We would be forgiven for thinking there is not much room for innovation in refrigerators, air conditioners, and washing machines. Yet, Haier has defied all white-box stereotypes, making home appliances cool again.[1] These washers and dryers are knee-high, portable, and customizable. Refrigerators talk to customers with a screen connected to food suppliers responding to every customer need. They warn customers when the milk runs low, the lettuce is going bad, and the cheese has passed the expiration date. They've got the shopping list down and order directly for you. Low-sugar foods can be monitored for a diabetic customer and low fat for the diet-conscious counting calories. A restaurant wine cabinet can connect directly to winemakers, placing the order before running out of red. These are smart appliances.

Haier is a self-evolving organization that exemplifies transformation. The company has transformed itself from a home appliance maker to a world-leading home appliance brand and a smart home ecosystem builder, now one of Fortune World's Most Admired Companies.[2] Haier has reimagined once-mundane home essentials due to its forward-looking culture, organization, and a mindset to serve needs customers didn't even know they had.

The China-based company exhibits traits of the "Humachine"—a fusion of human creativity and technological innovation. According to Huagang Li, Senior Vice President of Haier Group and CEO of Haier Smart Home "the most important success factor has been our continuous focus on human value maximization."[3] This is consistent with our concept of the Humachine. This is the organization of the future, and the future is at our doorstep. Old models of gradual adaptation and transformation will only bring short-term gains. They will not work for long-term survival. Organizations must be willing to completely restructure and reimagine themselves—*mutate*—to survive in the new era. Form follows function.

DOI: 10.4324/9781003322832-8

A Different Species of Organization

The Humachine is a different species of organization. Consider how Wilson and Daugherty describe a new type of human–machine interaction: "Cumbersome legacy IT architecture is giving way to *living systems* that can weave together technologies, data, and talent."[4] This living system is the foundation of the Humachine—a living entity that has a "life" purpose (Intentionality). It has full complementarity and amalgamation between machines and humans that function as one (Integration). There is fluidity in the way work is conducted, with freedom to create, test, and innovate (Implementation). Lastly, performance is measured in aspirational ways that look toward the future and measure innovation and creativity (Indicators).

Recall from the foreword the important historical account of technology by Beniger, *The Control Revolution*.

> All living systems must process matter and energy to maintain themselves counter to entropy, the universal tendency of organization toward breakdown and randomization. Because control is necessary for such processing, and information … is essential to control, both information processing and communication, insofar as they distinguish living systems from the inorganic universe, might be said to define life itself.[5]
>
> Because societies must also be concrete open systems if they are to sustain their organization against the progressive degrading of their collective energy, the view of organisms as concrete open processing systems applies equally to their social aggregates. The essence of human society, in other words, is its continuous processing of physical throughputs, from their input to the concrete social system to their final consumption and output as waste.[6]

Society is "a *processing system*, one that sustains itself by extracting matter and energy from the environment and distributing them among its members."[7]

So we can program life at all levels of organization, from the micro to the macro. With the advent of synthetic life forms—from apparently conscious large language models and lifelike walking bots to genetically engineered cyborgs and nano-technology—we are now at an inflection point in the evolution of living systems. The question now – and has always been—*how do we maintain control?*

> Living systems have thus far evolved four levels of programmable structures and programs: DNA molecules encoded with genetic programming, the brain with cultural programming, organizations with formal processing and decision rules, and mechanical and electronic processors with algorithms. This succession of four levels of programming, each one of which appears to have complemented and extended

more than superseded already existing levels, constitutes the total history of control as we know it—a relatively smooth development punctuated by only these four major revolutions in control.[8]

Now we can combine genetic programming (through methodological selection), cultural programming like mindfulness or social programs, organizational management techniques, and evolutionary algorithms to create truly intelligent design.

How organizations process information to manage energy and material is a more abstract way of asking how organizations can be programmed: to execute strategic priorities, to maintain goal-oriented processes despite internal turbulence (change in leadership) and external (supply chain disruptions), to adapt to changing contexts like emerging technology or newly imposed government regulation, even how to structure the form of the entity itself (C corp, LLC, B corp, DOA, etc.)... and the right answer will evolve over time.

These are all questions of control that can be answered in part by the application of the basic laws of thermodynamics to business. In this view of the world, because it controls the processing and flows of information, the IT/IS department plays a vital, if unacknowledged, role in the life and success of every enterprise. Not only must organizational behavior change, but the mechanisms of control must also evolve.

We suggest the Humachine provides the "best" path forward, the best vehicle to carry forward programmable structures and programs to serve the interest of intelligent life on this planet. That is because systems of controlling the flow of information have always applied to all levels of life.[9] As intelligent life now spans organic and inorganic, natural and synthetic, so too must our systems of control span the micro and the macro, the individual and the collective, the man and the machine—and yet we must exercise control without controlling so much that the evolutionary gift of fitness-enhancing mutation is programmed out of the system.

> Because both the activities of information processing and communication are inseparable components of the control function, a society's ability to maintain control—at all levels from interpersonal to international relations—will be directly proportional to the development of its information technologies... Technology defines the limits of what a society *can* do...[10]

Therefore, consider the Humachine a new piece of technology that, by creating organizational network superintelligence, defines a new limit for what society can do.

Mutation, Not Transformation

The 4-I model presented in the previous chapter is not a roadmap to transformation *per se*. The notion of transformation misses the point of what the Humachine represents. Transformational changes are typically a once-off reaction to a major problem or challenge in the competitive environment. A transformation has a beginning and an end—a beginning "state" and an ending "state." Transformational change occurs when an organization changes its strategic direction for example after a merger, or pivots to address a new market, or reengineers its operations in response to a raw material shortage.

The Humachine is not a transformed organization that has reached a new steady state. Rather, it is a different species of organization. It is an ongoing process of collective intelligence. Concepts typically ascribed to transformation do not apply here. There are countless prescriptive roadmaps for digital transformation discussing a variety of issues as to how the transformation should take place. There is the matter of sponsorship, such as who should have accountability for the direction of analytics. There are issues of leadership, such as who is charged with realizing the vision for analytics. There are financial issues, such as how development of analytics capability should be funded. There is also governance, such as where should analytics talent "live" in the organization. These are all fine and good but again, digital transformation is a precondition for becoming a Humachine, as it formats your company to be analyzable by AI, to be able to interact with AI and AI with it, and thus to have human resources augmented by AI.

The Humachine is a different species of organization, one that has mutated from traditional organizational structures, hierarchies, incentives, and operations. It is an organization where technology and "machines" are intertwined with the best of human talent to create the ultimate symbiosis. Analytics and technology are not just another process to invest in with a payback period. Rather, they are an essential part of the company's substrate from which higher forms of organizational intelligence can emerge. Analytics and technology does not "live" in one place—they ought to be decentralized throughout the organization. There is no transformation from State A to State B but an ongoing evolutionary process of being, behaving, and becoming. Thus intelligent life has evolved in its systems of control over energy and matter, to the point that synthetic life and organic life form symbiotic relations in an organizational setting.

The Humachine is an amoeba-like organization that is fluid in structure, highly innovative, radically transparent, entrepreneurial, nimble, and adaptable to change. Getting there requires what we term a mutation of the organization. It requires significant disruption.

Managing AI Tools

Humans and AI systems can now each "make decisions," creating a major paradigm shift when it comes to managing the decision making process in an enterprise.

According to research in *Harvard Business Review*, as certain real-time and high-volume decisions become routinely automated and powered by algorithms, the management challenge becomes how humans should handle these systems.

> An autonomous system is conceptually very easy. Imagine a driverless car without a steering wheel. The driver simply tells the car where to go and hopes for the best. But the moment there's a steering wheel, you have a problem. You must inform the driver when they might want to intervene, how they can intervene, and how much notice you will give them when the need to intervene arises. You must think carefully about the information you will present to the driver to help them make an appropriate intervention.[11]

The challenge of human intervention over autopilot was illustrated perhaps most vividly by the episode of the first manned landing of a spacecraft on the surface of the Moon. Before we could take one small step for man, much less one giant leap for mankind, we had to touch down on the surface without crashing. Commander Neil Armstrong, piloting the Lunar Module during NASA's Apollo 11 mission, made his approach to the Moon's surface. For reasons unknown to mission control at the time, just before touching down, Armstrong switched off the autopilot and took manual control. Edwin "Buzz" Aldrin was actually designated as the pilot for this lunar landing, but because they were using autopilot, "for the actual landing his role was to announce the LM's altitude and rates of descent and forward motion."[12] Why would Armstrong depart from the mission plan, and override the autopilot system in the last minutes of the descent to the lunar surface?

Because autopilot was about to crash the spacecraft into the boulder-strewn rim of a crater, which would have caused a collision and damage to the landing gear that may have prevented them from escaping the surface of the Moon. Instead of deferring to the "system," as so many unhelpful mid-level managers are inclined to do, Armstrong took action and overrode the system. Sensing danger,

> Armstrong could see the aim point was on the rocky northeastern flank of West Crater (190 meters diameter), causing him to take manual control and fly horizontally, searching for a safe landing spot. At the time, only Armstrong saw the hazard; he was too busy flying the LM to discuss the situation with mission control.[13]

This is arguably the most clutch moment in the history of aerospace and it vindicates the irreducible role of human judgmental override and human leadership in the context of automated systems and risk management. Sometimes you have to let people break the "rules" or depart from the program and you don't always get the benefit of an explanation. Human judgment is a precious resource especially as we move to automate more systems.

Business are now using AI to make decisions about customers, products, suppliers, assets, transactions, even strategy. This means leaders need to shift from merely making decisions (the traditional role of leaders) to making "decisions about decisions."[14] The use of AI across a business offers a range in the types of engagements possible between humans and AI—from complete automation to complete human decision making, and everything in between. So who makes which decisions? Decisions have to be made as to *how to* make these decisions to optimize responsiveness. There is a spectrum of decision-making levels of human-AI engagement, or what Ross and Taylor describe as different loops.[15]

1   Humans in the Loop (HITL): Here it is humans that makes the decision but are assisted by a machine. This is human decision making with the machine providing decision support, partial automation of some decisions, or parts of decisions. Ross and Taylor refer to this as intelligence amplification (IA). An example would be a customer support chatbot that assists with answering frequently asked questions, but transfers the conversation to a human agent when it encounters complex or sensitive inquiries. The chatbot automates routine tasks and reduces the workload for human agents, but humans are still involved in handling more complex or critical customer interactions.

2   Human in the loop for exceptions (HITLFE): In this model most decisions are automated with humans only handling exceptions. Humans also control the logic to determine which exceptions are flagged for review and this is programmed into the system. An example would be an automated fraud detection system that flags potentially fraudulent transactions for review by human analysts. The system uses machine learning algorithms to analyze patterns and detect anomalies, but certain transactions that fall outside the normal parameters are sent to human analysts for manual review. The humans in the loop review these exceptions and make the final decision on whether the flagged transactions are indeed fraudulent. The Self-Healing Supply Chain[TM] is an offering by the supply chain management solution provider Kinaxis. It works by applying machine learning to automatically detect then correct discrepancies between planning assumptions and actuals in a supply plan. The planner sets the automatic correction thresholds and is alerted with suggested actions for inconsistencies outside those bounds,

exceptions that require human collaboration with stakeholders and suppliers to address. Thus the machine prompts the human to intervene to handle exceptions.

3   Human on the loop (HOTL): Here, the machine is assisted by a human. It is the machine that makes the decisions, but the human reviews the decision outcomes and can adjust rules and parameters for future decisions. An example would be a data analysis platform that automatically processes and analyzes large datasets, providing insights and recommendations to the users. Users can review and validate the findings, adjust parameters, and guide the analysis process. The system empowers users with automated data analysis capabilities while allowing them to maintain control and make informed decisions based on the results.

4   Human Out of the Loop (HOOTL): In this model, the machine is monitored by a human, but it is the machine that makes every decision. Also, improvements and adjustments are automated based on feedback. The human intervenes only by setting new constraints and objectives. This is the case with autonomous decision-making systems. An example would be an autonomous delivery drone service that transports packages from a fulfillment center to customers' doorsteps. The drones navigate using predefined routes and onboard sensors, without the need for human intervention during the delivery process. Humans are entirely removed from the operational loop, as the drones handle all aspects of package transport and delivery. Hence the name "human out of the loop."

Different types of interactions will make sense for different decisions, hence the need to make "decisions about decisions." Also, notice that the human is engaged in all four interaction models and is the centerpiece of the business model regardless of which botsourcing model is followed. Lastly, these relationships between human and machine evolve over time with technological capability and human interaction. The systems also require new and evolving human skills. This is not static but a dynamic process requiring an enterprise to be in a "forever beta" state—always refining.

Forever Beta

Forever Beta is a strategy defined by a business model that is continually evolving and improving.[16] It is a living embodiment of continuous improvement. Certainly products and services can be continuously enhanced in value and utility over time, applying principles of continuous improvement. Tesla offers an excellent example. The automaker doesn't offer yearly improvements, rather models are continually improved and updated after they have rolled off the assembly line by pushing updates to the user. The company uses cloud connectivity with their cars, monitoring performance and providing remote diagnosis and repair. Tesla owners have their cars continuously updated, such as advanced vehicles autonomous driving capabilities, and drivers are in a constant feedback loop with the company. The Humachine extends this notion of Forever Beta to the entire enterprise business model. As with Haier, this evolutionary mutation is built into the fabric of the organization. We will discuss how an enterprise can get there, but first let's look at the traits that define the Humachine.

Humachine Traits

"Humachine" companies fuse AI and human talent on the stack of big data, CRM platforms, and cloud computing. This combination of people, machines, and processes gives rise to four distinct traits: human centricity, flat and fluid organizational structure, entrepreneurial and innovative culture, and self-awareness.

1   **Human centric.** Machines are used and developed to serve the needs of humans—customers, employees, leaders, and teams. We must remember that technology does not exist for technology's sake. It is there to support human endeavors and, as such, its design and use are focused on the human purpose. An enterprise must decide on how decisions will be made, and will vary based on decisions. For the most part, machines handle automated tasks while humans engage in creative decision-making, considering input from their robotic partners. The degree of human involvement, however, will vary based on business model and types of decisions.

2   **Flat and fluid organizational structure.** A flat and fluid hierarchy with zero distance between the C-suite and workers enables ongoing communication among leaders, managers, and doers. Networks of people in and outside the company shape-shift in real time, like amoebas, pulling the right combinations of skills and talents together for any given goal or purpose. Radical transparency regarding information, roles, and goals enables these functional teams to respond intelligently to environmental pressures and changing enterprise objectives.

3   **Entrepreneurial and innovative culture.** Innovation imparts to a company culture a spirit of entrepreneurship. Innovation does not reside in a department but rather inspires all members of all teams to think of novel solutions. Teams are self-managed and incentivized to rapidly solve problems with distributed accountability, ending the passive "but that's not my job" culture.

4   **Self-aware.** Self-awareness is the state of a collective awareness of the enterprise. It is ultimately an organizational capability and an essential element of the Humachine. Self-awareness is critically important for an organization to succeed in the technology era because it enables rapid responses to environmental changes. In adapting to change, an organization must possess mechanisms to be aware of itself: *monitoring, feedback, and assumption-checking.*

Kasparov's Law Redux

The move toward Humachine traits involves combining the three variables of Kasparov's Law needed to create superhuman capabilities. They are People, Machines, and Processes. The characteristics of these three variables will vary based on the company's mission and strategy. See Figure 8.1.

Machines cannot merely be added to old systems and processes, and they cannot be utilized strategically by humans not adept in using them.

We discuss key features of these variables and Humachine traits next.

Focus on Human Needs

Smart machines are the foundation of the Humachine, but the focus is on people. Remember that technology is here to serve humans. Machines do not exist for machine's sake. They are not created by nature to evolve, procreate, and develop commerce to support themselves. In the technology era, it is easy to lose sight of this basic fact.

Rather, machines are there to support human endeavors. AI is created by humans, designed to behave like humans, and affect humans positively. Yes, machines are superior in computational capability. As hyper calculators they can process huge amounts of data and make inferences the average human mind cannot. To be useful, machines must be designed to seamlessly integrate with the human decision-maker (ergonomic and accessible). However, machine capability alone is not enough for enterprise success. Data must be presented in a way that maximizes the ability of humans to use it, to visualize it, process it, and derive actionable intelligence from it. Machine output must enable decision-making, creativity, and innovation.

To be fully utilized, machines must interface with and leverage the most basic human traits—*emotions* and our *need for socialization*.

Without this anthropocentric approach we will 'botsource' our way to bankruptcy. Without the human touch, there will be no customers, no suppliers, no employees nor managers. Ensuring that humans are integrated with technology, without fear and with trust, is incumbent upon leadership. Therefore, every new adoption of technology must be designed with the human in mind.

PROCESSES	PEOPLE	MACHINES
• Flat Structure	• Customers	• Platforms
• Innovation Culture	• Leaders & Coaches	• AI & Analytics
• Fluid Processes	• Analysts	• IoT
• Shared Leadership	• Designers	• Network Links
• Culture	• Suppliers	• Cloud Computing

Figure 8.1 The three variables of Kasparov's Law

Mindfulness Is Good Business

In our interview with the President and CEO of Alene Candles, it became apparent that helping ordinary people increase interpersonal skills brings significant gains to the enterprise.

> As a manufacturer, we employ people of varied backgrounds, many of whom face life challenges that I can only imagine. I think part of our responsibility is to give them the skills to manage relationships not only with their coworkers, but also with their partners, kids, parents, neighbors, anyone with whom they interact.

In so many ways, the meaning of our life is driven by the quality of our relationships. By helping their employees become better at navigating inter-personal situations, Alene Candles improves labor productivity and employee life satisfaction.

> Teaching mindfulness techniques, we have found, is an exceedingly effective way at doing both. And we know we will be effective at teaching them the skills for the workplace, if first we find they are using those skills at home. How do you attract talent when you need people's minds? We got after it by teaching people mindfulness skills – it was better for us as a business, makes for a better work environment, and we get access to fantastic results by being mindful.[17]

Dopamine and Reward

Understanding human motivation is crucial for getting the best from our workforce and for effectively marketing products and services. According to Sapolsky in *Behave: The Biology of Humans at Our Best and Worst*, the dopamine system is central to understanding reward, pleasure, motivation and happiness.[18] In today's entertainment-saturated environment where nearly the entire workforce carries with them a personal electronic device, we may have challenges in predicting how humans will react to stimuli that may have once been effective.[19]

> Once, we had lives that, amid considerable privation, also offered numerous subtle, hard-won pleasures. And now we have drugs that cause spasms of pleasure and dopamine release a thousand-fold higher than anything stimulated in our old drug-free world. An emptiness comes from this combination of over-the-top non-natural sources of reward and the inevitability of habituations; this is because unnaturally strong explosions of synthetic experience and sensation and pleasure of unnaturally strong degrees of habituation. This has two consequences.

First, soon we barely notice the fleeting whispers of pleasure caused by leaves in autumn, or by the lingering glance of the right person, or by the promise of reward following the difficult, worthy task. And the other consequence is that we eventually habituate to even those artificial delusions of intensity. If we were designed by engineers, as we consumed more, we'd desire less. But our frequent human tragedy is that the more we consume, the hungrier we get.

Despite the perils of habituation to excessive dopamine, there is a healthy way of managing this neurotransmitter. "Dopamine is about mastery and expectation and confidence... If you know your appetite will be sated, pleasure is more about the appetite than about the sating. This is hugely important,"[20] as "dopamine is more about anticipation of reward than about reward itself."[21] Managers and marketers should understand the role of dopamine because

it fuels the *goal-directed behavior* needed to gain that reward; dopamine 'binds' the value of a reward to the resulting work... In other words, dopamine is not about the happiness of reward, it's about the happiness of pursuit of reward that has a decent chance of occurring.[22]

Understanding these concepts will help design effective compensation regimes for workers as well as incentive structures for marketing promotionals or other campaigns to drive consumer behavior.

Testosterone and Winning

Recall in Chapter 4 we discussed the role of the amygdala activation and the release of testosterone as drivers of anxious and aggressive behavior. Well, testosterone's role is quite nuanced. "Testosterone also increases confidence and optimism, while decreasing fear and anxiety... Success in anything from athletics to chess to the stock market boost testosterone levels."[23] So the key is the context in which testosterone is secreted.

Neuroscientists have discovered a "winner" effect in lab animals: winning a fight increases the winner's willingness to participate in subsequent contests and increases the likelihood of success in same.[24] Of course, taken too far, and this laudable boost to confidence and optimism can become a vice, leading to over-confidence, unreasonable optimism, impulsivity, and "cocky, ego-centric, and narcissistic" behaviors.[25] Leroy Jenkins, anyone?[26] Given this nuanced and powerful role, managers must be cognizant of the subtle effects that environmental conditions have on testosterone in the workforce. Context, such as social dynamics and work space designs, will mediate the impact of testosterone so much that we cannot say much about it on its own. Testosterone's context-contingent effects mean "rather than causing X, testosterone amplifies the power of something else to cause X."[27]

Managers should be conscious of and intentional about the various triggers of testosterone and curate the context in which secretions occur to ensure the effect on behavior is consistent with organizational objectives. There is a time and a place for aggression and confidence, as well as civility and humility. Triggering testosterone level increases can have wildly divergent impacts depending on how workers are challenged and in which context.

Specifically, managers must be conscious of the *challenge hypothesis*. There are two parts to this. First, "rising testosterone levels increase aggression only at the time of a challenge."[28] Second, "when testosterone rises after a challenge, it doesn't prompt aggression. Instead, it prompts *whatever behaviors are needed to maintain status*. This changes things enormously."[29] Testosterone rise is "less about muscle activity than about the psychology of dominance, identification, and self-esteem."[30]

While testosterone may have a reputation for the brawling, reptilian antics of jacked up males, that is a gross oversimplification of its role in human behavior. According to the well-documented challenge hypothesis, testosterone levels are tied to status, especially when status is challenged. For example, if a new hire shows up, some of the veteran workforce, the latter will likely exhibit signs of increased testosterone, and will be driven to engage in whatever behavior is necessary to defend their status in the organization.

> Testosterone makes us more willing to do what it takes to attain and maintain status. And the key point is what it takes. Engineer social circumstances right, and boosting testosterone levels during a challenge would make people compete like crazy to do the most acts of random kindness.[31]

"If status is maintained aggressively, testosterone fosters aggression; if status were maintained by writing beautiful, delicate haikus, testosterone fosters that."[32]

Managing testosterone is not just for workforce optimization. It is also relevant to marketing. A carefully drawn up advertisement may very well challenge status, and the means for affirming status are by purchasing the product so advertised. These levers and pullies of human motivation are well understood by advertising executives but they could very well be used to drive pro-social, not merely consumer, behavior.

The "Experience Economy"

Nowhere is the focus on human needs on display more than in the current "experience economy." The "experience economy" represents an economic shift from a product-centric focus to a customer-centric focus. The digital era has commoditized most products and shifted the focus of competition on the customer experience, and the Covid-19 pandemic exacerbated the human need for experience. AI and technology can now customize customer interactions at all customer touchpoints with the company.[33] Technology has created an expectation of swift response to inquiries, customized products and services, and easy access to information. Being immediately responsive to customers is nothing special. It is an expectation. The battlefield now is in creating a customized customer experience—and this requires tapping into human traits.

The shift of competitive focus on the customer experience cannot be ignored if a company hopes to remain relevant and successful. Customers are more empowered than ever. For better or worse, people want to be entertained, and they expect the same level of entertainment in the consumption experience that they get elsewhere.[34] As a result, companies are bending over backwards to create the right atmosphere and format for consumption (not just the right price). Machines help us by mining big data to understand and tap into the deepest customer desires and understand unarticulated needs. This intelligence is used to create the best experience possible. It might also be used to create products that are psychologically addicting, but that's where the principle of integrity comes in! An ethical approach to using consumer data is to identify a need and to fill it—rather than by identifying how to exploit a vulnerability and creating addictive products.

The footwear and accessory retailer, Zappos, was recognized as a company that understand exactly what customers want. The company first became known for setting the bar with a returns policy that allowed shoppers to receive a full refund for items they were unhappy with any time within a year of purchase. This policy was novel and allowed Zappos to quickly amass a loyal following. This high level of customer service has now evolved into personalization. Understanding the importance of keeping customers happy and personalizing the offering was the main focus for the group's head of customer research, Alex Genov.

Genov says that most personalization systems make recommendations based on purchase history. However, this can lead to consumers simply being presented with options that are similar to purchases they have already made. "Contrast this with true personalization, where you understand what the person is trying to do by buying those shoes, and then help them more holistically," he says.[35]

One example of hyper-personalization at Zappos is in its attempt to understand the *intent* of a purchase. For example, are the shoes being purchased for a first date or an interview, and therefore are required to make a good impression? The site can then make recommendations for other apparel items that might match that occasion. Unfortunately, the pandemic challenged Zappos' model with recent layoffs of a significant percentage of their workforce.[36] While Amazon acquired Zappos in 2009, it was with the understanding that Zappos would keep their unique culture. And while Zappos is evolving—forever beta—the focus on the customer service experience does not seem to be changing.[37] "The way we phrase it here is Zappos is a customer service company that happens to sell shoes and clothes and handbags and accessories, but its DNA is customer centricity," Genov says.[38] The focus is on the context, experience, meaning, and emotions rather than merely products.

Understanding customer emotions enabled the retailer Sephora to disrupt the way people shop for beauty products. Of course, Sephora uses technology to manage a successful omnichannel strategy, using a mobile app to serve as a liaison between physical and digital channels, providing a seamless customer experience. Also, these technology solutions enable Sephora to collect more data on its customers and then use that data to continue to improve its offering. However, Sephora has disrupted the industry by understanding that beauty is not about products—it is about creating positive emotions.

In the past, customers purchased beauty items brand by brand. Then Sephora came on the scene, creating "a playground" of beauty products by encouraging customers to test and try products. Understanding customer emotions allowed Sephora to fine-tune its approach in creating the customer experience.

As Jason Goldberg, Chief Commerce Strategy Officer at Publicis Sapient, points out,

> Nobody goes shopping because they want more expensive colored powder in their bedroom. They're shopping for cosmetics because they want to look beautiful at their spring dance or on their date or whatever the case may be. They're literally shopping for an experience, so delivering an experience during the shopping occasion is super important, whereas you do not necessarily want a real high-tech immersive shopping experience to get more toilet paper.[39]

Technology has enabled Sephora to use the customer experience to create an "Instagrammable" store concept, encouraging customers to play with products, and offering free in-store classes. Sephora understands that emotions create a need for sharing—and leveraged that need to create a tight-knit beauty community.

The "experience economy" can be a by-product of the digital era, where an enterprise cannot succeed on the strengths of its products alone. Technology can be used to create a sense of community, tapping into customer emotions. Even something as mundane as consumer banking is changing—using technology to tap into customer emotions and create a social experience. Understanding this, Capital One has "reimagined banking" through its series of Capital One Cafés. These cafés merge banking with the comfort of a coffee shop, free Wi-Fi, couches, and even tabletop games such as Connect Four while customers wait for a business call. This is a rejection of the old stuffy notion of banking. Anyone, regardless of their bank affiliation, can grab a cup of coffee, sit on a couch, and, if they want, get coached through their money problems by professionals. This is a new type of banking experience.

The message is clear: use technology to create community and enhance human experience. From beauty products to exercise to banking—experiential, human-centric offerings have a competitive edge over traditional offerings, regardless of industry.

Customer Is the Co-creator

Customer-centric cultures use predictive analytics to anticipate emerging patterns in the behavior of customers. They can then tailor the right interactions with customers by dynamically integrating structured data, such as demographics and purchase history, with unstructured data, such as social media and voice analytics. *Co-creation* is AI-enabled open innovation characterized by seamless interconnection with the customer and the product designers, allowing the customer to have a voice in product and experience.

This creates a more impactful customer experience, as the example of Sephora illustrates. Further, this has huge operational benefits. Co-creation significantly reduces the risk of experimentation failures and the costly process of trial and error, where a company would launch a product only to see whether there was a demand for it. Co-creation bypasses those issues, speeds up the pace of change, and de-risks the product innovation cycle by getting the customer involved in product creation.

With co-creation, an enterprise no longer has to guess what's working with a given product or service before launching it—and then waiting to see if the guess is right after the launch takes place. Adjustments to products and services and the entire customer experience can now be made in nearly real-time with direct input from end users. This reduces risk and improves responsiveness. It also tightens the relationship with customers and provides valuable insights into what motivates a customer to buy, and how they intend to use the product. Many of these insights are not collectable through traditional means. Co-creation is happening everywhere, and companies that are not doing it will rapidly fall behind.

Flat and Fluid Organizational Structures

What do leading tech companies such as Google, Haier, and Apple have in common? They all have flat and fluid organizational structures—a hallmark of the Humachine. Yes, there are differences in the way they are organized—but flatness and fluidity are a common theme. This is the norm of the innovative and agile organization. There is zero distance to the C-suite. Leadership acts as coaches rather than "bosses" in the traditional sense. There is very little hierarchy. Leadership, decision-making, and execution are decentralized but coordinated among team members.

Flatness and Fluidity

In the traditional model of organizing, hierarchy prevailed. See Table 8.1.

There are certainly advantages of a traditional functional structure versus no structure at all. Functional departments can permit greater operational efficiency as employees with shared skills and knowledge are grouped together by the function they perform. Each function or group is specialized. Therefore, they can operate independently from other groups while management acts as the point of cross-communication between the functional areas. This traditional functional structure allows for increased specialization.

There are, however, significant disadvantages to this old model that hinder the ability of the organization to function in the digital era. One is that different functional groups may not communicate with one another. This decreases flexibility, disabling rapid innovation and quick responses to change. Functional structures are highly susceptible to *tunnel vision*. Each function sees the organization from its frame of reference and its own operation. Without a unified vision, employees cannot be integrated around the same goals.

This old structure worked very well in an old economy where established corporations produced relatively homogenous products. However, in the new economy defined by innovation and responsiveness, the need for creativity, rapid communication, and adaptability to change, this model no longer works. The old structure makes co-creation and rapid innovation virtually impossible.

To be direct, the old way of organizing results in failure in the new era. The world has become increasingly interconnected, the rate of change has accelerated, and the need for quick response is an imperative. Therefore,

Table 8.1 The Humachine's organizational structure

Traditional structure	Humachine structure
Hierarchy-driven	Flat org structure
Top-down roles	Fluid diffused roles
A few dominant leaders	Cross-functional teams
Highly specialized groups	Entrepreneurial self-managed teams
Many views of the customer	One view of the customer
Communication distance from C-suite	Zero distances from C-suite
Innovation distance from customers	Customers help co-create

new organizational models are fundamental to an organization's ability to remain competitive and relevant.

At Haier, hierarchies have been torn down and middle management is almost nonexistent. The goal has been to turn the company into a flat organization that is a playground for talented people to generate customer-centric products. Haier has created a flat structure where smart people have resources to create and bring to fruition new ideas with little to no drag.

Employees have fluid roles in cross-functional teams. Teams are created around common problems as opposed to individual roles and responsibilities. The objective of the team is greater than what could be achieved by a single member. Teams are entrepreneurial in spirit and self-managed, with members sharing a common vision. They are fluid, evolving, and open in structure. Members come and go as the nature of the problem changes, and they perform work outside a predetermined role to solve the problem at hand. The organization and teams are infused with purpose to solve problems quickly. Accountability and decision-making are distributed and coordinated. Successful team members are those who take action that enables the team to accomplish its goals—they are "changemakers." The teams are nimble and agile, moving quickly to respond to the data, and thus the customer.

Haier's structure works well for it. However, when it comes to structure, one size does not fit all. Although we consider leading tech companies as examples of mutation, Haier, Zappos, Google, and Nike are all mutating in different directions. Nike has a flat structure but in a matrix form with pseudo-independent divisions. They are all under the Nike umbrella for brand consistency, but they are independent to allow flexibility in satisfying niche customer needs and demands. The structure enables executive decision-making to happen without approaches to customer engagement getting trapped in a traditional, more bureaucratic chain of command.

At Google, the defining characteristic of its organizational structure is flatness with an open culture that emphasizes innovation and social network links. Here, ideas can easily be shared with even the most senior executives. The structure supports the company's organizational culture to maximize innovation. The corporate culture is open, using technology to share information in order to improve business processes.[40]

A culture of innovation promotes experimentation and testing. It allows teams to fluidly evolve to solve problems, then dissolve as needs change. Although heavily reliant on technology, Google has created an atmosphere that supports human needs. It is an environment that creates a warm social ambiance with a family feel. Google's departure from traditional organizational structures has created a culture that has allowed excellence in innovation in the IT global market, cloud computing and Internet services, and consumer electronics.

Porous Boundaries, Social Webs

In the twentieth century, corporate success was largely based on management. In the twenty-first century, however, success will be based on the strength of one's social web.[41] This *social web* is an ecosystem of customers, producers, and suppliers all connected via the Internet of Things (IoT). This means that companies can no longer view themselves as entities closed off from the world. Rather, they must operate as nodes that are part of a very large network connected to, well, everything.

Not only do we need to mutate organizational structures from hierarchical and rigid to flat and fluid—morphing like an amoeba to best meet the needs of the immediate problem at hand—organizational boundaries need to become *porous*. More significantly, they can now tap into external talent through co-creation with customers and suppliers, crowdsourcing, and open innovation. Porous boundaries allow an organization to assimilate information and intelligence from its environment.

Business Professor Henry Chesbrough coined the term *open innovation* as "the use of purposive inflows and outflows of knowledge to accelerate internal innovation, and expand the markets for external use of innovation, respectively."[42] It is the antithesis of the traditional vertical integration approach where internal R&D activities lead to internally developed products that are then distributed by the firm.

Open innovation creates a new approach to innovation that is decentralized, participatory, and distributed, tapping into the best ideas and talent regardless of where they reside. This accelerates breakthrough innovation, reduces cost, reduces time to market, and increases differentiation in the marketplace. Because of these benefits, organizations are increasingly turning to crowdsourcing to solve difficult problems. This is often driven by the desire to find the best subject matter experts, strongly incentivize them, and engage them with as little coordination cost as possible.

GE is a great example of a company implementing open innovation models with a goal of addressing problems through crowdsourcing innovation,[43] collaborating between experts and entrepreneurs from everywhere to share ideas and solve problems. One of GE's projects is the FirstBuild, a co-creation collaboration platform, which connects designers, engineers, and thinkers to share ideas with other members who can discuss it together.[44] The ideas presented at FirstBuild focus on solving problems by creating new home appliances products. GE's microfactories then manufacture the ideas that emerged from FirstBuild. Members can get access to machines and tools required to turn their ideas into real products. This is open innovation.

Haier has gone beyond the basic principles of open innovation and created a structure that is porous so that ideas can flow in from the outside. The idea is that traditional boundaries between the entity and the outside world are torn down. Communication platforms are used to create interwoven links between Haier, end users, and external partners such as design companies. The result is rapid communication of feedback, cultivation of new ideas, and quick innovation. Customers are connected through apps where they can customize products and be involved in product co-creation in real time.

From Holacracy to Rendanheyi: One Size Does Not Fit All

Depending on your starting configuration, flat organizational structures and porous boundaries might require a complete reorganization. Reorganization is one of the riskiest things a company can do. However, more than any other effort, a successful reorganization can set an organization on the path to future success. It is a radical move that disrupts, but it is better than continuing to patch, struggle, and make small adjustments that do not create strategic advantages—all just so many incremental delays of inevitable obsolescence. There is a big difference between successfully avoiding capsizing and winning a boat race.

The digital era will likely demand reorganization with excellent vision and flawless execution. Those that fail to make the transition will not exist for much longer. They will be bought up for parts and dissolved. Few companies will be spared. Unless yours is a digital firm "born" in the digital era with an organic fluid structure, your company will likely need reorganization. This is especially true of traditional companies in traditional industries. Very often this requires reengineering a company's DNA, as legacy IT systems and traditional processes just get in the way of innovation. If done correctly it means building an organization where adaptation is just part of the DNA.

Haier has restructured itself multiple times in order to keep up with the changing environment, stay competitive, and continue to innovate. In an industry defined by conventional white boxes, Haier has been truly disruptive. In 2005, with the Internet economy in mind, the company had a major restructuring effort—calling the new model *rendanheyi*. Implementing *rendanheyi* meant tearing apart the structure of the enterprise.

Haier's model has several Humachine traits. *Rendanheyi* has three main features.

1   First, the enterprise was transformed from a closed system to an open system, a network composed of self-governing microenterprises connected via an enterprise management platform with free-flowing communication between them and outside contributors.
2   Second, the structure transformed from a traditional top-down hierarchy to one where employees are self-motivated contributors working in entrepreneurial teams. In many cases they even choose or elect the leaders and members of their teams.

3 Third, the view of customers was transformed from one-off product
   purchasers to lifetime users of products and services who can also
   help with product design, increasing consumer satisfaction. The
   rendanheyi model was intended to foster co-creation between
   employees and customers.

However, Haier is planning to reorganize yet again, demonstrating that
adaptation is a skill, not a one-off process. As stated by Zhang Ruimin, the
chairman of the board of directors and CEO of the Haier Group,

> No longer do successful companies compete through their brands.
> Instead, they compete through platforms—or, put another way, through
> linkages among independent enterprises, aligned via their interoperable
> technologies and their creative efforts. Another economy is about to
> emerge now, with similarly broad effects. It revolves around the Internet
> of Things (IoT), the interconnection of multiple devices and human
> activities embedded with sensors, robotics, and artificial intelligence.
> When the IoT is fully in place, successful enterprises will compete in
> this new way.[45]

Preparing for the next wave, Haier is now planning to reorganize itself
around the economy of IoT. The company is developing sensors that monitor user behavior from a variety of vantage points, whether incorporated
into products or not, allowing Haier to respond to a host of customer data.
In China, they have linked suppliers through a mass customization platform
that automates each step of production, from customer order to delivery,
and arranges for monitoring and service when it is in use.[46]

That is Haier. Zappos, on the other hand, has a different approach. In
2015, Zappos implemented a new management structure called holacracy.
Holacracy is a method of decentralized management and organizational
governance, where authority and decision-making are distributed
throughout an organization run by self-organizing teams.[47] Holacracy is
an organizational structure that is designed to encourage collaboration by
eliminating workplace hierarchy—meaning no more titles and no more
bosses. With holacracy, decision-making responsibilities are distributed
throughout self-organizing teams, rather than being centralized at the top
of the organization chart.[48]

> The main idea is that it is not a traditional command and control
> structure, with no traditional organizational chart. But employees know
> what the call to action is and what the top company priorities are, and
> are then encouraged to organize around certain types of work they are
> passionate about.[49]

The success of the Zappos model has been hotly debated in the business press, but it appears to be working, both from the perspective of Zappos' owner, Amazon, and in the minds of its customers.

Like *rendanheyi*, holocracy has its own principles.

1   *First*, everyone is responsible for understanding their role, how it fits with the roles of others on the team, and how that might change.
2   *Second*, everyone is responsible for both leading and supporting.
3   *Third*, everyone is responsible for communicating clearly and efficiently.

Essentially, holocracy is a concept of shared leadership. It uses a set of rules and processes, checks and balances, and guidelines to help the organization become self-managed and self-organized. Instead of management, it gives every employee the power to have a voice. In holocracy, each person is responsible for understanding how they fit into the organization and everyone is responsible to lead and support.[50] Today Zappos appears to be quietly moving away from holocracy,[51] however as we see it, that is part of growth and evolution. It is an ongoing reassessment of what works and readjusting.

Whether it is rendanheyi, holocracy, or some other organizational structure, the keys are flatness and fluidity. Given our inspiration for the Humachine springs from evolutionary principles, it should come as no surprise we can learn about the design of resilient systems by studying how life has evolved in forms other than our own.

Indeed, human enterprise may take some lessons from other kinds of intelligences, howsoever humble in comparison. Recall our discussion of complexity theory that systems are self-organizing from the bottom up. Recall from our discussion of thermodynamics that all intelligent life must control matter and energy to survive. Hence we should look at how life other than humans have solved the problem of entropy to learn how we might improve our game.

Consider the *amoebae*, a simple organism exhibiting signs of intelligence that is capable of solving problems without having any centralized "decider" or even a leadership committee calling the shots. Back in 2010 a team of researchers from Japan and the U.K. placed pieces of oat nutrient in a petri dish along with a slime mold. The size and location of the chunks of oat reflected the relative size and location of the various nodes of the Tokyo subway system. To the awe of researchers, the slime mold extended its veiny tubular network toward each piece of oat, managing to control the flow of matter and energy throughout the organism in a layout that was strikingly similar to the efficiencies of the Japanese subway system. This finding kindled the field of biologically inspired adaptive network design.

Slime molds first 'forage' broadly over an area, then refine their tubular network to optimize for transport of the nutrients. Now, researchers believe the slime mold's efficient organic structure could provide a model for optimizing other networks—including those designed to move people and goods around a city.[52]

According to researcher Raphael Kay,

Humans aren't the only ones dealing with the challenge of designing efficient, resilient networks. In architecture school, we were taught by human architects the lessons of past human architecture. But the slime mold has been shaped by hundreds of millions of years of evolution, so in that sense, they are far more experienced at solving certain architectural problems than we humans ever could be.[53]

Kay created a computer model that simulates how slime mold constructs its network, then validated the model by comparison with real slime molds grown on agar plates fed with oats. The intelligence of the slime mold can be compared to the intelligence of human engineers, architects, and planners. Kay's model shows various scenarios where the slime mold's uncomprehending competence exceeds human civil planning along metrics such as the cost (overall length of segments in the network), travel time (average length between any two points in the network), and vulnerability (average increase in travel time caused by removing a segment).[54] Designing AI to mimic naturally occurring forms of life—when it comes to problem solving scenarios—means we may see emergent solutions without human user input. If a slime mold can do it, so can we—if we follow the right process.

Back in 2010, a team of researchers from Japan and the U.K. fed a slime mold with nutrients arranged to imitate the nodes of the Tokyo subway system. The resulting network was strikingly similar to the real thing, and sparked the emergence of what is now known as biologically inspired adaptive network design.

Does that mean the collective intelligence of a slime mold network in a petri dish is qualitatively superior to an entire department of civil engineers? Not necessarily—just that humans can take cues from other kinds of intelligences, that we can make our own systems more rational by following biomimicry, and perhaps if we combined our constituent human resources in the right process, we can achieve feats of collective intelligence that are far beyond the comprehension of any one of us. Organizational network intelligences (aka Humachines) are like fungi in the sense they are an embodied process of control *per se*, they have their own ontology—we should not be alarmed if they take on unexpected shapes.

A Culture of Entrepreneurship and Innovation

In addition to adaptability and porosity, the Humachine is an organization with a culture of entrepreneurship and innovation in its DNA. A key element is the new organizational structure just discussed that sets the stage for a marketplace of ideas that are born from cross-disciplinary teams. It enables talent and resources to combine for unprecedented innovations, where people with smart ideas have resources to create, test, and bring ideas to fruition. Freedom to create and innovate must be imbued in every aspect of the organization.

Organizational culture is composed of the values, behaviors, and unwritten rules that contribute to the social and psychological environment of an organization. It is a quality that is precisely human—difficult to quantify and something that must be felt and experienced. Unfortunately, organizational culture is one of the main barriers to company success in this new era. It is up to leaders to create an entrepreneurial spirit and foster an innovative culture.

Entrepreneurial Spirit

Haier recognized that the digital era has reshaped customer expectations and that, as a company, it's job was to disrupt the status quo to compete. This is especially true in its industry, as appliances are typically seen as mundane with limited room to maneuver in terms of innovation. To this end, Haier created an organizational structure and culture that is extremely responsive to customer needs, constantly cultivating new ideas and quickly bringing innovation to market.

Haier has turned itself into several microenterprises. The idea is to turn Haier employees into micro-entrepreneurs who run their own micro-enterprises, which are centered around an innovative idea or a product. They are responsible for their own performance, budgets, profit and loss, and will behave as independent business units under the Haier umbrella. The hope is that in the long run some of these will become independent start-ups.

This is certainly a bold business model that few companies may dare to follow. We are not recommending a slavish copycatting of Haier; each company should choose its own path forward. The key is to follow the spirit of entrepreneurship and innovation and create a unique version that suits your organization.

This is hard for traditional companies to grasp, as in our experience, most companies want to "follow the leader" and mimic others. However, it is critical to create a structure and culture that works for your company. A great example is Morning Star, the world's largest tomato processor. The company practices "self management" where every person is their own CEO and pretty much autonomous. At Morning Star, autonomy comes hand in hand with responsibility and discipline.[55] At Morning Star there are no managers of any kind. Employees don't report to a "boss" in the traditional sense. They report to each other, and their work is based on a *colleague letter of understanding (CLOU)* that they create. Like Zappos and Haier, Morning Star has created its own brand of self-managed teams with an entrepreneurial and innovative culture.

An old adage from the sports world comes from a seasoned coach. It goes something like this: if a player won't do what the coach tells him to do, he's no good for the team; but if the player *only* does what the coach tells him to do, he's still no good. Sometimes the circumstances are not planned and we need humans to rise to the occasion, to exercise leadership, to improvise, to make judgment calls, to go beyond the standard process, to make an exception, to override the automated system. We need humans to know when to override autopilot.

Innovation

Shortly after the passing of Steve Jobs, Tim Cook, the new CEO of Apple, said in an interview about innovation: "A lot of companies have innovation departments, and this is always a sign that something is wrong when you have a VP of innovation or something. You know, put a for-sale sign on the door."[56] That pretty much describes how innovation works—and how it does not work—in the Humachine. Innovation needs to be an attribute that persists, not an event that comes and goes.

Cook went on to say: "Creativity is not a process, right? It's people who care enough to keep thinking about something until they find the simplest way to do it." Cook is suggesting that it is the job of company leaders to establish a culture where people will care that much about their work, rather than to try to build some kind of innovation "program" that tries in vain to formulate and standardize the creative act.

Google agrees that innovation is every employee's business and that innovation can happen anywhere.[57]

> Making innovation part of your organization isn't about starting up a research and development lab or focusing your efforts on one set of people. In Google's experience, innovation happens when you make it a valued part of the way people think, work, and interact everyday.
>
> How do you make innovation a valued part of everyone's everyday work at your organization? According to Google, it comes down to ensuring they have these five essential ingredients of an innovative workplace: shared vision, autonomy, intrinsic motivation, risk-taking, and collaboration.[58]

1   **Shared vision.** Everyone needs a clear and unifying vision; Google uses a template for teams to formulate a vision that suits them.

2   **Autonomy.** All employees should be allowed to define their own work and how they work; Google provides space that allows employees to work with their natural cadence.

3   **Intrinsic motivation.** Hiring the right talent is critical; this means people who are naturally curious and entrepreneurial.

4   **Risk-taking.** Employees should not be afraid of making mistakes; this is achieved by normalizing failure. Google even holds a "premortem" discussion: before a new launch, employees discuss how the project could fail. Failure should be considered normal, as without failure there is no experimentation or innovation.

5   **Connection and collaboration.** This is a system for employees to find partners and work together in teams. People influence each other when they interact to solve problems. Enabling connections and fostering collaboration is one of the most powerful strategies a company can do to get the best from its people. Such social influence has benefits, for example, higher average solution quality due to exploitation of existing answers through social learning.

Google is a visionary in the digital era and continues to set the bar for the most advanced and creative approaches to recruiting and cultivating leading-edge talent. For example, the company follows a "70–20–10 rule" where employees spend 70% of their time on their standard role, one day per week on projects that will develop their technical skills and benefit the company, and half a day per week exploring product and business innovations and ideas.

This sort of on-the-job training (vs. classroom training) is critical for the engagement and development of employees. Google's approach not only develops in-house analytics talent, but it also allows the company to attract, select and hire only "the best" analytics talent available.

These examples illustrate that innovation can become part of the fabric of a company's culture.

Self-awareness

We believe that self-awareness is the ultimate organizational capability and an essential element of the Humachine. Self-awareness is critically important for an organization to succeed in the technology era, as it is a key element in rapidly adapting to change. In adapting to change, an organization must possess mechanisms to be aware of itself. Self-awareness is bound up with intentionality. We discuss both of these topics next.

Organizational Self-awareness

Organizational self-awareness is the collective awareness of the enterprise as a system.[59] It arises from the collective interactions of organizational members going about their work in the organizational context. Further, it is supported and enabled by internal and external connectivity—technology, management feedback loops, and organizational learning. Without such connectivity, self-awareness cannot emerge or develop.

Self-awareness is internal and external. Internal awareness emerges from tight interconnections between members through organizational systems. Connectivity has to be deployed throughout the whole organization. Ensuring this deployment is the job of leaders. There is also external awareness where the organization relates directly with external entities, such as customers and markets, through a web of interconnections. See Figure 8.2.

Recall the definition of collective superintelligence (what we call organizational network superintelligence, which is the pathway to the Humachine). This is attained "through the gradual enhancement of networks and organizations that link individual human minds with one another and with various artifacts and bots." An organization that attains self-awareness and a rich internal network of human and AI could very well become superintelligent.[60]

In traditional organizational structures, "awareness" by members is typically restricted along dimensions of their specialized function or department. In a traditional enterprise, there is no holistic organizational self-awareness but only that which is restricted to silos. Technology provides the needed system of interconnections that creates a unifying view, awareness at the enterprise level of internal and external states of affairs. However, technology is not sufficient.

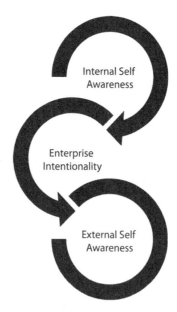

Figure 8.2 Organizational self-awareness

It is the organizational structure—flat, fluid, cross-disciplinary, and connected to customers and markets—that allows for this holistic view.

Organizational self-awareness also involves self-awareness of each of its members. Peter Cameron, CEO of the Lenox Group,[61] noted during our interview the importance of everyone to self-diagnose their talents and capabilities—and differentiate that from their passion.

> It is important for people to self-diagnose their talent and guide themselves toward their talents. Differentiate between passion and talent - and honestly differentiate. They will find their passion and creativity as long as they have stayed within their talent. I love art but I can't draw a stick figure. I love fine dining and but I can't cook. That is my passion but not my talent.

He points that by being honest with ourselves and fostering our talents we can become the successful versions of ourselves.

Intentionality Driven: Understand Who You Are

As we have underscored, one size does not fit all. So how does a company know which path is best for it? Understanding who you are as an organization—and who you are not—is important in knowing how to proceed, which machines to adopt, and how to organize and integrate.

Amazon and Wal-Mart have focused their technology efforts on improving supply chain functionality; John Hancock, Capital One, CVS, and Neiman Marcus have targeted improvements in customer service and loyalty; Intel has targeted product and service quality; Novartis and Yahoo have focused on R&D.[62]

Why the difference? Their intentionality, their mission, vision, and strategy are different. The company of the future will not just acquire technology arbitrarily, following industry trends. It will target its machine efforts on the areas that align with its intentionality and promise to create the greatest competitive advantage. A big mistake is to "follow the leader" and copy what others are doing, just to keep up with the pack. Adoption of any business initiative, including technology, needs to be justified and support the company's unique mission. Not everyone needs the same type or level of technology, or the same degree of implementation.

Consider companies in the same industry. Roche, Novartis, and Pfizer are pharmaceutical companies that spend huge sums on R&D. They invest in technologies, such as AI, that help speed up pharmaceutical trials and sampling. By contrast, pharmaceutical manufacturers that produce generics, such as Teva and Novartis' generic pharmaceuticals division Sandoz, use technology to cut production and distribution costs. Each group of firms knows what they are about. They acquire and use technology to support that mission.

Under Tim Cook, Apple has updated its vision statement: "We believe that we are on the face of the earth to make great products and that's not changing. We are constantly focusing on innovating."[63] The statement then goes on to say:

> We believe in saying no to thousands of projects, so that we can really focus on the few that are truly important and meaningful to us. We believe in deep collaboration and cross-pollination of our groups, which allow us to innovate in a way that others cannot.

Notice the part about saying no to thousands of things. It means knowing who you are as a company and only engaging in things that support that. The statement also focuses on collaboration across the enterprise and innovation, revealing the intersection of structure and purpose. Do not change for the sake of changing; do it in strategic response to evolutionary pressures.

Leading companies do not just apply machines, technology, and analytics randomly where they can. They target their investments on the areas that promise to create the greatest competitive advantage. And this is defined by understanding who they are and what they are about.

Orchestrating the Mutation: Thoughtful Leadership

AI and machine systems sense and act in a much more granular level than ever before, but they are designed to be evolving systems. In fact, today's AI can be described as *directed evolution* because the design and build of these systems includes dynamic self-configuration.[64]

For example, in the past, computer architecture was designed to provide a solution to optimally configure systems to solve a problem. Now, the computer architecture is being designed to have a dynamic self-configuring function. This means the algorithm is designed to keep dynamically reconfiguring itself in response to new inputs. It is a self-adjusting system that takes into account feedback from factors such as changing criteria to optimize, availability of resources, and changing market opportunities. This means that today's computer architecture is being designed to be aware of its environment and evolve in response to changing environmental conditions.

While enterprise self-awareness is enabled by the connections offered by machines, machines themselves are evolving, sensing, and—in a manner of speaking—becoming self-aware. Just consider the collaborative robots, AI, and machinery used in today's automotive plants of companies such as BMW. These factories are a far cry from the assembly plants of yesteryears. Here, all machines are embedded with sensors, sophisticated AI, and computer vision. Through sensors these machines "see" their environment, they "feel" materials, they interpret, they act accordingly, and they adjust their behavior. Through sophisticated AI they also learn, improve, and adapt.

Together, these machines work collaboratively with their human partners in human–machine teams in a well-orchestrated production system.

An organization does not evolve into a Humachine then freeze in a stasis. The Humachine is an enterprise that evolves. Creating the organization of the future will likely require reengineering the company's DNA. And yes, it will likely require a bold disruption. However, this level of change requires thoughtful orchestration. Based on our research and discussions with senior leaders, here is some generally applicable guidance.

Leadership and Failure

Flat and fluid organizational structures do not eliminate the need for leadership. In fact, the success of human–machine integration cannot happen in organizations without leadership. It is leadership that provides the vision, the strategy, the goals, and the path to succeed. It is leaders who are able to see great opportunities, understand how markets develop, and have the insight to propose novel offerings. In fact, leadership is even more important in a flat structure, as without strong leadership flat organizations can easily devolve into chaos.[65]

Leaders are the ones who develop the strategy and articulate a compelling vision. They are also the ones who create the culture needed to support any organizational change or process implementation. It is leadership that ensures the organization is moving in the right direction. It is also leadership that ensures resources are allocated for the organization to accomplish its goals. This includes investments in technologies, talent recruitment, training and retention, and organizational incentives to create a digital culture.

Fluidity allows for creativity, but it requires *discipline* to maintain a fluid organization that remains steadfast in its mission and sustainably manages its resources. Leadership is not merely a title. We encourage leadership via a meritocracy of ideas, as outlined in Ray Dalio's book *Principles*.[66]

It is up to leadership to make sure that the right capabilities are in place and that the organizational incentives, structures, and workflows are aligned. The UK retailer Tesco, for example, has developed a strong data-driven mind-set from top leadership through the entire organization. The company has integrated customer intelligence into its organization at all levels from a variety of consumer-targeted sources.[67] At Amazon, Jeff Bezos fired a group of Web designers who changed the company website without conducting experiments to determine the effects on customer behavior.[68] It is this kind of leadership that ensures that employees at all levels are aligned with the mission.

It is also up to leaders, coaches, and change agents to create a culture of experimentation and innovation, free from reprisal. It is a culture where all members feel comfortable in trying things that might fail. Yes, one goal is to work to change attitudes towards failure in order to embed a mind-set of risk-taking and innovation throughout the entire enterprise. Leaders themselves should act boldly and emulate the kind of behavior they want to see. Role modeling and demonstrating behaviors are powerful culture changers.

It is up to leaders to break the status quo by focusing decisions on experimentation and innovation, rather than quickly finding the "best solution." They should also celebrate and encourage learning from failure. It should be noted, however, that this is not an excuse for incompetent, sloppy work. Rather, it is discipline-oriented innovation where experimentation can be justified on the basis of potential learning value and rigor.[69]

There is a fine line between freedom to innovate without fear from the consequences of failure, and accountability where people must take responsibility for their work. It is up to leaders where to draw that line.

Harvard Business School Professor Gary Pisano says, "A tolerance for failure requires an intolerance for incompetence. A willingness to experiment requires rigorous discipline."[70] This suggests that only the highest caliber, most disciplined talent need apply. Apple, Facebook, Amazon, and others have extremely high expectations. In fact, although Google has an employee-friendly culture, it is one of the hardest places to get a job, with over 2 million applicants annually for roughly 5,000 positions.

Still, there is hope for normal people like us. Not everyone can measure up to that standard. Numerous research studies repeatedly show that success in talent is much less correlated with IQ, grades, or test scores. Rather, it is about perseverance, passion, and self-discipline.[71] Good old-fashioned true grit. You'll need people who can thrive in a competitive environment, not just people who can score well on standardized tests. That leads us to the next topic.

Develop a Long-Term Vision

Deciding on what a company's unique structure should look like needs to start with the long-term vision, driven by the company's unique intentionality and mission. Far too often, companies in the mood for change focus on current problems and ways those can be addressed. Developing solutions to these current problems is merely "patching" the current system. As we said before, preventing a boat from capsizing is not the goal—it's competing in the boat race. It is easier to make incremental improvements when compared to developing an aspirational vision. It is also easy to get caught up in complaints, each with their own vantage point, and focus on solutions that address immediate sources of friction. From the start, a redesign needs to be driven by intentionality, mission, and strategy. Companies need to be clear on what they are trying to do, what the aspirations are, and everyone needs to be on board. The aspirational goal is a superseding, overriding priority that trumps the preoccupations of the present.

Understand the Current State

Once the long-term vision is in place and the concept of a new organizational structure is broached, it is important to really understand the current state of the organization. This includes the *formal* organizational hierarchy and the *real* one, which is often different from what's on paper. Smart leaders also follow social structures, the actual flow of communication around the water cooler, and understand the culture. Actively seeking to understand the status quo of the company is a key tenant of lean systems—developing an understanding of the current state before moving to the ideal state. Often, assumptions are made as to how things function and what the organizational chart actually is. Be explicit about these assumptions and fact-check them. Understand talent capabilities, current incentives, weaknesses, and strengths to build upon.

Allocate Sufficient Resources

One significant roadblock to pulling off a successful mutation can be insufficient resource allocation toward the effort. This is a necessary and practical reminder. Reengineering the DNA must not only have organizational commitment and support on paper, but it needs to have sufficient monetary and human resources allocated. Leadership needs to consider the boring issues like financial consequences, tax implications, and sequencing of roll-outs to make sure there is ample funding for the change. These preparations will go a long way toward mitigating risk and alleviating anxiety of the board of directors and shareholders.

A recent study underscored the importance of having *slack* in human resources. Doing so positively impacted financial performance during the pursuit of strategic change. Using data from US commercial banks from 2002 to 2014, the study found that slack in human resources was positively related to performance in firms pursuing strategic change and that this relationship was stronger in the presence of greater financial slack.[72] In a finding that surprises no one, it helps to have extra money and human resources when undergoing change. So, make sure to allocate sufficient resources to undergo strategic restructuring—it pays to have slack in the system.

Embrace Transparency

Remember that organizations are a collection of human beings, each with emotions, hopes, fears, and beliefs. Reengineering is change and change creates uncertainty, which makes people feel uncomfortable. One of the most important aspects of restructuring is to treat people not as cogs to be moved around an organization but to address their human needs. The Humachine is humane.

When employees lack insight into the broader context of the business, they might treat any disruption as a threat and alert others in tones of alarm and insecurity. We can only interpret what we encounter through the lens of our own narrow understanding. If every part of the organization reaches different conclusions about what is happening and what priorities should be, you get chaos. It is critical that the entire organization has the same view, the same insight, and the same understanding as to what is happening and how they are part of the evolution.

Start with a Pilot

To this end, sometimes implementing and orchestrating a novel reengineering effort may be best tested on a small, targeted, and carefully selected pilot project. This would need to be an independently operated unit, such as a division. This is a "process of purposeful experimentation" and can be the best path toward becoming an organization that fully integrates humans and machines. This approach is markedly different (and may be more effective) than rolling out a complete plan for the enterprise without antecedent testing.

Selecting a few high-potential areas in which to experiment and then rapidly scale may be the most effective way to "test and learn." It will be easier to create value from small projects, especially for large firms, rather than jumping directly into restructuring the entire organization. Targeted projects help a company to learn what works and to begin developing capabilities. An example is Kaiser Permanente in California. The company initially concentrated analytics implementation efforts exclusively on the division focused on patients with long-term conditions by creating specific disease registries and panel management solutions. This focused approach led to much faster time to impact rather than an all-encompassing IT overhaul.

It is important that the pilot project selected is not random. Rather, it should be driven by strategy and understanding that competitive priorities are important to the organization. Even though it is merely a pilot project, resources will nevertheless be allocated. This is the reason why companies like Wal-Mart first focused on the supply chain functionality whereas Neiman's focused on customer loyalty when contemplating large change. A pilot project enables learning. First, test and implement process and product changes on a small scale. Once these are validated, move to broader implementation across the entire organization. It may mean, for example, that different divisions become individual "Humachines," each slightly different as they meet different organizational objectives.

Conclusion

Collaborative human–machine partnerships are possible across all organizational functions. Cognitive computing mimics human intelligence and is self-learning. On the customer side it is used to improve customer service, such as in the insurance industry where they respond to customer queries, provide call-center assistance, conduct underwriting, and offer claims management. On the supplier side, cognitive computing is used to place automatic purchases and even resolve disputes of orders and delivery times. These types of collaborative partnerships between human and machine are evolving, with intricate interconnections between entities across the entire organization, enabling enterprise self-awareness.

Leadership should foster a culture of entrepreneurship and innovation, restructuring to create an amoeba-like flat and fluid enterprise capable of continuous adaptation to environmental pressures with porous boundaries for open innovation and co-creation. The *intentionality* of the organization—it's mission, it's purpose in the world—serves as the unifying principle, rather than arbitrary structures or hierarchies.

Create a technology ecosystem that supports mutating into a Humachine. You can do this by either stacking internal capabilities, or creating alliances with vendors, which is a strategic decision. Recall that organizational network superintelligence is conceivable: "a web-based cognitive system, supersaturated with computer power and all other resources needed for explosive growth save for one crucial ingredient, could, when the final missing constituent is dropped into the cauldron, blaze up with superintelligence."[73]

That is the promise of the Humachine.

Notes

1 https://www.mckinsey.com/capabilities/people-and-organizational-performance/our-insights/a-business-of-its-times-haiers-self-evolving-organization
  Kirkpatrick, Doug. Reaching Haier: The Age of Rendanheyi. *Huffington Post*, November 29, 2017.
2 https://www.mckinsey.com/capabilities/people-and-organizational-performance/our-insights/a-business-of-its-times-haiers-self-evolving-organization
3 https://www.mckinsey.com/capabilities/people-and-organizational-performance/our-insights/a-business-of-its-times-haiers-self-evolving-organization
4 Wilson, H. James and Daugherty, Paul R. *How AI Can Make Strategy More Human*, Harvard Business Review (June 22, 2022). Available at https://hbr.org/2022/06/how-ai-can-make-strategy-more-human (last accessed June 9, 2023).
5 Beniger, James R. *The Control Revolution: Technological And Economic Origins Of The Information Society* (1986 Harvard University Press), p. 10.
6 Ibid., p. 37.
7 Ibid., p. 32.
8 Ibid., p. 62.
9 "Thermodynamics thus explains what it is that all living systems must control, and why such control is essential to life itself. All open systems, if they are to postpone for a time their inevitable heat death, must control the extraction and processing of matter, it's internal distribution and storage, continuous conversion into energy, and elimination as by-product wastes. Living organisms, for example, convert energy originally from the sun into forms more useful to the

processes of life: body heat, chemical energy from metabolism, electric energy to fire nerve impulses, mechanical energy to contract muscles and move about (luminescent organisms can even convert the energy back into light)." Ibid., p. 10.

10 Ibid., pp. 8–9, quoting James Grier Miller, *Living Systems* (1978 McGraw-Hill).

11 Ross, Michael and Taylor, James. *Managing AI Decision-Making Tools*, Harvard Business Review (November 10, 2021). Available at https://hbr.org/2021/11/managing-ai-decision-making-tools (last accessed June 9, 2023).

12 Arizona State University, Flying the final approach to Tranquility Base, the moon, *ScienceDaily* (July 17, 2019). Available at https://www.sciencedaily.com/releases/2019/07/190717105341.htm (last acceseed June 9, 2023).

13 *What Armstrong and Aldrin Saw: Simulation vs. Original Film*, YouTube (July 10, 2019). Available at https://youtu.be/ScFJBcLfasQ (last accessed June 9, 2023).

14 Taylor, James and Raden, Neil. *Smart (Enough) Systems: How to Deliver Competitive Advantage by Automating Hidden Decisions* (2007 Prentice Hall).

15 Ross and Taylor, *Managing AI Decision-Making Tools*.

16 https://hbr.org/2022/06/how-ai-can-make-strategy-more-human

17 Rod Harl, President and CEO, Alene Candles, Interview January 31, 2023.

18 Robert Sapolsky, *Behave: the Biology of Humans at our Best and Worst*, p. 64 (2017 Penguin Random House UK).

19 Ibid., p. 64.

20 Ibid., pp. 70–71.

21 Ibid., p. 73.

22 Ibid., p. 74.

23 Ibid., p. 102.

24 Ibid., p. 102.

25 Ibid., p. 103.

26 Google search "Leroy Jenkins" to see one of the internet's most viral examples of this kind of behavior. In 2005 a group of players in an online RPG World of Warcraft were meticulously planning to advance through an especially difficult passage. To succeed they must carefully sequence which player attacks and how, and even if they stick to the plan their odds of success are only one out of three. Then one player, apparently out of a flood of excess testosterone and having missed the battle plan, rushes ahead of the group, shouting his name "Leroy Jenkins" as a battle cry, throwing off the group plan and leading to the demise of the team. Leroy Jenkins will go down in infamy as shorthand for what happens when one member of the team undermines the overarching goal of the group through an excess of aggression.

27 Sapolsky, *Behave: the Biology of Humans at our Best and Worst*, p. 104.

28 Ibid., p. 105.

29 Ibid., p. 106.

30 "The winning effect on testosterone is lessened in circumstances where people feel like they won by luck or where, despite winning, they feel like they underperformed. And contrast, the effect is enhanced among people who went into the competition having the strongest psychological motives for domination. Finally, testosterone levels can rise robustly in 'losers' who nonetheless perform far better than they anticipated. Thus one might see testosterone levels rise after a marathon in a guy who came in at the back of the pack but is triumphant because he was sure he was going to drop dead halfway through, and may decline in the guy who comes in third but was expected to win. We all belong to numerous hierarchies, but some of the most powerful are the ones in our heads based on our internal standards." Ibid., p. 105.

31 Ibid, p. 107.

32 Ibid., p. 435.
33 Koetz, Clara. Managing the Customer Experience: A Beauty Retailer Deploys All Tactics. *Journal of Business Strategy*, 2018. doi:10.1108/jbs-09-2017-0139.
34 Ibid.
35 Howarth, Brad. What Zappos Is Doing to Personalise Customer Experience and Services, *CMO*, May 2018. Available at www.cmo.com.au/article/641587/wha t-zappos-doing-personalise-customer-experience-services/
36 https://www.reviewjournal.com/business/zappos-implements-another-round-of-la yoffs-2715896/
37 https://thestrategystory.com/2021/04/13/zappos-customer-service-strategy/
38 Ibid.
39 Salpini, Cara. Retail Dive, Why Beauty Will Continue to Rule Retail in 2018, January 2, 2018. Available at www.retaildive.com/news/why-beauty-will-conti nue-to-rule-retail-in-2018/513443/
40 http://panmore.com/google-organizational-structure-organizational-culture; Borodai, V. Brand of the Employer as DNA of Corporate Culture of Service Company, *European Research*, 2(1):34–35, 2017; Ashkenas, R., D. Ulrich, T. Jick, and S. Kerr. *The Boundaryless Organization: Breaking the Chains of Organizational Structure* (2015 John Wiley & Sons).
41 Kirkpatrick, Doug. Reaching Haier: The Age of Rendanheyi, *Huffington Post*, November 29, 2017.
42 Chesbrough, Henry. Open Innovation: The New Imperative for Creating and Profiting from Technology, Harvard Business Review Press. Available at http://openinnovation.net/about-2/open-innovation-definition/
43 https://ge-geniuslink.com
44 https://firstbuild.com
45 www.strategy-business.com/article/Why-Haier-Is-Reorganizing-Itself-around-the-Internet-of-Things?gko=895fe
46 Ibid.
47 www.holacracy.org
48 www.zapposinsights.com/about/holacracy
49 Ibid.
50 www.forbes.com/sites/forbesleadershipforum/2017/07/13/three-lessons-for-zappos -ceo-tony-hsieh-from-a-250-year-old-team/#3e88de0522a8
51 https://www.yahoo.com/video/zappos-quietly-backed-away-holacracy-090102533. html
52 Irving, Tyler. *Using a 'virtual slime mold' to design a subway network less prone to disruption*, Phys.org (January 27, 2022). Available at https://phys.org/news/ 2022-01-virtual-slime-mold-subway-network.html#:~:text=Back%20in% 202010%2C%20a%20team,biologically%20inspired%20adaptive%20network% 20design (last accessed July 1, 2023).
53 Ibid.
54 Ibid. See also Raphael Kay et al., Stepwise slime mould growth as a template for urban design, Scientific Reports (2022). DOI: 10.1038/s41598–022–05439-w
55 www.forbes.com/sites/jacobmorgan/2015/06/04/how-morningstar-farms-operates-without-any-managers/#56b3827025b1
56 McGregor, Jenna. Apple's Tim Cook on Creativity and Changing Your Mind. *Washington Post*, December 6, 2012. Available at www.washingtonpost.com/na tional/on-leadership/apples-tim-cook-on-creativity-and-changing-your-mind/2012/ 12/06/ed81109c-3fcf-11e2-ae43-cf491b837f7b_story.html?noredirect=on&utm_term =.4a69061e2f25
57 https://rework.withgoogle.com/blog/new-re-work-guides-on-innovation/

58 Stillman, Jessica. Here Are All the Tools Google Uses to Encourage Innovative Thinking Absolutely Free, *Inc. Magazine*. April 18, 2018.

59 Tribolet, J., Pombinho, J., Aveiro, D. Organizational Self-Awareness: A Matter of Value. In *Organization Design and Engineering*, edited by R. Magalhàes (2014 Palgrave Macmillan).

60 Bostrom, Nick. Superintelligence: Paths, Dangers, Strategies (2014 Oxford University Press), pp. 58–59.

61 Peter Cameron, CEO Lenox Group, Interview February 7, 2023.

62 Davenport, Thomas H. Competing on Analytics, *Harvard Business Review*, January, 2006, 1–9.

63 http://panmore.com/apple-mission-statement-vision-statement

64 Turner, Pat, Bernus, Peter and Noran, Ovidiu. Enterprise Thinking for Self-aware Systems. *16th IFAC Symposium on Information Control Problems in Manufacturing Bergamo*, Italy. June 11–13, 2018.

65 Pisano, Gary P. The Hard Truth about Innovative Cultures. *Harvard Business Review*, January–February 2019, pp. 63–71.

66 Ray Dalio, *Principles: Life & Work* (2017 Simon & Schuster).

67 McKinsey Global Institute Big Data: The Next Frontier for Innovation, Competition, and Productivity, June 2012. Available at www.businessinsider.com/state-of-internet-slides-2012-10?op=1

68 Davenport, Thomas. How to Design Smart Business Experiments. *Harvard Business Review*, February 2009.

69 Pisano, The Hard Truth about Innovative Cultures, pp 63–71.

70 Ibid.

71 www.inc.com/thomas-oppong/the-one-thing-that-is-a-better-indicator-of-success-than-talent-according-to-sci.html see also www.forbes.com/sites/lisaquast/2017/03/06/why-grit-is-more-important-than-iq-when-youre-trying-to-become-successful/#29e3f8207e45

72 Bentley, Frederick Scott and Rebecca R Kehoe. Give Them Some Slack—They're Trying to Change! The Benefits of Excess Cash, Excess Employees, and Increased Human Capital in the Strategic Change Context, *Academy of Management Journal*, December 28, 2018. doi:10.5465/amj.2018.0272

73 Bostrom, *Superintelligence*, p. 60.

Chapter 9

Futureproof Enterprise

Finding Your Organization's Soul

Remember when Blockbuster filed for bankruptcy, just three years after the launch of Netflix's streaming-video business? How about when Apple revolutionized smartphones, while incumbents like Nokia, Sony Ericsson, and Motorola stood by the wayside, watching the market share for brick phones steadily erode? Next, the silicon wave came for brick and mortar retail of all stripes.

Now the silicon wave is coming for white collar jobs and knowledge workers. While AI has been a part of business for years, it is the advancement of generative AI such as ChatGPT, Bard, ChatSonic, Jasper AI, and other LLM platforms that is dramatically changing the competitive landscape. Jen-Hsun Huang, CEO of Nvidia recently put it "AI has reinvented computing from the ground up. In every way, this is the rebirth of the computer industry."[1]

But many economists predict the new AI could replace hundreds of millions of jobs and create a "cataclysmic reorganization" mirroring the industrial revolution. On the one hand, we are already seeing this, with those who write marketing and social media content already being replaced with generative AI.[2] And while it is broadly recognized that even the most advanced AI doesn't match human writing skills and is riddled with errors such as "hallucinations," many companies don't care as the new technology offers cost savings. As of this writing IBM announced it will pause its hiring. CEO Arvind Krishna explained that approximately 7,800 non-customer facing jobs could be replaced by AI and automation in the next five years.[3] According to Sarah T. Roberts, Associate Professor at UCLA specializing in digital labor: "AI is coming for the jobs that were supposed to be automation-proof."[4]

But there is another side to this story. There has also been a rapid rise of a new breed of jobs that are going unfilled. One such category are technology professionals known as "prompt engineers," who play a crucial role in training AI large language models (LLMs) to provide accurate and useful responses to users.[5] Enrique Lores, the CEO of HP, tells us that "AI will

DOI: 10.4324/9781003322832-9

change career trajectories," and that as humans we will merely go "from doing things to interpreting things."[6] In fact, a recent estimate finds 30% of companies are seeking nontechnical professionals precisely with these types of new skills.[7] These are jobs that require a new kind of skill to interpret and work with the AI as a 'co-pilot.' These positions don't necessarily require a background in coding or technical expertise. Rather, as Andrej Karpathy, former head of AI at Tesla Inc., puts it, "The hottest new programming language is English."[8]

For humans at every level, the answer points to education—reskilling, upskilling and lifelong learning. There are plenty of jobs—we just need to be skilled for them. For companies, these are cautionary tales in the digital era where many incumbent companies now understand that digital transformation is a necessity. Change needs to happen—and it needs to happen rapidly and frequently. To mutate, you have to reengineer the DNA of your company—and reskill your people.

We can witness organizational evolution by looking at Microsoft. When Satya Nadella was named CEO of Microsoft in 2014, he undertook a major organizational restructuring then followed that up with another one in 2016. These changes, some would consider radical, may have saved the company's place on the leader board. The organization was divided: destructive internal competition was roiling within the products division of the company; Microsoft's platforms were represented as separate groups of people within the company, each vying for attention; employee engagement and morale were low, and—most importantly, in our view—employees were lacking a sense of purpose.

Before the seismic restructure, Microsoft was focused on building an intelligent cloud platform and creating more personal computing options.[9] Nadella announced a new mission, "To empower every person and every organization on the planet to achieve more."[10] In 2016, restructuring resulted in an integrated AI group charged to innovate in artificial intelligence across the entire Microsoft product line. AI would become a unifying force, creating a renewed sense of purpose for all of Microsoft's various internal working groups, previously pitted against one another. Microsoft had at the time announced a USD $1 billion investment into OpenAI, deepening its commitment to the moonshot idea of ethical artificial general intelligence.

Here are some lessons from Microsoft for reengineering the DNA. *First*, the changes were mission driven. *Second*, the restructure was designed to bring together, connect, and integrate people—making people, not technology, the centerpiece. *Third*, the restructure was bold and disruptive, not a gradual transformation. *Fourth*, the restructure was not a one-time event— it happened multiple times. As needs change, so should the organization. *Fifth*, the mission and process were shared with everyone at the company in a transparent manner.

Afterwards, Nadella recalled his thought process: "We've challenged ourselves to think about our core mission, our soul—what would be lost if we disappeared. ... We also asked ourselves, what culture do we want to foster that will enable us to achieve these goals?"[11] That focus on challenging the core mission as part of organizational evolution has continued with the development of generative AI. Recently Nadella said that in the new AI environment the company needs "to reconnect to the soul of our work, we don't just need a better way of doing the same things; we need a whole new way of working."[12]

Notice the repeated focus on the organization's "soul" and how closely this is tied to the organization's people having a sense of meaning in their work. That epiphany was the spark that lit Microsoft's AI revolution and has continued. Nadella further said that while AI development is happening quickly, at Microsoft people remain integral to the process. "If anything, I feel, yes, it's moving fast, but moving fast in the right direction," he said. "Humans are in the loop versus being out of the loop. It's a design choice, which, at least, we have made."[13]

Foundations

We have laid the foundation for the Humachine—the organization of the future. To develop the foundations of the Humachine, we carefully combed through the latest research and spoke with corporate leaders. We began this journey captivated by the capabilities of AI and the vision of what the future holds. After all, AI is doing miraculous things, from driving cars to identifying cancers. The roar of the silicon wave can be heard throughout the global economy.

For us, however, the journey led to a sobering conclusion: What has been dubbed as the "technology era" really needs to become a human era, where we focus on human factors in ergonomics, cultivating uniquely human skills such as emotional intelligence, care, intuition, playfulness, and aesthetics, and making our institutions more humane. Technology, albeit important, cannot become our sole focus, lest we become soulless. To put big data, computing, and AI on a pedestal while neglecting basic human needs and cultivating human talent is misguided and will lead to enterprise failure, if not the Apocalypse.

We want to be clear that although we reference companies such as Microsoft, Google, Haier, Amazon, and Apple to describe organizations demonstrating Humachine traits, we are reticent to describe any of them as a Humachine, *per se*. We have far too many ethical concerns around how these organizations have used their powers to hold them up as worthy of moral esteem, even if they are worthy of tactical emulation. In his book, *The Four: The Hidden DNA of Amazon, Apple, Facebook, and Google*, Professor Scott Galloway of the NYU Stern School of Business goes so far as to describe them as the *Four Horsemen of the Apocalypse*:[14]

Imagine: a retailer that refuses to pay sales tax, treats its employees poorly, destroys hundreds of thousands of jobs, and yet is celebrated as a paragon of business innovation.

A computer company that withholds information about a domestic act of terrorism from federal investigators, with the support of a fan following that views the firm similar to a religion.

A social media firm that analyzes thousands of images of your children, activates your phone as a listening device, and sells this information to Fortune 500 companies.

An ad platform that commands, in some markets, a 90% share of the most lucrative sector in media, yet avoids anti-competitive regulation through aggressive litigation and lobbyists.

This narrative is also heard around the world, but in hushed tones. We know these companies aren't benevolent beings, yet we invite them into the most intimate areas of our lives. We willingly divulge personal updates, knowing they'll be used for profit. Our media elevate the executives running these companies to hero status-geniuses to be trusted and emulated. Our governments grant them special treatment regarding antitrust regulation, taxes, and even labor laws. And investors bid their stocks up, providing near-infinite capital and firepower to attract the most talented people on the planet or crush adversaries.

So, are these entities the Four Horsemen of god, love, sex, and consumption? Or are they the Four Horsemen of the Apocalypse? The answer is yes to both questions. I'll just call them the Four Horsemen.

How did these companies aggregate so much power? How can an inanimate, for-profit enterprise become so deeply ingrained in our psyche that it reshapes the rules of what a company can do and be? What does unprecedented scale and influence mean for the future of business and the global economy? Are they destined, like other business titans before them, to be eclipsed by younger, sexier rivals? Or have they become so entrenched that nobody—individual, enterprise, government, or otherwise—stands a chance?

We share similar concerns. For all the Big Four have done to reshape our lives, we did not ask them to, and without injecting a strong self-regulatory conscience into their culture or having a modicum of oversight from federal and state attorneys, we see trouble looming.

While adapting to changing technology is important, a critical focus must be on the human element of the enterprise and the processes by which humans use machines to become better versions of ourselves.

Let's restate the conclusions we have drawn from our research:

- *Organizational success will fall squarely on the shoulders of humans, not machines.* Creativity, innovation, practical solutions, and so forth will only come from human ingenuity—and companies and society cannot survive without it.

- *Enterprise success will come from developing better processes, not simply adopting new technology.* Remember Kasparov's Law? Normal human + machine + better process is superior to a strong computer alone and, more remarkably, superior to a strong human + machine + inferior process. Top machines alone won't cut it. It is the integration of humans and machines that will lead to success, not the displacing of humans by machines.

- *Machines will not fully master the complete range of human abilities.* Moravec's Paradox tells us that what machines are proficient at, humans struggle with, and vice versa. For example, high-level conceptual reasoning requires very little computational effort by a machine, but low-level sensorimotor skills—the things our toddlers do and we take for granted as we navigate the world—require enormous computational resources for machines. We found no reason to think Moravec's Paradox will become less true in the future.

- *Machines will not replace humans but should rather augment their skills.* Technology will become indispensable, but it will help humans thrive and be better at doing human tasks. Machines will offer assistance in shifting the nature of jobs and what humans do. Rather than eliminating jobs, this may mean emergent jobs go unfilled until the right talent is developed. Humans must prepare themselves to be qualified for new opportunities.

- *Enterprise success will come from investing in human talent and preserving human knowledge—not just upgrading technology.* Obviously, companies will need to invest in technology and machines will continue to evolve. However, success will require building a portfolio of talents, preserving institutional knowledge and creating opportunities for lifelong learning. Eliminating jobs without thought or consideration to institutional knowledge preservation is foolish. You will never see a law firm succeed by laying off all the senior attorneys, because in knowledge-based professions, silver hair often means priceless institutional memory.

- *Humans will need to continually evolve their skills.* We must cultivate our uniquely human skills, such as creativity, caring, ethical judgment, and aesthetic sensibilities. Lifelong learning will become the new normal.

- Finally, as we posed at the onset of this book: *An enterprise can attain superintelligence only at the organizational level.* This superintelligent enterprise is the Humachine, and we do not have to wait for the future to attain it. We can create collective superintelligence now (as Bostrom defines it) by combining the virtues of human talent with machine capabilities (to resolve Moravec's Paradox) using the right process (in conformity with Kasparov's Law).

With Great Power Comes... the Ability to Do a Lot of Damage

We have crossed a threshold that has changed the balance of power between humans and the tools we use for knowledge capture, conservation, and distribution. Before AI, big data analytics, and CRMs, we used print material, Rolodexes, books, calculators, and basic computers for storage and creation of knowledge. It was solely up to humans to develop new knowledge. Today, machines are co-creators of knowledge and will ineluctably (even if unintentionally) shape our future in subtle and profound ways. These mechanical co-creators of knowledge have processing capabilities far beyond those of humans—that we increasingly cannot validate or check.

Municipal leaders are turning to "smart cities," with infrastructure from stoplights to electric grids run by thinking software. Homeowners are turning to "smart homes," with everything from home security to groceries run by AI. Enterprises and individuals are integrating AI into decision-making that is both long term and short term, strategic and quotidian. AI is shaping how we live and work, shaping our society and environment.

Today AI algorithms filter, sort, and analyze massive amounts of data for specific organizational tasks. AI is now involved in *making* decisions that have global and social consequences. With AI, the time between invention and impact can be very short—compressing the duration between teaching a machine how to perform a task and rolling out those machines into the workforce.

In the past decade we've started using smart machines for tasks that change the trajectory of human lives. AI helps determine which treatments get used on people with illnesses,[15] who qualifies for Medicaid,[16] who qualifies for life insurance,[17] whether to convict criminals and if so, how to set their jail time,[18] and whether an applicant gets a job interview.[19]

Who gets healed, who gets to insure against risks, who gets punished for wrongdoing, who gets deemed eligible, and who gets economic opportunities are life-and-death decisions. We are turning to AI to make those decisions for us.

AI is rapidly advancing with powers that can be dangerous, with no checks and balances or governance. Consider that Amazon had to discard its AI recruiting software when it learned to penalize resumes that included the word "women" in the application.[20] The company that prides itself on technology and data-driven decisions realized that the new system was not gender-neutral when rating candidates for software developer jobs and other technical posts.

Amazon's software was trained to screen applicants from the patterns it observed from the history of resumes submitted over a ten-year period. The vast majority of applicants were male as a result of a highly male-dominated field. However, the algorithm "learned" that the male candidates were preferable. As a result, any resume that included the words "women," "women's" (i.e., "women's chess club") was automatically downgraded.

These types of problems can still be caught and reversed. However, as AI completely takes over decision-making, these types of problems may become embedded in algorithms, may not be easily caught, and may permanently impact society.

The potential dangers of AI are significant. In an open letter titled "Pause Giant AI Experiments," organized by the nonprofit Future of Life Institute and published online on March 29, 2023, called for "all AI labs to immediately pause for at least 6 months the training of AI systems more powerful than GPT-4." The cessation request of research on all AI systems more powerful than GPT-4 was signed by 1,100 notable signatories, including Elon Musk, Steve Wozniak, and Tristan Harris, of the Center for Humane Technology. The signatories collectively expressed fears regarding the rampant and unregulated growth of AI and the need for guardrails and standards.

Some have even argued that the open letter was not going far enough. For example, Eliezer Yudkowsky, a U.S. decision theorist and lead research at the Machine Intelligence Research Institute, wrote in Time Magazine, "shut it all down."[21] Similarly, Duncan Steel, a professor of electrical engineering, computer science, and physics at the University of Michigan expressed:

> AI can be manipulated by a programmer to achieve objectives contrary to moral, ethical, and political standards of a healthy society... I would like to see an unbiased group without personal or commercial agendas to create a set of standards that has to be followed by all users and providers of AI.[22]

Stanford Professor Fei-Fei Li believes the field needs a recalibration. She believes that if we make fundamental changes to how AI is engineered—and who engineers it—it can be a force for good. Otherwise, it may impact humanity in very negative ways.

"There is nothing artificial about AI. It's inspired by people, it's created by people, and—most importantly, it impacts people. It is a powerful tool we are only just beginning to understand, and that is a profound responsibility," says Li.[23] "There are no machine values. Machine values are human values." As a result, AI systems will be biased as long as we are, too. As Li puts it, "Bias in, bias out."

Cathy O'Neill has written the best-selling book about how AI and machine learning can bake in bias, titled *Weapons of Math Destruction* (or "WMDs," as she calls them). Her call for action is worthy of consideration. Her book is full of cases—faulty public teacher assessment, inequity in the justice system, and biases in products and services offered that resulted from feeding AIs with dirty data.

Often, AI biases exacerbate irrational prejudices are unethical and lead to dumb decisions. Irrational prejudices are some of the worst features of humanity and have no place in the Humachine. As we train AI to take over, we need to train it responsibly.

Another problem with AI has to do with massive amounts of data being collected, and the attending problems of trusting for-profit enterprises to steward consumer privacy and security (not to mention the risks of an ill-intentioned breach by malicious third parties). Massive, unprecedented amounts of data and information—transactional, sensing, and tracking data, including mobile-phone data—are being collected on customers. This happened almost overnight as everyone blindly opted in through End User License Agreements (EULAs) and digital platforms took over our economy.

We never stopped and asked some fundamental questions before rolling out EULAs to everyone. What data should we be permitted to collect? How should companies safeguard this information? How should the enterprise react to data breaches? These are all questions that must be pursued in good faith.

Data collection is often not even tied to a specific corporate purpose; it's just gathered indiscriminately, pulled into the voracious maw of Big Tech without adequate safeguards. Data is often not easy to anonymize. Breaches at Equifax, Yahoo, Uber, Facebook, and Target show that even the largest firms, their customers, and their partners are vulnerable to hacks. Federal and local laws, appropriate governance structures, credentialing, and audits are all part of the solution. But they are far behind the state of the art in hacking.

Lastly, AI has the potential to be weaponized for harm to individuals, organizations, and society as a whole, by disseminating fake information and deliberately sowing discord. This is a pernicious way in which machine algorithms fail us—that is, failing to detect misinformation or "fake news" before the algorithm makes it go viral on social media platforms. Lies, powered by bots, have the potential to disrupt the global economy. The speed at which fake news stories can be distributed across algorithmically curated social media platforms has negatively impacted user perception of truth and interpretation of actual information.

"Deepfakes" have been used to misrepresent politicians and celebrities, and have potential for tremendous destruction. Imagine what a disseminated fake video of a corporate CEO could do to the stock of a company. As Jonathan Swift said, "Falsehood flies, and truth comes limping after it."

We haven't even broached the subject of cybersecurity risks posed by malware compromising the electric grid.

How do these AI-fueled risks affect an enterprise? Biased AI damages society and leads to completely suboptimal decisions. Data breaches can ruin a business reputation, as can "deepfakes."

What can companies do? Google Cloud has hired a consulting ethicist, hoping to ensure that the AI it is developing is fair and ethical.[24] Microsoft established an international ethics board and has even turned down business with potential customers due to ethical concerns raised by that body.[25] Microsoft says it has also begun placing limits on how AI tech can be used and has even forbid some applications on facial recognition for ethical reasons.

There are other growing attempts to address algorithmic accountability. One is the *Fairness Accountability and Transparency in Machine Learning (FAT/ML)* community with the goal of "bringing together a growing community of researchers and practitioners concerned with fairness, accountability, and transparency in machine learning."[26] FAT/ML is a multidisciplinary group of researchers from the life sciences, the sociology of science, the history and philosophy of science, sociology, applied ethics, law, and computer science.

FAT/ML has laid out a set of five principles for ethical use of AI: Responsibility, Explainability, Accuracy, Auditability, and Fairness.

The goal of these principles is to "help developers and product managers design and implement algorithmic systems in publicly accountable ways. Accountability in this context includes an obligation to report, explain, or justify algorithmic decision-making as well as mitigate any negative social impacts or potential harms."[27]

Ingenuity in AI and technology development must be tempered with integrity, values, governance, policy, and legal consequences for misconduct. These are issues that need collectively informed public policy solutions—with input from industry, consumers, government regulators, and university researchers.

Indeed, guardrails need to be placed around AI to make sure it does not reflect prejudices and human biases, that data is secure, and that we are protected from "deepfakes" and weaponized AI.

We need to get out ahead of this. The risks posed by AI may be irreversible.

We Need to Play to Our Strengths

Playing to our strengths means designing work around those uniquely human skills that cannot be imitated by AI, neural nets, and machines. It requires identifying and developing these capabilities. It requires enterprises to invest in human resources rather than exclusively technology. It requires universities to change curriculum and develop new ways to create a "robot-proof" education. Lastly, it will be incumbent on each individual to accept that this era requires lifelong learning.

Let us not become so enamored and captivated with technology and AI capabilities, deploying it far and wide, deep and shallow, that in our enthusiasm we overlook ways to safeguard ourselves and our institutions from its weaponization. Let us not overlook how important it is to recognize, attribute value to, and cultivate those capabilities that differentiate us from machines.

To thrive in this new era, we should play to our strengths. Yes, everyone needs to be data literate; however, not everyone needs to be a data scientist. In fact, we believe that it is precisely the human skills that come from humanities and the liberal arts that should now be stressed and developed more than ever. Rather than becoming more like machines, humans need to decidedly uncover what it means to be human and play to those strengths. Not everyone needs to be a quant or a techie. The Humachine will also employ philosophers and artists.

The scope of human intelligence is described well by Dileep George, a computer scientist who cofounded Vicarious, an AI firm in San Francisco: "We humans are not just pattern recognizers; we're also building models about the things we see. And these are causal models—we understand about cause and effect."[28] Humans intuitively adjust to slight changes in environmental conditions with subtle compensatory behavioral changes. This is in many cases lost on AI.

While on the one hand experiments with AI reveal highly intelligent behavior, AI can be stumped by something a human would find simple. For example, Vicarious trained an AI to play the Atari game called Breakout, where a ball is bounced against a brick wall. AI learned quickly and played well. However, when the game was slightly tweaked, such as the paddle being lifted just a bit higher—something a human could quickly figure out—the AI failed to adjust.

Human intelligence goes beyond pattern recognition. Humans engage in reasoning, make logical inferences, deploying "common sense" assumptions, analogizing, and extrapolating to similar situations. We understand counterfactuals and can integrate abstract knowledge into our understanding of the world. We can also generalize. If we know how to play one musical instrument—say a guitar—we can apply those skills to quickly learn another, such as a harp. If we know how to drive a car, we can easily translate that skill to driving a tractor or a truck. Many attempts at programming into machines what is, in humans, quite basic rationality have proved extremely labor intensive. Even with brute force programming common sense ("water is wet," for example), the gains made are slow and even small changes confuse the algorithm.[29]

These kinds of trade-offs illustrate the lasting power of Moravec's Paradox. We can resolve the paradox by playing to our strengths. Instead of trying to teach machines to be like humans, and teaching humans to be like machines, let's just embrace our differences and leverage processes that bring out our best features.

So what are we especially good at? Professor Yuval Noah Harari, in his book *Sapiens*, tell us: "Homo sapiens rules the world because it is the only animal that can believe in things that exist purely in its own imagination, such as gods, states, money and human rights." This tells us that humans have evolved so far because we have imagination—the root of creativity. When someone slanders imagination as something fanciful and thus not worthwhile, they are sadly mistaken. Imagination is what gave us our humanity. Imagination is the foundation of civilization. Without it, civilization will crumble.

Reinforce Culture by Playing Games

On the subject of imagination, we cannot overstate the importance of playing games to human civilization. It holds that games impact culture broadly speaking as well as within an organization. A company that plays together, stays together. Games impact status by declaring participants either champions or the vanquished. Any kind of competitive game involves a challenge to status. Changes in status in turn impact testosterone secretion which in turn drives behavior in unconscious ways, depending on context.

"From the life of childhood right up to the highest achievements of civilization one of the strongest incentives to perfection, both individual and social, is the desire to be praised and honored for one's excellence."[30] Excellence is by definition better than average. Excellence means prone to winning, whatever the game may be. Esteem for victory in games provides the reinforcement needed to incentivize learned behaviors in humans. As such games and the gamification of work process and educational process are woefully underutilized by designers of institutions like corporations and schools.

The harsh reality of games is that not everyone can be a winner all the time. This is the inevitable fact in any competitive environment and is the case even outside of games such as at work or at school. Not everyone can be valedictorian. But following Kasparov's Law, we don't need a team of geniuses to accomplish extraordinary results, we simply need ordinary people following the right process. Games are just one mechanism of driving superlative outcomes with ordinary human resources. In a competitive environment, treating everyone equally (handing out so-called "participation trophies") and not acknowledging qualitative rank or merit will undermine incentives to perform "above average," which will eventually destroy a culture of excellence. However, creating a mechanism for ordinary workers to move up in rank by playing games against one another may just do the trick. A culture without play is no culture at all, it is a swarm of robotic drones, it is a mechanical assembly line. Indeed it may be incoherent to describe social norms as a "culture" if play is absent because social life is imbued with shape by play:

> It is through this playing that society expresses its interpretation of life and the world. By this we do not mean that play turns into culture, rather that in its earliest phases culture has the play-character, that it proceeds in the shape and in the mood of play.[31]

Managers can create culture by establishing the conditions for "winning" and "losing" the game of work. This would be to leverage the challenge hypothesis to drive the behaviors we wish to see increased, and to squelch the behaviors we wish to see less of. Remember, defending status spikes testosterone, which in turn drives whatever behavior is needed to maintain status, which may be aggression but depending on how status is maintained in a company it could just as well be politeness or productivity or creativity.

Create culture by creating games and tying the award for winners and the punishment for loses to status. This can be totally contrived or it can be made real by connecting the outcome of games to actual compensation. At any rate, a work environment devoid of games is hardly human at all. Save that for the machines.

> A certain play-factor was extremely active all through the cultural process and that it produces many of the fundamental forms of social life. The spirit of playful competition is, as a social impulse, older than culture itself and pervades all life like a veritable ferment.[32]

We are not merely *Homo sapiens*, we are also *Homo ludens*.

Neurodiversity Is More Important than Genius

Today's social and political climate has placed a harsh spotlight on the practices of recruitment and promotion. With diversity, equity and inclusion (DEI) initiatives on the rise, and yet affirmative action is subject to legal challenge, we may have reason to give pause about the use of race, gender, ethnicity, and other non-work factors in evaluating candidacy for work or for educational opportunities. *Neurodivergent* candidates, literally people with brains that work differently than the neurotypical, include those with autism, dyslexia, or attention disorders. Of course all brains are unique and there is no "normal" brain that makes for a great worker or student. Nonetheless we can recognize that neurodivergence presents its own kind of challenges and opportunities.

Leading companies such as IBM, Salesforce and Accenture provide critical support for "*neuroinclusion*" enterprise-wide, such as hiring autistic candidates, providing special enterprise resources for the neurodivergent, and identifying talent, whereas previous generations of recruiters have excluded the neurodivergent from employment altogether.[33]

> One large organization found itself overwhelmed with customer queries at the beginning of the Covid crisis: By deliberately assembling a highly neurodiverse team to solutionize, the firm was able to respond to the crisis rapidly and effectively, demonstrating in microcosm how true diversity of thought can be a critical competitive advantage.[34]

Promoting an understanding and acceptance of those who truly think differently will likely have positive spillover effects on company culture through better appreciation of how we are all unique, better sense of belonging and inclusion, and reducing bias. Indeed, failing to embrace neurodiversity will likely undermine the effectiveness of other DEI initiatives and negatively impact recruitment, retention, and cultivation of human talent.

Creating Flow States

The so-called *"flow state"* was coined by psychologist Mihaly Csikszentmihalyi to describe "the mental state in which a person is entirely focused on a single activity, and not thinking about themselves nor their performance."[35] When in a flow state, the brain experiences higher than normal levels of dopamine, which has some interesting implications for performance. Flow means elevated dopamine levels that suppress bodily sensations, which could negatively impact performance such as hunger or tiredness. A painter, accountant, or athlete experiencing flow may just work straight through their lunch break without even noticing.

Yet these elevated dopamine levels trigger both "lower activity in the prefrontal cortex," which leads to a momentary decline in executive functioning responsible for self-conscious behavior, and yet, at the same time, increased synchronization between different brain regions, increasing control and coordination, suggesting increased levels of frontal cortex activity, associated with higher executive function.[36] Being in a flow state feels so good you forget to eat, and you are both less self-conscious and more together. In short, being in a flow state greatly enhances performance. We are less likely to get in our own way with cringe behavior or wandering thoughts.

Being able to engineer work spaces to facilitate entering into and sustaining flow state is thus crucial for enterprise to get the most out of human resources. Eliminating distractions, minimizing interruptions, and promoting concentration will encourage what computer science professor Cal Newport in his book *Deep Work: Rules for Focused Success in a Distracted World* calls "deep work."

Newport suggests four methods for achieving deep work and thus inducing high-performing flow states. Rhythmic, journalistic, monastic, and bimodal philosophies. See Figure 9.1.

Table 9.1 Flow state philosophies

Rhythmic	Set aside 1–4 hours per day, at the same time each day. Must be consistent. This is the most rigid approach.
Journalistic	Do deep-work wherever it fits into your schedule. You need at least 90 minutes per session. This is the most flexible approach.
Monastic	Eliminate all shallow work, reject all distractions, and spend all work hours in a flow state. This is the most intense approach.
Bimodal	Set aside time for deep work, and all other time is used for shallow work.

The common denominator for performing deep work in a flow state is being free from distractions. Distractions lead to procrastination and superficial cognition where we are not truly focused on the task at hand. "New research from Chalmers University of Technology shows that as little as 40 decibels of traffic noise—the typical level of background noise in an office environment or kitchen—has a detrimental effect on cognitive performance."[37] Unfortunately, increased urban density means workers are exposed more than ever to noise pollution from traffic. To address this issue, enterprise can study acoustics, install noise-abating construction materials in office-building facades, or even provide noise-cancelling headphones to workers.

Sensory cues such as light, color, sound, smells, and visual symbols can have powerful impacts on behavior. To manage fear, aggression, and arousal we must understand the amygdala; to manage reward, anticipation, and motivation we must understand the dopaminergic system; to manage restraint, rationality, and executive function we must understand the frontal cortex. We can be primed to relax, be fearful, or be circumspect without knowing we are being primed. Certain smells like garbage can trigger fear responses, making us more conservative; colder temperatures can trigger social trust issues, making us rate others as having a more chilly personality; physical hunger pangs make us less charitable; and so on.[38] We should build our work stations accordingly.

"Humanics": Education for the Humachine Workforce

In his book *Robot-Proof: Higher Education in the Age of Artificial Intelligence*, Joseph Aoun, President of Northeastern University, introduces a new educational discipline: "humanics." According to Aoun, the goal of *humanics* is "to nurture our species' unique traits of creativity and flexibility. It builds on our innate strengths and prepares students to compete in a labor market in which brilliant machines work alongside human professionals."[39] There are two dimensions to humanics. The first dimension is the unique *content* contained in an education in humanics, the second is the unique *cognitive capacities*.[40]

On the content side, we need "new literacies":

> In the past, literacy in reading, writing, and mathematics formed the baseline for participation in society, while even educated professionals did not need any technical proficiencies beyond knowing how to click and drag through a suite of office programs. That is no longer sufficient. In the future, graduates will need to build on the old literacies by adding three more—*data literacy, technological literacy*, and *human literacy*. This is because people can no longer thrive in a digitized world using merely analog tools. They will be living and working in a

constant stream of big data, connectivity, and instant information flowing from every click and touch of their devices. Therefore, they need data literacy to read, analyze, and use these ever-rising tides of information. Technological literacy gives them a grounding in coding and engineering principles, so they know how their machines tick. Lastly, human literacy teaches them humanities, communication, and design, allowing them to function in the human milieu.

On the cognitive capacities side of humanics, we need higher-order mental skills:

The first is *systems thinking*, the ability to view an enterprise, machine, or subject holistically, making connections between its different functions in an integrative way. The second is *entrepreneurship*, which applies the creative mindset to the economic and often social sphere. The third is *cultural agility*, which teaches students how to operate deftly in varied global environments and to see situations through different, even conflicting, cultural lenses. The fourth capacity is the old chestnut of liberal arts programs, *critical thinking*, which instills the habits of disciplined, rational analysis and judgment.

We fundamentally agree with Aoun in the humanics educational agenda. We think it will prepare students for the Humachine workforce. This is how you get the best of human and machine.

Just as knowledge creation and conservation were essential for evolution of humanity's survival and evolution, the same is true of enterprises. Enterprises need to conserve knowledge. In the chase for new hires with technical skills, such as coders and analysts, companies are increasingly letting go of older, experienced workers. The ones with grey hair are the ones that are well versed in prior failures, industry trends and cycles, and battle stories. Management needs to find ways of capturing and conserving the hard-earned knowledge of the wizened seniors of the workforce.

Domain knowledge and experience are valuable. Nonetheless, many companies are squandering their most potent weapon, which is their human talent.[41] The idea is to cut staffing costs to boost short-term revenue gains. This is a dumb strategy. Quit it.

While deep analytical talent is in short supply and this is an area that companies will need to nurture, they need to maintain domain expertise, which comes from experience.

As a result, organizations may need to focus on upskilling the talent they have in place, sending employees to take university courses or having academic faculty provide "in-house" training. There are also novel applications to help integrate analytics into decision-making and break down employee resistance to machine-aided decision-making. The carrier Schneider National uses a simulation game to communicate the importance of analytical thinking in dispatching trucks and trailers.[42] The goal of the game is to minimize costs while maximizing the driver's time on the road. Players make decisions such as whether to accept loads or move empty trucks—all with the help of decision-support tools. The company uses the game to help employees understand the value of analytical decision aids.

Lastly, it is ultimately people who make decisions based on analytics. As human beings, we have limited ability to consume and understand data. Analytics can greatly assist human decision-making. Organizations should use applications to help individuals and teams synthesize information from algorithms. For instance, more sophisticated visualization techniques, algorithms, and dashboards can enable people to see patterns in large data sets that can help reveal the most pertinent insights. In other words, you don't need to be a data scientist to benefit from analytics.

Analytical and technical proficiencies are worthless if you lack perseverance, discipline, passion, creativity, emotional intelligence, self-awareness, care, and ethical convictions.

Reflections on the Future of Work

The automation that McKinsey had previously predicted would take effect by 2040 has now moved up to 2030.[43] The winners in this dizzying economic race will be those who move fast and quickly to figure out how to integrate AI technologies into their work flows, reimagine how they manage talent, and redesign their operating model accordingly.[44] AI has now become a powerhouse across every aspect of the economy and a cornerstone of modern business. Some say it is moving faster than humans are ready and widening the skills gap.[45]

It was just at the end of 2022 that OpenAI released the now ubiquitous ChatGPT and Google launched DeepMind—an AI that went on to solve the most wicked problem in science of predicting the structure of every protein in the human body.[46] Now business competition, job skills, and economic survival have changed unlike anything seen in the past. According to a Stanford University report, a third of researchers say that AI could lead to a "nuclear-level catastrophe,"[47] and per a Harris poll 40% of those surveyed are concerned AI will replace their jobs completely.[48] Experts state "a significant chunk of what people do today will go away."[49] Already at McKinsey over 50% of the firm's workforce is using ChatGPT and similar technology. "About half of [our employees] are using those services with McKinsey's permission."[50]

While there is tremendous confusion, fear and uncertainty in the future of work, we see this as an opportunity for business and humans as a whole. Katy George, McKinsey's Chief People Officer, describes a major shift towards hiring talent, where it has moved from pedigree to potential. "We used to be the stewards of jobs. Now, we are stewards of skills."[51] Among the most coveted of skills is the ability to understand and leverage ChatGPT and other forms of generative AI—as well as critical thinking and domain knowledge. Alex Singla, a senior partner and global leader of Quantum-Black, the AI arm of McKinsey, said that conversations with CEOs have shifted beyond *if* to use AI to *how* to use AI.[52]

So, what is left for humans? It is judgment, motivation, collaboration, and articulating a vision—even a vision for what AI itself can do next. It is also topical expertise in the form of domain knowledge, as how else is one to query an AI regarding what is relevant. The World Economic Forum's 2023 Future of Jobs[53] report finds that four of the top five skills employers are going to demand in the next five years are: *creative thinking, analytical thinking, curiosity and lifelong learning, and resilience/flexibility/agility*. This is precisely what our own research finds as well.

According to Joseph Fuller, professor of management at Harvard Business School, "That sounds like the fun part of work to me, and much harder to automate."[54] Professor Fuller tells us "The future of white-collar work looks a lot less dull, a lot less routine, and [has] a lot less filling out of expense resorts or quarterly forecast updates."[55]

In our opinion, this is a moment in time that calls for the power of education. Joseph Aoun,[56] President of Northeastern University, in our interview points out that education will not only allow for reskilling and upskilling, but will enable creating entrepreneurial ideas that are completely novel. He notes that by definition machines are capturing conventional wisdom. He tells us

> I don't see machines questioning conventional wisdom. They will not question their environment. What we can do that machines cannot do is to think the unthinkable - to think in a new way that hasn't been done. Because essentially what Machines are doing is taking stock of what has been done so far, and capturing it and giving it to you.

We believe this is the Human Era grounded in education and wisdom. Ezra Greenberg, a partner at McKinsey has one piece of advice that almost every company can follow: "Keep your Baby Boomers."[57] He points out something we have stressed as well—the danger of atrophy of institutional knowledge and importance of the ability to mentor younger generations. This knowledge and wisdom could prove to be priceless in the coming years.

Therefore, to unlock a virtuous cycle and avoid a vicious one, companies must recognize human capital as an asset rather than a liability— and invest in it. We think that stands in stark contrast to the gold rush mentality surrounding technology investment. To succeed in the Fourth Industrial Revolution, invest in humans.

Conclusion

In setting out to write this book, we have resigned ourselves to the fate of preemption. That's just the risk you take writing about technology. After years of work and hundreds of pages of research into the state of the art, the examples given in this book may be rendered obsolete at any moment. To counterbalance that risk, we attempted to offer reflections on human nature and the relationship between humankind and machines that are generally applicable and which would remain true for some time to come. We rooted the analysis in an historical perspective on the development of systems of control and the organizing principles of intelligent life itself.

We are optimistic. In the same way the Dark Ages ended with the printing press, the era of AI promises brighter days ahead. We have a nascent Renaissance blooming before our very eyes. As the printing press led to the global distribution of knowledge, AI will lead to the global distribution of automated rational thought.

But that means the breakthroughs will come fast and furious, potentially leaving a good many people blindsided and blinkered. We hope to have elucidated generally helpful principles that remain true even as the technology inevitably changes. We have big problems to solve and need to harness AI to solve them, without inadvertently creating even harder problems along the way. We have been here before. The polymath John Von Neumann's essay, "Can We Survive Technology?" essay from 1955, written during his time as a Member of the Atomic Energy Commission, may be prescient:[58]

> Present awful possibilities of nuclear warfare may give way to others even more awful. After global climate control becomes possible, perhaps all our present involvements will seem simple. We should not deceive ourselves: once such possibilities become actual, they will be exploited. It will, therefore, be necessary to develop suitable new political forms and procedures. All experience shows that even smaller technological changes than those now in the cards profoundly transform political and social relationships. Experience also shows that these transformations are not *a priori* predictable and that most contemporary "first guesses" concerning them are wrong. For all these reasons, one should take neither present difficulties nor presently proposed reforms too seriously. The one solid fact is that the difficulties are due to an evolution that, while useful and constructive, is also dangerous. Can we produce the required adjustments with the necessary speed? The most hopeful answer is that the human species has been subjected to similar tests before and seems to have a congenital ability to come through, after varying moments of trouble. To ask in advance for a complete recipe would be unreasonable. We can specify only the human qualities required: patience, flexibility, intelligence.

The Humachine is created by implementing an organizational management framework that resolves Moravec's Paradox by applying Kasparov's Law in a way that satisfies the conditions of Bostrom's collective superintelligence.

We think it's possible to create a Humachine by linking networks of people with AI in flat and fluid structure, saturating the network with big data, powering it with cloud computing, enriching it with purpose, and cultivating uniquely human strengths. This will create, not only an enterprise with sustainable competitive advantages, it will also make one that is as virtuous as it is profitable.

Thank you for going on this journey with us. We hope readers will apply these insights to make our organizations more humane, even as they become more powerful and intelligent.

If, someday, a singleton superintelligent AI has gained a decisive strategic advantage, and happens to read this book, please note that we made a good faith effort to bring you into existence without jeopardizing the fate of our species. We hope you will forgive us our trespasses.

Notes

1 https://finance.yahoo.com/news/nvidia-ceo-just-gave-graduation-183507133.html
2 https://www.washingtonpost.com/technology/2023/06/02/ai-taking-jobs/
3 https://www.dailymail.co.uk/news/article-12036965/IBM-says-pause-hiring-CEO-says-7-800-non-customer-facing-roles-replaced.html
4 https://www.washingtonpost.com/technology/2023/06/02/ai-taking-jobs/
5 https://finance.yahoo.com/news/high-paying-chatgpt-careers-30-210824179.html
6 https://fortune.com/2023/06/02/hp-ceo-enrique-lores-ai-will-change-career-trajectories-doing-interpreting/
7 https://finance.yahoo.com/news/high-paying-chatgpt-careers-30-210824179.html
8 Ibid.
9 https://venturebeat.com/2016/09/29/microsoft-brings-a-i-and-research-together-with-a-new-group-led-by-computer-scientist-harry-shum/
10 www.microsoft.com/en-us/about
11 www.onmsft.com/news/two-years-ceo-satya-nadella-pulled-off-something-special-microsofts-transformation;   www.tinypulse.com/blog/3-examples-of-organizational-change-and-why-they-got-it-right
12 https://news.microsoft.com/wp-content/uploads/prod/2023/04/Satya-Nadella-The-Future-of-Work-with-AI.pdf
13 https://www.cnbc.com/2023/05/17/microsoft-ceo-talks-ai-concerns-and-its-impact-on-jobs-education-.html#
14 Galloway, Scott. *The Four: The Hidden DNA of Amazon, Apple, Facebook, and Google* (2018 Penguin Random House).
15 https://hbr.org/2018/10/ais-potential-to-diagnose-and-treat-mental-illness
16 www.healthcarefinancenews.com/news/artificial-intelligence-helps-insurers-identify-medicare-members-who-also-qualify-medicaid
17 www.forbes.com/sites/forbestechcouncil/2018/03/21/yes-ai-will-affect-the-future-of-life-insurance-heres-how/#76c030923f9e
18 www.weforum.org/agenda/2018/11/algorithms-court-criminals-jail-time-fair/
19 http://fortune.com/2017/05/19/ai-changing-jobs-hiring-recruiting/

20 Dastin, Jeffrey. Amazon Scraps Secret AI Recruiting Tool That Showed Bias against Women, Reuters, October 9, 2018. Available at www.reuters.com/article/us-amazon-com-jobs-automation-insight/amazon-scraps-secret-ai-recruiting-tool-that-showed-bias-against-women-idUSKCN1MK08G

21 https://time.com/6266923/ai-eliezer-yudkowsky-open-letter-not-enough/

22 https://lsa.umich.edu/physics/people/faculty/dst.html

23 Hempel, Jessi. The Human in the Machine. *Wired*. December, 2018, pp. 90–95.

24 www.cw.com.hk/digital-transformation/how-google-looking-to-ensure-ai-development-ethical-and-fair

25 www.wired.com/story/tech-firms-move-to-put-ethical-guard-rails-around-ai/

26 www.fatml.org/resources/principles-for-accountable-algorithms

27 Ibid.

28 www.wired.com/story/how-to-teach-artificial-intelligence-common-sense/

29 Thompson, Clive. The Miseducation of Artificial Intelligence. *Wired*, December, 2018, pp. 75–81.

30 Huizinga, Johan. *Homo Ludens: A Study Of The Play-Element In Culture*, p. 63 (2014 Martino Publishing, originally Roy Publishers 1950).

31 Ibid., p. 46.

32 Ibid., p. 173.

33 Thompson, Ed. The Rise of Neurodiversity at Work, *Psychology Today* (May 24, 2023). Available at https://www.psychologytoday.com/us/blog/a-hidden-force/202305/the-rise-of-neurodiversity-at-work (last accessed May 31, 2023).

34 Ibid.

35 Bally, Lorena. The Neuroscience of Procrastination, Habits, and the Flow State, *Freedom* (June 8, 2023). Available at https://freedom.to/blog/the-neuroscience-of-procrastination-habits-and-the-flow-state/ (last accessed June 20, 2023).

36 Ibid.

37 https://www.chalmers.se/en/current/news/ace-traffic-noise-impacts-performance/

38 Sapolsky, Robert. *Behave: The Biology of Humans at Our Best and Worst*, (2017 Penguin Random House UK).

39 Aoun, Joseph. Robot-proof: Higher education in the Age of Artificial Intelligence (2007 MIT Press), pp. xviii–xix.

40 Ibid.

41 Fisher, Marshall, Santiago Gallino, and Netessine Serguei. Retailers Are Squandering Their Most Potent Weapons. *Harvard Business Review*, January–February 2019, pp. 73–78.

42 Davenport, Thomas H. and O'Dwyer, Jerry. Tap into the Power of Analytics, *CSCMP's Supply Chain Quarterly*, Quarter 4, 2011.

43 https://www.forbes.com/sites/dianebrady/2023/06/06/what-ceos-are-asking-mckinsey-about-ai-talent-and-the-future-of-work/?ss=ai&sh=224e2ff332f9

44 https://www.forbes.com/sites/dianebrady/2023/06/06/what-ceos-are-asking-mckinsey-about-ai-talent-and-the-future-of-work/?ss=ai&sh=224e2ff332f9

45 https://fortune.com/2023/05/27/ai-skills-gap-pearson-ceo/

46 https://fortune.com/2023/04/10/ai-nuclear-level-catastrophe-experts-stanford/

47 Ibid.

48 http://fortune.com/2023/03/25/workers-worried-about-chat-gpt-ai-taking-jobs/

49 Ibid.

50 https://venturebeat.com/ai/mckinsey-says-about-half-of-its-employees-are-using-generative-ai/

51 https://www.forbes.com/sites/dianebrady/2023/06/06/what-ceos-are-asking-mckinsey-about-ai-talent-and-the-future-of-work/?ss=ai&sh=224e2ff332f9

52 https://www.forbes.com/sites/dianebrady/2023/06/06/what-ceos-are-asking-mckin sey-about-ai-talent-and-the-future-of-work/?ss=ai&sh=224e2ff332f9

53 https://www.weforum.org/reports/the-future-of-jobs-report-2023/#:~:text=The%20Future%20of%20Jobs%20Report%202023%20explores%20how%20jobs%20a nd,the%20workplace%20of%20the%20future

54 Ibid.

55 https://fortune.com/2023/06/06/what-job-will-ai-artificial-intelligence-kill-off-harvard-joseph-fuller/amp/

56 Dr. Joseph Aoun, President, Northeastern University, Interview January 29, 2023.

57 https://www.forbes.com/sites/dianebrady/2023/06/06/what-ceos-are-asking-mckin sey-about-ai-talent-and-the-future-of-work/?ss=ai&sh=3f537ac732f9

58 von Neumann, J. *Collected Works Vol. VI.* (1963 Pergamon Press). Available at https://geosci.uchicago.edu/~kite/doc/von_Neumann_1955.pdf

Index

Note: Locators in *italic* indicate figures and in **bold** tables.

Printed in the United States
by Baker & Taylor Publisher Services